Hymes Ln 1

Educational Linguistics - TESOL
University of Pennsylvania
Graduate School of Education
3700 Walnut Street/C1
Philadelphia, PA 19104

THE MELODY
OF LANGUAGE

THE MELODY
OF LANGUAGE

edited by

Linda R. Waugh
Associate Professor of Linguistics
Cornell University, Ithaca, New York

and

C. H. van Schooneveld
Professor of Slavic Languages and Literature
Indiana University, Bloomington

University Park Press
Baltimore

UNIVERSITY PARK PRESS
International Publishers in Science, Medicine, and Education
233 East Redwood Street
Baltimore, Maryland 21202

Copyright © 1980 by University Park Press

Typeset by the Composing Room of Michigan, Inc.
Manufactured in the United States of America by
The Maple Press Company

Library of Congress Cataloging in Publication Data
Main entry under title:

The Melody of language.

Bibliography: p.
1. Prosodic analysis (Linguistics)—Addresses, essays,
lectures. 2. Bolinger, Dwight Le Merton, 1907-
I. Waugh, Linda, R. II. Schooneveld, Cornelis H. van.
III. Bolinger, Dwight Le Merton, 1907-
P224.M4   416   79-23657
ISBN 0-8391-1557-1

Contents

Contributors

Isamu Abe
Language Research Laboratory
Tokyo Institute of Technology
2-12-1 Ookayama
Meguro-ku
Tokyo 152, Japan

Charles-James N. Bailey
Institut für Linguistik
Technische Universität Berlin (TEL-9)
Ernst-Reuter-Platz 7 (Zi. 815)
1000 Berlin 10, East Germany

Evá Berard
Institut d'Etudes Linguistiques et
    Phonétiques
19, rue des Bernardins
75005 Paris, France

M. Chafcouloff
Université de Provence
Institut de Phonétique
29, avenue Robert-Schumann
13621 Aix-en-Provence, France

Y. R. Chao
1059 Cragmont Ave.
Berkeley, California 94708

Heles Contreras
Department of Linguistics GN-40
University of Washington
Seattle, Washington 98195

David Crystal
Department of Linguistic Science
University of Reading
Whiteknights, Reading RG6 2AA
England

G. Faure
Université de Provence
Institut de Phonétique
29, avenue Robert-Schumann
13621 Aix-en-Provence, France

Ivan Fónagy
Institut d'Etudes Linguistiques et
    Phonétiques
19, rue des Bernardins
75005 Paris, France

María Beatriz Fontanella de Weinberg
Universidad Nacional del Sur
Colón 80
8000 Bahia Blanca, Argentina

Kerstin Hadding
Lund University
Department of Linguistics
Kävlingevägen 20
S-222 40 Lund, Sweden

D. J. Hirst
Université de Provence
Institut de Phonétique
29, avenue Robert-Schumann
13621 Aix-en-Provence, France

Wiktor Jassem
Pracownia Fonetyki
Akustycznej IPPT PAN
ul. Noskowskiego 10
61-704 Poznań, Poland

Katarzyna Kudela-Dobrogowska
Instytut Językoznawstwa
Universytet im. A. Mickiewicza
Matejki 49
60-769 Poznań, Poland

D. Robert Ladd, Jr.
Department of Modern Languages
    and Linguistics
Cornell University
Ithaca, New York 14853

W. R. Lee
English Language Teaching Journal
16 Alexandra Gardens
Hounslow, Middlesex TW3 4HU
England

Ilse Lehiste
Department of Linguistics
204 Cunz Hall of Languages
Ohio State University
Columbus, Ohio 43210

P. R. Léon
Experimental Phonetics Laboratory
Graduate Department of French
University of Toronto
39 Queens Park Crescent East
Toronto, Ontario M5S 1A1
Canada

Philip Lieberman
Department of Linguistics
Brown University
Providence, Rhode Island 02912

J. Derrick McClure
University of Aberdeen
Department of English
Taylor Building
King's College
Old Aberdeen AB9 2UB, Scotland

P. Martin
Experimental Phonetics Laboratory
Graduate Department of French
University of Toronto
39 Queens Park Crescent East
Toronto, Ontario M5S 1A1
Canada

Anthony Mulac
Department of Speech
University of California
Santa Barbara, California 93106

Rose Nash
Department of Humanities
Inter-American University of Puerto
    Rico
San Rey, Puerto Rico 00919

Kerstin Nauclér
Lund University
Department of Linguistics
Kävlingevägen 20
S-222 40 Lund, Sweden

Emily Rando
10 Newbury Terrace
Newton, Massachusetts 02159

Maria Schubiger
Hochstrasse 81
8044 Zurich, Switzerland

Berthe Siertsema
Meander 767
Amstelveen, Holland

Henri Wittmann
Syndicat des Professeurs
Université de Québec a Trois-Rivières
Case postale 500
Trois-Rivières, Québec
Canada

Henning Wode
Englisches Seminar der Universität
    Kiel
Olshausenstrasse 40-60
D-2300 Kiel, West Germany

Preface

This volume deals with the melody of language—with everything that falls under the rubric of intonation and prosody, one of the areas of linguistics that, perhaps, offers the explorer more difficulties and unsolved problems than any other. The topics covered reflect the breadth of this area and include such phenomena as stress and accent, pitch contours and intervals, rising and falling of pitch, fundamental frequency, pressure and intensity, duration and length, rhythmic structure, pause, and breath groups. No attempt has been made to standardize terminology across contributions (both "intonation curves" and "intonation contours," for instance, are used in the text and index); it was felt that this would also help to show the diversity that exists in this area today.

The authors interpret the larger aspects of intonation and prosody in discussions that range from animal communication to human language; from phylogenesis and glottogenesis to ontogenesis; from questions of innateness to questions of language acquisition; from close instrumental study to wide-ranging comparative analysis and further to questions of universals; from dialects to standard languages; from the emotive (attitudinal) to the cognitive (intellectual) elements of speech; and from the "phonetic" to the "functional" aspects of intonation. More intensive facets are explicated in papers that range from the articulatory and muscular to the acoustic and auditory; from the segmental and suprasegmental through the syllable, the word, the phrase, the clause, the sentence, and finally to discourse; from the "grammatical" to the "lexical" function of prosody; from assertions to commands; from yes-no questions to "wh"-questions; from binarism ("all-or-none") to gradience; and from obligatoriness to optionality. The languages subjected to analysis include English (several varieties), Japanese, Cantonese, Spanish (several varieties), French, Hungarian, Swedish, Russian, German, and Dutch.

Thus, the volume gives a representative selection of the present state of the art for the investigation of prosodic phenomena. It is hoped that these studies by some of the world's leading experts will serve both as a springboard for future work in this fecund and exciting field, and as an index of Dwight L. Bolinger's impact on research in intonation and prosody.

Linda R. Waugh
C. H. van Schooneveld

This book is dedicated to our friend and colleague, Dwight L. Bolinger, one of the most original and imaginative of American linguists

who over several decades of work has made a monumental contribution to our understanding of intonation and prosody;

whose ability to transcend narrow theory has led to broad outlooks;

who has never forgotten the complexity and the versatility of language;

whose work touches the edge of language as well as central questions of form and meaning;

who has been a stimulating "devil's advocate" for scholars of various persuasions;

whose inexhaustible creativity has blazed ever novel trails in linguistics;

whose humanism and work will be an inspiration for many generations to come.

THE MELODY
OF LANGUAGE

1/ How Vocal Pitch Works

Isamu Abe

Melody is part and parcel of language, and the various problems pertaining to it have further stirred the curiosity of the linguist, the psychologist, and the physicist alike in recent years. A great deal of exploration is currently being attempted in order to grasp its nature, and still more remains to be done in the future. The aim of this paper is to answer some of the basic questions, such as: For what purpose does man use his vocal pitch and under what conditions? What factors of vocal pitch thus employed are linguistically operative or relevant? Therefore, I try to provide a panoramic picture of the human voice, and then see how it relates to our daily lives when we whisper, shout, speak, read, and sing.

BIOLOGICAL FACTOR

Vocal pitch is more or less inseparably associated with the speaker's biological condition. Normally, the speaker's articulatory muscles begin to lose their elasticity as he grows tired, with the result that his voice becomes lower and his pitch range narrower. Conversely, when he feels cheerful and inflated, his general tone of voice tends to rise—an inevitable consequence of the behavior of his muscles, which refuse to stay idle. In an unidentified radio play, I once heard a man disposing of waste cans one by one in the yard of his house, as dictated by his wife. He was heard to be counting each of the cans as he threw it away in the dump in the following manner:

"One (rising), two (rising), three (rising), ..."

This was a deliberate method of counting things, as was shown by the rising terminal intonation of each enumerated item. However, the man had hardly finished disposing of all the cans when he was told to go through the entire process again from the very beginning. The second time he was going about the same business of counting, he was heard to be mumbling to himself in an obviously weary voice:

"One (falling), two (falling), three (falling), ..."

1

This falling intonation, coupled with other phonic features such as huskiness and break, was typical of his exhausted condition. Had he continued the counting job, he might well have altogether stopped even mumbling to himself. The same thing may be said of a man who is making a long speech. His voice grows huskier as he talks on, until he finds it extremely painful—and at the last stage of his speech even difficult—to speak cogently. For example, at certain locations in his utterances a falling intonation, or rather an abrupt sinking of the voice, is likely to take over as he desperately gropes for immediate relaxation of his muscular activity.

PHYSICAL FACTOR

Vocal pitch is constrained by physical circumstances. Typical of this fact is a proxemic factor that dominates tunes. Proxemic factors primarily determine the physical space in which a person manipulates his voice in his communication with another person or with his audience. One of the proxemic factors is distance. When a person addresses or calls someone who is a considerable distance away, he has to use a tone of voice that is different from the one he is accustomed to using when the other person is right before his eyes. For example, the intonational patterns

may indicate that "Johnny" is not (at least in the speaker's mind) standing close by, whereas the patterns

may indicate that the two persons are actually standing face to face. According to Bolinger (private communication, March 9, 1973), "[An intonation such as]

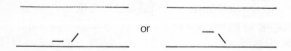

could hardly be a question without the most powerful gestural cues. For instance, you might be calling to me at a considerable distance, and I have had difficulty hearing you. I use that intonation not because it is appropriate to a question but because it carries well and enables you to hear me; you perhaps see me cup my ears, so you know I am trying to hear you. That is enough for you to interpret my utterance as a question, in spite of the intonation.''

On the other hand, there are circumstances where something must be communicated to a specific person but not to any other person, and with the least ''noise.'' It is at such times that one begins to talk in a very low tone of voice—in a whisper. Whispering is characterized by reduced volume and pitch, and distance between the two speakers is kept to a minimum. In a whisper, one's vocal cords are not vibrating, and instrumentally there is no voice pitch. The apparent impression one has of its presence is due to the working of other phonic features, such as voice quality. Whispering is in a sense the direct opposite of whistling or a loud call, which are used in certain languages as a means of communication. A good example of a whistled language is a dialect used in Kuskoy, a mountainous region near the Black Sea in eastern Turkey. An article from the *New York Times* (March 1, 1964) tells how it works:

> Whistling will be taught, along with the Turkish language. But Kushoy parents teach their boys and girls to whistle about the time they learn to talk. The whistler forms his 'speech' with tongue curled around his teeth so that the 'words' are forced through lips that are not puckered in the conventional whistling style; they are tensely drawn flat across the face. The palm of the left hand is cupped about the mouth, and high pressure is applied from the lungs. The result, to one who has not heard it before, is terrifying. The sound is of steam locomotive proportions. Whistling is so developed that men and women speak, argue and woo in whistles. A village sage recently disclosed that when a young couple elopes, the news is broadcast over the 'mountain telephone'—whistle. And the romantic escapade is quickly brought to an end.

Whistling is used as a language among the inhabitants of the Canary Islands, among American Indians, and elsewhere. It is considered a language in that it is speech *minus* its segmentals. It is a language that works, as Bolinger (1955, p. 21) aptly points out, with ''no assist from accompanying words.'' Whistled language is a verbal melody formed from real speech that is used to carry across vast distances, hence its ''steam locomotive proportions,'' as we have observed in Kuskoy, and the observation that a ''well-pitched whistle may be heard through a fog and through the pines for five miles around.''

Silbo, a whistled language used in La Gomera in the Canary Islands, is actually whistled Spanish. ''The Silbador,'' says Critchley, ''while whistling, strives to articulate words as in speech. . . . and as local residents informed me it is possible to transmit across long distances fairly elaborate messages which can be picked up and interpreted by those who are within earshot'' (Critchley, 1970, pp. 345–347).

Critchley also refers (1970) to some of the drum languages of Africa and Melanesia. In this case, African talking-drum signalers use one or two drums to produce a tone-and-rhythm code that mimics the tones and rhythms of human speech, so here again the talking drum is speech *minus* its segmentals. Drum language is different from whistled language in that the former is speech produced instrumentally, whereas the latter is speech produced physiologically.

AFFECTIVE FACTOR

Vocal pitch also serves to reveal specific emotions and attitudes on the part of the speaker. The affective function of pitch is probably the most significant of the uses to which it is put. A man's feelings of joy, sorrow, and so forth are expressed in a variety of ways. Just by way of experiment, a quasi-lexical item containing the nasal sound [m] and its variants, with or without an oral sound accompanying it, can be examined in relation to how it will be intoned. The nasal is chosen because it is a voiced sound and is capable of being lengthened to carry pitch with it, and is a kind of tabula rasa on which the many emotional tunes may be jotted down. The [m] sound thus used has ceased to function as a segmental that forms a part of lexical meaning; instead, it now works as a carrier of some affective meaning.

James Kirkup, a British poet and essayist, says that "one of the first things I noticed, in talking to American shop-assistants, was that in reply to 'Thank you' they say 'Uh-huh' in a sort of disinterested tone of voice. I think this is meant to indicate: 'I don't require your thanks. I'm doing you no favour, so don't thank me.' Again, this rather hostile response seems to show that every American resents being treated as an inferior. The 'uh-huh' so casual in tone hides fierce independence. Of course, one sometimes receives, in answer to one's polite 'Thank you', the Americanism 'You're welcome.' But this is now becoming rare" (1970, p. 23).

I am not at all sure that Kirkup's interpretation of the melody of the American "uh-huh" and its implication is correct. It seems from the recording by Kirkup of this particular passage that this "uh-huh" ("uh" is high, and "-huh" is low) is interpreted to mean "No, I don't require your thanks," or "No, don't thank me." However, the usual pattern associated with this expression is just the opposite—that is, a low tone followed by a high tone, which means "yes," obviously an indication that the person responding is willing to accept the words of appreciation. The "uh-huh" expression can be intoned in more than one way depending on whether it means yes or no. For more details, see E. T. Anderson, "The Intonation of American English" (M.A. thesis), translated into Japanese by Abe (1971).

Sometimes intonation may reverse meaning. Vance E. Johnson (1973) states that "around 1900 people described some thing or person or feeling that interested them and they liked as 'swell.' It has stayed in the language, but as it has lost its freshness it is more often used with the opposite or negative meaning." Literally, the expression "that's swell" is a complimentary phrase, and it can still be used in that sense with the first syllable starting on a mid-level pitch and the second syllable sweeping up and down:

However, no one would now deny its ironic meaning when it is pronounced with the second syllable placed lower than the first syllable:

Intonation

What, then, is intonation? This is the question Bolinger asked in 1955. He stated at that time that it was easy to answer the "what" in physical terms. "Intonation is the melodic line of speech, the rising and falling of the 'fundamental' or singing pitch of the voice, as distinguished from the 'overtones' which our vocal organs shape into the vowels and certain of the consonants, and from other noises of the speech apparatus." Again, "physically it is the most uniform element that the phonetician has to deal with; but this, instead of making for simplicity makes for complexity for, with its lack of contrast, intonation cannot be sliced up as other segments are" (1955, p. 20).

Indeed, as Bolinger has reiterated since then, this "more-or-less" (i.e., gradient) nature of intonation, as opposed to the "all-or-none" nature of segmentals, makes intonation the tricky subject that it is. In addition to this, there is another difficulty that we encounter in decoding intonation thus defined on a "pragmatic" level—that is, in the way a person takes it. There is no decisive method for ascertaining that people are responding to something more than pitch curves when we think that they are responding to intonation. Pragmatically, intonation is actually more than one thing: it is speech melody. "Basically," says Stokowski, "melody is a combination of frequency and duration." Here the duration feature is admitted as an added prosodical dimension. If more dimensions are added—for example, tempo, loudness, voice register and quality—we shall be dealing with the whole prosodics of speech, and, needless to say, it is not necessarily easy to decode a message in terms of pitch curves alone, if that is instrumentally possible.

The fundamental pitch has something it goes with and this something has a host of informational data—the whole prosodics, in fact. Hence, we sometimes come across an apparently incongruous, but pragmatically relevant, statement such as "the intonation patterns of the two expressions are the same, but they mean two different things depending on other features of speech." Pike's example from Rumanian, "Kum te kyama" (What is your name?), is pronounced with an identical intonation (2 3 34, with 1 for the highest and 4 for the lowest relative pitch level), yet it ceases to be a normal unemotional question when it is spoken "rapidly and irritably, as by a nervous teacher or a harried clerk" (Pike, 1964).

Kinesics must also be taken into account to describe the pragmatic import of speech melody. Bolinger (1968) reminds us of the important role gestural (i.e., kinesic) cues play along with intonation.

More recently, Tibbitts (1973) has conducted some experiments in an attempt to see what prosodic parameters other than intonation or in addition to intonation are actually at work to produce some specific attitudinal meaning. He hypothesizes tentatively that, although pitch characteristics have traditionally been accorded primacy of place in expounding attitude, this is a mistake.

GRAMMATICAL FUNCTION

Vocal pitch is also used to differentiate sentence types, as shown by the following passage:

> "Ich bin Herr McLane," he said, after a pause. "So?" she replied, with a questioning inflexion. "Ja, ich bin Herr Grant's Bruder." "Ach, so!" she said, with a downward inflexion. (Hamlin Garland, *Up the Coolly*)

Statement and question tunes are the most representative of grammatical intonation. Statements may be changed into questions asking for the answer "yes" or "no" by using a question particle or marker or by altering syntactical word order or simply by using a different kind of intonation. "The most usual question contours as contrasted with ordinary statement tunes would appear to be either (1) rising or raised (i.e. higher in pitch as a whole) than those for statements or (2) less falling (i.e. than the corresponding pattern for statements). Either the entire sentence or the relevant portion of the sentence is in this way modified" (Abe, 1972).

This principle appears to underlie most of the world languages, and to that extent intonation here may be regarded as a universal trait of language. Each language has recourse to each of these question-signaling devices or it has preference for one or another. For example, Russian appears to prefer intonation to a question particle or marker in changing a statement into a yes-no question; hence the statement "это ваша книга" (lit., it your book) becomes "это ваша книга?" (sharp rise on "кни-" and fall on "га"). In the same context, the corresponding English question would have a straight rising intonation on the element "book." If pronounced after the Russian fashion, the English question "Is it your book?" may sound like a question with added emotional colorings instead of a straight yes-no question.

PHONOLOGICAL/MORPHOLOGICAL FUNCTION

Vocal pitch is also used to differentiate meanings of words or phrases. In a large number of languages, such as Chinese, Vietnamese, Zulu, and Mixteco, there are pairs or groups of words or phrases that sound identical except for tone. Japanese is also one such language, although it differs from Chinese in that Japanese monosyllabic words do not have any inherent pitch per se, whereas Chinese lexical items each possess either one of the four or five (as the case may be) specific syllabic tones. For example, the Mandarin word spelled "yu" in Romanized letters may have four different meanings depending on what kind of tone is applied to it:

Yu (high level tone) means "excellent"
Yu (mid-rising tone) means "oil"
Yu (low falling-rising tone) means "exist; possess"
Yu (falling tone) means "right" (as opposed to "left")

A monosyllabic Japanese word used in isolation, on the other hand, reveals no such phonological contrast. I have done an experiment using some sample monosyllabic words such as "hi," which were pronounced in randomized order and at different times. Visual recordings were made of the "tones": for example, compare (1 + 5 + 6 = fire; 2 + 3 + 4 = sunbeam):

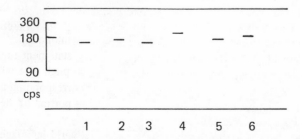

As is evident in the pitchgrams, Japanese words are phonetically "neutralized" as to tone or pitch level at the monosyllabic level. In a larger phonetic context, however, the two *hi*'s given above immediately reveal their "tonal" distinction. Compare the use of the two *hi*'s in this context:

> Hi ga deta.   (The sun came out)
> Hi ga deta.   (The fire broke out)

In the first example, "hi" is lower in pitch than "ga"; in the second example, "hi" is higher in pitch than "ga" ("ga" is a subject indicator).

Phenomena of "tonal sandhi" are quite common in Japanese, as they are in many tone languages. The words "asa" (morning) and "gohan" (meal) are both head-high words, but when combined they become a phrase, "asagohan" (breakfast), that is no longer a combination of two head-high words but is now a body-high one, with or without the change in quality of the segmental sound [g] from the plosive to the nasal. If the two words are merely juxtaposed, a possible implication of "asa gohan" is "rice for morning meal (breakfast)." Hunter and Pike reported (1969) that in Molinos Mixtec the phrase "so¹ko¹ ži¹či¹" (dry spring) is derived from the two separate basic forms "so¹ko¹" (spring) and "ži³či¹" (dry), where 1 is highest and 3 is lowest.

TONE AND INTONATION

"On top of these tonal differences," says Bolinger (1955, p. 21), "the speaker adds intonational changes that show attitudes and emotions, just as in English we may add an emotional stress to the word 'incénsed' on top of the verbal stress. As might be expected, there is a good deal of friction between the two levels. Fortunately, . . . English, French, German, Spanish, Russian, and most other West European languages are not 'tone languages' like Chinese or Mixteco."

Apropos of tone-intonation interplay, Siertsema's view is worth noting. She assumes that in tone languages it is the scale of the contour that has intonational function; in nontonal ones it is the shape of the contour, but the boundary of the two is not clear-cut (1962). This observation attests to the fact that the tonal backbone is in the main solid enough to resist perturbation by intonation. This sometimes leads one who is not familiar with a certain language to perceive different intonational patterns in the two utterances below when what sounds different on the surface actually concerns tones, not intonation. The two utterances are intonationally the same:

Amega furu asa (The morning the rain
            falls)

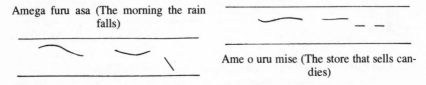

Ame o uru mise (The store that sells candies)

In the first example, the three elements "ame" (rain), "furu" (fall), and "asa" (morning) are all head-high words, and, except for the tones that are deflected upward at phrase boundaries, as shown in the pitchgrams, the utterance as a whole describes a descending curve. On the other hand, in the second example we have no distinct downward tonal shift, and the slight drop on the final syllable "-se" is intonational. The elements "ame" (candy), "uru" (sell), and "mise" (store) are all tail-high words.

To go more into the details of tone-intonation interplay, the following three relational models are presented, which at this stage of analysis are still regarded as highly hypothetical:

Model I: the relation is cumulative. For example, a mid-tone is brought up to a yet higher level by a "high" intonation, or the downglide of a falling tone is arrested by a "rising" intonation.

Model II: the relation is successive. For example, a falling tone is followed by a "rising" intonation.

Model III: the relation is conflictive. The original tone is either heavily modified by intonation or is utterly destroyed.

According to Ole Kjellin, the word "Stockholm" in Swedish has a pitch accent with a double crest in a statement

and the crest goes up to a higher level when the word is used in a yes-no question

This is a Model I example. In Japanese, on the other hand, the word "ame" (rain) in a staement

is made into a question with the linear addition of a rising intonation

This is a Model II example.

According to Kiyoshi Nasu of Kyushu University, Japan, the Chinese word "hao" (good) has a tonal shape 214 (1 for the lowest level and 4 for the highest). Used in a normative type of statement, the word is pronounced with a 213 intonation, with the rising tone (14) being affected by a "falling" intonation, thus producing the cumulative result 213. This is apparently a Model I example. However, Nasu informed me that the audience watching a play may get excited and applaud in a loud voice "Hao!", which has a 51 intonation. (The numeral 5 is the highest pitch level in Nasu's system of pitch notation.) This would appear to be a Model III example. Likewise, Nasu points up the existence of the pattern 51 of the expression "yu" (Yes; I'm present), which may be used in answering the roll-call. The original tonal shape is 214.

Another Model III example is the Norwegian word "utmerket" ['u:tmærkət] (excellent), which shows diametrically opposite melodic forms according to whether the word is pronounced in a placid manner or in an excited manner (Popperwell, 1963). Norwegian words are generally described as belonging either to Tone 1 or Accent 1 or to Tone 2 or Accent 2. Very briefly stated, the former is marked by rising tonality and the latter by falling tonality, albeit the fact that in either case the terminal syllable is rising. According to Kloster-Jensen of Bergen University (private communication, December 17, 1970), this terminal rise becomes less of a rise (Model I) or the rise is turned into a fall (Model III) as it occurs in a plain statement. What does not happen, in his view, is a successive fall after the rise (Model II). Personally he seems to prefer Model I. He states that "in my dialect, which is the one most often used for demonstration of Norwegian tones, the tonemes always (in both cases, tone 1 and tone 2) are rising at the end. Intonation does not seem to interfere with tones. Tones are expressed in stressed syllables; intonation, it would seem, mostly on unstressed syllables. This was exemplified in my Prague paper: there therefore seemed to be very little 'interference' between intonation and word tones."

INDIVIDUAL DIFFERENCES

Vocal pitch serves to tell us who it is that is speaking or what his or her stock in trade is; it works as a kind of class or occupational tune. Bolinger says, "Politicians, college professors, army sergeants, housewives, hucksters, newsboys, and especially, ministers of the Gospel, have their peculiar ways of intoning the English language, ways which they may use habitually or only when hawking their wares, but which are typical enough to brand their occupation even when we cannot understand a word they say. Individuals are similarly branded, and we associate the humor or whimsicality of a person's speech with his particular manner of inflecting it, as actors and announcers know only too well, &c." (1955, p. 19). A minister who appears in one of Walpole's novels—*Jeremy*—is appraised as a man who has a rich voice by those who like him, and is branded as an affected ass by those who don't. Walpole describes the way of his addressing a lady in the five-level quasi-musical staff:

Everyone has a way of speaking or dialect, whether he is aware of the fact or not, and it is the mark of his occupation or personality. This is true of people of any nationality. Some profit from it (they even draw heavily on it for a living), and some suffer from it because their voices do not sound the way they should. Among those who use the tone of their voices as assets are professional mimics and entertainers. For example, they sometimes play the roles of little children by using a falsetto voice. These people not only reproduce on the stage the appropriate phonemes of the entire phonological inventory possessed by the person they happen to be imitating verbally, but they also go into superphonetic (i.e., noise) details of these phonemes—which is something that simply is not attempted in the average classroom.

Some people use tones of voice peculiarly their own, so that when we hear them, we immediately notice what they are doing, as Bolinger pointed out, although we may not understand a word of what they are intoning. It is the melody that does the trick.

A Japanese goldfish vendor walking down the streets will intone "Kingyo-o-e Kingyo" (with "kin-" starting on a mid-level pitch, "-ngyo-o-" on a high level and stretched, and "-e" coming down in pitch). The second "kingyo" is almost the same as the first, but lacks the terminal "-e." The interesting thing about this melody is that it is not a dutiful rendition of the spoken melody used in natural conversation—that is, "ki" (high) and "ngyo" (low). This phenomenon of pitch displacement has its equivalent in Spanish, although this time it is stress rather than pitch that is involved. Vendors use calls such as "limonés" and "melonés" with a shift of stress before a pause in many instances (Wallis, 1951). In English, a greengrocer who appears in Betty Smith's novel *Tomorrow Will Be Better* "put his hand to the side of his mouth and sang a strange song. 'Straw-bebbs! Lawn-I'll-dadoes! Spinch! Tur-rumps! Green led-duz!' He sang 'led-duz' the way the priest sang 'Amen' at High Mass. Women came out of houses, bargaining briefly but passionately with the wandering greengrocer." Bolinger informed this writer that the "Amen" here consists of two syllables of level pitch; the "a-" is higher than "-men."

MELODY AND CHANT

I have already touched on a few illustrative specimens of melody akin to distant calls—all of these attest to the presence of melody that falls some-where between true speech and true song. This may be termed a chant or, when it takes on a more pious nature, an incantation. Everyone knows that song has prosodic laws of its own, just as speech has its own suprasegemental laws, and it is readily conceivable that "sound" and "sense" do not always get along together as we might expect.

Here is a passage from Jean Webster's well-known novel, *Daddy-Long-Legs*. Jerusha, the heroine, happened to hear Tommy Dillon, who had recently joined the choir in the orphanage where she was also living, coming up the stairs to tell her that Mrs. Lippett, head of the orphanage, wanted to see Jerusha at her office. This is the way Tommy intoned his message to Jerusha:

> Je-ru-sha Ab-bott,
> 2 2 2   1   2
>
> You are wan-ted
> 2   2   1   2
>
> In the of-fice.
> 2   2 1 2

(The passage was read at the request of this writer by a Catholic nun residing in Japan. The numerals indicate pitch levels; 1 is higher than 2.) According to Webster, Tommy "piously intoned" the message, which was referred to as "his chant." One of the major features of this chant is its rather simplified intonational pattern composed of two pitch levels and syllable/time-oriented rhythm.

Commenting on the quoted lines, Bolinger (private communication, August 22, 1959) stated that "my guess is that the singer is pretty much on his own except when major accents occur. The would-be differences between one singer and another is how responsive they would make their music to the speech melody; some might make a musical contrast at a number of musical points; for instance, in the first line, I can conceive of either

Jerusha Abbott   or   Jerusha Abbott
2 1 2   2 3   2 2 2 2 3
(3 for the lowest pitch; 1 for the highest)

"The latter would seem to be the least contrast that could be shown, but there is still the possibility of none at all, i.e. with a perfectly level tone through the whole first line and no contrast in pitch until the second or even the third line.

Jerusha Abbott,   You are wanted   In the office.
2 2 2 2 2   2 2 2 2   2 2 2 3

"The way the writer uses hyphens in the first three lines suggests that there must be at least this one pitch contrast, on the very last word, but there would not have to be any others. What you [Abe] say about the lengthening of final syllables [is correct]; this is strikingly true of English, for the musical cramping of unaccented syllables has to give way to the rhythm of the chant, in which I think every final syllable would have maximum length—i.e., in this example the words *Abbott, wanted,* and *office* would have double length.

Webster's *Daddy-Long-Legs* was made into a radio play for school children and was broadcast on the NHK (Japan Broadcasting Corporation) network. On this program, the boy who played the role of Tommy intoned the passage in question in the following manner:

Ji---ru ↑sha---- ↑A↓botto---
inchoo↑sensee go ↑yoo↓datte↑sa---

(Unless otherwise transcribed, initial syllables begin on a mid-pitch level; the arrow signs ↑ and ↓ indicate that the following syllable or syllables shift one step higher or lower and continue on that level, respectively.) As far as the Japanese rendition of this passage is concerned, many of the same phonetic features may be observed—notably, lengthened terminal syllables and the flow of pitch on a sequence of notes that is more faithful to musical rules, although traces of speech tone remain to retain the meaning of the message, which would otherwise be lost (Abe, 1960).

There seem to be different styles of chant in different cultures. The type as represented by the *Daddy-Long-Legs* example is what Chao terms as "singsong," which is "a style of use of the language which is neither the algebraic addition of tone and intonation, resulting in ordinary speech, nor singing of a musical melody, but something intermediate, which is based largely on the phonemic tones of the words, spoken in stereotyped manner" (1967).

George List made a very detailed analysis of the vocal pitch problems relating to speech and song, and his recitation chants are both twofold affairs proceeding either to a monotonous melody with its negation of intonation or to a melody labeled as "sprechstimme," which refers to the type of elevated or heightened speech characteristic of the melodrama—with its expansion of intonation (1967). So a chant actually ranges from a monotonous one like a religious liturgy or a monk's incantation or a reading of Japanese classical poems at the Imperial Palace at New Year's time to a *haka* sung by the Maoris of New Zealand in which "speech intonation seems to have been amplified and developed into a free form" (List, 1967).

As for the exploitation of speech melody in music, languages that have phonological tones are bound by their nature to pose problems of some kind. To quote Herzog (1934),

> The songs [i.e., in Navaho] illustrate a constant conflict and accommodation between musical tendencies and the curves traced by the speech tones of the song-text. Even when the speech tones prevail, the musical impulse is not quelled but merely limited—urged, perhaps, for discovering devices it had not used before. The best proof of this is that often a turn which was evoked by speech melody immediately begins to lead its own melodic life, calling for repetition or balance, whether this agrees with the following speech-curve or not. The melodic element which is strong in 'tone-languages' intrudes upon the music of the peoples speaking such languages. In our languages, such an influence is much less definite. But accent (stress) is, with length, the important 'musical' element of our languages that has figured in our musical development.

Examples illustrating this abound. The words in the poetic text

(with their too mechanical alteration of strong and weak stresses) may be set to music, but ordinarily not like

but rather like

according to Bainbridge Crist (1934), who thinks that the words "when" and "day" have weak beats, and the words "hour" and "numbered" are not emphasized and that a weak beat in poetry should not be assigned to a strong beat in music unless dramatic requirements justify it.

In Japanese songs, deviations from the normal word pitch accent patterns may be tolerated insofar as they do not seriously affect the meaning of the song contents or do not sound offensive to the ear. The minimum requirement is that meaning be inferred from the context. For example, compare

mi-tsu-ba-chi

from *Dandelions,* composed by Nagayo Motoori, with

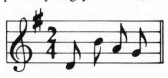

mi-tsu-ba-chi

from *Buzzing Bees,* composed by Ichiro Hosoya. The second "mitsubachi" (honeybee), which is a body-high type with the crest coming on the syllable "-tsu," is a more faithful rendition of normal word melody. However, both forms are comprehensible in song.

The expository, or narrative, style of reading or interpretative reading of a piece of prose is something that comes very near to spontaneous speech. One does not necessarily read as one talks: for one thing, different styles of language are used in reading and speaking. In Japanese, men and women lose their characteristic verbal mannerisms used only in speech when they compose and read a written piece of work, so that reading and speaking habits have their own peculiar flavor. In general, spontaneity of natural speech is tempered and subdued in reading. A Japanese example from *Yane no ue no Sawan* (Sawan on the Housetop)—a short story written by Masuji Ibuse—will suffice to illustrate the case in point.

"Sawan" is the name of a goose that the person who appears in this story has caught and grown attached to, but finally decides to release. In the story the bird is called and addressed by the person in more than one way under different circumstances. For example,

1. "Sawan! Don't cry loud!" (The heroine or hero of the story opening the window and calling the bird, which is outside on the housetop.)
2. "Sawan! Don't you ever leave me! Don't be so cruel to me!" (The woman saying this imploringly while feeding the bird, which is just standing by her side.)

If a proxemic factor is taken into account, it is inconceivable that the two "Sawans" should be read in a more or less identical tone of voice, but even a professional narrator, much less a nonprofessional, sometimes falls into the trap of verbalizing the two in the same manner. The several persons who happened to read the passage in question actually pronounced the word "Sawan" more or less like

in all environments, but had their roles been not merely those of a narrator, but of people really trying to establish a perfect communicational tie with the bird, they would discover at once that the address contour used in example 2 would not reach the bird's ear, and he would then have to revert to the call contour in example 1. Thus the contours that are likely to be used in examples (1) and (2) are, respectively,

and

REGIONAL AND NATIONAL DIFFERENCES

Just as each person has his own peculiar vocal mannerisms, so does a member of each nationality or region. These mannerisms are called dialects or national traits, as contrasted with idiolects. For example, it can be inferred from hearing a single utterance whether the speaker is British or American or a non-native speaker of English, despite the fact that the utterance is grammatically and even emotively structured alike. Yukihiro Yamada pointed out, according to Shin Kawakami's private communication to me, that "there seem to exist some dialectical differences in the intonational patterns used by people residing in the hilly districts near Toyohashi, which is in central Japan. For example, a plain yes-no question "Akaika?" ("akai," red; "ka," question particle; thus, is it red?) is either pronounced

or

but the implication is the same." A more or less analogous observation is made of the German dialects spoken in Volmerange and Haut-Clocher, according to Guentherodt (1969).

VOCAL PITCH AND SEX

It has been claimed—and justly—that there are subtle differences in the speech of men and women. Those differences are due in part to cultural and in part to biological factors. For example, women usually use a higher register of voice and a wider pitch range, particularly when they are excited, than men do. (There is a period in one's life, regardless of sex, when one's voice begins to change into a lower register—when the voice "breaks"—but this is a purely physiological matter and need not concern us here.) In some societies certain verbal taboos exist that put restrictions on women's speech in terms of vocabulary or syntax.

As far as I know, the written literature on male and female speech is not plentiful. Haas gave a description of men's and women's speech in the Muskogean language spoken in southwest Louisiana. Referring to the expression that in English means "I am lifting it," she says, "if the women's form has the falling pitch stress on its final syllable and ends in a short vowel followed by l, the men's form substitutes the high pitch stress for the falling pitch stress and an s for the l. E.g. 'lakawwîl' (female) vs. 'lakawwís' (male)" (1944).

Key says as part of her explanation of the use of segmental patterns that "both men and women use basic patterns without male/female differences, except perhaps quantitatively. Some individuals use a high percentage of patterns that communicate such traits as coyness, bull-headedness, cheerfulness, and sarcasm. It is likely that linguistic features correlate with personality types. It is also quite likely that women use patterns of uncertainty and indefiniteness more often than men—patterns of PLIGHT" (1972). She also remarks that in an experiment in which 3rd, 4th, and 5th grade children were asked to retell a story, the girls used a very expressive intonation, while the boys toned down intonational features even to the point of monotony, "playing it cool." Perhaps this is analogous to Bolinger's remark that "women are less inhibited in their intonational range" (1968, p. 136).

Brend (1972) cites some examples of intonational patterns preferred or solely used by women under specific circumstances, attesting to the existence in English of some male/female intonational differences.

In Japan, as Richard Halloran says in his humorous book, *We Japanese* (note that he is including himself as a Japanese) that "we Japanese men like to be masculine by talking abruptly and with guttural sounds while Japanese women, especially those well brought up, like my wife, speak a lovely, melodic language. We Japanese can tell in a minute where a foreigner learned to speak Japanese, particularly G.I.'s who learn some from Japanese girls. They talk like women, which sounds very funny to us." I doubt that Japanese men always behave like ancient warriors: they often start by acting out their masculine roles as though they were the politest persons on earth! Conversely, some Japanese women, particularly women of the younger generation, just do not mind talking like men, although they still cannot deviate from the diction and verbal mannerisms that are special to them. One of my American friends once told me that Japanese women talk as though they were always asking a question or were shocked at something. This is probably because of the high-pitched emotive particles that Japanese women customarily use—or rather overuse—at the end of an utterance.

VOCAL PITCH AND AGE

There are questions as to how vocal pitch is correlated with age. Do children use intonational patterns different from those of adults? How does a child begin to learn the melodic patterns of his native tongue? These are subjects worth exploring.

Crystal (1969, 1970) has recently reviewed the whole issue of the child's acquisition of intonation, and so has Nash (1973). I have not as yet made any exhaustive or systematic investigation of the way a child picks up nonsegmental sounds, so the following observation I made of the development of my son's melodic patterns is tentative and fragmentary. This child was 2 years old in June, 1956. Early in that year his speech was, as can readily be imagined, just piecemeal baby talk and babbling, and if any interpretation could be made of this, it was something in the nature of broad, undefinable reference to the things around him. He did not make, for all intents and purposes, any differentiated use of intonation despite the constant impact on his speech of more than one pattern from the people who came in contact with him. A careful listening to his "speech," however, made one aware that he was using a uniform level tone or something resembling that contour. It may well have been merely an immature and imperfect imitation of the prosodic forms of the words that he perceived. For instance, he used "wan-wan" (dog), "daji" (radio), and "de-de" (let me out) all on a level pitch. Some of the contours he obviously imitated according to the way in which they were provided to him—deliberately distorted on occasion to perhaps make it easier for the child to mimic. For instance, he was able to say "iya" (I don't like it) (an expression he used when something displeased him) in a rising tone that was faithful to the pitch accent of the word. However, this rising tone was different from the rising intonation that the adult might use in a yes-no question. In fact, he did not use this type of rising intonation (nor did he appear to be trying to imitate it at this stage), despite the fact that he often heard people around him address him by using such interrogative sentences as "Raji?" (Is it a radio?) or "Nanshii?" (Do you want the doll "Nancy"?). This was probably because he did not care to ask or because the use of the adult's rising pattern was still a physiological and muscular burden; I have no means of knowing the real reason.

After 2 years of age, he began to discriminate the various patterns of lexical pitch accent. Surprisingly, he also began to use both the rising and the falling intonation as he wished, and he continued to elaborate his patterns until he started to pronounce words with a falling intonation in reply to his parents' queries of the type "Is this . . . ?" He even started to say on his own initiative "Kore buu buu?" (Is this a car?) or "Dare?" (Who is it?)—all with a rising intonation when he either wanted to elicit the answer "yes" or "no" or to ask for a piece of information. Although the child was a rather slow starter and learner as compared with the average child of his age, his tempo and manner of developing nonsegmental sounds may be considered to match for the most part the Crystal theory of speech development.

More recently, a very systematic and well-organized study of four Japanese children's language development from birth to the fifth year was done by Etsutaro Iwabuchi et al. In Chapter 2 of this book, Ichiro Kirikae and Masayuki Sawashima (1968) describe the development of infant speech. Some of the interesting points they have come up with are:

A child starts life with a birth cry, a reflexive sound, his first respiratory motion, and this birth cry is immediately followed by a series of crying—a physiological symbol for a new life at work. This cry (ranging in frequency from 400–500 Hz) is rather monotonous and not varied, but at 1–2 months the child begins to undergo a change both in rhythm and frequency and duration. It is at this point that he begins to 'speak to himself.' This is called a babbling or vocal play stage. From the articulatory point of view, this is important in that the child has now at his command two kinds of voice—crying and non-crying. At 6 months, his voice range is 200–600 Hz, and his shriek may reach the note of 1000 Hz—a note which is higher than the highest note of a soprano singer. That means that he has by now considerably developed his physiological potentials for producing both high and low voices. Nevertheless, the pitch variations the child has as his own are for the most part unconsciously and accidentally produced, and the child does not yet possess at this stage (i.e. up to the first year) the ability to sing a given melody by deliberately modulating the pitch height. About the time of his first birthday, he begins to dance and sing to music, but his melody is usually off key and falls within a very limited musical range. It is said that the child can manage to sing a melody as it ought to be sung at 2–3 years.

After 6–7 months, the child proceeds from the babbling period to the period of imitation. He tries to imitate and reproduce the sounds he hears and the words spoken to him in addition to his babbling and crying. As for the imitative process, it appears that the child is taking in the entire speech chain including its rhythm and intonation rather than the separate phones.

In this connection, we may well cite W. von Raffler-Engel's reasoning (1972), which runs like this: In the infant, the first stage of verbal communication is melodic. Control of the movements of the vocal cords begins very early in life whether for purposes of kinesic imitation or vocalization. The baby learns to alter the shape of the mouth resonator before he uses his articulators, so with the child, the vocal cords, which produce pitch and a resultant vowel as well, are of primary importance for communication. Kirikae and Sawashima go on to say

Then the child begins to learn speech as a meaningful something, and at 10 months to one year, he says 'uma' [meal] pointing to the food. He is now emitting a meaningful sound, and with the maturation of his articulatory mechanism, the child manages to pronounce the 'serviceable' vowels of his mother tongue (this is at 3 years) and he finally succeeds in pronouncing all the consonants at about 6 years, and this, with some children even earlier. In other words, a three-year-old child can carry on a conversation which somehow enables him to go along with adults no matter how poor his pronunciation or enunciation may be.

So we may be justified in concluding after all that it takes the child at least 3 years to have a fairly good command of his vowel and nonsegmental systems.

Children of more advanced years have a well-set melodic system except for their occasional use of intonation that is branded "childish." For example, Bolinger mentions the intonation of the expressions such as "He doesn't want to" and "He doesn't like it"—the type that is used by spoiled children (1955, p. 24). There are obviously some intonational mannerisms coupled with children's "formula" diction, like "I won't tell." [This time, the example is from Pike (1949) with a ^{02}-2- ^{03}-1- ^{02}-2- ^{03}-3- contour.] Japanese children also use melodies and expressions comparable to the English ones just cited, e.g., "Yadaai" (I won't do that) or "Boku yukuu" (I wanna go). The two sentences may be intoned in this manner:

and

MEDICAL ASPECTS

Vocal pitch serves as a good index to the pathology of the speaker, as medical science has revealed in recent years. Linguistically, it is interesting that more communication is likely to be lost, particularly communication dealing with abstract thoughts and ideas, when the ear—rather than the eye—is impaired. These days audiologists and speech therapists are endeavoring to lay more stress on the salvation of whatever is retained of the impaired capacity for hearing for the education of the deaf(-mute) than on the once all-powerful method of instruction, lipreading.

The deaf often find it very difficult to control the intensity and frequency patterns of the speech sounds that they use, and their vowels and consonants are sometimes not clearly distinguished because of the absence of normal feedback activity. It is a well-known fact that, even when a person has normal hearing capacity, his vocal pitch begins to falter and gradually ceases to function as intended if he is made to continue to hear what he is saying not at the same time but a fraction of a second later. Helen Keller is said to have managed, after intensive training, to pronounce the sentence, "I am not dumb now."

It was through the untiring efforts on the part of her first teacher, Anne Sullivan, that Helen learned to speak. The first word she pronounced as taught was "i-t" (it). Carol Hughes says in her article on Helen Keller (1947) that "she must accept the discouraging reality that her voice could never sound normal. Today her voice is low-pitched and somewhat difficult to understand, but with people who know her well she converses with ease." There is a film version of the way Miss Sullivan went about teaching this deaf and blind child. Helen "heard" what was being said to her by placing her thumb on the speaker's throat, the first two fingers on the lips and the third finger on the base of the nose. She "read" by placing her hand on the hand of the speaker so lightly as not to impede its movements as the speaker signed the message. The position of the hand was to her as easy to feel as it was to see. She did not feel each letter any more than one sees each letter separately when one reads. In both cases, tactile devices were used to their best advantage.

In Japan, Naomichi Kaneko, a teacher of English, trained a deaf Japanese student to speak English. Reminiscing about the method of teaching a foreign language to the deaf—a method that in this student's case turned out to be very successful— he said:

> A deaf person on the whole is not good at intonation, or rather he is totally ignorant of it. He reads sentences in a monotone, and occasionally he goes out of tune or lapses into unsteady notes. He knows how to amplify his voice but not how to modulate it. He does sometimes emit a high-pitched voice, but it is a kind of shriek—somewhat like a falsetto voice. I have had the most difficulty with the teaching of intonation. Intonation should however form the basis of full articula-

tory drills. It is necessary to let more than a normally required amount of air flow through the articulatory organ for the satisfactory vibration—hence increased tension—of the vocal cords. Mere tightening of the vocal cords, however, is not enough—it will only lead to a falsetto voice. (1966)

In teaching pitch sensations to the student, Kaneko made the student place the palm of one hand on the instructor's throat—somewhere on the Adam's apple—and the palm of the other hand on the student's own throat, which helped the learner to feel with the palms of his own hands the movement and tension of the Adam's apple, thus somatically associating it with, say, a rising intonation. Oddly enough, Kaneko found it less easy to teach accent (or stress) to the deaf student. He assumed that the deaf have a sense of rhythm and, although they cannot hear sound, they can easily and quickly grasp through their somatic receptors its rhythm. The result was that, as in the Kaneko experiment with the deaf student, stress accent was often overemphasized.

More serious trouble with prosodics of this kind arises when dealing with mentally retarded or deranged persons. Here the issue seems to concern this point: how vocal pitch does *not* work. Ostwald says that "there are patients who speak like dogs, cats, chickens, billy-goats, monkeys, and other animals. Sometimes this is due to a degree of mental deficiency plus social isolation which in effect keeps the sick person from learning any human language" (1964). Ostwald's report on a patient (a woman who had been hospitalized for 40 years) who uses bleats and grunts and another patient who communicates only by humming and song-like tunes as well as repetitious, monotonal hums compares—very aptly, I think—the mentality of some patients with that of animals. As for intonation, Ostwald observed two diametrically opposed types among the patients—monotonal and overworked, histrionic tone.

COGNITIVE ASPECT

There is a very difficult question as to how pitch per se is related to the melody of language in the cerebral cortical region of the brain. Luria (1970) pointed out that "behavioral processes that seem very similar or even identical may not be related to one another at all. For example, it turns out that the mechanism for perception of musical sounds is quite different from that for verbal sounds. A lesion of the left temporal lobe that destroys the ability to analyze phonemes leaves musical hearing undisturbed. I observed an outstanding Russian composer who suffered a hemorrhage in the left temporal lobe that deprived him of the ability to understand speech, yet he went on creating wonderful symphonies!"

We know that even a habitual stutterer does not necessarily find it hard to sing a song, especially a hummed tune, or he may show little, if any, symptoms of verbal inhibition when talking to his pet bird or dog or even when he is "talking" with himself. One of the severely retarded children that I met during World War II did not speak a syllable of a coherent, intelligible word, but he found tremendous pleasure in listening to or attempting to seek sound—any sound, but especially one he made by knocking on some hard object with a stick or with his own fist. He was sometimes heard to be muttering to himself as if tuning in to the melody of the sound he created in this way. So, even deprived of speech, the patient holds on to his melody.

CONCLUSION

There is good reason to believe from what I have discussed in the preceding sections that, with humans, melody has in the course of history separated into many avenues and alleys, but these lead from two major pathways—one that informs, like our lexical and grammatical intonation, and one that inspires and that we attribute to the various forms of animal life (and, paradoxically, elaborated thereon in artistic life as well). Nevertheless, melody has never lost its primordial characteristics, and it will surely continue to go with our thinking and feeling as an exponent of "nature and nurture" when we whisper, shout, speak, read, and sing.

NOTES

My wish to do more work on vocal pitch problems was inspired by the numerous pieces of written literature that have appeared in recent years. Some of the most significant and informative ones are: Ilse Lehiste, *Suprasegmentals,* MIT Press (1970); David Crystal, *Prosodic Systems and Intonation in English* (Cambridge Studies in Linguistics, Vol. 1), Cambridge University Press (1968); D. B. Fry, "Prosodic phenomena," in *Manual of Phonetics,* edited by B. Malmberg, Elsevier-North Holland Pub. Co., New York (1968); D. L. Bolinger, "Melody of language," in Modern Language Forum, Vol. XL 1 (June, 1955); and P. R. Léon, "Où en sont les études sur l'intonation?" in the *Proceedings of the VIIth International Congress of Phonetic Sciences,* Mouton & Co., The Hague (1972). For source materials I also drew on my book, *Eigo Intonation no Kenkyuu* (A Study of English Intonation), Kenkyusha Publishing Co., Tokyo (1958), and some of my papers on intonation.

REFERENCES

Abe, I. 1960. Chant melody. Rising Generation CV 1:348–349.
Abe, I. 1971. Translation of E. T. Anderson, The Intonation of American English, 2d ed., pp. 98–99. Kenkyusha Publishing Co., Tokyo.
Abe, I. 1972. Some remarks about the formulation of question tunes. Acta Univ. Carol. [Philol.] 1:17–19.
Bolinger, D. L. 1955. The melody of language. Mod. Lang. Forum XL 1:19–30.
Bolinger, D. L. 1968. Aspects of Language. Harcourt, Brace & World, New York.

Brend, R. 1972. Male-female intonation patterns in American English. In: A Rigault and P. Charbonneau (eds.), Proceedings of the Seventh International Congress of Phonetic Sciences. Mouton & Co., The Hague.

Chao, Y. R. 1967. Tone, intonation, singsong, chanting. In: M. Halle et al (eds.), For Roman Jakobson. Mouton & Co., The Hague.

Crist, B. 1934. The Art of Setting Words to Music, Chpt. II. Carl Fischer, New York.

Critchley, M. 1970. Aphasiology and Other Aspects of Language, pp. 344–347. William Clowes & Sons Ltd., London.

Crystal, D. 1969. Non-segmental phonology in first language acquisition. Working paper for private circulation.

Crystal, D. 1970. Prosodic systems and language acquisition. In: P. R. Léon et al. (eds.), Prosodic Feature Analysis, pp. 77–90. Studia Phonetica, Vol. 3, pp. 77–90. Didier, Paris.

Guentherodt, I. 1969. Der melodieverlauf bei Fragesätzen in zwei Lothringer Mundarten. Phonetica 19:156–169.

Haas, M. R. 1944. Men's and women's speech in Koasati. Language 20:3.

Herzog, G. 1934. Speech melody and primitive music. Musical Q. 20:452–466.

Hughes, C. 1947. Coronet, May.

Hunter, G. G., and Pike, E. V. 1969. The phonology and tone sandhi of Molinos Mixtec. Linguistics 47:24–40.

Johnson, V. E. 1973. Stud. Curr. Engl., Aug., pp. 24–25.

Kaneko, N. 1966. Some phonetic observations on teaching English to the deaf—especially on its learning process. In: Study of Sounds, Vol. 12, pp. 166–180. Phonetic Society of Japan, Tokyo.

Key, M. R. 1972. Linguistic behavior of male and female. Linguistics 8:15–31.

Kirikae, I., and Sawashima, M. 1968. In: E. Iwabuchi et al. (eds.), Kotoba no Tanjoo (Birth of Language), pp. 45–76. Nippon Hoosoo Shuppan Kyookai, Tokyo.

Kirkup, J. 1970. American Themes & Scenes, p. 23. Ashai Press, Tokyo.

List, G. 1967. Boundaries of speech and song. Ethnomusicology 7:1–16.

Luria, A. R. 1970. The functional organization of the brain. Sci. Am. 222:66–73.

Nash, R. 1973. Turkish Intonation, pp. 24–29. Mouton & Co., the Hague.

Ostwald, P. F. 1964. How the patient communicates about disease with the doctor. In: T. A. Sebeok et al. (eds.), Approaches to Semiotics. Mouton & Co., The Hague.

Pike, K. L. 1949. The Intonation of American English, p. 71. University of Michigan Press, Ann Arbor.

Pike, K. L. 1964. Tone Languages, p. 16. University of Michigan Press, Ann Arbor.

Popperwell, R. G. 1963. The Pronunciation of Norwegian, p. 443. Cambridge University Press, Cambridge, England.

Siertsema, B. 1962. Timbre, pitch, and intonation. Lingua 11:388–398.

Tibbitts, L. 1973. Prosodies of *Impatience* of three statements. Phonetics Department Report No. 4, pp. 14–27. Leeds University, England.

von Raffler-Engel. W. 1972. The relation of intonation to the first vowel articulation in infants. Acta Univ. Carol. [Philol.] 1:197–202.

Wallis, E. 1951. Intonational pattern of contemporary Spanish. Hispania 34:2.

2/ Evidence for Variable Syllabic Boundaries in English

Charles-James N. Bailey

The first linguist to propose an alternative to the straitjacket of static, nongradient frameworks of linguistic analysis was Dwight Bolinger—in writings dating as far back as 1958. Since those days, other linguists have found gradience in areas of language not mentioned by Bolinger. One may mention Labov's work, Keenan and Comrie's hierarchies of accessability, and John Ross's morphosyntactic squishes (although static and idiolectal, these are gradient and can be made dynamic by allowing the line dividing used and unused items to slide back and forth for different stylistic, age, regional, class, and other lects). Bailey (1978c) follows Bolinger's lead in intonation. The writer has also found that more than 40 percent of the (more than 120) segmental rules of English phonetology are variable (i.e., their outputs are implicationally arranged), and that over 30 of these rules depend on the position of the syllable boundary. This paper discusses 33 of these rules, and shows with various examples that the syllabic boundary is variable according to tempo and other factors. This writing is, then, one more example of the gradience that pervades language that Bolinger called linguists' attention to so long ago. I regard as thoroughly lamentable attempts to straitjacket linguistic analysis into the old-fashioned and counterintuitive nongradient frameworks that have so long prevailed. These strike me as antecedently fruitless approaches to the analysis of natural languages as we actually know them.

The present paper is written from notes (mostly) made for the University of Colorado Symposium on Segment Organization and the Syllable. It briefly summarizes and updates past work done by me, including some rules discovered and some problems solved since the time of the Symposium. I would like to thank Joan Hooper for valuable comments on the Symposium manuscript and for the invitation to attend that Symposium. I am also indebted to two Bells— Alan Bell, who co-organized the Symposium and co-invited me to it, and the Bell Laboratories and I. Fujimura for inviting me there to discuss the syllable. Both the Symposium and the visit to the Bell Laboratories provided profitable occasions for thinking about the syllable and for getting my ideas clearer.

Since the first part of Bailey, 1978b, discusses the general issues involved in an investigation of this sort, present comments can be limited to observing that, until neurophonetics establishes the truth (or falsity) of the surmise (see references in Kim, 1971) that the brain sends motor signals to the speech organs in syllable-sized bundles, there is little phonetic evidence for syllabization, i.e., for locating syllabic boundaries. Chest pulses mark the onset of stressed syllables, but not others (Ladefoged, 1967). The most reliable present-day evidence for syllabization comes from phonology: there is evidence from the manner in which phonetological rules apply and sometimes evidence from stuttering and spoonerisms. The distinction between phonological and phonetic syllabization is discussed in Bailey, 1978b, where I also point out that when syllabization is viewed as a gradient phenomenon the disagreements of various scholars over the syllabization of given items can easily be reconciled. It must be emphasized that, although some writers speak of floating styles or syllables, it is really only the syllable boundaries that "float"! I do not wish to maintain that no scholars have recognized variation in syllabization—on the contrary, expressions like "mostly" or "more often than" and discussions of different syllabizations in different styles can be cited—but only wish to point out that the frameworks of such analysts absolutely rule out such comments as invalid, since the frameworks are static and idiolectal (in every case known to me).

At this juncture, an illustration may clear up what is meant for the reader unaccustomed to gradient frameworks. The word <u>Wisconsin</u> has two pronunciations: 1) [(ˌ)wɪsˈkhɛ̆t$^?$sn̩], and 2) [wəˈscɛ̆tsn̩]. Pronunciation 2 occurs in many tempos when the word is very frequently used by a speaker; otherwise, it is the allegro pronunciation, whereas 1 is the lento one. The manner in which rule evidence is used to ascertain the phonetic syllabization can be succinctly stated. In 1, the velar [k] is aspirated because it is syllable-initial here; in 2, however, one hears [c] instead, unaspirated because it is not syllable-initial and fronted to the palatal articulatory position because it follows tautosyllabic [s].[1] (The glottalization of [t$^?$] in 1 is irrelevant for syllabization; see below.)

The role of # (word boundary) has also, in my opinion. been much misunderstood by writers on the syllable. The evidence suggests that it plays no role in all but perhaps the most monitored styles when an unstressed syllable follows; it does play a role when a fully stressed or mid-stressed syllable follows. Although <u>mistake</u> can group [st] together in the following

---

[1]In the afterpart of the syllable, however, //k// becomes [c] after tautosyllabic //s// only if the preceding syllabic nucleus ends in a front vowel.

syllable in an allegro pronunciation, this is not true of dis#taste. And //t// in point can never begin the next syllable in point##out the way it may in Toronto, nor can [tr] be tautosyllabic in night#rate the way they must be in retreat and may be in controvert ([t~r] with a syllabic division is impossible in the first item; note that ~ is a syllabic boundary). What has just been said about # must be qualified by the observation that # can rule out a given part of the environment as relevant to a rule's operation, although the examples that follow seem to be more phonomorphological than phonetological (morpho-phonic). Although some of the phenomena depend on a distinction between heavy and light consonantal clusters, this distinction has developed out of a historical distinction between closed and open syllables. Note that the //ē// of pēnal is lightened in pĕnal+ty, but not in pēnal#ize; and also that the /ĕ/ in the adjective clean+ly contrasts with the /ē/ in clean#ly. There are further complications in the rule that lightens nuclei before heavy clusters, since the nucleus is lightened in wĭd+th and deal+t and fŏrt+y, but not in fōur+th; nor is the nucleus in hāst+n lightened, although the one in mĕtr+ic is light-ened—before -ic, since //tr// is a light cluster (cf. //ē// in mēter). Although the word boundary and the syllable boundary play major roles in the phoneto-logical rules of English, the role of the formant boundary is negligible (see the rules for degemination and interconsonantal apical-stop deletion). Few assi-milations cross word boundaries, but //d// does become a dorsal or labial be-fore #g, #b, and so on. Furthermore, an apical sibilant becomes a lamino-palatal before # plus a laminopalatal or palatal. Note also that //s// is changed to [z] before ~m in plas~ma and spas'modic.

SYLLABIZATION RULE EVIDENCE

Before giving the syllabization rules, the evidence for them is presented below in the form of phonetological rules. The rules that precede the stress rules (rules 1–6) presume an un-English syllabization in which open syllables are maximized. Most of these look like phonomorphological rules rather than rules with genuine phonetological motivations. If such is indeed the case, then these rules cannot offer any evidence for the facts of phonetic syllabization. The rules that follow the stress rules (rules 7–33) presume the phonetic syl-labization of English, in which a consonant (liquids and glides have special provisos) adjacent to a nucleus that is stressed prefers to be syllabized with it rather than with a preceding or following unstressed nucleus; e.g., Wis'con-sin, ec~stra ("extra"), ac~rid, and mys~tic. (Cases like motto, pronto, and "th" in Dorothy are discussed later.) Moreover, progressively more distant consonants clustered with the one that is adjacent to the more heavily stressed nucleus are syllabized with it as the tempo (or the frequency and familiarity of the item) progressively increases; e.g., Wi'sconsin, ex~tra and ext~ra, acr~id, myst~ic. It is very important to observe that the "English" principles of syllabization summarized above do not apply to the syllable-timed rhythm heard in Shakespearean and other poetic recitation.

1. The rule diphthongizing //ŭ// requires an open syllable; e.g., augury, communal, tabular, Lilliputian. Note that the rule cannot operate after //l// clustered with a consonant in the same syllable, even in lects where it may otherwise operate after //l//, e.g., flute. The cluster //st// will not always close a word-initial syllable for purposes of this rule, e.g., Eustace, Houston; contrast mustard, custard.

2. The rule that changes velar stops into sibilants in regent and electricity before underlying //ĭ ĕ//. Unlike the change in rule 20 below, which requires the underlying velar to be tautosyllabic, this rule effects the change even when the velar is heterosyllabic. (One assumes that, except in the North of Great Britain, pairs like brig and bridge and rig and ridge are not related for speakers of English.)

3. The rule deleting /ɫ/ before a nonapical (and not always) requires a closed syllable; compare palm, calm, and alms (which normally have no lateral) with palmetto, calmative, and almoner (which may have a lateral), and also compare the nouns salve, calves, and halves (which normally have no lateral) with the verbs salve, calve, and halve (which may have a lateral). The lateral has been or is being restored in many words in which it was formerly lost (Ralph, help, calk, chalk, calm) or in which it never existed (soldier, solder). Uncultivated English often lacks a lateral in such words as help and self, and cultivated English may have no lateral in Holborn, golf, and so on.

4. A rule very similar to the preceding that is found in some "r-less" lects treats //a// as //ar// before //f θ s// (and certain clusters) if these consonants are tautosyllabic with the nucleus; cf. popular spellings like marster, arsk, and larf. The development is heard in pass, graph, and class among many speakers who retain the output of light //a// in passage, graphic, and classic, where the following fricative at some time was or is not now tautosyllabic with this vowel. There may not be enough alternations of this type in contemporary English to allow us to speak of even a minor "rule," but formerly the situation was more evident (Jespersen, 1961, pp. 298–304).

5. The rule that sibilantizes and palatalizes the apical stops before tautosyllabic //r// in some lects probably comes here; e.g., train, drain, mattress,

string.[2] In Hawaiian English, because of the phonetic open-syllable syllabization, this rule operates in bath-room ['baₜt˅sum].

6. It is not entirely clear how to discuss the evidence for deleting //r// clustered with a tautosyllabic consonant in the forepart of the syllable; cf. Hawaiian bath-(r)oom, vernacular Black English buvva (for brother), and White and Black vernacular Southern States th(r)ob, th(r)row, and th(r)ough. Such a rule can be variously ordered, but does require a tautosyllabic cluster, since //r// is not deleted in the diagnostic lects in bathₜroom when so syllabized.

At this point, the stress rules—probably morphological—operate. In many analyses, the concept of strong cluster—defined so as to maximize open syllables—is employed. Whatever the truth of the matter may be, the surficial syllabization of English depends on the position of the stress. Although the ordering of the following rules cannot be demonstrated here (see Bailey, 1973b, and Bailey and Maroldt, manuscript in preparation), these rules all follow the stress rules and depend on the "English" syllabization principle summarized above, a principle that depends on syllabic stress.

7. The palatalization of apicals (other than //l θ ð//) requires that they be tautosyllabic with the following /y/ or /ɥ/. It occurs in tenure, mania, and menial, but not in Spañada [ˌspæn'yɑdə]. In allegro Goodyear, Neptune, and menu, where /dy tɥ nɥ/ go with the preceding syllable, palatalization is heard,[3] but in the lento pronunciations of these words, where a [ₜ] intervenes to make the palatalizing clusters heterosyllabic, the rule does not operate.

8. Between a nasal and a tautosyllabic obstruent, English introduces an "epenthetic" stop that has the place of articulation of the preceding nasal and the heavy or light order of the following obstruent; e.g., warmth ['wɔ:pθ] (with deleted //m// by rule 12), respon[t]se, prin[t]ce, Sampson, sempstress, Thompson, contempt, bumpkin, presumption. Although epenthesis occurs in U.S. barytonic princess, it does not occur in British prin'cess nor in tramₜcar, where the environmental consonants are heterosyllabic to begin with. They become heterosyllabic after epenthesis, one of a number of syllabic changes resulting from the rules—

---

[2]In Hawaiian English, this rule stands prior to the pre-stress rule that changes an apical sibilant to a laminopalatal sibilant when a palatal follows, e.g., string ['št˅siŋ]. For the absence of [r] in string and bathroom, see rule 6.

[3]In Bailey, 1978b, I give evidence for syllable-final clusters that cannot occur word-finally. The glides /y/ and /ɥ/ are probably not syllabized with preceding labials (see premium below); but contrast the [c] in allegro ocular ['ɐcɥ~ɫ~lə] with the [k] in lento ocular ['ɐk~yɫ~lə].

this suggests to some that syllabization rules are "anywhere" rules (see below).

9.   The rule deleting interconsonantal apical stops under certain conditions does so only when they are syllable-final (e.g., in ves(t)~ment and exac(t)~ly, but not in ves~try and elec~tric); at least, this is the inference to be drawn from deletion behavior. In environments in which the rule operates variably under slightly complex conditions, deletion behavior correlates with the variable lento and allegro syllabizations that other evidence has already led us to expect. Thus, the deletion occurs for many speakers in conversational tempos in ban(d)-width, las(t) one, trus(t)worthy, ol(d) yeast, jus(t) yet, lan(d) rights, gol(d) rights, and las(t) rites, where we may safely assume that # preserves a syllabic division; but the deletion requires much more unmonitored styles to be heard in landward, sandwich, Baldwin, and eastward, where # would not serve to preserve a syllabic boundary before an unstressed vowel anyhow. Examples like land rights and last rites are especially to be compared and contrasted with laundry and vestry, where the deletion never occurs.

The rule that deletes interconsonantal //t θ d// under the appropriate conditions is part of a large and very complex rule that stipulates where stops are unreleased. Lack of release triggers the glottalization of the heavy (i.e., underlying voiceless) stops (//t// becomes /tʔ/ or /ʔ/, depending on the context). Glottalization is thus generally complementary to release in such stops. The vastly misunderstood rule of glottalization—far too complex to state here (see Bailey, 1979, and Bailey and Maroldt, manuscript in preparation)— has been alleged to provide evidence for syllabization. That the relationship is not simple can be seen by examining the tempo-variable behavior of /p k c/ before //s//. In slow tempos, one hears [cʔ] in axe and [pʔ] in cops; in faster tempos, the glottalization is replaced by release. Note, however, that where interconsonantal //t// is replaced by length in acts ['æcʔ:s] and Copts ['khapʔ:s], glottalization is heard in faster tempos than those in which /c/ and /p/ deglottalize in axe and cops (although in yet faster tempos acts and Copts can sound like axe and cops). A failure to understand this gradient variability is responsible for the lack of success of the static analyses I have seen.

10.   The change of syllable-final //t// (thus in at#all, but not in a't+all) to [d] (regularly in North American English and under different conditions elsewhere) occurs if the following vowel is unstressed, regardless of the stress on the preceding nucleus; e.g., formative. The syllabization is seen to be especially relevant in the contrast between lento Plato and motto, (with syllable-initial aspirated [ˌth]) and allegro Plat,o and mott,o

(with syllable-final [d]). In some lects, the change is to a tap; compare Tok Pisin wara for water and Bislama garem (apparently) for got 'em (though -em may also come from an aboriginal transitive formative). Id'ly for Italy is explained in Bailey, 1973b, p. 239.

11.   The allegro deletion of //t// under the conditions exemplified in plenty and twenty in U.S. English (//nt// become /nd/ when flanked by un-stressed vowels, as in seventy) provides evidence for syllabization, since it evidently occurs syllable-finally (as in inter), not syllable-initially (as in in'ter, i.e., "bury"). Since //t// is deleted in allegro Toronto and pronto, but not in the lento pronunciations of these words, we are justified in concluding that the syllabizations are allegro To'ron(t,)o and pron(t,)o and lento To'ron,to and pron,to. The aspiration of [th] in the lento examples confirms this surmise (see rule 12 below). Apoin(t)'ee is a further example that, like tau[d]'ology (i.e., tautology, relevant to the preceding rule), shows that the syllabization rules are sometimes ig-nored. Further evidence for such phenomena is mentioned in connection with rule 15 below.

12.   The deletion of a nasal between a stressed nucleus (which becomes nasalized) and a tautosyllabic heavy obstruent occurs in bent, continent, and temple, but does not occur when the obstruent is heterosyllabic, as in con'tain and tem,po. Concerning panther, it may be observed that although the //θ// goes with the stressed nucleus—this is shown by the loss of //n// as well as by the effects of rule 16—the epenthetic stop that results from rule 8 (before rule 12 operates) causes the output to be syllabized thus: ['phǽt(ʔ)~θə].

13.   Syllable-initial occlusives are aspirated, e.g., [th] in contain, but [t] in stop. The second of the three syllabizations of extra—ec~stra, ex~tra, ext~ra—is the only one that has [th]. Since this rule precedes schwa deletion for some speakers, support may differ from sport in that the former may have [ph].

14.   In various lects, the outputs of /ī ū/ have older and newer variants. In some of these lects, the newer variant occurs before syllabic boundaries (e.g., psy'chology, mi'gration) and light consonants other than //g// or nasals plus a heavy obstruent. The newer variant heard in psychic and migrant, no less than in mike and pint, shows that /ī/ is tautosyllabic with the following consonants. Variation, as expected, turns up in psy,cho and cy,clone, but not if # intervenes (contrast nitrate, with variable output of /ī/ before variable syllabization of //t//, and night#rate—always 'night,rate).

15.   An //n// (normally not other nasals) is assimilated to the place of articu-lation of a following tautosyllabic obstruent, but usually not to that of

one that is heterosyllabic.[4] Contrast [ŋ], [ɱ], and [m] in congress, conversation, and in between, respectively, with [n] in con'gressional, con'verse, and in 'bed. Tempo-dependent variation in the syllabization of 'mon͵goose (lento): mong͵oose[5] (allegro) and similar examples create [n]:[ŋ] alternations, although the issue is complicated by orthography (Bailey, 1973a, p. 28). Like rule 11 above, the conditions in this rule can be completely ignored in some very unmonitored styles, so that one hears one ['wʌm] 'moment, and the like, as noted in Bailey, 1978b. Examples like one ['wʌm] moment might be analyzed as an avoidance of [nm], just as [db] is avoided in English (cf. goob-bye, goob boy); although this may well be true, it won't explain oddities like li[ŋ]'guistics, which may be due, however, to the orthography. Allegro raimbow and hempecked may be due to treating the second syllable in each example as though it were unstressed in such tempos, rather than merely mid-stressed.

16. In some lects, the interdental fricatives become labiodental fricatives in the afterpart (but not the forepart)[6] of a syllable. The result is [f] in syllable-final position in panther and [v] in mother.

17. After a tautosyllabic nucleus, nondorsal stops become dorsals in slips of the tongue and regularly in Jamaican English. That this occurs in neegle (for needle) and many similar examples shows that the stop goes with the stressed nucleus. The history of Caribbean fraekn ("frighten") is instructive; [t] was syllable-initial in English so long as syllable-final [ç] existed, but later became syllable-final when [ç] disappeared; after which, it could change to [c].

18. Postnuclear liquids are vocalized—//l// becomes /ɫ/ and //r// becomes /ɚ/—when no tautosyllabic vowel follows.[7]

19. Although English syllabic nasals may follow only /ʔ/ and apical (also laminopalatal in British) sibilants under any and all conditions, they may follow stops provided that they are *heterosyllabic*—i.e., not pre-

---

[4]Changes like that of in- to im- in im'pose are the result of morphological rules derived from Latin and are not English phonetological rules. When //m// is followed by an obstruent or lateral, English prefers epenthesis (see rule 8) to assimilation.

[5]Mong͵oose, but not mon͵goose, may have [ɔ] in the first syllable if the rule effecting this (see rule 24) is ordered after the assimilation rule; otherwise, it may not.

[6]In Cockney English, the change of the inderdentals to labiodentals occurs syllable-initially as well as in the afterpart of the syllable. This lect is therefore not diagnostic for syllabization with respect to the evidence of rule 16.

[7]In lects outside of North America and northern Great Britain, [l], not [ɫ], is heard after the nuclei illustrated in school, gules, mule, goal, drawl, and cowl. Contrast Southern States boil ['bɔ(ᵉ)ɫ:] with ball ['bɔl 'bɒᵒl] and with Northern States ball ['bɔɫ:].

ceded by an obstruent, an unstressed nucleus, or a word boundary. Contrast the two pronunciations of golden: [ˈgoᵘldən] (where [d] is clustered and [ɾ] may not follow) and [ˈgoⱡːdn̩] (where [d] is unclustered and [n̩] is allowed). An exception permits [n̩] for <u>and</u> in <u>hundred-and-one</u>. <u>Sentence</u> can either delete //t// by rule 11, above, or [n̩] is permitted after [ʔ], e.g., [ˈsɛ̃ʔn̩s].

20.   A [w] is inserted between nuclear elements if the first is rounded and the second is heterosyllabic, but not if the second nuclear element has been made a satellite on the first nucleus. Thus, lento <u>fluid</u> [ˈfluwɪd], <u>poet</u> [ˈpoᵘwɪʔ], and <u>fuel</u> [ˈfüᵘwⱡ] have a [w] that is absent in allegro [ˈflⱨⁱd ˈphoⁱʔ ˈfⱨuⱡː]. For similar reasons, <u>mow#er</u> ("one who mows"), <u>low#er</u> (comparative of <u>low</u>), and so on have a [w] not heard in <u>mow+er</u> (a machine), low+er (the verb), etc. (in conversational tempos these sound like <u>more</u> [ˈmoᵊː], <u>lore</u> [ˈloᵊː], etc.).

21.   In the Southern States and adjacent areas of the Northern States, front /æ ɛ ɪ/ (heard in <u>sack</u>, <u>speck</u>, and <u>sick</u>) and central /ɐ ə ⱨ/ (heard in <u>cot</u>, <u>cut</u>, and <u>put</u>) are retracted respectively to /ɐ̣ ə̣ ⱨ̣/ and /ɑ ʌ ɯ/ when, <i>inter alia</i>, a tautosyllabic grave consonant follows. The retractions in <u>happy</u>, <u>Debbie</u>, <u>socket</u>, <u>lucky</u>, and <u>bookie</u> provide evidence that the medial consonant in each case is syllabized with the preceding stressed nucleus.

22.   Some lects of "r-ful" English change syllable-final /ɑ/ to /ɔ/; e.g., <u>hurrah</u>, <u>pa</u>, <u>Panama</u>, <u>Arkansas</u>, <u>Utah</u>, <u>praline</u>, <u>Chihuahua</u>. The last two must be pra~line and Chiˈhua~hua.

23.   Southern States English changes /æ/ to [æⁱ] before a variety of tautosyllabic consonants, among which is //s//; the change is absent if the consonant is heterosyllabic. Compare <u>lasso</u> lento [ˈlæˌsoᵘ] and allegro [ˈlæⁱsˌoᵘ].

24.   A change very similar to the foregoing changes /ɑ/ to /ɔ/ when tautosyllabic //s θ f g// or /ŋ/ follows. (The rule has disappeared for younger speakers in various areas.) As the result of tempo-variable syllabizations, <u>Chicago</u> may be heard as lento [šəˈkhɑˌgoᵘ] (also [ˌšəˈkhɔˌgoᵘ] where rule 22 is operative) and allegro [š̩ˈkhɔgˌoᵘ].[8]

25.   The first type of detriphthongization (Bailey, 1973b, pp. 230–231) deletes /e o/ before /ⱡ ɚ ᵊ/, which in some lects come from tautosyllabic liquids (in some of these lects this has been generalized to further environments). The change could occur in <u>sour</u>, <u>cowl</u>, and <u>toil</u>, but not in

---

[8]The phenomenon in which speakers have [ɐ] in <u>Roscoe</u> and <u>Moscow</u> but [ɔ] in <u>Ross</u> and <u>moss</u> is hardly to be explained by means of variable syllabizations!

dowry, cowling, or toilet (unless the liquid has been geminated in the lect in question; see below).

26. The deletion of syllable-final glides in shepherd, (h)e, (h)im, (h)er, Durham, forehead, Greenwich, unstressed will, would, and Michael—with additional examples in noncultivated speech like Dan'el, back'ards, and innards. This rule has apparently been replaced in the speech of most English users by a rule deleting glides before unstressed vowels, since word-initial glides are no longer deleted (e.g., historic), except in clitics.

27. The rules that result in shorter nuclei and longer tautosyllabic postnuclear heavy obstruents versus longer nuclei and shorter light consonants indicate in sŭpp̄er and rŭb̄ber, no less than in săf̄e and săv̄e, that the consonants [p b f v] are tautosyllabic with the preceding stressed nuclei in these examples.

28. The preservation of the tautosyllabicity of the peak plus satellite that is created out of prevocalic heavy nuclei (as in mire and paranoia, from underlying //mīr//, in which //r// is eventually vocalized in most kinds of English, and //para+nǖə//) creates a contrast with the syllabization heard in certain lects in Maya and lawyer. Contrast, for example, Southern States ['pærə'nɔ^eə] with ['lɔ~yə] or ['lɒ^o~yə], and note the syllabization also of Southern States Ma~ya and Ga~wain. (In various other lects, glide gemination affects these words, and then /y/ in Maya is deleted following a geminate [^e], effectively changing the syllabization to May~a.)

29. The change of the dorsal stops to [c ɏ] next to a tautosyllabic front vowel in cycle and regal shows that the internuclear stops are syllabized with the preceding stressed nuclei (see also footnote 3).

30. The change of //k// to [c] following tautosyllabic //s//—not in slower [wɪs'khētsn̩] (Wisconsin), but in faster [wə'scē^ʔsn̩]—is another test of syllabization.

31. Devoicing of liquids and glides that occurs after tautosyllabic heavy fricatives (but not after aspirated occlusives); e.g., in slow, fly, smoke, and swipe, but not in ice-locker, life-like, policeman, or housewife.

32. The deletion in "r-less" lects of //r// when not followed by a tautosyllabic vowel leads to alternations like the following Southern States examples:

bar ['bɑ:]   barrister ['bærəstə]
par ['phɑ:]   parity ['phærədɪ]
car ['khɑ:]   carriage ['khærɪdž]
war ['wɔ:]   warrior ['wɑrɪə]
abhor [əb'hɔ:]   abhorrent [əb'hɐrə̃ʔ]
err ['ɜ:]   error ['ɛrə]

These alternations depend on which syllable //r// belongs to. Note the difference between demurr+er [də'mərə] (the result of demurring) and de-murr#er [də'mɜːrə] ("one who demurs"), where the boundary is relevant, since forward gemination (which I have treated in a number of writings; cf. Bailey, in press) occurs when //r// is followed by #.

33.   In some varieties of English, syllable-initial nonsibilant fricatives be-come homorganic stops, either in emphatic speech only (in many lects), or, in the case of the interdentals, quite generally (in some lects). The change of //θ// to [t̯] implies that of //ð// to [d̯]. Examples are: these, those, thin, first, vote.

SYLLABIZATION RULES

The phonetological rules that have been examined point consistently to the following set of rules for English syllabization:

Ia.   Provided that clusters that are not permitted word-initially are excluded (and this condition may vary with the tempo in question, although dn, dm, dl, tn, tm, tl, and usually θl are generally ruled out), and provided that clusters of stop-plus-r are not divided (e.g., la'trine), more conson-ants are grouped with a following stressed nucleus than with a preceding nucleus as the tempo increases and the monitoring decreases; however, # creates a syllabic division (e.g., dis#taste; contrast "X-L", i.e., X#L, with excel). (In fast tempos, English allows many clusters not permitted in slower tempos; e.g., 't's me, m'rine, p'tato, f'tigue, y'know, and even T'ledo and n'night!)

Ib.   Internuclear single obstruents and nasals, as well as cluster-initial con-sonants, are syllabized with a preceding nucleus (even an unstressed one) if an unstressed nucleus follows (e.g., pat~ron, fath~er, Doroth~y). (This principle is disregarded for internuclear liquids and glides, which go with the next syllable always; however, gemination may obscure this fact, as a comparison of ['lɔᵉ~ə] with ['lɔ~yə] for lawyer or of ['sɪ̯~li] with ['sɪ~lɪ] for silly shows.) Formerly the English language syllabized glides (but not liquids) with a preceding stressed syllable, as in steward, seaward, leeward, mayor, and so on.

Ic.   Since the stress is weaker on a nucleus following a stressed nucleus (e.g., the second nucleus of center is weaker than that of cen͵taur, and menu and Neptune have second nuclei that may be weaker or stronger), more consonants between the two nuclei are likely to be syllabized with the preceding stressed nuclei, and this tendency is increased as the tempo accelerates. Apical-grave clusters (e.g., God~frey, Ox~ford, Cos~ grave) remain heterosyllabic; also, # is relevant before a mid-stressed nucleus, but not before an unstressed one, in maintaining a syllable division (cf. night#rate with nitrate).

Note i: The considerations mentioned under Ia concerning stop-plus-r clusters are of no relevance to principle Ic; however, another principle is—clusters of nasal plus homorganic heavy obstruent do syllabize with a preceding more heavily stressed nucleus (e.g., simp~er, simp~ly). In fast tempos, clusters not allowed word-finally do go together with a preceding heavily stressed nucleus (e.g., acr~id, doubl~et, sequ~ence, acc[ɥ]~urate, crumb~le, ang~le, but not dn, dm, dl, tn, tm, tl); the rule disallowing syllabic nasals after tautosyllabic [d] assumes in London the syllabization, Lon~don.

Note ii: As for consonants preceded by a fully stressed nucleus and followed by a mid-stressed one, the latter is treated more like a stressed syllable in slower tempos (e.g., 'mo͵tto, To'ron͵to), but more like an unstressed syllable in faster tempos (e.g., 'mo[d]͵o, To'ron(t)͵o. Between unstressed nuclei, such syllabic divisions as these are found: seven~ty, Coven~try.

II.   Single glides and liquids between nuclei go with the following nuclei, as noted above. Not only may gemination (and the subsequent loss of /y/) obscure this, but the rules must be ordered or otherwise arranged so that the change of unstressed i to y in billion and that of unstressed u to ɥɵ in failure yield glides that stay in the same syllable as a preceding l (cf. Southern States lento ['bɪ~lyən], allegro ['bɪ~yən], and lento ['fɛ^l~lyə], allegro ['fɛ^l~yə]); only when the rule that changes preconsonantal //l// to /ɫ/ is ordered after the other rules just mentioned, as in Northern States and Scottish English, do we hear heterosyllabic [ɫ:y] in billion ['bɪɫ:~yən] and failure ['feɫ:~yɚ]. Note that this rule does not apply to glides and liquids clustered with a preceding apical or palatal consonant, at least in the faster tempos; this is shown by examples under Ic above, such as acrid, doublet, sequence, and accurate.

III.   Between any nuclear segment and a following nuclear peak, there exists a syllable boundary. (This leads to a difference between underlying and phonetic syllabization; compare monosyllabic dual ['dɥuɫ:] with underlying disyllabic //du~al//, and compare slower trisyllabic prem~i~um with faster disyllabic prem~[y]um.)

Principle Ic above is worded in such a way as to capture the presumed generalization that consonants preceding unstressed vowels are treated alike, regardless of the stress on the preceding nucleus (except that liquids and glides go with the second of the nuclei). It may seem counterintuitive to let non-stress be so determinative; the stress of a preceding stressed nucleus would seem to be what determines the syllabization. What we probably have here is a generalization from the environment 'V _____ ~V to the environment _____ ~V.

The evidence for the syllabization of a single obstruent·or nasal between unstressed nuclei is less clear than one might wish. Some of the evidence favors a V C ~ V syllabization in faster tempos and a V ~ C V syllabization in slower tempos:

1. In multiple and moniker, the stop between the unstressed nuclei is unaspirated in allegro tempo and aspirated in lento tempo (see rule 15 above).
2. In monarchy and moniker, one hears in lento tempo [c] and [k], respectively, agreeing with the following nucleus and suggesting V ~ C V; in allegro tempo, one hears [k] and [c], respectively, agreeing with the preceding nuclei and suggesting V C~ V (see rule 29 above).

Other evidence favors V C ~ V:

3. Dorothy has [f] for //θ// in lects that are diagnostic for rule 16 above.
4. The change of syllable-final //t// to [d] is heard in monitor and formative (see rule 10 above).

I do not know whether these //t//'s are replaced by velars (see rule 17) in the diagnostic lects. The fact that unassimilated [n], not assimilated [m], precedes [b] in Normanby suggests (see rule 15 above) the syllabization [n~b]. In Bailey, 1978b, I concluded that tempo differences cause the syllable boundary to float in mimicry, amnesty, tapestry, Coventry, and 'Kerensky. I suggested an ordering principle to account for the difference between the syllable-final and syllable-initial stops in multiple and moniker.

Some writers have used the concept of *ambisyllabicity* to indicate a segment's simultaneous membership in both adjacent syllables. The above evidence clearly shows that such a concept is not suited to English—and probably not to any other language, either. If the term has any valid use, it is to indicate a consonant that in one style belongs to the following syllable and in another style to the preceding one. This phenomenon suggests writing *phonological stress* with an acute (full stress) or grave (mid-stress) accent over the appropriate peak and *phonetic stress* with the ticks [' ˌ] at the actual point of onset of stress in the given style being presented. The accents are fixed, but the ticks "float" from style to style in some examples that have been considered.

Resyllabization is discussed in Bailey (1973a, 1978b).

The different operation of liquid gemination between a fully stressed nucleus and a mid-stressed one in "r-ful" Southern States and Northern States

English (if the preceding nucleus is /ō/, there is no difference), creates different results in hero, pharaoh, Cairo, tyro, Pyrex, Truro, and bureau (but not in moron or Chlorox), as noted in Bailey, 1978b, p. 28. (In that article, gemination was wrongly treated as part of syllabization, and the manner in which # preceding a liquid or glide blocks its gemination in some lects in America and Britain was not made clear.)

A FINAL PROBLEM

A question arises as to whether or not syllabization is an "anywhere" rule that applies after every other rule. Some evidence indicates that this is true; see the results of epenthesis discussed under rule 8, the derivation of frighten and fraekn mentioned in connection with rule 8, and the discussion of premium following rule III. On the other hand, the discussion of billion and failure in connection with rule II shows that the Southern States (lento) examples would be a problem for "anywhere" applications of the syllabization principles. This is not the place to decide the issue, and I leave it for subsequent investigations. It is clear that "anywhere" syllabizations would have to follow the stress rules in English. The vocalization of //l   r// to /ɫ   ɚ/, respectively, which is intimately connected with syllabization and the rules that depend on syllabization (see the discussion of golden, above, under rule 19)[9] is itself a problem for rule ordering.

REFERENCES

Bailey, C.-J. N. 1973a. Variation and Linguistic Theory. Center for Applied Linguistics, Washington, D.C.

Bailey, C.-J. N. 1973b. Variation resulting from different rule orderings in English phonology. In: C.-J. N. Bailey and R. W. Shuy (eds.), New Ways of Analyzing Variation in English, pp. 211–252. Georgetown University Press, Washington, D.C.

Bailey, C.-J. N. 1978a. Four low-level pronunciation rules of Northern States English. IPA J. 8:1–2.

Bailey, C.-J. N. 1978b. Gradience in English Syllabization and a Revised Concept of Unmarked Syllabization. Indiana University Linguistics Club, Bloomington, Ind.

Bailey, C.-J. N. 1978c. System of English Intonation with Gradient Models. Indiana University Linguistics Club, Bloomington, Ind.

Bailey, C.-J. N. 1979.   English Phonetic Transcription for Teachers. Center for Applied Linguistics, Arlington, Va.

[9]However, speakers changing //t// to [d] after a lateral in shelter and Walter do so regardless of whether it is /ɫ/ (as in shelter) or /l/ (as in Walter in the lects mentioned in footnote 7). One would expect an implicational relation such that the change after /l/ would imply it in the environment following /ɫ/— a vowel.

Bailey, C.-J. N. The patterning of sonorant gemination in English lects. In: R. Fasold and R. Shuy (eds.), Papers from NWAVE meetings. Georgetown University Press, Washington, D.C. In press.

Bailey, C.-J. N., and Maroldt, K. Grundzüge der englischen Phonetologie. In preparation.

Jespersen, O. 1961. A Modern English Grammar on Historical Principles: Part I, Sounds and Spellings. George Allen & Unwin Ltd., London.

Kim, C.-W. 1971. Experimental phonetics. In: W. O. Dingwall (ed.), A Survey of Linguistic Science, pp. 16–128. University of Maryland, Linguistics Program, College Park.

Ladefoged, P. 1967. Three Areas of Experimental Phonetics. Oxford University Press, London.

3/ Chinese Tones and English Stress

Yuen Ren Chao

It is a well-known fact that speakers of Chinese, whether literate or illiterate, feel unconsciously that a tone is such an integral part of the word that a syllable of the same consonantal and vocalic makeup but spoken in a different tone sounds like a totally different word. This attitude is usually carried over to the study of a nontonal language, such as English.[1]

To the Chinese ear a single stressed syllable, such as yes, no, you, or good, sounds like a 4th tone, or a 1st tone merging into a 4th tone. A learner of those words pronounced in that intonation tends to pronounce them always the same way, even though they may have quite different pitch patterns in actual sentences. When an American speaker says, "Will you have a cup of tea?" the last syllable may have one of the following pitch patterns[2]:

$$45 \ \urcorner \quad 55 \ \urcorner \quad 52 \ \searcorner$$

(The last form is for contrasting stress and sounds about the same as it does when pronounced alone.) However, it is usually very difficult for a Chinese speaker to learn the British intonation and say:

> Will
>   you
>   have
>   a
>   cup of
>   -a?
>   te-

with the word "tea" sounding as if it were in the Chinese 3rd tone.

Such intonation sometimes occurs in American English also. For example, a Chinese girl working as announcer in Station XGOA in Nanking started a sentence with:

---

[1] For a discussion of English stress and frequency and other factors, see Wang, W. S-Y. 1961. Stress in English. Lang. Learn. XI:3–4, 69–77.

[2] I am here using the five-point system of indicating relative syllabic pitch, which seems to be fairly widely used now.

this
In sit- -tion,
-u-
-a-

and was criticized for putting the stress on the wrong (last) syllable. I was asked why she did this even though she had been born and raised in America, and I had to go to some lengths to explain to her boss that she did not have the wrong stress, but had simply used an unusual intonation because it was a phrase of suspense. It was hard for her Chinese-minded boss to understand that the word ''situation'' had any other intonation but mid–half-low–high–low, which was of course the pattern in which he had learned the word in isolation.

Because of such association of stress with pitch, a phrase of several words will tend to follow the pitch pattern of the separate words. For example, ''apple cider'' is usually pronounced by a Chinese student with the tonal pattern of high–low–high–low, instead of the normal high–high (or half-high)–high–low. A name like ''Scalapino'' is usually given as high–low–high–low instead of the normal high–high (or half-high)–high–low.

So much for Chinese learners of English. As for transliteration of English names into Chinese characters, most writers from North China have taken no account of tone and stress. However, the Cantonese do make more use of tones for indicating stress, possibly because of the richness of tones in Cantonese. Thus, we have:

Oakland	屋崙	ok-lön	high–low
Watson	屈臣	wat-san	high–low
Pacific	怕思域	p‘a-si-wik	mid–high–low
unit[3]	么匿	iu-nik[3]	high–low
Detroit	積彩	tik-t‘oi	low–high

the last being in the T'oishan variety of Cantonese, in which Canton city affricates are pronounced with pure stops.

A low- or half-low–tone syllable is often used to transliterate voiceless sibilants. For instance:

---

[3]A final voiceless stop is often given a wrong place of articulation by Cantonese learners of English.

| sport | 士砵 | shi-po:t | half-low–mid |
| Stockton | 士德頓 | shi-tak-tön | half-low–high–mid |

or, in the T'oishan variety of Cantonese,

Stockton	士作頓	shi-tok-tön	half-low–mid–mid
Richmond	列治文	lit-chi-man	half-low–half-low–low
stamp	士 □	shi-ta:m	half-low–high

with the last character being undetermined, since I have only heard this, and not seen it in print.

Another feature of Chinese transliteration of foreign names is the avoidance of monosyllables, which are felt somehow to be too short for place names. Thus, whereas the disyllabic forms "Shanghai" and "Nanking" are spoken as they are, a place with the name of "Ting" (seat of James Y. C. Yen's Mass Education movement) has to be spoken of as "Ting Hsien" ("the District Ting"). For the same reason, my hometown is spoken of as Ch'angchow ("the Prefecture Ch'ang") even though the administrative unit of the prefecture has long been abolished. A foreign place like "Bonn" is rendered as:

| Bonn | 波昂 | po-ang | high-level–high-rising |

although theoretically it could be rendered something like:

| the Bonn city | 邦城 | pang-ch'eng | high-level–high-rising |

In the case of people's names, a monosyllabic form connotes great familiarity, such as that used between husband and wife or in calling the children. When one knows someone too well to call him "Wang Hsien-sheng," one does not simply drop the "Mr." and call him Wang, but adds a prefix "Lao" and calls him "Lao Wang," corresponding in degree of familiarity to calling someone "Smith." In the case of transcribing foreign names, a monosyllabic surname is usually broken into two syllables. For example, the name "Dean" is commonly rendered as:

| | 第安 | ti-an | falling–high-level |

not because the translator does not know that "Dean" is one syllable, which he probably does, but because possible monosyllabic forms

ting   丁   high-level

tien   典   low-rising

do not sound like free words.

Although tones are all important and constant with Chinese names and words in general, this does not mean that there is no distinction of stress, especially in Mandarin. For example, in a verb-object form, the verb has secondary stress and the object has the main stress. Once, my daughter Lensey was feeding our black cat, which hesitated at first and then started to eat, whereupon she said:

黑 貓 '吃, ,黑 ,貓

hei mao 'ch'ih, ,hei ,mao
(The black cat eats, it does)

I pretended to misunderstand her and said:

hei mao ,ch'ih 'hei 'mao?!
(The black cat eats the black cat?!)

She did not even realize the quasi-ambiguity, however, since with a different stress pattern it did not sound like the same sentence at all.

To sum up, a tone in Chinese is felt as so much a part of the word, as much as consonants and vowels are, that this attitude is carried over when stress patterns of English words are associated with fixed tones. Moreover, in Cantonese transliteration of English, not only are high and low tones associated with stressed and unstressed syllables, respectively, but even voiceless sibilants are usually transcribed by a low- or half-low–tone syllable. Finally, ubiquitous and important as tones are, stress does play an essential part in Chinese, too, and sometimes makes a difference in meaning or structure.

4/ Sentential Stress, Word Order, and the Notion of Subject in Spanish

Heles Contreras

There are two opposing views of sentential stress in the literature. The first, which we might refer to as syntactically based, assumes that sentential stress is assigned on the basis of syntactic criteria. Proponents of this view are Chomsky and Halle (1968), and Bresnan (1971). The second view, which I call informational, holds that sentential stress depends not on syntax, but on the informational content of the utterance. This view has been argued for by Bolinger (1954, 1958, 1961, 1972), Daneš (1960), and Hultzén (1956), among others.

The problem of word order, which is closely related to sentential stress, has also been dealt with in purely syntactic terms by linguists like Chomsky (1965) and Bach (1962), whereas Prague school syntacticians, e.g., Mathesius (1924), Daneš (1964), and Firbas (1964, 1966), and in this country Bolinger (1952, 1954–5), Hatcher (1956a,b), and more recently Kuno (1972), have maintained that, in addition to syntactic factors, word order is determined by the informational content of the sentence. Other linguists who hold positions at odds with classical transformationalism in this respect include Staal (1967), who argues for a deep structure without concatenation, and Dover (1960), who maintains that word order is determined by a variety of factors in addition to the purely syntactic ones.

In this paper I present evidence from Spanish in support of the view that both sentential stress and word order depend, at least partially, on the informational structure of the sentence, in other words, on the kind of units that are referred to in the literature as *topic* and *comment*, or *theme* and *rheme*.

Crucial to my argument is an elucidation of the nature of functional notions like "subject" and "object." In classical transformational grammar, "subject" is defined as the Noun Phrase dominated directly by the Sentence (Chomsky, 1965, p. 68). In case grammar (Fillmore, 1968), the subject is similarly defined, except that it does not start out in that position but is moved to it by a SUBJECT FORMATION (SF) rule. Goldin (1968, p. 69), on the other hand, has proposed to identify subjects and objects in terms of transformationally inserted features rather than in terms of configuration. The significance of this question for our purposes is that, if subject and object are configurationally defined, it is possible to talk about an unmarked word order, which may in turn provide the basis for the operation of syntactically determined rules of sentential stress assignment. On the other hand, if subject and object are identified by means of features, the motivation for positing a basic word order, and consequently assigning stress by syntactic criteria, is considerably weakened.

Limiting myself to the notion of "subject," I here present some arguments in favor of a feature analysis for Spanish. Before presenting these arguments, however, let me restate Fillmore's SF rule:

> The highest ranking case—the hierarchy being Agent, Experiencer, Instrument, Object, Source, Goal (Fillmore 1971, p. 251)—is moved to the left of the verb under the direct domination of the Sentence.

For my purposes, it is immaterial whether this movement is simultaneous with the deletion of the original occurrence of the case moved, i.e., the rule is a chopping rule, or the movement stage precedes the deletion stage, i.e., the rule is a copying rule.

The first argument against this version of SF is based on examples like (1) and (2):

(1) Salió el sol. (The sun came out.)
(2) Mi padre salió. (My father went out.)

both of which are felt to be in the normal noninverted order, with the main stress on the last element.

In Fillmore's treatment, however, only example (2) would show the normal word order, whereas example (1) would be interpreted as an inverted sentence that, in addition to SF, had undergone a rule of SUBJECT-VERB INVERSION. This counterintuitive difference need not be imposed under an interpretation of SF as a feature-assignment rule, independent of the principles that account for word order.

However, even if we are willing to tolerate the undesirable consequences of the movement analysis for examples (1) and (2), there are equational sentences like those in examples (3) and (4),

(3) a. El jefe soy yo. (*I* am the boss.)
    b. *El jefe es yo.
(4) a. Los jefes somos nosotros. (*We* are the bosses.)
    b. *Los jefes son nosotros.

where the verb agrees not with the preceding, but with the following, Noun Phrase. If "subject" means the Noun Phrase with which the verb agrees, these examples clearly show that the "subject" defined in this sense is not always the preverbal Noun Phrase, and that a rule that moves a Noun Phrase to the preverbal position precisely so that it can be picked up by the rule of SUBJECT-VERB AGREEMENT does not make much sense for Spanish, in view of the fact that special provisions must be made for sentences like those in examples (3) and (4) anyway.

It could be argued that examples (3) and (4) are inverted, and that agreement takes place at the stage where they still show the "normal" order, as in examples (5) and (6):

(5)   Yo soy el jefe.
(6)   Nosotros somos los jefes.

However, examples (5) and (6), read with normal intonation, i.e., with the main stress on *jefe(s)*, are not equivalent to examples (3) and (4), respectively. Whereas the latter answer the questions:

(7)   a.   ¿Quién eres tú? (Who are you?)
      b.   ¿Quiénes son Uds.?

the former answer the questions:

(8)   a.   ¿Quién es el jefe? (Who is the boss?)
      b.   ¿Quiénes son los jefes? (Who are the bosses?)

Consequently, we must reject an analysis where examples (3) and (4) derive from examples (5) and (6), respectively.

A similar example is (9),

(9)   La demás chusma del bergantín son moros y turcos.
      (The rest of the mob in the ship are Moors and Turks.)

where the verb again agrees not with the preceding, but with the following Noun Phrase. This sentence cannot at all be considered an inversion, since

(10)   *Moros y turcos son la demás chusma del bergantín.

is ungrammatical with normal intonation.

Although examples like (3), (4), and (9) could be accounted for within a theory of SF as a movement rule by considering them as exceptions to the rule of AGREEMENT, they lend some support to the competing theory of SF as a feature-assignment rule, since within this theory it is to be expected that the verb will agree with other than preverbal Noun Phrases.

Within this theory, the criteria for assigning the feature [+Subject]— which simply identifies the Noun Phrase (NP) with which the verb will agree and, consequently, does not always fall on the traditionally recognized subject—are varied and may interact in complicated ways. The most important one is, of course, case hierarchy, in Fillmore's sense. Thus, in example (11),

> (11) Los cuidadores abrieron la puerta con la llave.
>   (The janitors opened the door with the key.)

with an Agent, an Instrument, and an Object, the Agent, which ranks the highest, receives the feature [+Subject].

In sentences with PRO-Agents, like example (12),

> (12) Se vende(n) zapatos. (Shoes are sold.)

the feature [+Subject] is assigned either to the PRO-Agent or to the Object. More is said about these cases in a later section of this paper.

In equational sentences, where the two NPs have the same rank, person and number seem to determine the choice of NP to be marked as [+Subject]. Consider the following examples:

> (13) a. El jefe eres tú. (You are the boss.)
>   b. Tú eres el jefe.
>   c. *El jefe es tú.
>   d. *Tú es el jefe.

These sentences, together with examples (3) through (6), suggest that in an equational sentence first or second person takes priority over nonpronominal NPs for the purpose of assignment of the feature [+Subject]. In equational sentences involving two nonpronominal NPs of different number, the plural takes priority over the singular:

> (14) La época más dichosa de la vida de Caldas fueron (*fue) los años en que gozó de la plena y pacífica posesión del Observatorio de Bogotá. (Ramsey, 1965, no. 31.9)
>   (The happiest time in the life of Caldas were the years when he indulged in the full and peaceful possession of the Observatory of Bogotá.)

After this brief interlude concerning the treatment of AGREEMENT under a feature-assignment rule of SF, let us consider a further argument against the theory of SF as a movement rule. Questions such as

> (15) ¿Qué quiere Juan? (What does John want?)

are derived in the following way within the theory of SF as a movement rule:

> (16) Querer Juan qu-algo (want John wh-something)
>   Juan querer qu-algo (after SF)
>   Juan quiere qu-algo (after AGREEMENT)
>   Qué Juan quiere (after QU-PREPOSING)

The last string in this derivation is ungrammatical, except in certain dialects like Puerto Rican Spanish. In order to make it grammatical, a rule of SUBJECT-POSTPOSING must apply, generating example (15). This rule is, of course, unnecessary within the theory of SF as a feature-assigning rule, since that analysis does not require the movement of the subject to the left of the verb.

Another difficulty with SF as a movement rule is that it also requires the application of SUBJECT-POSTPOSING in cases like the following:

(17) a. Ven acá - dijo Juan. ("Come here"—said John.)
      b. *Ven acá - Juan dijo.

Notice that this rule would have the very odd condition of applying only when the quotation precedes the identification of the speaker, not when it follows it, as indicated by example (18):

(18) a. Juan dijo: 'Ven acá.'
      b. *Dijo Juan: 'Ven acá.'

It could be argued that SUBJECT-POSTPOSING is needed anyway for sentences like those in example (19):

(19) a. Mi padré comió. (My father ate.)
      b. Comió mi padre.

I doubt, however, that such a rule exists, and I would hypothesize that examples (19a) and (19b) are not mere stylistic variants of each other, but differ in their semantic interpretation. This can be shown by embedding similar sentences under a verb like *preferir* (to prefer):

(20) a. Prefiero que mi padre coma.
          (I prefer for my father to eat [rather than, say, drink].)
      b. Prefiero que coma mi padre.
          (I prefer for my father [rather than, say, my mother] to eat.)

These examples provide us with the final and, in my view, conclusive argument against the theory of SF as a movement rule. It is clear that this theory predicts that examples (20a) and (20b) are synonymous sentences, since the only way to generate example (20b) under this analysis is via a stage like example (20a), where the subject of the embedded sentence is in preverbal position. The falseness of this prediction is a particularly strong argument against the theory in question..

Now, if SF is not a movement rule in Spanish, i.e., if the subject is not topologically defined, the motivation for assigning word order on a syntactic basis is weakened. In particular, if in some cases the subject follows and in others it precedes the verb under normal intonation, and if there is no

SUBJECT-POSTPOSING rule to relate these two different constructions, then it must be the case that word order is determined by other factors.

Bolinger (1952, 1954, 1954-5) and the Prague linguists (Mathesius, Firbas, and Daneš in particular) have argued for rules of word order based on the information content of the different elements in the sentence. More specifically, they have argued that the more informative elements (rheme) normally go at the end of the sentence and carry the main stress, whereas less informative elements (theme) normally occur at the beginning of the sentence and do not carry the main stress. Granted the lack of preciseness in the definition of these notions, the idea seems to be applicable to word order and sentential stress in Spanish. Thus, in example (1), the Noun Phrase *el sol* is located in final position and carries the main stress because it constitutes the information "point" of the sentence. We are not interested in what the sun did or did not do; we are interested in whether it is sunny or not. On the other hand, the corresponding negative sentence will normally show the reverse order:

(21)   El sol no salió. (The sun didn't come out.)

This fact, which would be hard to explain in purely syntactic terms, has a reasonable explanation within an "informational" theory: the negation normally constitutes new information, i.e., it is the rheme, and consequently it occurs in final position and carries the main stress.[1]

The facts illustrated by examples (17) and (18) also have a natural explanation within the informational theory. In this kind of construction, the verb is clearly the least informative element, the most informative being the direct object. Following Firbas (1966), I consider the subject, the verb, and the direct object as the theme, the transition, and the rheme, respectively. In example (18a), these elements occur in what is considered to be the normal order. In example (17a), the rheme has been preposed, and thereby given more prominence. If we assume the following decreasing scale of "prominence,"

Initial element with main stress (foregrounded rheme)
Final element with main stress (normal rheme)
Initial element without main stress (normal theme)
Final element without main stress (postposed theme)
Middle element (transition)

we can explain the relative position of the three elements in examples (17a) and (18a) simply thus: the object, being the rheme, always occupies the highest position in the scale, and the verb, being the transition, the lowest.

---

[1]Strictly speaking, the main stress goes on the Verb Phrase, and within the Verb Phrase, on its rightmost constituent, the Verb.

This explanation seems to extend to other sentence types as well. Consider, for instance,

(22) El sol (theme) salió (transition) por la tarde (rheme). (The sun came out in the afternoon.)

Note that if the rheme is foregrounded, the subject must come in final position, which is predicted by our hierarchy:

(23) a. Por la *tar*de salió el sol.
      b. *Por la *tar*de el sol salió.[2]

Lest the reader object that I am dealing with matters that are somehow different from normal syntactic facts and can be casually swept under the rug of "performance" or "stylistic variation," I close this paper by showing that the theme/rheme organization of the sentence may be crucial both for the semantic interpretation of the sentence and for the operation of certain syntactic rules.

Concerning the relevance of the thematic organization of the sentence for semantic interpretation, I refer the reader to examples (20a) and (20b). In example (20a) the rheme of the embedded clause is the verb *coma* (eat), whereas in example (20b) it is the Noun Phrase *mi padre* (my father), and this fact correlates with a crucial semantic difference that is clearly brought out when the clauses are embedded under a verb like *preferir*. There is no question that the semantic difference between these two sentences goes beyond what is normally dismissed as merely stylistic difference.

Concerning the relevance of thematic organization for the operation of syntactic rules, I offer two examples. The first one involves agreement in sentences like:

(24) a. Se vende zapatos. (Shoes are sold.)
      b. Se venden zapatos.
      c. Los zapatos se venden. (The shoes are for sale.)
      d. *Los zapatos se vende.

In examples (24a) and (24b), where the Object is in final position, the verb may agree with it or with the PRO-Agent, i.e., either NP may be assigned the feature [+Subject]. In example (24c), where the Object is preposed, the verb agrees with it obligatorily. However, it is not simply a matter of position but of thematic organization: in examples (24a) and (b), *zapatos* is the rheme, whereas in examples (24c) and (d) it is the theme. This distinction is crucial, for if the rheme *zapatos* is preposed, the agreement facts remain the same as in (24a) and (b):

---

[2]The underlined syllable constitutes the intonation center of the sentence.

(25) a. Za*pa*tos se vende.
      b. Za*pa*tos se venden.

In order to determine, then, which NP is to be marked [+Subject], i.e., which NP the verb may agree with, it is necessary that the theme and the rheme be identified, for it is only with a rhematic Object that an impersonal sentence will show optional agreement with the Object or the PRO-Agent.

The second example concerns the interrelation between the thematic organization of the sentence and the applicability of the rule of Conjunction Reduction. The simplest statement of Conjunction Reduction is found in Chomsky (1957, p. 36):

> If S_1 and S_2 are grammatical sentences, and S_1 differs from S_2 only in that X appears in S_1 where Y appears in S_2 (i.e., $S_1 = \ldots X \ldots$ and $S_2 = \ldots Y \ldots$), and X and Y are constituents of the same type in S_1 and S_2, respectively, then S_3 is a sentence, where S_3 is the result of replacing X by $X + and + Y$ in S_1 (i.e., $S_3 = \ldots X + and + Y \ldots$).

This rule applies to (20a) and to:

(26) Prefiero que mi madre *co*ma. (I prefer for my mother to *eat*.)

which generates

(27) Prefiero que mi padre y mi madre *co*man.
      (I prefer for my father and my mother to eat.)

If the thematic organization of the sentence is not taken into account, however, the rule of Conjunction Reduction will also apply to example (20a) and to

(28) Prefiero que mi *ma*dre coma. (I prefer for my *mo*ther to eat.)

and generate example (27). This is clearly wrong, however, since (27) is not ambiguous: it can only be interpreted as a reduction of examples (20a) and (26), not of examples (20a) and (28).

Information about the thematic organization of the sentence must be available to the grammar, then, at the point where Conjunction Reduction applies.

In conclusion, the facts presented in this paper suggest that, since ''subject'' is not topologically defined in Spanish, a theory that assigns an unmarked order to Spanish sentences on a purely syntactic basis is to be viewed with suspicion. The same is true of a theory that uses unmarked word order as a basis for assigning sentential stress. Conversely, a theory that assigns word order and sentential stress on the basis of the thematic, or ''informational,'' structure of the sentence becomes more attractive. Additional support for this alternative comes from the fact that the thematic organization is relevant for semantic interpretation and interacts with the operation of syntactic rules.

REFERENCES

Bach, E. 1962. The order of elements in a transformational grammar of German. Language 38:263–269.

Bolinger, D. 1952. Linear modification. PMLA 67:1117–1144.

Bolinger, D. 1954. English prosodic stress and Spanish sentence order. Hispania 37:152–156.

Bolinger. D. 1954–5. Meaningful word order in Spanish. Bol. Filol. [Universidad de Chile] 7:45–56.

Bolinger, D. 1958. Stress and information. Am. Speech 33:5–20.

Bolinger, D. 1961. Contrastive accent and contrastive stress. Language 37:83–96.

Bolinger, D. 1972. Accent is predictable (if you're a mind reader). Language 48: 633–644.

Bresnan, J. 1971. Sentence stress and syntactic transformations. Language 47:257–281.

Chomsky, N. 1957. Syntactic Structures. Mouton & Co., The Hague.

Chomsky, N. 1965. Aspects of the Theory of Syntax. MIT Press, Cambridge, Mass.

Chomsky, N., and Halle, M. 1968. The Sound Pattern of English. Harper & Row Pubs., Inc., New York.

Daneš, F. 1960. Sentence intonation from a functional point of view. Word 16:34–54.

Daneš, F. 1964. A three-level approach to syntax. Trav. Linguist. Prague 1:255–240.

Dover, K. J. 1960. Greek Word Order. Cambridge University Press, Cambridge, Eng.

Fillmore, C. J. 1968. The case for case. In: E. Bach and R. T. Harms, Universals in Linguistic Theory. Holt, Rinehart & Winston, Inc., New York.

Fillmore, C. J. 1971. Some problems for case grammar. Working Papers in Linguistics, No. 10. Ohio State University, Columbus, Ohio.

Firbas, J. 1964. On defining the theme in functional sentence analysis. Trav. Linguist. Prague 1:267–280.

Firbas, J. 1966. A note on transition proper in functional sentence analysis. Philol. Praguensia 8:170–176.

Goldin, M. G. 1968. Spanish Case and Function. Georgetown University Press, Washington, D.C.

Hatcher, A. G. 1956a. Syntax and the sentence. Word 12:234–250.

Hatcher, A. G. 1956b. Theme and underlying question. Two studies of Spanish word order. Word 12, Suppl. 3.

Hultzén, L. S. 1956. "The poet Burns" again. Am. Speech 31:195–201.

Kuno, S. 1972. Functional sentence perspective. Ling. Inquiry 3:269–320.

Mathesius, V. 1924. Několik poznámek o funkci podmětu v moderní angličtině. CMF 10:244–248.

Ramsey, M. M. 1965. A Textbook of Modern Spanish. Holt, Rinehart & Winston, Inc., New York.

Staal, J. F. 1967. Word order in Sanskrit and universal grammar. Foundations of Language Supplementary Series, No. 5. Reidel Publishing Co., Hingham, Mass.

5/ The Analysis of Nuclear Tones

David Crystal

The analysis of the pitch movements that expound the tonic syllable (or nucleus) of a tone unit has been much neglected in recent theoretical discussions of intonation, although this issue was very much to the fore in early pedagogical studies, and a number of phonetic classifications have been made. The approach presented in Crystal (1969a) argues that the range of nuclei in a language is best seen in terms of the interaction between two systemically distinct features—*syllabic pitch range* and *tone*. The former refers to the relative pitch height of a syllable, syllable onset, or syllable termination in relation to preceding or subsequent syllables; the latter refers to the pitch direction followed throughout a tonic syllable. For example, the traditional concept of a "high rising tone" is seen as the product of two separate systemic selections: high (versus mid or low) and rising (versus falling, level, falling-rising, and so on). It is clear that there are in principle a very large number of phonetic possibilities that a language might use—high falling, high falling-rising, high falling-level, high level-falling, and so on. The problems are to determine the number of basic phonological categories required, to provide a model for their interrelationship, and to give adequate recognition to the range of functions that they possess.

Methodologically, this is probably the most difficult area of all for the intonation analyst; some of the reasons for this are discussed in Crystal (1969a, Ch. 7). However, this book did not pay sufficient attention to the underlying malaise in this area of intonation study, which is a failure to think theoretically about the subject: crucial theoretical terms tend to be used loosely, and their implications are missed. Three terms in particular are widely used, but their status remains largely uninvestigated; *context, system,* and *connected speech*. These terms are fundamental to any general explanation of intonation, but they must be used carefully and precisely in order for the explanation to succeed. As a general indication of my attitude, I would say that the concept of context has been much overrated, that of system much underestimated, and the complexity involved in constructing a model of intonation for connected speech largely ignored.

Statements referring to the importance of context in intonation analysis are found throughout the literature. They reflect a movement away from the view that a nuclear type (e.g., low rise) expounds a single, "basic" meaning, always present regardless of context (although contextual variations may add certain overtones), to a view that there is no common meaning underlying all instances of its use, the interpretation of each instance being totally dependent on the context in which the tone occurs. Certainly it is difficult to defend the first position, in any strong sense. A collection of instances of any tone bring to light a large number of possible attitudinal implications, and identity between the different instances seems possible only by a process of simplification (in which some attitudes are selected as being more fundamental than others, which are considered marginal) or by a process of generalization, whereby all the implications are subsumed under some extremely broad attitudinal label (e.g., "emphasis," "self-involvement"). Neither of these processes is desirable: the first approach may have pedagogical value, but it begs crucial theoretical questions as to what is central and what is marginal; the generality of the labels in the second approach is such that they are vacuously applicable to almost every nuclear type one might find. In any case, one might add, why *should* one be looking for a single meaning that can be traced through all instances of a given category? No one would expect this for other kinds of formal categories. The point has been much discussed, in linguistics, philosophy, and elsewhere, and I do not go into it further here.

The second position seems to have a lot in its favor. In particular, there is the difficulty of finding a single sentence with a *totally* unacceptable nuclear tone: it is always possible to think up some context that makes the sentence appear quite normal, even though the context discovery procedure may itself be an involved process, as Haas has pointed out (1973). Analysts asterisk intonationally transcribed utterances at their peril, as Bolinger regularly shows, and much of the discussion in recent years has taken the form of criticism of proposed semantic generalizations on grounds of contextual inadequacy. However, this position is not as clear-cut as it seems. For instance, it ignores the important question, discussed by Haas (1973), that contextualization is itself a complex process, involving various procedures and degrees of intuitive confidence: the degree of difficulty encountered in thinking up a context is itself a significant factor in deciding the overall acceptability of that utterance. More important than this, the position remains unintelligible without clarification of the term "context." It is a term that has been used in a variety of senses—or so it would seem, for it is rarely explicitly defined. It has been used to include some or all of the following: the concurrent formal structure of an utterance (whose intonation is being analyzed), the formal structure of utterances preceding or following the focal utterance, the intonation patterns preceding the focal utterance, the observable situation in which the utterance takes place, factors in the observable situation preceding the focal utterance, the presuppositions in the mind of the speaker or hearer, and other things besides. Given such a broad interpretation, it would not be surprising for the meaning of an intonation pattern to be wholly dependent on context, but of course this says nothing, until the specific conditioning claimed to be operating within each kind of context is explained and some kind of criteria are set up. "Finding a context" for intonation patterns by adding a previous utterance or giving a brief cue specification in brackets provides pedagogic plausibility, but no explanation.

When one looks closely at the various possible senses of context, however, one finds that certain of them are quite inoperable or irrelevant for the specification of intonational meaning. One may, to begin with, dispense with general appeals to mental presuppositions and unobservable aspects of "the situation" in which the utterance occurs. It should be obvious that unless we are provided with some objective linguistic, visual, or other evidence to indicate that a presupposed state of affairs or a change in the concurrent situation is conditioning the structure or interpretation of an utterance, we have no alternative but to assume that nothing contrastive is presupposed, that no change is taking place, that mutual attitudes are constant, and that the process of interpretation based on an appeal to observable characteristics of the situation (see below) should continue unaltered. For example, if in a conversation the mood of one of the participants changed (e.g., boredom setting in), but at the time there was no formal sign that this had happened within the pattern of the utterance and retrospective analysis of a tape failed to produce any consistent interpretation of boredom at this point, then this information must be disregarded. (The fact that it is often not disregarded is due to the speaker-oriented approach to intonation, whereby the analyst uses his own intuition to interpret his own usage, and thereby frequently fails to realize which aspects of his semantic introspection were expounded in his utterance and which were not, which were a reflex of aspects of his personality, and so on. The danger is always to read too much meaning into a pattern.) The same reasoning applies when questions of ambiguity are raised: an utterance is not intonationally ambiguous until such time as the participants recognize it and accept it as relevant for the conversation. If A sees a possible ambiguity in B's utterance, but discounts it (as unintentional, or for some other reason), then it would be misleading to extract the feature concerned and refer to it as "potentially ambiguous," or something similar. A fortiori, if none of the participants detect any ambiguity at all, and retrospective analysis fails to produce any consistent interpretation of an utterance as ambiguous, appeals to potential ambiguity must be disregarded. (References to such notions are usually the result of looking at sentences in isolation instead of in connected speech. Of course many sentences are intonationally ambiguous in isolation: to take these and then to say that "context resolves the ambiguity" is questionable, to say the least, since if connected speech had been studied in the first place, the question of ambiguity would never have arisen. Similar views have been expressed over the supposed ambiguity of sentences like "Flying planes can be dangerous," e.g., Noss, 1972.) Most of the time, we produce or interpret an utterance's intonation using the assumption that it will be unambiguous, and that there is no change taking place in the concurrent situation that could affect the process of interpretation. Only when there is clear evidence to the contrary do we need to talk about the notion of context.

Eliminating such matters from our discussion reduces the notion of context to more manageable proportions. Specifically, five senses of context need to be distinguished:

1. The concurrent syntactic and lexical pattern of utterance. There are a number of formal notions (e.g., sentence final versus nonfinal) that are prerequisite for any semantic analysis of nuclear types. This aspect of contextual influence is discussed further below.
2. Preceding and subsequent syntactic and lexical patterns. I have not explored discourse organization as a whole in relation to the selection of nuclear types, but in principle it should be clear that there could be a considerable influence here, e.g., a sequence of parallel sentence structures (as in a series of rhetorical questions) would strongly motivate a corresponding sequence of parallel choices of nuclei.
3. Preceding and subsequent intonational patterns (see further below).
4. Relevant concurrent and preceding semiotic behavior, especially facial expression but including all forms of kinesic and proxemic behavior. The importance of context in this sense is well known, although underestimated (see Crystal, 1969a, Ch. 7).
5. Concurrent and preceding observable alterations in situation. This is the traditional core of the notion of context in intonation studies. The choice of intonation is related to such situationally conditioned attitudes as politeness, surprise, anger, and so on; and it is this aspect of context that has been overrated. The range of "attitudes" to be considered under this heading is very wide, and it is the multiplicity of semantic labels and the problems of quantifying affect that have led to pessimism in the semantics of intonation and the extreme reliance on the notion of context. Doubtless it will be possible to make much progress in these areas once we have available more adequate analyses of affective states and their linguistic categorization, so that the idea of situational context might become more explicit. In the meantime, it is important to realize that this

aspect of context is by no means the cornerstone of intonational semantics: it is in fact very much dependent on the other senses of context (1–4) above.

The following dialogue provides an example of the interrelationship of the various senses of context:

A /you've got something in your HÂIR/ (said in a jocular tone, thinking that it is no more than a fallen leaf)
B /HÀVE I/

The low falling tone here, where one might have expected a livelier reply (such as a high rise) to suit A's jocular mood, provides a contrast that indicates B's displeasure—let us call the tone "offended." However, it would now be most misleading to say, as is often said, "One of the meanings of the low falling tone is 'offended'." It would be absurd to see the low falling tone as "containing" a range of meanings, one of which is "selected" at this point in context, because obviously the range of meanings the low fall (or any other tone) could contain are as many as there are contextual conditions, and hence no analytic progress would have been made. Rather, this example shows the importance of the other contextual factors in accounting for a particular effect. Sense 1 is relevant, because with a less abrupt syntax and lexis there would be less likelihood of an interpretation of "offended." Sense 2 is relevant, since if B had been replying in this manner in previous discourse, A would have grounds for discounting the interpretation of "offended." The relevance of sense 3 has already been referred to—the contrast between A's and B's intonation—and sense 4 is relevant because the interpretation of "offended" could disappear entirely if an appropriate facial expression or gesture were involved. Indeed, when one considers senses 1–4, it is difficult to see what need there is to refer to sense 5 of context at all.

I would in fact want to argue that sense 5 is largely irrelevant to the semantic analysis of intonation. It is only occasionally that one may make a confident prediction of an intonational pattern from an observed situational event, and vice versa. There is no guarantee that, for example, an angry situation will produce an attitude of anger in any individual, and none that an angry attitude will produce an "angry" intonation pattern. The controlling variables are personality (e.g., some people are more controlled than others) and sociolinguistic (e.g., some social situations are more conducive to angry scenes than others). Even on the basis of a clearly observable situation, then, it would be misleading to assume that the interpretation of the situation should be allowed to influence one's semantic analysis of the intonation. Indeed, we are aware of this, because we say such things as "John kept very calm—there wasn't even a tremor in his voice," which indicate the possibilities of intonational disassociation from the accompanying situation [or "displacement," in the terms of Hockett and Altmann (1968)].

The observable situation probably has an important role to play in the initial stages of any discourse, where it establishes norms (e.g., of formality, intimacy, or excitement) for the dialogue. It then proves unnecessary to refer again to situation unless major variations in it arise. There have been in fact only a handful of occasions in my own conversational data where an observable change in the accompanying situation directly influenced the intonation. One occasion was when a third speaker entered the room; since he was a stranger to one of the participants, the speech became more formal and the intonation altered. Another was when the doorbell rang, and a puzzled tone came into one participant's voice. These occasions were isolated. For the most part, one can listen to a tape without referring at all to the ongoing situation. (The impression of the opposite is probably due to the emphasis on the more action-packed kind of situation found to be important in foreign language teaching, which motivates so much of available intonational materials.) The language is self-contained, and the interpretation of the intonation depends essentially on the semiotic (linguistic and nonlinguistic) contexts. (The analysis of nonvocal semiotic features is not dealt with further in this paper.) The problem for the intonation analyst, therefore, is to develop an adequate model of the contrastive possibilities operating as one moves from nuclear tone to nuclear tone in the stream of connected speech. In order to do this, he has to clarify what is involved in the other vague theoretical notions mentioned above—the notion of an intonation *system* in relation to *connected speech*.

The concept of system is generally discussed with reference to three criteria: a system contains a finite number of members; it is reciprocally exclusive (two or more members may not be selected at a particular point in a syntagm); and it is reciprocally defining, i.e., the most precise and economical statement of the meaning of an item is in terms of the other members of the system of which it forms a part. The set of nuclear tones in English is normally referred to as a system, but little attempt seems to have been made to show that these conditions have been met. The notion of reciprocity of definition is particularly important. What this implies is that attempts to define the meaning of a nuclear tone cannot be successful until we know two things: what tone the previous discourse (or, in a discourse-initial position, the previous observable situation, semiotic frame, and so on) lead us to expect; and what tone we actually get. Regarding the first point, one might construct an arrangement of tonal possibilities such that, given a sequence of tone units and tonic syllables, the selection of any tone is made dependent on the selection of the previous tone or tones. Given the selection of the first tone in a string, one may then see a progressive influence of the type

A-B
B-C
C-D...

such that a primary factor influencing the selection of any tone is going to be functional compatibility with the previous one(s). For example, one might expect, given the occurrence of a rising-falling tone, to find clusters of such tones at a particular point in discourse; this is in fact what one finds (as reported in Crystal, 1969a, p. 241, where the notion of ''tonal reduplication'' is introduced, but the value of the statistical analysis reported in this earlier work is extremely limited, because little account was taken of the grammatical contexts of the various tones). A more important illustration of functional compatibility emerges from the statistical fact that, for any sample of data, between 50 and 60% of the nuclei will be falling tone, with the vast majority being low falling in type—in other words, the ''neutral'' intonation for statements, as generally reported. As Quirk et al. (1972, p. 1044) say, ''a tone unit has a falling nucleus unless there is some specific reason why it should not.'' Of the remaining 40% of nuclei, half of these are low or mid-rising or level tones whose use is wholly conditioned by the accompanying syntax (see below) for the signaling of dependent nonfinal structures. In other words, between 70 and 80% of nuclei are semantically ''neutral.'' The problem is in accounting for the remaining tones, and the non-neutral use of the low falling and rising tones. However, as a general principle, I would wish to argue that the vast majority of tones in connected speech carry no meaning—that is, they communicate no new information because their occurrence is syntactically predictable. The problem of specifying nuclear meaning comes when a tone is used unpredictably in a specific syntactic context, or when (as stated above) the discourse leads us to expect a particular tone and we are given another. Both of these cases involve us in looking at the nature of tonal relationships within the nuclear system.

For the rest of this paper, I restrict the discussion to the following nuclei:

Low fall   (symbolized as $\downarrow$`)

High fall   (symbolized as $\uparrow$`)

Low rise   (symbolized as $\downarrow$′)

High rise	⌐	(symbolized as ↑′)
Level	=	(symbolized as ⁻)
Rise-fall	∧	(symbolized as ^)
Fall-rise	∪	(symbolized as ˇ)

The other phonetically distinct nuclei in English are not dealt with here (e.g., fall-level, rise-fall-rise): statistically they are a very minor group, and semantically it will probably be possible to see their analysis as a straightforward extension of that suggested for the major tones. Certainly, if the approach is not plausible for the above seven categories, it will not work for the others.

In this approach, then, we are given a tone unit and tonic syllable, along with all concurrent syntactic and lexical information. [These notions are introduced and justified theoretically in a separate paper (Crystal, 1973).] The first task is to determine the extent to which grammatical factors have to be taken into account in arriving at a semantic specification of the tones. Here one has to be very rigorous over what is to count as a grammatical function of intonation. If the criteria are not exact and explicit, the grammar quickly becomes overloaded with spurious categories and artificial distinctions (for example, degrees of "exclamatory force" or "personal commitment"). This is the difficulty that I find with Halliday's approach to intonation, for instance (see Crystal, 1969b). To avoid this difficulty, the present approach uses a much more restricting criterion: one allows as grammatical only those uses of intonation that can be shown to expound categories *already required* by a grammar. Given a grammar of English that uses such notions as dependent clause, negation, restrictive and nonrestrictive, and sentence completion, for instance, if one can show intonation expounding these concepts, this can then be said to be a genuinely grammatical function of intonation for this grammar. Note, too, that in all such cases we are dealing with a grammatical system in the strict sense—a finite, mutually defining and mutually exclusive membership, e.g., restrictive versus nonrestrictive, positive versus negative. In this way, one would need to establish six conditions for the use of nuclear tone, in order to account for the following grammatical distinctions (all of which are taken from recently published grammars of English):

⁻ or ′   Nonfinal tonic in sentence: *syntactic dependence,* e.g.,
　　　　　　/what he sᴀ̄ɪd/ was are you cómɪɴɢ/
　　　　　　/he won't go hóme/ until she comes bᴀ̀ᴄᴋ/

  ´   Final tonic in sentence: *continuity,* e.g.,
           incomplete listing:
             /would you like TÉA/ or CÓFFEE/ (cf. ... TÉA/ or CÒFFEE/)
         Final tonic in setence: *expectation of response,* e.g.,
           tag question:
             /he's CÒMING/ ÍSN'T he/ (cf. ... ÌSN'T he/)
           question (versus exclamation):
             /weren't they PÚNCTUAL/ (cf. ... PÙNCTUAL/)
             */how WÈLL she sings/ DÓESN'T she/
  ↑´   *Contrastive question,* specifically
           echo utterance marker (cf. Quirk et al., 1972), e.g.,
             A /John's going to the ÒFFICE
             B /to the ↑WHÉRE/
           also in certain types of rhetorical questions, and indicating the
           penult in a list, e.g.,
             /we want ÉGGS/ BÚTTER/ ↑BRÉAD/ and TÈA
  ↑`   *Contrastive focus,* e.g.,
             /he's HÀPPY/ in fact he's ↑VÈRY happy/
  ˇ   *Contingency,* especially negative implication, where the polar con-
           trast is clear, e.g.,
             /I didn't give her ǍNYTHING/ (cf. ... ÀNYTHING/)
             /I SHǑULD go/ (but I won't) cf. ... SHÒULD ...)
             /we do admit STǓDENTS/ (but not ÀNY STÚDENTS/)
             /it's GǑOD/ (but not THÀT GÓOD/)
             /John won't sit still until the TǍXI comes (cf. ... STÍLL/
             ... TÀXI ... /)
  ↓`   Final tonic in sentence: *unmarked*
         Nonfinal tonic in sentence (see below under attitude)

It may be possible, with further study, to add to this list, but meanwhile it would seem prudent to restrict one's claims about grammatical function—which are extremely strong claims to make—to those cases about which there is clear and extensive evidence.

By distinguishing the three phonetic variables that underlie the above nuclei [general pitch direction (falling-type versus rising-type), pitch range (high versus low start) and complexity (viz. ˆ, ˇ, the following systemic relationship might be hypothesized between tonal type and grammatical functions:

    ` *Neutral* ⌒ +↑ = *contrastive focus*

    ´ *Continuity* ⟨ +↑ = *contrastive question*
                      +complex = *negative implication*

NOTE: 1) There seems to be no grammatically conditioned equivalent to fall-rise under the heading of falling-type tones. Rise-fall cannot be predictably related to any grammatical contrastivity, and its description thus falls under the heading of attitude, below. 2) Labeling` as FINALITY, as is sometimes done, is to be misled by the labels used, with the term CONTINUITY suggesting its opposite. The only clear sense for which the term FINAL might be applicable, in a grammatical context, is "final in a string," such as a sentence, and this would handle only a small proportion of the low falling tones in the data.

Specifying further semantic differentiation for the tones in the above contexts is a purely attitudinal matter, and here the problem of labeling arises. As I pointed out in an earlier work (Crystal, 1969a, Ch. 7), descriptive labels in intonation are generally unclear. It is often uncertain, for example, whether a label like *interrogative* is being used to refer to an attitude, a syntactic pattern or category, or a speech act. Likewise, labels tend to be used in a fairly arbitrary way, such that one is uncertain of the structural meaning relations that may be operating between them—a pair of labels, such as *sarcastic* and *ironic*, may be being used synonymously, hyponymously, incompatibly, and so on (see Lyons, 1968, p. 403, for these relations). In the absence of explicit criteria and an agreed semantic theory, it is not surprising that descriptions of nuclear meanings do not take us very far, and are often contradictory. However, although a great deal of empirical psycholinguistic work remains to be done on the use of these labels by judges, it should still be possible to develop some theoretical ideas about the way in which our semantic interpretations are organized and how they are arrived at, and thus reduce somewhat the amount of arbitrariness in our descriptions. One suggestion toward this end is developed below: it is based on the view that any explanation of intonational meaning cannot be arrived at by seeing the issues solely in either attitudinal or grammatical terms. It is precisely the interplay between the interpretation of an intonation pattern in grammatical terms and its interpretation in semantic (attitudinal) terms that is of interest, since there are grounds for believing that the two sets of "meanings" are to some extent mutually defining. A low rising tone, for example, may in syntactic terms be given an interpretation as "marker of syntactic continuity," but in attitudinal terms one might talk of "inconclusiveness" and a range of related labels. Likewise, the fall-rise might in a grammatical context be defined with reference to a category of contingent negation; attitudinally, it might be defined with reference to such labels as "uncertainty" or "doubt" (see below). There would seem to be a certain analogousness between the two dimensions of interpretation, which any analysis should take into account. The present approach insists on a dual account of the meaning of any nucleus that distinguishes, but interrelates, its grammatical and its attitudinal roles. In this way, it is hoped, one might arrive at a solution to the problem of nuclear meaning posed at the beginning of this section by postulating a stable ''core'' of meaning (partly grammatically and partly attitudinally defined) and a ''periphery'' of attitudinal nuances that rely for their interpretation on the concurrent lexis, semiotic features, and so on (see Crystal, 1969a, p. 284, for examples).

A first attempt at specifying the attitudinal core of the above tones is as follows:

‾   Final tonic in sentence: *absence of emotional involvement,* which may be interpreted as sarcasm, irony, or boredom, e.g.,

/it was a F̄ASCINATING lecture/

Nonfinal tonic in sentence: *implication of routineness*—perhaps arising out of the dominant sense of the level tone in final position.

↓´   Final tonic in sentence: *personal inconclusiveness* (cf. the continuity sense above)—specific labels used here are noncommittal, unaggressive, and so on, which are a short remove from polite, respectful, and so on.

Final tonic in sentence: *social openness,* perhaps arising from the interest and so on implied in the expectation of response sense given above (p. 63)—specific labels used here are casual, friendly, persuasive, and (with appropriate kinesic accompaniment) warning, grim, and so on.

↓`   Nonfinal tonic in sentence: *attitudinally neutral.*

Final tonic in sentence: *attitudinally neutral.*

Nonfinal tonic in sentence: *personal definitiveness*—specific labels used here are abrupt, insistent, and so on.

Nonfinal tonic in sentence: *unsociability*—specific labels being cool, irritated, rude, and so on.

↑`   In any position: *definite emotional commitment*—specific labels being emphasis, surprise, warmth; selection depending very much on kinesic accompaniment.

↑´   In any position: *definite emotional inquiry*—specific labels being query, puzzlement, surprise, and so on.

˅   In any position: *uncertain outcome*—doubt, hesitation, and so on leading to suspicion, threatening, and so on.

˄   In any position: *definite outcome*—impressed, satisfied, smug, and so on, or the reverse, depending on kinesic accompaniment.

In the same manner as above, the systemic relationship between these tones may be outlined as follows:

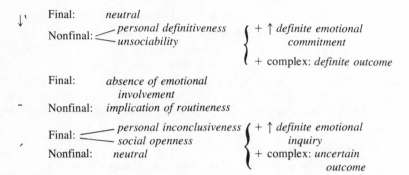

NOTE: The complexity and pitch range features are continuously variable (cf. Trim, 1971): the wider the overall tone, and the higher the beginning or end points of the tone relative to the preceding utterance, the more intense the attitude.

Figure 1 presents a schematic account of the main English nuclei, in the light of the discussion so far. The various tones are given a preliminary classification into two general types, the general directions being falling and rising, respectively. Various grounds for such a distinction were discussed in Quirk and Crystal (1966), but there was no discussion of the general theoretical implications. Level nuclear tone is placed at the top, rather than being midway between fall and rise phonetically; it takes on the functions of either fall or rise, depending on its distribution. Within each phonetic type, the tones are ordered on the basis of their twofold potential function—grammatical and attitudinal. The scale of *specificity of grammatical function* refers to the degree of restrictiveness of the syntactic conditions that predict the occurrence of a tone: some of these conditions are fairly general (e.g., "occurring finally in statements"), whereas others are quite specific (e.g., "occurring on words beginning with the morpheme *any-*"). The further down the scale a tone appears, the more specific the definition of the grammatical conditions required to predict it. *Degree of affective involvement* refers to the amount of attitudinal implication carried by a tone, with "amount" here referring to the consistent use of a range of descriptive labels (angry, pleasant, very . . .). The further down this scale a tone is placed, the more labels are needed for its complete semantic specification. The line A-A indicates the extent of the area of grammatical function: in other words, this model claims that all other nuclei in English can be described without reference to further grammatical constraints, and are assumed to be attitudinal intensifications of the attitude types already described. (Attitudinal intensification applies only within a phonetic type, however—e.g., ~ intensifies, ˇ, ˄ intensifies ˆ, and so on.) Grammatically, all that can be said about complex tones is that they are

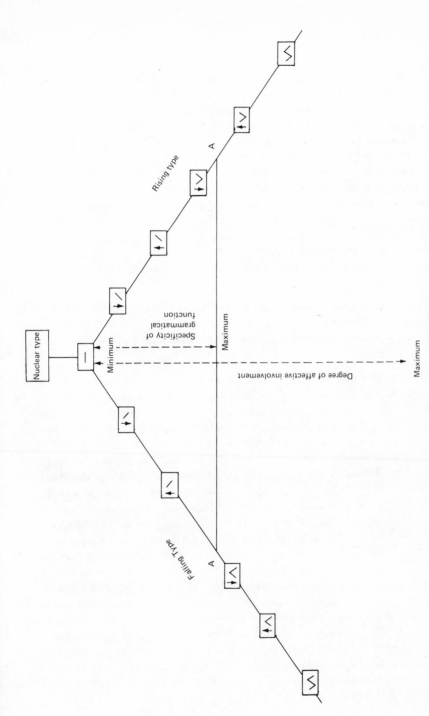

Figure 1. Nuclear-type interrelationships and functions.

distributionally restricted to the ranges of the simple tones of the same phonetic type: for example, ˆ may be used in all places where ↓ˋ or ↑ˋ go, and simply adds attitudinal information to the utterance. However, if ˆ were to replace, say, ↓ˋ, then there would be a corresponding change in grammatical function, but this would result not from the pitch complexity of the tone, but from its status as being basically falling in type.

There is no evidence of any grammatical constraint operating on syllabic pitch range, apart from the basic high versus low distinction used above. Rather, the three independent scalar values involved (pitch height of tonal beginning, pitch height of tonal termination, and overall width) should be seen as producing formal contrasts capable of being interpreted semantically as sets of gradable antonyms. For example, width can be seen as a contrast between maximally *wide* and minimally *narrow,* with a semantic specification as follows:

Wide: increased positive implication, definitiveness of commitment, and emotional involvement.
Narrow: increased negative implication, noncommitment, and emotional noninvolvement.

However, these comments at present are no more than suggestive.

So far we have been talking about the semantic interpretations as produced by an ideal intonation user who takes a syntactic context and uses the predicted tones above to produce the stated result. However, there are some 5% of cases in my data where the user did not produce the predicted tone in the syntactic context. How are these to be handled? To consider them as performance errors would be both naive and erroneous, as the very deliberate use above (p. 59) suggests. Clearly, the model has to be extended to account for such cases, and I would propose the following. By "expected tone" (E), I mean the tone that the grammatical context normally requires, as outlined above (p. 62); by "obtained tone" (O), I mean the tone that actually occurs in the data. Where there is identity between E and O (which happens 95% of the time), no further semantic specification is required to that given above. Where there is not, a further dimension must be added to Figure 1. The three phonetic variables of pitch direction, complexity, and range are interrelated, as in Figure 2, and a possible formalization given in Figure 3. An arbitrary value of 1 is assigned to each feature, and the tones are matched in terms of increasing differentiation, using the model as a basis. The higher the number, the greater the point of formal divergence; and it is then hypothesized that this will be the maximum semantic divergence also. In this way, some interesting hypotheses are generated, e.g.,

$$E = \text{ˇ}, O = \downarrow\text{ˋ} \equiv E = \downarrow\text{ˋ}, O = \text{ˇ}$$

Input

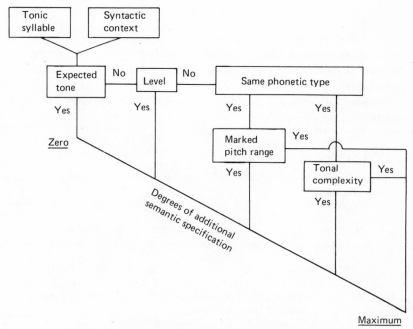

Figure 2.   Additional semantic specification for nuclear types.

O

	↑↘	—	↓↗	↑↗	∨
↑↘	E=O	1	2	3	4
—	1	E=O	1	2	3
↓↗	2	1	E=O	1	2
↑↗	3	2	1	E=O	1
∨	4	3	2	1	E=O

E

Figure 3.   Hypothetical values for nuclear differentiation.

(i.e., replacing a more marked tone by a less marked one is equivalent to replacing a less marked tone by a more marked one), and

$$E = \downarrow' O = ^- \equiv E = \uparrow' O = \downarrow'$$

The testability of these hypotheses now needs to be investigated. Equivalence might be measured in terms of quantity of labels, interrelated in semantic structure, or by obtaining reactions to sets of labels using Osgoodian differential techniques. It is to be hoped that analysts will now turn their attention to such matters, if the present hypothesis is felt sufficiently plausible to warrant the effort.

REFERENCES

Crystal, D. 1969a. Prosodic Systems and Intonation in English. Cambridge University Press, London.
Crystal, D. 1969b. Review of M. A. K. Halliday, Intonation and grammar in British English. Language 45:378–394.
Crystal, D. 1973. Intonation and linguistic theory. In: K.-H. Dahlstedt (ed.), The Nordic Languages and Modern Linguistics, pp. 267–303. Almqvist & Wiksell, Stockholm.
Haas, W. 1973. Meanings and rules. Proc. Aristotelian Soc., pp. 135–155.
Hockett, C. F., and Altmann, S. 1968. A note on design features. In: T. A. Sebeok (ed.), Animal Communication: Techniques of Study and Results of Research, pp. 61–72. Indiana University Press, Bloomington.
Lyons, J. 1968. Introduction to Theoretical Linguistics. Cambridge University Press, London.
Noss, R. B. 1972. The ungrounded transformer. Language Sci. 23:8–14.
Quirk, R., and Crystal, D. 1966. On scales of contrast in English connected speech. In: C. E. Bazell et al. (eds.), In Memory of J. R. Firth, pp. 359–369. Longmans, London.
Quirk, R., Greenbaum, S., Leech, G., and Svartvik, J. 1972. A Grammar of Contemporary English. Longmans, London.
Trim, J. L. M. 1971. Some continuously variable features in British English intonation. Proceedings of Xth International Congress of Linguistics, pp. 267–272. Éditions de l'académie de la republique socialiste de Roumanie, Bucharest.

6/ Rhythm in English: Isochronism, Pitch, and Perceived Stress

G. Faure, D. J. Hirst, and M. Chafcouloff

Few linguists today would find fault with Dwight Bolinger's affirmation (1958) that "the primary clue of what is usually termed STRESS in the utterance is pitch prominence." Thus the experimental work on synthetic speech carried out by D. B. Fry (1958) confirms that a change in pitch may outweigh any other clues all together. Other experiments (see Faure, 1962, p. 138) have shown that it is virtually impossible for a speaker to deliberately increase the intensity of one syllable in a series ("ma ma ma" for example) without a corresponding change in pitch. The results of this type of research, however, do not seem to have been consistently applied to research on an allied topic, that of rhythm. Thus, for example, in an interesting recent article Skalickova (1970, p. 72) concluded that rhythm does not depend on the regularity of recurrence of stressed syllables, but on "the duration of both the positive and negative sound manifestations."

We take a closer look in this paper at this double question:

1. How true is it to say that the rhythm of English is characterized by the *regular recurrence* of stressed syllables?
2. How far is it possible for a rhythmic pattern to be established *without any accompanying variation in pitch?*

Since the introduction of mechanical means of measuring and recording acoustic data, few linguists have gone so far as to claim that rhythm in English is based on *strictly* identical intervals between stressed syllables. It is, however, noteworthy that, although for most linguists rhythm is considered a by-product of stress, for at least some linguists the rhythmic pattern of an utterance seems to be one of the factors that contributes to the perception of stress. Thus for Abercrombie (1964, p. 217) "English utterances may be considered as being divided by the isochronous beat of the stress pulse into feet of (approximately) even length."

In most standard textbooks on English phonetics the issue is obscured by a reference to an *impression* of regularity. The use of such terms as "as nearly as possible at equal distances" (Jones, 1918, p. 237), "à intervalles sensiblement égaux" (Faure, 1948, p. 101), "a fairly regular pace" (Stannard Allen, 1964, p. 3), "fairly equal intervals of time" (Gimson, 1962, p. 238), and "feet of (approximately) equal length" (Abercrombie, 1964, p. 217) is inherently ambiguous. To say that the intervals separating stressed syllable onsets are "roughly equal" (Halliday, 1970, p. 3) can mean either:

1. The intervals seem equal because they only vary within certain definable limits (in the same way that different examples of the "same" phoneme will vary).
2. The intervals seem equal, despite considerable variation, because the perception of rhythm is based on the alternation of stressed and unstressed syllables, and not on the duration of the intervals.

Once the two hypotheses have been formulated in this way it is evident that, although either might a priori be true, both cannot be correct.

To test these hypotheses, we asked two British subjects to read a number of sentences (taken from Skalickova, 1970; see Appendix One) in an anechoic chamber. The resulting recordings were submitted to three specialists of English phonetics who were asked to mark, independently of one another, the stressed syllables of the sentences and any pauses that might occur. Having asked for a definition of "pause," they were told to consider as a pause any break in the rhythm of the utterance, including any type of segmentation with or without an accompanying silence.

For the purpose of our experiment we counted as effectively stressed all those syllables that were marked as stressed by at least two of the three phoneticians. In the same way we counted only the pauses marked by at least two of the three.

The recordings thus obtained were analyzed by means of an oscillograph (Siemens Oscillomink) and the resulting documents were used to measure the duration between the onsets of succeeding stressed syllables. When a pause had been marked between two syllables, the duration between these two syllables was not measured. Altogether, 114 intervals were measured in this way and durations were found ranging from 0.14 to 1.26 seconds.

Since the recordings had been made by two different speakers, we calculated the t of Student in order to see whether there was any significant difference between the two sets of data. For the data given in Table 1 we calculated t to -2.520, which is below the level of significance (2.617) at 0.01 for 120 df (two-tail test). We could thus treat the data as if they came from a single source.

Table 1.   Variation between speaker 1 and speaker 2

	Number of intervals (N)	Mean duration (M)	Variation (S²)
Speaker 1	60	42.92	322.38
Speaker 2	54	52.50	509.65
Total	114	47.61	

A second possible source of variation, however, seemed to come from the number of syllables included in the interval measured, contrary to the principle of isochronism, according to which the number of syllables should have no influence on the duration of the interval. Table 2 shows the calculation of the t of Student between one and two syllables, two and three syllables, and so on. It is to be noted that this coefficient is largely significant (beyond 0.01) for all pairs except 4/5 and 5/7. These last figures are no doubt due to the small numbers involved. Even when we calculate t for 4/7, it comes out no higher than 1.337. Since the duration varies significantly with the number of syllables, we can consequently calculate the mean duration *of the syllables,* which gives the results shown in Table 3.

It seems, then, that, although it is simply not true that stressed syllables are separated by even "roughly equal" intervals of time, our results tend to confirm the impressions of numerous linguists that

> Plus nombreuses sont les syllabes et plus rapide est leur articulation (Faure, 1948, p. 101).

> The speed at which the unstressed syllables are uttered and the length of them will depend upon the number occurring between the strong beats (Gimson, 1962, p. 238).

Table 2.   Variation due to number of syllables

Number of syllables	Number of intervals (N)	Mean duration (M)	Variation (S²)	Level of significance (0.05; 0.01)	t
1	6	22.00	19.600	2.00; 2.70	−3.374
2	48	35.75	95.894	1.98; 2.66	−5.506
3	37	50.03	198.721	2.00; 2.70	−2.746
4	14	68.50	1182.269	2.09; 2.86	−0.846
5	7	80.71	520.238	2.37; 3.50	−1.256
7	2	102.00	8.000		

Table 3.   Mean duration of syllables

	Number of syllables					
	1	2	3	4	5	7
Mean duration	0.22	0.17875	0.16676	0.17125	0.16143	0.1457

> If there are more syllables in the foot they will need to be spoken more quickly (Halliday, 1970, p. 3).

This should not, however, be taken as definitive, since we might suggest another explanation and assume that in fact there is no reduction at all, but that stressed syllables are simply longer than unstressed syllables. Indeed, if we take the average duration of stressed syllables to be 0.22 seconds throughout the recordings, we may decompose the mean durations as shown in Table 4.

As can be seen from Table 4, the evidence seems to point to a fixed (average) duration for stressed and unstressed syllables (0.22 seconds and 0.14 seconds, respectively, here), but further experimental work will be necessary before this can be affirmed with any greater certainty. In any case it seems certain that hypothesis (1) that we outlined above must be rejected in favor of hypothesis (2).

To test whether or not it is possible to perceive rhythmic patterns in English without any accompanying variation in pitch, we designed an experiment that would neutralize the effect of pitch change in an utterance without necessarily having any effect on intensity duration or vowel timbre. For this experiment we placed a number of minimal pairs, such as 'black 'bird / 'blackbird, in a sentence-final, postnuclear position in the context.

"I know very well \ well it's a ＿＿＿＿＿＿＿＿＿."

where normally there would be no further change of pitch from low static. We chose eight such minimal pairs:

Spanish-teacher	Spanish teacher
greenhouse	green house
blackbird	black bird
paper-bag	paper bag
hot-pot	hot pot
tallboy	tall boy
darkroom	dark room
heavyweight	heavy weight

Table 4. Mean duration of unstressed syllables

Number of syllables	Duration of interval	Duration of stressed syllable (estimated)	Total duration of unstressed syllables	Number of unstressed syllables	Mean duration of unstressed syllables
1	22.00	22	0	0	—
2	35.75	22	13.75	1	13.75
3	50.03	22	28.03	2	14.01
4	68.50	22	45.50	3	15.00
5	80.71	22	58.71	4	14.68
7	102.00	22	80.00	6	13.33

We then established the two lists, A and B (see Appendix Two) each composed of one expression from each of the eight pairs, interspersed with other expressions like "empty box" and "windscreen wiper." These two lists were recorded, with each expression being pronounced in the context "It's a _____." Recording A was subsequently played back to a second subject seated in an anechoic chamber via a pair of SOCAPEX headphones. The subject was asked first of all to repeat each sentence as faithfully as possible, with his responses being recorded on a second tape recorder (Philips EL 3503; microphone Philips LBB 9061; recording speed 7.5 i.p.s.). Once the subject had completed this task he was requested to listen to the following sequence:

It's an empty box. — I know very *well* it's an empty box.
It's a windscreen wiper. — I know very *well* it's a windscreen wiper.

and then to reply in the same way to each sentence of recording A, which was then played back to him once again. His responses were recorded once more on the second tape. After a period of one week, the same subject was requested to repeat the same experiment, the only difference being that recording B was substituted for recording A.

We thus had recordings of each pair of expressions in the contexts "It's a _____" and "I know very *well* it's a _____," without the speakers having been aware at any stage that they were recording minimal pairs.

We decided to submit these recordings to 10 English-speaking subjects, asking them to choose each time between, for example, "Spanish-teacher" and "Spanish teacher." To do this we made a recording of 32 sentences of the context, "It's a _____" (each expression thus occurred twice) in random order separated by an interval of two seconds. This recording constituted test one. Test two was a similar recording of the expressions in the context "I know very *well* it's a _____." The two recordings then were played back to a group of English-speaking students (eight British and two American). Before listening to the recordings, the subjects read through a number of definitions to make sure that they could distinguish the two senses of each pair.

As was to be expected, the sentences of test one were decoded much more easily than those of test two (92.8% correct identification versus 58.1%, respectively). Table 5 shows for each stimulus the total number of correct identifications (x) in each test out of a total of 20 (10 students and each stimulus occurring twice). If we test the hypothesis that in both tests the subjects were giving random responses, the theoretical mean (μ) will consequently be 10. We calculated t as 15.859 for test one and 1.654 for test two. Since the levels of significance for 15 df at 0.05 and 0.01 are, respectively, 2.131 and 2.947, we may conclude that this test shows beyond any doubt that,

Table 5.   Correct identifications of stimulus

Stimulus		Test one		Test two	
		x	$(x-M)^2$	x	$(x-M)^2$
1	paper bag	18	0.31	10	2.64
2	paper-bag	13	30.91	12	0.14
3	tall boy	20	2.07	14	5.64
4	tallboy	20	2.07	8	13.14
5	green house	20	2.07	15	11.39
6	greenhouse	20	2.07	14	5.64
7	black bird	19	0.19	8	13.14
8	blackbird	14	20.79	9	13.14
9	heavy weight	20	2.07	17	28.89
10	heavyweight	19	0.19	3	74.39
11	dark room	20	2.07	9	6.89
12	darkroom	20	2.07	10	2.64
13	Spanish teacher	17	2.43	14	5.64
14	Spanish-teacher	19	0.19	19	29.89
15	hot pot	19	0.19	16	19.14
16	hot-pot	19	0.19	11	0.39
	Σ	297	69.88	189	232.74
	m	18.56		11.625	
	s^2	4.659		15.449	
	s	2.159		3.93	

without the acoustic information provided by pitch change, listeners obtain no better than random scores in a test on which they score nearly 100% when pitch change information is available.

We therefore conclude that a rhythmic pattern depends above all on the recognition of a sequence of two types of syllables, stressed and unstressed (for an account of the binary nature of stress, see Hirst, 1976), and that, without pitch variation, stress judgments are virtually impossible. It is the recognition of a pattern of recurrent stressed syllables against a background of unstressed syllables that accounts for the fact that widely different intervals between stressed syllables appear to the listener to be "approximately" equal.

APPENDIX ONE

The university.
Robert must do it.
The manager is the one who purchased it.

The teacher is interested in buying some books.

Buy her a pretty new dress.

I know you didn't mean to hurt.

Wearing a funny old hat.

That's not the way to fold a coat.

The teacher was interested in buying some books, but the manager was the one who purchased them at the university.

I know you didn't mean to hurt by wearing a funny old hat.

The price of pictures moreover had if anything gone up, and he'd done better with his collection since the war began than ever before. Air-raids, also, had acted beneficially on a spirit congenitally cautious. His wife was always out when she was in town and his daughter would flibbertigibbet all over the place like most young women since the war.

APPENDIX TWO

List A	*List B*
empty box	empty box
windscreen wiper	windscreen wiper
Spanish-teacher	Spanish teacher
garden shed	golden eagle
greenhouse	green house
wastepaper basket	Irish stew
black bird	blackbird
empty vase	young girl
paper-bag	paper bag
frying pan	narrow road
hot pot	hot-pot
filing cabinet	stamp collector
tallboy	tall boy
quiet street	operating theatre
dark room	darkroom
dog basket	famous dancer
heavy weight	heavyweight

REFERENCES

Abercrombie, D. 1964. Syllable quantity and enclitics in English, In: D. Abercrombie et al. (eds.), In Honour of Daniel Jones, pp. 216–220. Longmans, London.

Bolinger, D. 1958. A theory of pitch accent in English. Word 14:104–149.

Faure, G. 1948. Manuel Practique d'Anglais Parlé. Hachette, Paris.

Faure, G. 1962. Recherches sur les Caractères et la Rôle des Éléments Musicaux dans la Prononciation Anglaise. Didier, Paris.
Fry, D. B. 1958. Experiments in the perception of stress. Language Speech I:126-152.
Gimson, A. 1962. An Introduction to the Pronunciation of English. Edward Arnold, London.
Halliday, M. 1970. A Course in Spoken English: Intonation. Oxford University Press, London.
Hirst, D. J. 1976. A distinctive feature analysis of English intonation. Linguistics.
Jones, D. 1918. An Outline of English Phonetics. Heffer, Cambridge, England.
Skalickova, A. 1970. On rhythm in English. Phonetica Pragensia II:59-74.
Stannard Allen, W. 1964. Living English Speech. Longmans, London.

7/ Bleu ou Vert? Analyse et synthèse des énoncés disjonctifs

Ivan Fónagy and Eva Bérard

Cette contribution est dédiée à Dwight Bolinger, qui a le mieux contribué à la compréhension de l'intonation en tant que langage à mi-chemin entre la communication prélinguistique et la communication linguistique proprement dit.

ANALYSE

1.1. L'analyse acoustique et perceptive des phrases assertives et interrogatives hongroises du type Kék vagy zöld (Bleu ou vert) et Kék vagy zöld? (Bleu ou vert?) a montré que la modalité interrogative n'est pas marquée d'une façon aussi nette et aussi conséquente dans les *questions alternatives* (disjonctives) que dans les questions totales. Les questions totales, non marquées par un morphème interrogatif, ont une configuration mélodique qui contraste nettement avec celle des phrases noninterrogatives (assertives, impératives, ou exclamatives). Cette opposition claire et constante exclut le chevauchement d'intonations modales, et par là des cas d'ambiguïté modale, tels qu'on les recontre en anglais (Uldall, 1962) ou en français (Mettas, 1966). La mélodie des questions alternatives, par contre, diffère peu de celle des assertions correspondantes, et les traits qui pourraient éventuellement distinguer les questions des assertions alternatives varient selon le locuteur et l'occasion. Les questions alternatives sont souvent prononcées sur un niveau plus élevé, le ton flotte généralement au-dessus du niveau de base dans la dernière syllabe (sauf dans les questions posées d'une façon catégorique); il peut monter dans les premières syllabes (cf. Figures 1 et 2). Au cours des tests de perception faits à partir de 50 variantes interrogatives et 50 variantes assertives présentées à 10 étudiants, il est apparu que le modèle interrogatif le mieux identifié—celui qui était marqué par une montée initiale—était très faiblement représenté dans le corpus (5 variantes sur 50). La distinction de la modalité semblait avoir un caractère plus ou moins improvisé.

Figure 1.   Transcription musicale des trois réalisations typiques de l'énoncé disjonctif hongrois Tejet vagy feketét (Du lait ou du café): (a) énoncé assertif; (b) et (c) énoncés interrogatifs.

L'analyse acoustique et perceptive des énoncés alternatifs russes (Fougeron, 1971) montre également que les distinctions modales n'existent que sous la forme de tendances dans le russe moderne.

1.2 Montaigne tâche de dissuader ses lecteurs vers la fin d'un de ses Essais savant et savoureux de chercher le "pourquoi" d'un fait encore mal établi. Avant de chercher les causes de cette curieuse lacune du système intonatif, attestée dans des langues non apparentées, nous avons présenté un corpus analogue, composé d'énoncés alternatifs (disjonctifs) à des sujets francophones.[1]

Contrairement aux résultats obtenus à partir des phrases hongroises analogues, il apparaît que la *modalité* des énoncés disjonctifs du français a été *correctement identifiée* dans la plupart des cas. Il y a toutefois un pourcentage d'erreurs très élevé dans l'identification des questions (lues) du sujet masculin allant jusqu'à 57%. Ce succès relatif (cf. Tableau 1) a lieu de surprendre non pas seulement par rapport aux résultats moins nets obtenus avec des phrases hongroises et russes, mais aussi en vue de la haute ressemblance des configurations mélodiques interrogatives et déclaratives (Figures 3, 4, et 14), et des divergences importantes entre les phrases appartenant à la même catégorie modale (Figures 5 et 9).

1.3 Quand nous avons présenté les courbes de fréquence fondamentale en tant que *graphies arbitraires* à des sujets invités à les diviser par groupe à partir d'analogies configuratives—d'abord en deux groupes, puis en un nombre indéterminé de groupes—il est apparu que les différences configuratives étaient nettement insuffisantes pour distinguer les deux ensembles. Les courbes des Figures 3 (énoncé assertif) et 4 (énoncé interrogatif) étaient rég-

---

[1]Nous avons enregistré avec quatre sujets—Mme F. R., Mme A. B., Mme Ch. L., et M. J.-P. L.—neuf phrases alternatives en contexte, interrogatives et déclaratives. Par exemple:

Tu peux le mettre où tu le veux: ici ou là-bas.
Il faut choisir: ici ou là-bas?

Les trois sujets féminins ont prononcé les phrases librement, après mémorisation. Le sujet masculin lisait le texte. Les énoncés disjonctifs ont été recopiés hors contexte, en ordre aléatoire sur la bande stimulus. Nous avons présenté 30 phrases à 30 sujets (étudiants des deux sexes) qui devaient déterminer la modalité de la phrase présentée. Nous avons constaté une fluctuation de 4.4% dans les jugements de trois phrases identiques (recopiées à deux reprises).

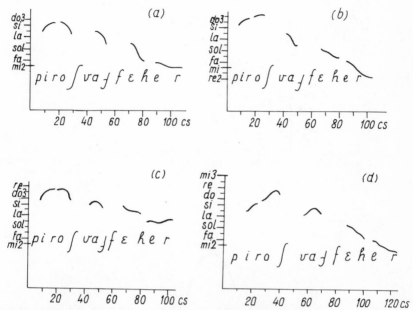

Figure 2.   Courbe de fréquence fondamentale dans quatre phrases hongroises contenant l'énoncé disjonctif <u>Piros vagy fehér</u> (Rouge ou blanc): (a) énoncé assertif (disjonction inclusive); (b) énoncé assertif (disjonction exclusive); (c) énoncé interrogatif (neutre); (d) énoncé interrogatif (catégorique).

Tableau 1.   Résultats des test d'identification des phrases assertives et interrogatives. Le nombre des réponses correctes est très élevé, la distribution est toujours hautement significative (S). ($N = 30$)

Prononcées par	Phrases assertives correctement identifiées	Phrases interrogatives correctement identifiées
Mme F. R.	202/210	148/150
Mme A. B.	192/210	149/150
M. J.-P. L.	207/210	106/150
Au total	601/630	403/450
Test binomial (z)	22.75	16.73
Probabilité	$p < 0.00003$	$p < 0.00003$
Validité	S	S

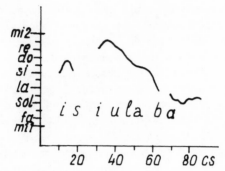

Figure 3.   Courbe de fréquence de l'assertion alternative (disjonctive) Ici ou là-bas.

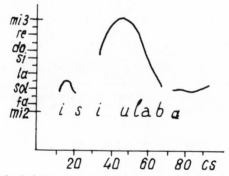

Figure 4.   Courbe de fréquence de la question alternative (disjonctive) Ici ou là-bas?

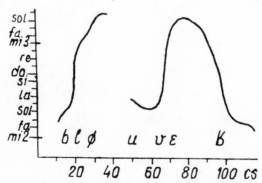

Figure 5.   Courbe de fréquence de l'assertion alternative (disjonction exclusive) Bleu ou vert.

ulièrement groupées ensemble, tandis que les courbes des Figures 5 et 9 (énoncés assertifs) étaient placées, sans exception, dans deux groupes différents. Le classement fait à partir de configurations visuelles était arbitraire par rapport à la modalité réelle des phrases en question.

1.4 En tenant d'expliquer le méchanisme du décodage modal, nous nous trouvons dans une situation assez semblable à celle des sujets du test graphique. On ne peut s'empêcher d'admirer la perspicacité des sujets du test auditif qui ont identifié, sans hésiter, des configurations disparates et distingué des courbes à peine différentes les unes des autres.

Nous avons rapproché les courbes de fréquence correctement identifiées dans 100% des cas à celles qui ont causé quelques difficultés. Les deux variantes de la phrase <u>Bleu ou vert</u>? perçues comme ''question'' dans 100% des cas (Figures 6 et 27) commencent par une montée considérable dans la première syllabe. Le montée est suivie d'une chute tonale dans la conjonction <u>ou</u>, et le ton flotte sur un niveau moyen dans le deuxième terme de l'alternative (dans le mot <u>vert</u>). La question <u>Ici ou là-bas</u>? des trois locutrices commence également par une montée rapide dans la première syllabe accentuée. L'écart entre le niveau de départ du mot et le sommet mélodique comporte 10 resp. 11 demi-tons. Cette montée sera suivie d'une descente plus légère dans la conjonction <u>ou</u>. Dans la dernière syllabe de la phrase, le ton ne descend guère au-dessous du palier initial sauf dans une question posée d'une façon très catégorique par l'une des locutrices (viz. Figure 12). Ajoutons que les phrases interrogatives des sujets féminins sont plus chantonnées, c'est-à-dire qu'elles ont un ''degré de musicalitée'' (Fónagy et Magdics, 1963) plus élevé que les phrases assertives.

La phrase assertive <u>Ici ou là-bas</u> du sujet masculin a été correctement identifiée par tous les sujets. La montée dans la première syllabe accentuée est

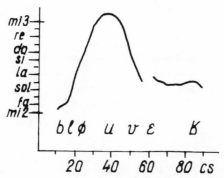

Figure 6.   Courbe de fréquence de la question alternative <u>Bleu ou vert?</u>

cette fois très faible (Figure 7); l'écart tonal entre les deux premières syllabes est inférieur à celui qu'on rencontre dans les questions correspondantes (cf. Figures 4 et 8). Cette faible montée est suivie d'une descente graduelle, à partir de la conjonction ou qui, en descendant, dépasse le niveau initial. Le palier de fréquence de la dernière syllabe est très inférieur à celui de la première.

La phrase déclarative Bleu ou vert de Mme A. B. a été cependant correctement identifiée par tous les sujets, malgré une montée très considérable (120 Hz, 9 demi-tons) dans la première syllabe. La pente de la montée est, toutefois, moins abrupte que celle des phrases interrogatives. Sa phrase se termine sur une note basse, avec une très légère remontée finale (Figure 9).

Pour en venir aux échecs partiels, la phrase assertive de Mme A. B., Ici ou là-bas (Figure 10), a été prise pour une question par 20% des sujets. Si on la compare à une variante correctement identifiée par tous (cf. Figure 7), on peut relever certains traits communs: note basse de la dernière syllabe, niveau moyen relativement bas. On trouve, en même temps, des traits nettement divergents: l'écart assez considérable entre le niveau de la première et de la deuxième syllabe, et le palier élevé de la conjonction. La montée dans la première syllabe semble moins rapide que dans les phrases enterprétées à l'unanimité comme questions.

Il faut noter, toutefois, qu'un écart encore plus considérable entre les deux premières syllabes d'une autre variante assertive de la même phrase (Figure 11) n'a pas empêché les sujets d'interpréter la phrase comme une assertion. Cette variante assertive se distingue de la phrase interrogative correspondante de la même locutrice (Figure 12) par une descente finale catégorique au niveau de base, et par une montée moins précipitée de la courbe dans la syllabe accentuée de la première alternative, ici. Dans les deux variantes, interrogative et assertive, le ton de la première syllabe atone est descendant.

La phrase interrogative Bleu ou vert? (Figure 13) de notre locuteur a été prise pour une phrase assertive par 57% des sujets. Après une montée importante, mais peu précipitée, la voix descend rapidement au-dessous du niveau de départ.

Certains traits intonatifs semblent donc favoriser les votes question:

1. Le niveau de fréquence moyenne de la phrase.
2. L'importance de la montée dans la première syllabe accentuée, et sa pente abrupte, c'est-à-dire, un quotient montée (demi-tons)/durée (centiseconds) élevé.
3. Le palier tonal de la conjonction est relativement élevé.
4. Le niveau de la dernière syllabe est plus élevé que celui de la première.
5. La dernière syllabe se termine par une montée.

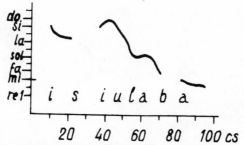

Figure 7.   Courbe de fréquence de l'assertion alternative <u>Ici ou là-bas</u>.

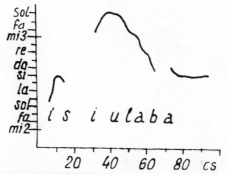

Figure 8.   Courbe de fréquence de la question alternative <u>Ici ou là-bas</u>?

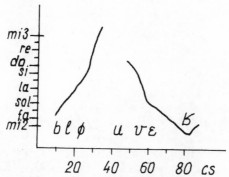

Figure 9.   Courbe de fréquence de l'assertion alternative <u>Bleu ou vert</u>.

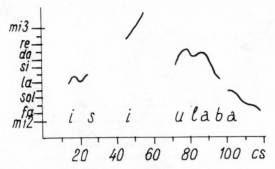

Figure 10.   Courbe de fréquence de l'assertion alternative Ici ou là-bas.

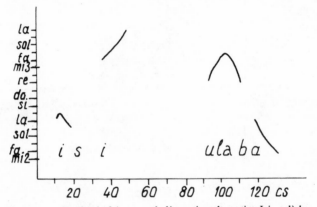

Figure 11.   Courbe de fréquence de l'assertion alternative Ici ou là-bas.

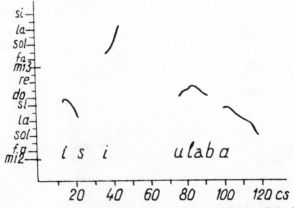

Figure 12.   Courbe de fréquence de la question alternative Ici ou là-bas?

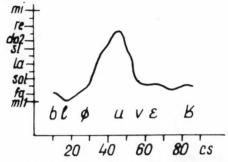

Figure 13.   Courbe de fréquence de la question alternative Bleu ou vert?

1.5. Nous avons déterminé par calcul les *courbes de fréquences moyennes* des phrase interrogatives d'une part, et des phrases déclaratives d'autre part (cf. Figure 14).[2]

1. Le *niveau tonal moyen* est effectivement *plus élevé* dans les phrases *interrogatives* que dans les phrases déclaratives (cf. Tableau 2). Les écarts moyens varient, selon les phrases et les sujets, entre 1.1 et 4.0.

2. Le *sommet* tonal des phrases interrogatives est relativement plus élevé. En d'autres termes, l'écart qui sépare le point le plus élevé de la première syllabe accentuée soit du niveau de départ, soit du niveau de base individuel, est plus grand dans les phrases interrogatives que dans les phrases déclaratives correspondantes. Le sommet de Bleu ou vert? dépasse de 3.5 demi-tons celui de Bleu ou vert, et pour Ici ou là-bas? le sommet dépasse de 4.4 demi-tons celui de la phrase déclarative. Le contraste est encore plus net entre les deux pentes: celle de la question est plus abrupte. Le *quotient montée/durée* moyen est de 1.21 dans les phrases déclaratives et de 2.93 dans les phrases interrogatives (Tableau 3).

3. Le ton descend moins bas dans la *conjonction* des phrases interrogatives. Il y a un écart de 9 demi-tons entre le point inférieur de la courbe de

---

[2]Nous avons divisé chaque syllabe en segments de 2–3 centisecondes pour déterminer la fréquence moyenne des segments, et calculé l'écart moyen en demi-tons entre le niveau le plus bas atteint par le sujet au cours des enregistrements. Le nombre des segments admis pour une syllabe devait être le même pour chacun des sujets, afin de pouvoir calculer la moyenne des changements de hauteur à l'intérieur de la syllabe. Nous avons calculé également le niveau moyen des syllabes, pour chaque sujet, et la moyenne de ces moyennes pour les trois sujets. Pour obtenir les schémas intonatifs (Figure 15), nous avons déterminé la hauteur moyenne des "points névralgiques" de la courbe: (1) départ (niveau moyen de la première syllabe dans Ici, resp. niveau initial dans Bleu, abstraction faite de l'occlusive); (2) sommet (le point le plus élevé atteint dans la première syllabe accentuée); (3) niveau terminal de la conjonction ou; (4) niveau initial du deuxième terme (vert, resp. ici); niveau terminal.

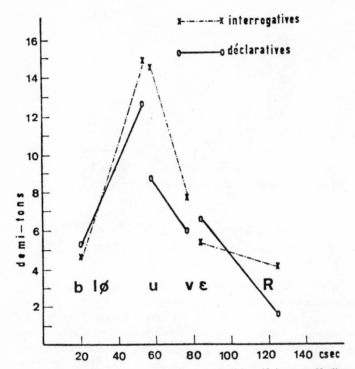

Figure 14.   Schéma de l'intonation moyenne des énoncés disjonctifs interrogatifs (ligne hachée) et assertifs (ligne pleine).

fréquence de <u>ou</u> et le niveau inférieur de la dernière syllabe. L'écart est de 8 demi-tons dans les phrases déclaratives (cf. Tableau 4).

4. Le niveau moyen de la *dernière syllabe* n'est pas plus élevé que celui de la première syllabe, ni dans les phrases déclaratives, ni dans les phrases interrogatives. Le niveau moyen de la dernière syllabe par rapport au niveau de base individuel est cependant *plus élevé* dans les *questions* que dans les phrases déclaratives (Tableau 5).

5. En divisant la dernière syllabe en deux parties égales, il apparaît que la hauteur moyenne de la deuxième partie est inférieure à celle de la première dans les phrases déclaratives. La *chute finale* moyenne est plus faible dans les phrases interrogatives (Tableau 6).

1.6 On peut se rendre mieux compte de l'influence exercée par ses paramétres prosodiques sur l'interprétation modale des phrases en comparant leur divergences en fonction du résultat des tests, c'est-à-dire en calculant les

Tableau 2.   Niveau tonal moyen (en quart de ton) par rapport au niveau de base du locuteur dans les phrases assertives et interrogatives; résultat du test t, seuil de probabilité (p), et validité (S = significatif)

	Phrases assertives ($N = 20$)	Phrases interrogatives ($N = 16$)
Niveau tonal moyen (en qu-t)	12.50	16.87
	4.298	4.545
Test t	2.93	
Probabilité	$p <0.005$	
Validité	S	

Tableau 3.   Moyennes du quotient de la montée dans la première syllabe accentuée (en quart de ton) et de la durée de la partie vocale de la syllabe dans les phrases assertives et interrogatives; résultat du test t, probabilité (p), et validité (S = significatif)

	Phrases assertives ($N = 20$)	Phrases interrogatives ($N = 16$)
Qu-t/csec	1.21	2.93
	0.643	2.081
Test t	3.18	
Probabilité	$p <0.005$	
Validité	S	

Tableau 4.   Ecart mélodique moyen (en quart de ton) entre le niveau mélodique inférieur de la conjonction et le niveau de base du locuteur dans les phrases assertives et interrogatives; résultat du test t, seuil de probabilité (p), et validité (S = significatif)

	Phrases assertives ($N = 20$)	Phrases interrogatives ($N = 16$)
Moyenne en qu-t	13.70	18.31
	5.813	5.641
Test t	2.41	
Probabilité	$p <0.025$	
Validité	S	

Tableau 5.   Niveau moyen de la dernière syllabe (en quart de ton) par rapport au niveau de base du locuteur; résultat du test *t*, probabilité (*p*), et validité (NS = non significatif)

	Phrases assertives (*N* = 20)	Phrases interrogatives (*N* = 16)
Moyenne en *qu-t*	7.78 6.025	9.38 6.152
Test *t*	0.78	
Probabilité	$p < 0.1$	
Validité	NS	

valeurs moyennes obtenues à partir des questions ou déclarations *univoques* (100% de réponses correctes) aux valeurs moyennes obtenues à partir des questions et déclarations *ambiguës* (moins de 85% de réponses correctes). En prenant les valeurs obtenues indépendamment du résultat des tests pour points de repère (ligne zéro), il apparaît que:

1.   Le quotient montée/durée est particulièrement bas dans les questions ambiguës par rapport aux questions univoques; de même, il est très bas dans les phrases déclaratives univoques par rapport au quotient des déclarations ambiguës (Figures 15 et 16).
2.   Le niveau tonal de la *dernière syllabe* est considérablement plus élevé dans les questions univoques que dans les questions ambiguës et, d'autre part, leur niveau est beaucoup plus bas dans les phrases déclaratives univoques que dans les déclarations ambiguës.

Tableau 6.   Différence entre le niveau moyen de la première et la deuxième partie de la dernière syllabe, en quart de tons. Le différence est significative selon le test *t* au seuil de probabilité $p < 0.0005$

	Phrases assertives (*N* = 20)	Phrases interrogatives (*N* = 16)
syll $\frac{n_1}{2} - \frac{n_2}{2}$	3.96 2.493	1.47 1.343
Test *t*	3.86	
Probabilité	$p < 0.0005$	
Validité	S	

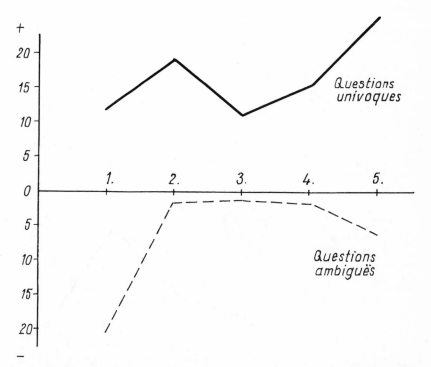

Figure 15.   Représentation schématique de l'importance relative de cinq paramètres prosodiques pour l'identification des questions alternatives: 1) le quotient montée/durée; 2) la fréquence moyenne; 3) l'écart entre le sommet mélodique et le niveau de base (niveau inférieur atteint au cours des enregistrements par le locuteur); 4) écart tonal entre le point inférieur de la courbe de fréquence de la conjonction et le niveau de base; 5) écart tonal entre le point terminal de la courbe et le niveau de base. Les écarts mélodiques sont déterminés en demi-tons. Questions univoques: reconnues comme telles par plus de 95% des sujets. Questions ambiguës: reconnues par moins de 85% des sujets. Les valeurs moyennes obtenues pour les différents paramètres constituent le niveau de référence (ligne 0); l'écart positif ou négatif par rapport à cette moyenne est déterminé en pourcentage (allant de + 25 à − 20). Le paramètre 1, quotient montée/durée, est particulièrement bas pour les questions ambiguës. Le paramètre 5, niveau terminal, dépasse pour les questions univoques de 25% la moyenne.

3.   Le *niveau moyen* de la phrase et le niveau de la *conjonction* sont également plus élevés dans les questions univoques que dans les questions ambiguës; ils sont plus élevés dans les phrases déclaratives ambiguës que dans les phrases déclaratives univoques (Figures 15 et 16). Ces écarts sont cependant moins importants que ceux des paramètres *montée initiale* et *niveau terminal*.

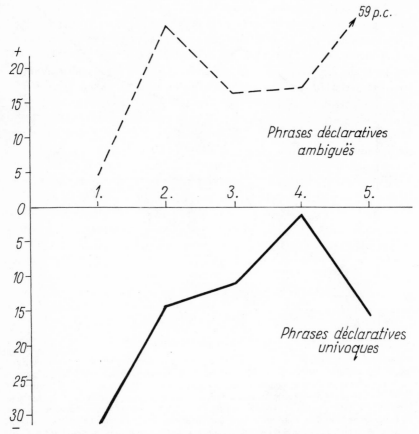

Figure 16.   L'importance relative des cinq paramètres prosodiques (cf. Figure 15) pour l'identification des assertions alternatives.

1.7 Nous nous sommes servis également de la méthode du *tronquage* afin de localiser les éléments distinctifs. Nous avons présenté à trente sujets francophones[3] l'un ou l'autre segment des phrases en question:

    (a)   Ici. . .   Bleu. . .
    (b)   Ici ou. . .   Bleu ou. . .
    (c)   . . .là-bas   . . .vert

Les sujets devaient déterminer la modalité des phrases tronquées.

---

[3]Les tests ont été faits sous la direction de M. George Kassai (CNRS). Les sujets étaient des étudiants en linguistique. Nous tenons à remercier M. Kassai de son aide très précieuse.

Les résultats semblent indiquer que la *première partie* de la *phrase interrogative* est plus pertinente que la deuxième (Tableau 7). C'est la première montée qui joue probablement le rôle le plus important; l'élimination de la conjonction ne diminue guère le pourcentage de réponses correctes. (Il y a une perte de 7.5% dans les phrases interrogatives.) La suppression de la première partie de la phrase rend la modalité méconnaissable (Figure 17). Dans ces conditions, le nombre des réponses correctes n'a jamais dépassé 60.0% pour les phrases interrogatives; il varie entre 11.5 et 60.0. Il ne faut pas oublier cependant que la partie finale présentée séparément, ne renseigne pas sur son niveau relatif (par rapport au début de la phrase).

La *phrase déclarative* souffre moins du tronquage de la première partie. Au contraire, elle en profite (Figure 17): 85.56% sont correctement identifiées à partir du dernier mot. Elle souffre plus de la suppression de la deuxième partie de la phrase: 95.3→76.1. Il semble qu'on est toujours tenté d'interpréter une phrase inachevée comme interrogative (cf. Karcevskij, 1930; Malmberg, 1966), une phrase dont on ne perçoit que la descente finale comme déclarative. La phrase (Ici ou) là-bas? n'a obtenu que 28.0% de suffrage "question" (Figure 12), et la phrase (Bleu ou) vert? seulement 11.5% (Figure 13); tandis que 60% des sujets ont correctement identifié la partie finale d'une phrase interrogative quand on leur a présenté là-bas dans une réalisation caractérisée par une montée finale audible (viz. Figure 4).

Dans certains cas, la première partie de la phrase a attiré plus de réponses corrects sans conjonction. Ce phénomène paradoxal s'explique dans ces cas-là par l'intonation "irrégulière," moins typique de la conjonction: par un niveau tonal trop élevé, un ton flottant dans les phrases déclaratives ou, inversement, par un ton brusquement descendant dans le cas des phrases interrogatives (cf. Figures 3 et 4).

1.8 Les hypothèses peuvent être, souvent, précisées, ou même partiellement infirmées ou confirmées à l'aide de la méthode de l'*identification automatique programmée*. Les essais d'identification peuvent apporter dans certains cas de très bons résultats (Fónagy et Bérard, 1973). Cette fois, les divergences individuelles ont rendu la tâche particulièrement difficile, voire impossible. En comparant les quotients montée/durée obtenus pour les deux phrases et leurs réalisations individuelles, on voit que le quotient montée/durée de Bleu est près du double de celui de (I-)ci. Il faudrait donc tenir compte de la structure rythmique des phrases, notamment du nombre des syllabes du premier terme (cf. Tableau 3). Il est évident qu'il faudrait fixer le seuil du quotient interrogatif—le niveau à partir duquel une phrase serait déclarée automatiquement interrogative—pour la phrase Ici ou là-bas moins haut que pour Bleu ou vert.

Le chevauchement individuel nous met dans une situation encore plus

Tableau 7. Tests d'interprétation modale avec 30 sujets à partir des phrases interrogatives et assertives tronquées

Phrases tronquées	Réponses correctes		Test binomial (z)		Probabilité (p)	Validité
	Assertive	Interrogative	Assertive	Interrogative		
Bleu ou . . . Ici ou . . .	137/180	156/180	6.932	9.764	<0.00003	S
Bleu . . . Ici . . .	142/180	139/180	7.677	7.230	<0.00003	S
. . . vert . . . là-bas	154/180	75/180	9.466	2.162	<0.00003; <0.01[a]	S

[a] Les résultats sont significatifs au seuil de probabilité p <0.00003, sauf pour les phrases interrogatives dont on n'a présentée que le dernier élément. Ici, c'est l'erreur des sujets (41% de votes corrects) qui s'avère être significatif au seuil de p < 0.01.

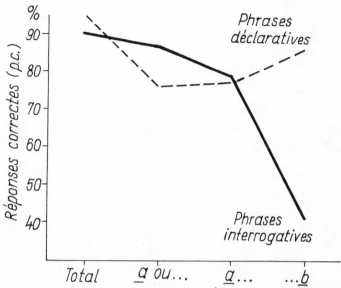

Figure 17.   Résultats des tests de perception pour les phrases tronquées (questions et assertions).

embarrassante. En fixant le seuil du quotient montée/durée pour la phrase <u>Ici ou là-bas</u>   à un niveau qui conviendrait aux énoncés de nos deux sujets féminins, la plupart des phrases interrogatives du sujet masculin seraient interprétées comme déclaratives. En le fixant à un niveau plus bas, la plupart des phrases déclaratives de Mme A. B. seraient considérées comme interrogatives.

SYNTHESE DE LA PHRASE <u>ICI OU LÀ-BAS</u>[4]

2.1 Afin de mieux évaluer l'importance relative des différents facteurs et pour pouvoir faire abstraction de l'influence éventuelle exercée par les variations de pression sonore, du débit, et du timbre, nous étions amenés à avoir recours à la synthèse. Nous avons repris et modifié les courbes de fréquence de deux variantes naturelles—de celles qui ont été identifées au cours des tests de perception à 100% soit comme question, soit comme assertion (cf. Tableau 8).

En reproduisant ces courbes sans autres modifications que celles imposées par la technique de la synthèse, la courbe interrogative non modifiée

[4]Les travaux de synthése ont eu lieu au laboratoire de Marcoussis de la Compagnie générale d'Electricité, sur un synthétiseur paramétrique, à circuits numériques, en collaboration avec Jacques Sap, que nous tenons à remercier de son aide précieuse.

Tableau 8. Perception de la modalité à partir de variantes synthétisées de la phrase Ici ou là-bas. La validité des préférences est déterminée à partir d'un test binomial (z). Préférence pertinente, S (significatif); préférence nonpertinente, NS (nonsignificatif); p, seuil de probabilité de la validité

| | Modalité | | Interprétations proposées par les sujets ($N = 54$) | | |
	Assertive	Interrogative	Test binomial (z)	Probabilité (p)	Validité
Variantes synthétisées d' Ici ou là-bas					
Q 1		54	7.22	<0.00003	S
Q 2	5	49	5.86	<0.00003	S
Q 3	17	37	2.59	<0.005	S
Q 4	12	42	3.95	<0.00005	S
Q 5	14	40	3.41	<0.0003	S
Q 6	13	41	3.68	<0.0001	S
Q 7	16	38	2.86	<0.002	S
Q 8	36	18	2.32	<0.01	S
Q 9	40	14	3.41	<0.0005	S
D 1	48	6	5.59	<0.00003	S
D 2	45	9	4.77	<0.00003	S
QD 1	18	36	2.32	<0.01	S
QD 2	38	16	2.86	<0.002	S
QD 3	7	47	5.31	<0.00003	S
DQ 1	38	16	2.86	<0.002	S
Q 4	15	39	3.13	<0.0009	S
Q 5	14	40	3.41	<0.0005	S
Variantes synthétisées tronquées					
Ici. . . (Q 1)	4	28	4.06	<0.00003	S
Ici ou. . . (Q 1)	4	28	4.06	<0.00003	S
. . . là-bas (Q 1)	25	7	3.00	<0.001	S
. . . ou là-bas (Q 1)	12	20	1.24	>0.1	NS
Ici. . . (D 2)	26	6	3.36	<0.0005	S
Ici ou. . . (D 2)	25	7	3.00	<0.001	S
. . . ou là-bas (D 2)	26	5	3.36	<0.0005	S

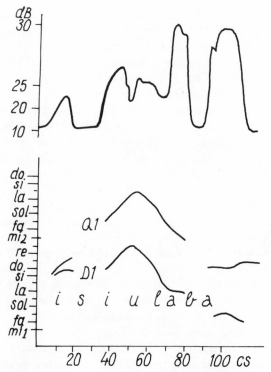

Figure 18.   Courbe de fréquence d'une assertion et d'une question alternative (disjonctive) synthétique (D 1 et Q 1).

Q1 a été identifiée par 54 sujets sur 54 comme phrase interrogative.[5] La phrase D 1, imitant la courbe de fréquence laryngée de l'énoncé assertif, a été reconnue comme telle par 48 sujets sur 54 (cf. Tableaux 1 et 8). Toutes les variantes présentées au cours des tests avaient la même courbe d'intensité, les mêmes durées, et la même structure formantique (Figure 18). Il est donc possible de changer le caractère modal des énoncés disjonctifs en ne modifiant que la fréquence fondamentale.

2.2 La variante Q 2 se distingue de Q 1 par une ligne mélodique descendante (de 130 à 110 Hz) dans la *première syllabe* (i-). Cette modification a eu peu d'influence sur l'évaluation de la modalité (perte de 5 votes ''interrogatives'').

---

[5]Les variantes synthétisées ont été présentées à deux groupes d'étudiants en linguistique des deux sexes (au département des Recherches linguistiques de l'Université Paris VII). La concordance des résultats nous a permis de réunir les données obtenues au cours des deux tests.

La courbe de fréquence (montante) de la *deuxième syllabe* (-ci) du modèle interrogatif est déplacée de 4 demi-tons (dt par la suite) vers le bas dans la variante Q 3 (Figure 19) toute en gardant l'intervalle mélodique (de 4 dt). Cette modification a eu plus d'effet sur les jugements (37 votes ''interrogatives'' sur 54, une perte de 17 voix) que la réduction de la gamme de la montée à 3 dt avec maintien du palier supérieur, variante Q 4 (Figure 19). Une montée d'un demi-ton à partir du même palier élevé dans la variante Q 5 a suffi pour assurer 40 votes ''interrogatives'' sur 54 (Figure 19).

2.3 Dans tous ces cas, la courbe de la deuxième motié de la phrase n'a pas été modifiée. Le point inférieur de la descente tonale dans la conjonction ''ou''—la *troisième syllabe* de la phrase ''*ou* n'a jamais dépassé,'' par exemple—le niveau de départ (170 Hz) de la deuxième syllabe (-ci). Si, par contre, le ton descend au-dessous de ce niveau, même légèrement (jusqu'à 162 Hz) comme dans la variante Q 6, cette modification entraîne la perte de 13 votes ''interrogatives'' (Figure 20).

Dans les énoncés disjonctifs, le ton ne descend guère dans la première syllabe du deuxième terme (là) qui suit la conjonction, au-dessous du niveau de départ de la première syllabe du premier terme (i-). Nous avons fait descendre la courbe de fréquence dans la *quatrième syllabe* (là) d'un demi-ton au-dessous du niveau de départ de i- dans la variante Q 7, le nombre de votes ''interrogatives'' descend de 54 à 38 (Figure 21).

2.4 Le caractère interrogatif de l'énoncé est supprimé par une sensible baisse du niveau tonal de la *dernière syllabe*. Si, au lieu de laisser flotter le mot bas légèrement au-dessus du niveau de départ de la phrase, on déprime le début de la courbe de 3 demi-tons et la fin de 6 demi-tons (variants Q 8,

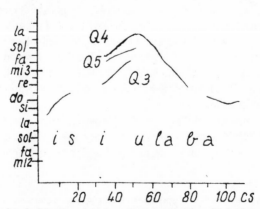

Figure 19.   Courbes de fréquence de trois variantes synthétiques (Q 3, Q 4, et Q 5) du modèle interrogatif.

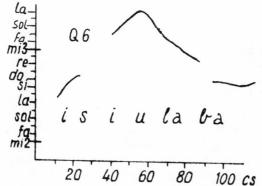

Figure 20.   Courbe de fréquence d'une variante synthétique (Q 6) du modèle interrogatif.

Figure 22), la balance bascule: en face de 18 votes "modalité interrogative," on aura 36 votes "modalité assertive." On pourrait penser que ce virage est partiellement dû à la ligne mélodique descendant de la fin de la phrase. En substituant, toutefois, une courbe montante à la courbe descendante (variante Q 9, Figure 22), on renforce le caractère déclaratif de l'énoncé: on obtient 40 votes "modalité assertive." Selon les tests perceptifs qui ont eu pour but de déterminer les attitudes suggérées par les différentes variantes, la variante Q 9 paraît exprimer une attitude nonchalante ("l'une ou l'autre, peu importe") qui s'associe très mal à la vélléité interrogative (Tableau 8).

La variante D 2 se distingue de D 1 (ayant élicité 48 votes "assertives") par son niveau tonal plus élevé, et une descente tonale plus progressive. Elle a obtenu 9 votes "interrogatives" (Figures 23 et 24).

La variante QD 2 suit dans la *première partie* (Ici) le modèle *interrogatif*

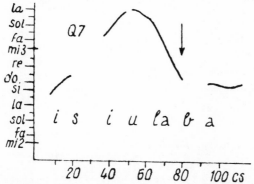

Figure 21.   Courbe de fréquence d'une variante synthétique (Q 7) du modèle interrogatif.

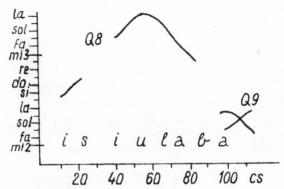

Figure 22.   Courbes de fréquence de deux variantes synthétiques (Q 8 et Q 9) du modèle interrogatif.

Q 1 et dans la *deuxième partie* le modèle assertif D 2: elle a obtenu une majorité de votes ''interrogatives.'' [La variante QD 1 réunit les mêmes éléments, avec la différence, toutefois, que la deuxième partie de la phrase est déprimée de 5 demi-tons en suivant la courbe de l'énoncé assertive D 1. Cette *dépression* fait basculer les votes: on obtient 38 votes ''assertives'' contre 16 votes ''interrogatives.'' Donc, malgré le caractère interrogatif de la première partie, une descente au ''niveau de base'' fait penser plutôt à une assertion qu'à une question (Figures 23 et 24).] La variante QD 3 combine la première partie et la conjonction de la variante interrogative Q 1 (Ici ou) avec le deuxième terme (là-bas) de l'énoncé déclaratif D 2: l'énoncé sera interprété par 47 sujets sur 54 comme une question. Ceci met en évidence le rôle que joue le

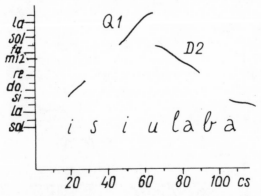

Figure 23.   Courbe de fréquence d'un énoncé alternatif synthétique combinant les modèles interrogatif (Q 1) et assertif (D 2).

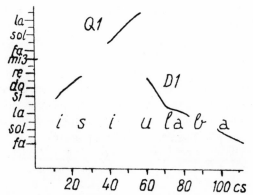

Figure 24.   Courbes de fréquence d'une phrase synthétique combinant les deux modèles, assertif et interrogatif (QD 1) et de sa variante (QD 2).

niveau tonal de la *conjonction* dans la caractérisation de la modalité inter-rogative.

La variante DQ 1 réunit le premier terme de l'énoncé déclaratif D 2 (Ici) à la deuxième partie de l'énoncé interrogatif Q 1 (ou là-bas). Cette variante est interprétée comme plutôt assertive (avec 38 voix sur 54). Ceci paraît indiquer qu'un début nettement déclaratif ne saurait être neutralisé suffisamment par une deuxième partie interrogative.

Nous avons soumis aux sujets du premier test des phrases synthétisées tronquées, notamment différentes parties des phrases Q 1 et D 2. Les phrases ont été perçues comme des *questions* quand on a présenté le premier terme de l'alternative (Ici) ou le premier terme et la conjonction (Ici ou) de la phrase Q 1. Le deuxième terme (là-bas) isolé de la même phrase Q 1 a été interprété, par contre, comme faisant partie d'une *assertion*. Quand on a fait précéder le deuxième terme de la conjonction, la phrase a repris son caractère interrogatif pour 20 sujets sur 33. Les parties isolées de la phrase D 2 ont toujours été prises comme celles d'une assertion par la majorité des sujets.

Il y a une contradiction apparente entre ces résultats et ceux obtenus avec les variantes de la phrase entière. Le niveau de la dernière syllabe semble avoir joué un rôle décisif dans l'identification de la modalité au cours de la présentation des variantes de la phrase entière, tandis que le fragment . . . bas? a été attribué à une phrase assertive. C'est, probablement, l'absence d'un niveau de référence qui a privé la phrase tronquée (-bas) d'un trait distinctif: le niveau moyen de la dernière syllabe, comme c'était le cas au cours des tests à partir de phrases tronquées naturelles (cf. "Analyse," 1.7). Dès qu'on a pu comparer le niveau du deuxième terme à celui de la conjonction, la majorité des sujets a interprété la séquence . . . ou là-bas comme la deuxième partie d'une phrase interrogative.

La gamme de la montée mélodique du premier terme (Ici . . .) a été, par contre, un indice suffisant pour l'identification correcte de la modalité interrogative (Tableau 8, Ici, Ici ou de Q1).

Nous pouvons donc inférer que c'est surtout le *niveau tonal* de la syllabe accentuée du *premier terme* (-ci) et de la conjonction qui caractérise la modalité *interrogative* dans les énoncés disjonctifs, et que la modalité *assertive* est caractérisée à la fois par le niveau (moins élevé) et la faible montée tonale de cette syllabe, et par le *niveau bas* du *deuxième* terme (bas). Le ton montant dans cette syllabe ne prête pas un caractère interrogatif à l'énoncé, mais ajoute un message secondaire ("attitudinal") au message primaire modal. Il est important de noter, toutefois, la variété et le caractère facultatif des indices modaux dans les énoncés disjonctifs qui contrastent avec la caractérisation relativement simple des questions dites totales en français, en russe, et, surtout, en hongrois. Ceci semble indiquer que l'intonation interrogative des énoncés disjonctifs est moins nettement formulée et moins intégrée à la grammaire que celle des questions totales.

MODALITE ET ATTITUDE

3.1 On peut distinguer du point de vue logique, dans le premier corpus (questions et assertions parlées, non synthétisées), deux sortes d'énoncés; ceux que sous-tend une *disjonction inclusive,* permettant que les deux alternatives soient également vraies ("J'aime les deux: bleu ou vert"); et ceux que sous-tend une *disjonction exclusive* qui n'admet pas la validité simultanée des deux ("Ah non, pas les deux ensembles: bleu ou vert"). Le corpus hongrois soumis au test entérieurement (Fónagy et Magdics, 1963, 1967) contenait également des énoncés disjonctifs concessifs et exclusifs.

Au cours de tests complémentaires,[6] nous avons présenté à deux groupes d'étudiants des questions et des assertions alternatives inclusives et exclusives hors contexts.

Les résultats hongrois et français ont été, cette fois, convergents. Les sujets français, tout comme les sujets hongrois, ont réussi dans la plupart des cas à distinguer les deux opérations logiques à partir de leur expression prosodique (Tableau 9). Un tel résultat semble indiquer que cette distinction logique

---

[6]Le questionnaire contenait une "définition" pratique des deux opérations logiques: "Inclusif: 'et/ou' les deux alternatives sont admises simultanément. Exclusif: ou l'un, ou l'autre, il faut choisir; les deux alternatives ne sont pas admises simultanément."

Tableau 9.   Rapports entre attitudes et catégories logiques; r = coefficient de corrélation, m = pente de la droite de regression, y = constante qui détermine la point d'intersection de la droite de regression sur l'axe y (l'ordonné). m et y permettent de visualiser le rapport entre les paramètres mis en corrélation. Seuls les rapports "volontaire/intéressé" et "indifférent/inclusive (disjonction)" sont significatifs au seuil de probabilité $p <0.001$. Le rapport entre attitude volontaire et disjonction exclusive reste légèrement sous le seuil de la pertinence

Volontaire/intéressé ($p <0.001$; S)		Volontaire/exclusive (disjonction) ($p >0.04$; NS)		Indifférent/inclusive (disjonction) ($p <0.001$; S)	
r	0.610	r	0.329	r	0.747
m	0.673	m	0.295	m	0.608
y	5.796	y	8.906	y	2.438

est mieux exprimée sur le plan prosodique que sur le plan segmental, où la conjonction ou (hongrois vagy) neutralise l'opposition.

Dans les deux langues, la disjonction *exclusive* favorise la *polarisation tonale:* le premier terme se déplace vers le haut, le deuxième vers le bas (Figures 2b, 5, 11, 25, 26). La tendance polarisatrice se manifeste également sur le plan syntagmatique (au long de l'axe du temps), en éloignant les deux alternatives à l'aide d'une pause plus ou moins longue. Les deux termes *se rapprochent,* par contre, au long de l'axe vertical, comme au long de l'axe horizontal, si la disjonction est *inclusive* (Figures 2a, 7, 9, 27, 28, 29, 30).

Hâtons-nous d'ajouter que la sensibilité de l'intonation aux distinctions de la logique formelle est trompeuse. En réalité, la prosodie, et en même temps le style articulatoire, reflètent des attitudes émotives et intellectuelles, souvent associées à ces oppositions d'ordre logique. La polarisation tonale,

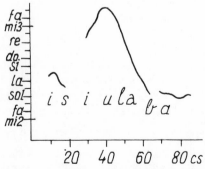

Figure 25.   Courbe de fréquence d'une assertion alternative catégorique ("exclusive").

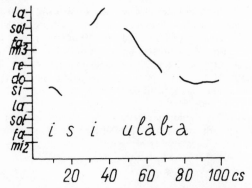

Figure 26.   Courbe de fréquence d'une question alternative catégorique.

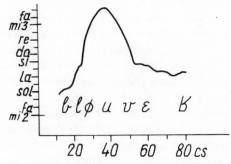

Figure 27.   Courbe de fréquence d'une question alternative neutre.

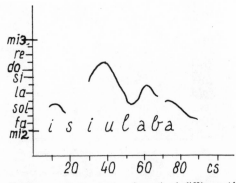

Figure 28.   Courbe de fréquence d'une assertion alternative indifférente (disjonction inclusive).

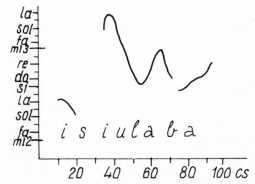

Figure 29.   Courbe de fréquence d'une assertion alternative hésitante, indifférente (disjonction inclusive).

les attaques fortes (occlusives glottales), les changements brusques du mouvement mélodique, les accents forts, et l'articulation tendue (prolongeant les consonnes nonvoisées au détriment des éléments vocaliques) reflètent une attitude énergique et catégorique; l'absence d'une polarisation tonale, les montées et descentes moins brusques, l'intonation ondulente (Figure 29), et les accents plus faibles où l'affaiblissement peut aller jusqu'à la suppression de l'accent du premier terme (Figure 30), répondent à une attitude plus hésitante et moins intéressée. Si la disjonction exclusive se combine avec une attitude peu énergique et peu intéressée, les sujets assigneront à la variante une structure logique inclusive. De même, il est probable que, si le locuteur pose, dans une question, l'alternative d'une manière nette, catégorique, les sujets seraient tentés de qualifier la disjonction comme exclusive, malgré la modalité interrogative qui n'admet guère une telle catégorisation logique. Une intona-

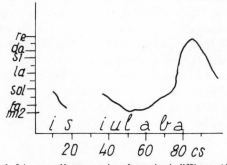

Figure 30.   Courbe de fréquence d'une assertion alternative indifférente (disjonction inclusive).

tion qui reflète directement une attitude émotive est associée, indirectement, à une structure logique. Il paraît, également, que les opérations logiques ont une affinité avec telle ou telle attitude émotive. Le rapport étroit entre information modale et expression émotive a été mis en évidence par Dwight Bolinger (1964).

Nous avons présenté le même corpus, composé d'énoncés exclusifs et inclusifs à deux groupes de sujets. Nous avons proposé au premier groupe un choix binaire entre énoncés disjonctifs inclusifs et exclusifs (cf. note 6, Tableau 10). Les sujets de l'autre groupe ont dû choisir entre des attitudes: volontaire vs. hésitant (indécis), et intéressé vs. indifférent. En comparant les résultats obtenus dans les deux groupes (Tableau 11), on trouve d'abord une bonne corrélation entre deux attitudes émotives—volontaire et intéressé— valable au seuil de $p < 0.001$; puis une corrélation, également valable au seuil de probabilité $p < 0.001$, entre l'attitude *indifférente* et la disjonction *inclusive*. Le rapport entre attitude volontaire et la disjonction exclusive n'atteint pas, cependant, le seuil d'une corrélation significative. Les résultats corroborent dans une certaine mesure nos doutes concernant le caractère purement logique de l'intonation des disjonction exclusives et inclusives. L'intonation "logique" se ramène très probablement à une distinction d'attitudes émotives caractérisées par des traits prosodiques et articulatoires. Ces traits paraissent être très proches dans deux langues nonapparentées, le français et le hongrois. C'est à partir de ces traits, essentiellement paralinguistiques, que douze étudiants français sur quinze ont correctement identifié huit (resp. sept sur huit) énoncés disjonctifs hongrois, dont quatre inclusifs et quatre exclusifs.[7] Le nombre des identifications correctes était 101 sur 120.

Il faut toutefois tenir compte du fait que, selon les résultats du même test, l'attitude volontaire ne recouvre que partiellement la catégorie logique de la disjonction exclusive, que cette dernière semble donc garder une certaine indépendance vis-à-vis des attitudes émotives sous-jacentes.

3.2 Il est surprenant qu'au cours du test préliminaire que nous venons de mentionner, la modalité interrogative de quatre questions disjonctives a été correctement identifiée en 51 cas sur 60. D'autre part, la modalité de quatre énoncés disjonctifs français a été reconnue dans 72 cas sur 88 par des sujets hongrois (étudiants en linguistique de l'Université Eötvös Loránd de Budapest). En attendant une corroboration de ces résultats provisoires, on pourrait hasarder l'hypothèse que la modalité interrogative des disjonctions hongroises et françaises a pu être identifiée à partir de traits prosodiques qui, d'habitude, reflètent des attitudes émotives ou intellectuelles, plus proches de

---

[7]Nous avons précisé aux étudiants (département de Recherches linguistiques de l'Université Paris VII) qu'il s'agissait d'énoncés disjonctifs du hongrois, et nous avons fourni la traduction des phrases.

Tableau 10. Réactions des sujets des tests de perception

Variantes d' Ici ou là-bas	Modalité (N = 50)				Aspect logique (N = 24)			
	Assertive	Interrogative	Test binomial (z)	Probabilité (p)	Inclusive	Exclusive	Test binomial (z)	Probabilité (p)
1	37	13	3.249	<0.0007 (S)	18	6	2.246	<0.01 (S)
2	49	1	6.638	<0.00003 (S)	4	20	4.696	<0.00003 (S)
3	50	—	6.921	<0.00003 (S)	15	9	1.021	>0.1 (NS)
4	47	3	6.073	<0.00003 (S)	16	8	1.429	>0.05 (NS)
5	48	2	6.356	<0.00003 (S)	20	4	4.696	<0.00003 (S)
6	48	2	6.356	<0.00003 (S)	4	20	4.696	<0.00003 (S)
7	47	3	6.073	<0.00003 (S)	20	4	4.696	<0.00003 (S)
8	33	17	2.119	<0.01 (S)	20	4	4.696	<0.00003 (S)
9	13	37	3.249	<0.0007 (S)	6	18	2.246	<0.01 (S)
10	—	50	6.921	<0.00003 (S)	6	18	2.246	<0.01 (S)
11	—	50	6.921	<0.00003 (S)	5	19	2.654	<0.004 (S)
12	—	50	6.921	<0.00003 (S)	7	17	1.837	<0.03 (S)
13	—	50	6.921	<0.00003 (S)	2	22	3.879	<0.00007 (S)
14	1	49	6.638	<0.00003 (S)	2	22	3.879	<0.00007 (S)

Tableau 11.   Choix des sujets au cours des tests de perceptions ($N = 30$). Quatorze variantes ont été proposées à 30 sujets qui devaient faire deux choix binaires, en assignant à la variante l'étiquette "volontaire" resp. "indécis," et l'étiquette "intéressé" resp. "indifférent." Les résultats ont été soumis à un test binomial (z). La validité est signalé par la lettre S (significatif), la nonpertinence par NS (non significatif). Le seuil de probabilité se trouve dans la colonne p. Deux des variantes sont synthétisées (sy)

Variantes d' Ici ou là-bas	Volontaire	Indécis	Test binomial (z)	Probabilité (p)	Intéressé	Indifférent	Test binomial (z)	Probabilité (p)
1	20	10	1.642	<0.05 (S)	7	23	2.737	<0.003 (S)
2	29	1	4.927	<0.00003 (S)	22	8	2.372	<0.009 (S)
3	6	24	3.102	<0.001 (S)	4	26	3.832	<0.0007 (S)
4	23	7	2.737	<0.003 (S)	24	6	3.102	<0.001 (S)
5	9	21	2.007	<0.02 (S)	5	25	3.467	<0.0003 (S)
6	27	3	4.197	<0.00003 (S)	25	5	3.467	<0.0003 (S)
7	19	11	1.277	>0.05 (NS)	13	17	0.547	>0.4 (NS)
8 (sy)	8	22	2.372	<0.009 (S)	5	25	3.467	<0.0003 (S)
9 (sy)	14	16	0.182	>0.4 (NS)	9	21	2.007	<0.02 (S)
10	12	18	0.912	>0.4 (NS)	22	8	2.372	<0.009 (S)
11	19	11	1.277	<0.05 (S)	21	9	2.007	<0.02 (S)
12	4	26	3.832	<0.0007 (S)	17	13	0.547	>0.4 (NS)
13	14	16	0.182	>0.4 (NS)	25	5	3.467	<0.0003 (S)
14	8	22	2.372	<0.009 (S)	5	25	3.467	<0.0003 (S)

Attitudes

la modalité interrogative que de la modalité assertive. Le niveau plus élevé, une montée plus importante et plus rapide, et l'absence d'une descente finale au niveau de base caractérisent à la fois l'excitation, le vif intérêt, et l'énoncé disjonctif interrogatif. De même, l'absence de la descente finale au niveau de base, exprime l'hésitation, et l'attente d'une conclusion en même temps qu'elle contribue à différentier la disjonction interrogative de la disjonction assertive. Le ton qui descend à la fin d'une phrase résolument au niveau de base implique, au contraire, l'absence du doute, suggère une attitude moins hésitante, et se prête mieux, par conséquent, à l'expression de l'attitude assertive. Ce rapport intime entre *modalités* et *attitudes* explique, d'une part, les analogies prosodiques qu'on peut relever en rapprochant les énoncés disjonctifs, interrogatifs, et assertifs, du hongrois à ceux du français, et, d'autre part, l'identification correcte de la modalité, malgré l'absence d'une configuration mélodique spécifique et permanente des questions alternatives.

On pourrait s'étonner à la vue du succès des sujets français qui ont réussi à identifier la modalité des énoncés disjonctifs hongrois que les sujets hongrois n'arrivent pas toujours à distinguer. En vérité, le fait que la modalité n'est pas marquée dans les questions alternatives par des traits constants déterminés par le système linguistique ne rend pas plus difficile leur identification à quelqu'un qui ignore le hongrois. Au contraire, l'improvisation basée sur l'expression des attitudes émotives est plus facile à interpréter vu le caractère motivé de cette expression.

Nous avons signalé au début un "trou" dans le système prosodique du hongrois. Il faudrait nuancer cette constatation, en l'envisageant du point de vue évolutif. Il paraît qu'en plusieurs langues—en français, en hongrois, en russe, et probablement dans bien d'autres langues—la modalité n'est pas marquée avec la même netteté dans les questions alternatives (disjonctives) que dans les questions totales. Dans l'acte de parole, les locuteurs arrivent néanmoins à distinguer les questions des assertions à l'aide de moyens prosodiques qui servent normalement à l'expression des attitudes (émotives et intellectuelles). Ses moyens *ad hoc* se transforment progressivement en traits distinctifs de la modalité. La transformation des traits prosodiques émotifs en traits distinctifs modaux semble être plus avancée en français qu'en hongrois ou en russe. C'est ce qui explique, probablement, que les hongrois qui ignorent le français arrivent moins bien à distinguer les questions alternatives des assertions que les sujets français à qui des énoncés disjonctifs hongrois sont présentés.

CONCLUSIONS

1. On constate dans plusieurs langues (le français, le russe, et le hongrois) un *trou dans le système prosodique:* l'absence d'une configuration intonative

permettant d'opposer sans ambiguïté les questions alternatives (du type "Bleu ou vert?") aux phrases assertives correspondantes ("Bleu ou vert").

2. Les locuteurs arrivent néanmoins à prononcer les questions alternatives d'une manière qui permet à la majorité des sujets de les *identifier,* hors contexte, comme telles. Cette majorité varie selon les diverses performances entre 77 et 90% pour le hongrois, et entre 43 et 100% pour le français. La moyenne des réponses correctes a été, toutefois, nettement plus élevée pour les phrases françaises naturelles (non synthétisées) que pour les phrases hongroises.

3. Nous avons essayé de déterminer et de localiser les traits prosodiques permettant la détermination de la modalité (interrogative ou assertive) des énoncés disjonctifs par diverses *méthodes:*

1. En calculant la courbe de fréquence moyenne des phrases interrogatives et assertives (cf. "Analyse," 1.4).
2. En comparant les traits prosodiques des variantes bien identifiées à ceux des variantes malidentifiées par les sujets de tests d'identification (cf. "Analyse," 1.3, 1.5).
3. En présentant différentes parties des variantes ("Bleu...?", "Bleu ou...?", etc.) aux sujets invités à déterminer la modalité des phrases tronquées (cf. "Analyse," 1.6).
4. En contrôlant les hypothèses formulées à partir de ces analyses à l'aide de variantes synthétisées (cf. "Synthèse de la Phrase 'Ici ou Là-bas' ").

4. Il paraît que l'identification modale se fait à partir de plusieurs critères:

1. Le *niveau* mélodique atteint dans la dernière syllabe du *premier terme* de l'alternative par rapport au niveau de départ.
2. L'*angle* de la montée dans cette syllabe.
3. Le niveau mélodique inférieur atteint dans la *conjonction* disjonctive ("ou").
4. Le niveau inférieur atteint dans la dernière syllabe du deuxième terme de l'alternative.
5. Le *niveau tonal* inférieur atteint dans la *dernière syllabe* de la phrase.
6. Le *niveau tonal moyen* de la phrase. Une valeur plus élevée de ces paramètres renforme le caractère interrogatif de l'énoncé.
7. Les indices contenus dans la *première partie* de la phrase (sans la conjonction) jouent un rôle majeur dans l'identification correcte des phrases interrogatives; ceux contenus dans la *deuxième partie* (conjonction y comprise) sont pertinents pour la caractérisation des énoncés assertifs. Toutefois, en ajoutant à la première partie d'une question alternative la deuxième partie d'une assertion, on arrive à prêter à la phrase un carac-

tère plutôt assertif à condition que la phrase assertive se termine par une chute grave au-dessous du niveau de départ de la phrase. D'autre part, on favorise également les votes ''assertives'' en faisant précéder la deuxième moitié d'une question alternative de la première moitié d'une phrase assertive (conjonction y comprise).

5. Il faut compter également avec le rôle qui paraît jouer la *microstructure* mélodique des syllabes: dans le français, comme dans le hongrois, les questions se distinguent par leur caractère chantonné, c'est-à-dire par un degré de *mélodicité* plus élevé dû à la plus haute régularité de la distribution des fréquences à l'intérieur de la syllabe. [Des recherches en cours devraient déterminer si un changement radical de la microstructure mélodique du degré de ''musicalité'' peut ou non changer l'aspect modal d'un énoncé d'une phrase synthétisée (cf. Tableau 12).]

Tableau 12.   Différents degrés de ''musicalité'' (m) des énoncés disjonctifs, interrogatifs, ou assertifs, à partir des impressions de 19 sujets qui se servait d'une échelle sémantique à 8 degrés (allant de degré de musicalité 0 à degré 7). La mélodicité moyenne ($\bar{m}$) des disjonctions interrogatives dépasse nettement celle des assertives. Cette différence est, selon le test t, significatif au seuil de probabilité (p) <0.005. La coéfficient de corrélation (r) entre ''caractère interrogatif'' (nombre des votes ''question'') de la phrase et son degré de musicalité est élevé.

Variantes d' Ici ou là-bas	Degré de musicalité (m)	Ecart type
1	1.37	0.895
2	2.05	1.393
3	1.89	1.329
4	4.47	1.210
5	4.05	1.508
6	2.79	1.182
7	6.00	1.247
8	2.05	1.129
9	1.05	1.021
10	5.74	0.806
11	4.95	1.223
12	6.21	0.918
13	6.16	0.958
14	4.84	1.258

	Disjonctions assertives	Disjonction interrogatives
$\bar{m}$	2.447	5.582
	1.227	0.652

t test = 3.191 p <0.005 (S)
r = 0.809

6. Certaines variantes des énoncés alternatifs (disjonctifs) permettent de distinguer les disjonctions *inclusives* des disjonctions *exclusives*. Il apparaît, cependant, que l'identification de la structure logique se fait par détour: on identifie l'*attitude* généralement associée à la disjonction exclusive (attitude énergique, ou catégorique) voire à la disjonction concessive (attitude hésitante, indifférente, ou permissive).

7. L'intérêt linguistique de la prosodie des énoncés disjonctifs réside surtout dans son imperfection, son incertitude. Nous pouvons assister à la transformation progressive des *intonations émotives* (ou plutôt: propres à certaines attitudes) en *intonation modale* proprement dite.

BIBLIOGRAPHY

Bolinger, D. L. 1964. Around the edge of language. Harvard Educ. Rev. 34:282–296.

Elekfi, L. 1965. Untersuchungen zu den Beobachtungsmethoden der ungarischen Sprechmelodie. Z. Phonet. 18:9–32.

Fónagy, I., et Bérard, E. 1973. L'intonation des questions totales simples et indirectes. Stud. Phonet. 8:53–97.

Fónagy, I., et Magdics, K. 1963. Das Pradoxon der Sprechmelodie. Ural-Altaische Jahrbücher 35:1–55.

Fónagy, I., et Magdics, K. 1967. A magyar beszéd dallama (L'intonation du hongrois). Akadémiai Kiado, Budapest.

Fougeron, I. 1971. De l'intonation dans les phrases nterrogatives russes. Thèse, Université Paris III, Paris.

Karcevskij, S. 1941. Sur la phonologie de la phrase. Trav. Cercle Ling. Prague 4: 188–277.

Malmberg, B. 1966. Analyse des faits prosodiques. Problèmes et méthodes. Cahiers Ling. Théor. Appliq. 3:99–108.

Mettas, O. 1966. Les facteurs ectosémantiques du discours et leur caractérisation par synthèse. Dans: A. Moles et B. Vallencien (éds.), Phonétique et Phonation, pp. 177–187.

Sedlaček, K., et Sychra, A. 1962. Hudba a slovo z experimentálního hlediska. Státní Hudební Vydavatelství, Praha.

Uldall, E. T. 1962. Ambiguity: Question or statement? Dans: Proceedings of the Fourth International Congress on Phonetic Science, Helsinki, 1961, pp. 779–783. Mouton, The Hague.

8/ Three Intonational Systems of Argentinian Spanish

María Beatriz Fontanella de Weinberg

Intonational differences are one of the most typical features of the regional varieties of Argentinian Spanish, and native speakers are fully aware of this fact.[1] These differences have not been dealt with systematically until very recently. In the last few years I have published brief accounts of two characteristic intonational systems, those of Cordoba and Tucuman[2], sketching in

---

[1]For example, with regard to Cordoba intonation, perhaps the most outstanding of all Argentinian intonations, the music and the popular literature of this province have reflected this peculiarity. Note the following sample, taken from a popular song by Chango Rodríguez called "El Cordobés":

> Adonde quiera que vaya
> me bautizan otra vez:
> porque hablo con la *tonada* [regional intonation]
> me dicen el Cordobés.

Also compare the following dialogues that appear together with drawings used in the publicity of a butter called *Tonadita:*

> —Vos sos de pura nata cordobesa.
> —Y, escuchame LA TONADITA.
> (*Hortensia* Review, Cordoba, No. 30, March 1973.)

A boy (to a very beautiful girl)—De todo lo que tenés, lo que más me gusta es la TONAAADITA. The girl—Es que soy cordobesa de pura nata.
> (*Hortensia* Review, No. 31, April, 1973.)

(Note that the graphic representation of TONAAADITA reflects their vocalic lengthening, which is discussed later in the paper.)

[2]Cordoba, capital of the province that bears the same name, is located in the central region of Argentina, about 700 km northwest of Buenos Aires; it has a population of over 600,000 and is at present one of the most important industrial and cultural centers of the country. Tucuman, an industrial city of more than 300,000 inhabitants, is the capital of the homonymous province, and is located about 1300 km from Buenos Aires in a northwest direction.

the latter study a short parallel between Tucuman and Buenos Aires intonations (Fontanella, 1966, 1971). In this paper, I present a comparative analysis of the three systems mentioned above, with the purpose of determining what their common features are and in what respects they differ from each other.[3]

The descriptions of the intonational systems of Cordoba and Tucuman are based in each case on the analysis of the tapes of spontaneous speech of four middle-age female informants. Two of the Tucuman informants had secondary education and the other two did postsecondary studies, and all of the Cordoba informants went through postsecondary studies.[4] This material was later completed with the observation of other speakers of similar characteristics and by means of several pronunciation and recognition tests that allowed me to elucidate some dubious aspects. With regard to the Buenos Aires intonation, I follow the description of Emma Gregores and Jorge A. Suárez in their Spanish adaptation of *A Course in Modern Linguistics,* by C. F. Hockett (Hockett, 1971, pp. 40–53). Although the authors do not specify the informants' characteristics, I checked their description with the intonations of Buenos Aires speakers that had the same characteristics as my Tucuman and Cordoba informants, and found that the intonational systems of my speakers coincided fully with the analysis of Gregores and Suárez.

In these three cases, an exclusively perceptual analysis was made, since I did not have at my disposal the instruments that would allow me to confront the auditive perceptions with the acoustic data. In any case, I consider that, although it would be ideal to make a complementary examination of both classes of data, the auditory analysis is fundamental in studies of this type and it is the starting point of all phonological interpretation.

In this paper, I confront the constituent elements of each intonational system without analyzing the values of each intonational contour in particular, since this analysis would be too lengthy. With respect to the theoretical approach adopted in this comparison, I apply, just as I did in my previous works, the analytical frame of pitch levels and terminal contours. The choice

---

[3]Comparative studies of regional intonations are not frequent in other Spanish-speaking countries either. In this respect it must be pointed out that the article by María Josefa Conellada (1941), in which the author compares certain aspects of the Extremeña intonation with the Castilian one, is an excellent pioneering work.

[4]In practice, both groups of informants may be considered equivalent, since no difference has been found at the level of analysis described here between the intonational systems of Tucuman speakers who have done secondary study and those who have done postsecondary study. I think that the fact that the speakers share the same characteristics is a basic requirement for the comparison of intonational systems of different areas—otherwise there would be a danger of confusing dialectal differences with sociolinguistic variations, since, although the study of sociolinguistic variation in intonation is an almost virgin field, the occurrence of intonational differences correlated with sociolinguistic factors are to be expected.

of this theoretical approach does not, of course, imply a disregard of the serious criticisms that have been made of it, among which stand out those of Dwight L. Bolinger (1949, 1958, 1971; cf. also, among others, Lieberman, 1965, 1967). However, since on the one hand the purpose of this study is not theoretical but comparative, and on the other I believe that no theoretical model has yet been formulated that is not subject in some way to these same objections, I choose to follow the same approach as in my previous studies. In any case, the phonological interpretation of each intonation is provided together with its phonetic representation, showing the relative voice height by means of a line above the examples, so that my phonological interpretation is not the only possible one and the data can be reinterpreted according to other theoretical approaches.

PITCH LEVELS

I call the sequence between certain rhythmic breaks that can be identified as pauses *macrosegments,* and the intonation that corresponds to each macrosegment the *intonational contour.* In the three dialects two phonological stresses can be distinguished: strong, /'/, and weak (unmarked).[5]

In Tucuman Spanish, each macrosegment has in principle four positions in which there can be tonal contrast: the first and the last unstressed syllables, and the first and the last stressed syllables. In fact, the first or the last unstressed syllable and/or the first stressed one may be missing if the macrosegment begins or ends with a stressed syllable, or if it has only one stressed syllable.

In these four positions there are three contrasting *pitch levels:* /1/ low, /2/ medial, and /3/ high. The height of a noncontrasting syllable is determined by the pitch level immediately preceding it. The stressed syllables, especially the first and the last ones in each intonational contour, are longer than the unstressed syllables and are higher at each pitch level. The following examples show the pitch levels and the relative height of each intonational contour:[6]

1) ¹Sa²có ócho cincuénta en la es²cri¹ta.

---

[5]Although I did not carry out an acoustic analysis, it may be assumed that, just as in other languages, this auditory impression cannot be identified with any acoustic feature in particular, but is a composite effect produced by the simultaneous action of several acoustic features. Cf., among others, the words of Kerstin Hadding Koch (1961) and David Crystal (1900). Also, in the physiological aspect the complex character of stress is pointed out: "Prominence appears to be implemented partly by varying laryngeal tension, partly by varying duration, and partly by varying subglottal air pressure" (Lieberman et al., 1900, p. 327).

[6]The height corresponding to pitch level /1/ is indicated with a little arrow at the beginning of the transcription.

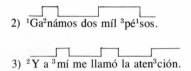

2) ¹Ga²námos dos míl ³pé¹sos.

3) ²Y a ³mí me llamó la aten³ción.

Besides these possibilities of contrast, in the first and last stressed syllables of
each macrosegment the voice can remain at a certain level or else rise to the
immediately higher pitch level. These glides are represented by an element of
a special kind, which I will call *internal inflection* and symbolize as +, and
whose phonetic realization is a rise of a pitch level from the initial pitch.[7] The
following examples show these glides:

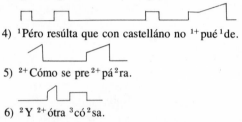

4) ¹Péro resúlta que con castelláno no ¹⁺pué¹de.

5) ²⁺Cómo se pre²⁺pá²ra.

6) ²Y ²⁺ótra ³có²sa.

In Cordoba Spanish, each macrosegment has in principle four points at
which tonal contrast can occur: the first unstressed syllable, the first stressed
syllable, the last stressed syllable, and the absolute end of the utterance. The
first two contrast points may be missing, as when the macrosegment begins
with a stressed syllable and/or has only one stressed syllable. However, the
last two contrast points occur obligatorily in every macrosegment because,
although the utterance ends with a stressed syllable, the final height of the
syllable is distinctive and acts as another contrast point.

Four pitch levels contrast in these positions: /1/ low, /2/ medial, /3/ high,
and /4/ extra high. The last has very low frequency and only occurs in intonational contours that have a certain emphatic character. The heights of the
syllables that are not placed in contrast positions is determined in this way: the
syllables subsequent to the first unstressed one or to the first stressed one have
the same height as these; in the syllables following the last stressed one, the
pitch moves gradually from its height to the final pitch level. There are almost
no differences in height between stressed and unstressed syllables of the same
pitch level. The following examples show simultaneously the phonological
pitch levels and the phonetic realization of each intonational contour:

---

[7]The occurrence of these glides obviously raises the problem of its representation. For the
reasons why this solution is chosen over alternative ones, see my above-mentioned paper (1966).

7) ... ¹que ¹tiénen múchas cósas que ha¹cér¹. ...

8) ¹Y me que² dé médio ²zónza¹.

9) ¹Las ²résmas de papél se a³cában¹.

10) ²Nó nos aguan⁴tábamos².

Buenos Aires Spanish displays the same obligatory points of tonal contrast in each macrosegment as Cordoba Spanish; it also has the possibility of a fifth contrast point between the first and the last stressed syllables.[8] The heights of noncontrasting syllables are determined in a manner similar to that in the Cordoba system, except that when there is a difference in height between the first unstressed syllable and the first stressed one the change is more gradual. However, in Buenos Aires Spanish there are only three contrasting pitch levels. The following examples illustrate these contrasts phonetically and phonologically:

11) ¹Es²tábamos en ²cása¹.

12) ²No es po³síble².

13) ²Hásta ²luégo².

TERMINAL CONTOURS

Apart from the positions that have been pointed out, the three systems show other contrasts at the end of the macrosegment, which are represented by means of *terminal contours*. Tucuman Spanish has two types of terminal contours /|/, which is indicated phonetically by a lengthening of the last syllable and/or a more or less prolonged pause, without perceptible rise or fall of the voice; and /↑/, which is represented by a sharp rise at the end of the last

---

[8]The occurrence of a fifth pitch level is not frequent. See, in this respect, the assertion of Gregores and Suárez: "La entonación con cinco niveles tonales ... parece ser menos frequente: el tercer nivel tonal es siempre el más agudo del macrosegmento y el significado que transmite es de énfasis o especial relieve de la palabra en que figura" (Hockett, 1971, p. 47).

syllable and an abrupt cut of the voice emission. The following are samples of terminal contours:

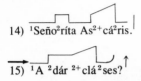

14) ¹Seño²ríta As²⁺cá²ris.

15) ¹A ²dár ²⁺clá²ses?

In the macrosegments ending in a stressed syllable, the voice rise in /↑/ is never confused with a possible internal inflection, because in /+/ the rise occurs throughout the syllable, whereas in the terminal contour it appears only at the end of the syllable. However, there is a contrast between a glide followed by /|/ or by /↑/:

16) ²Us²⁺téd.

17) ²Us²⁺téd!↑

In Buenos Aires Spanish and in Cordoba Spanish, there are three terminal contours: /↓/, indicated phonetically by a gradual cessation of the emission of voice and a fall of the pitch of the voice below the last pitch level[9]; /↑/, which is then realized by a pitch rise above the last pitch level; and /|/, which is indicated by the cessation of the voice emission, followed by a more or less brief pause and without perceptible change in height. The following samples are taken from Cordoba Spanish:

18) ²Désde el áño que viéne son ²trés² . . .

19) ²Háy que metér la ²máno?² ↑

20) ²Són dós ²áños². ↓

---

[9]Phonetically, the fall indicated by /↓/ is more outstanding in Buenos Aires intonation than in Cordoba Spanish and can affect not only the last syllables, but the whole macrosegment, as it appears in the markedly falling intonational contours that are characteristic of Buenos Aires Spanish: ''Cuando la curva tonal es descendente, sobre todo cuando se presenta como una sucesión de niveles /1/, el descenso es muy marcado y se da progresivamente a lo largo de toda la emisión, de tal modo que el /1/ con que ésta termina es más grave que cualquier otro /1/ de la misma. La relajación de la fuerza articulatoria es también más marcada, hasta el punto de que en algunas ocasiones las últimas sílabas se oyen casi como un susurro'' (Hockett, 1971, p. 44).

21) ²Puéde írse ²sóla¹.

OTHER CONTRASTS

Apart from the contrasts already analyzed, there are other kinds of contrasts in Cordoba and Tucuman intonational systems. In Tucuman Spanish, the initial unstressed syllable of the first or last tonic word of the macrosegment can be clearly higher and longer than the preceding or following unstressed syllables, and can have a slight optional rise of pitch. This fact can be attributed to a phonological element represented by /`/ and called *secondary pitch level:*

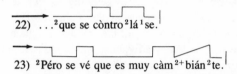

22) . . .²que se còntro²lá¹se.

23) ²Péro se vé que es muy càm²⁺bián²te.

The phonological value of /`/ is evident because there are intonational contours that are only differentiated by the presence or absence of this element. The following utterances, for instance, contrast with the preceding pair in the lack of a secondary pitch level:

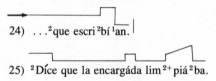

24) . . .²que escri²bí¹an.

25) ²Díce que la encargáda lim²⁺piá²ba.

The possibilities of occurrence of the secondary pitch level would point out the existence of a word juncture in Tucuman Spanish.¹⁰ If this fact is accepted, the distribution of /`/ can be formulated in this way: the secondary pitch level can occur in the initial unstressed syllable or in the first unstressed syllable following the word juncture immediately above the first or last stressed syllable of the macrosegment.

---

¹⁰The existence of word juncture, which, as is shown below, would also be determined by suprasegmental features in Cordoba Spanish, is corroborated by segmental features in both dialects, such as the defective distribution of the phoneme /r/, which does not occur after word juncture, and the presence of [h] as an allophone of /s/, which appears, besides other positions, before word juncture. Thus, the presence or absence of this juncture, for instance, would determine the following contrast:

/las-ádas/ "las hadas"   /lasádas/ "lazadas"
[lahádas]   [laṣádaṣ]

In Cordoba Spanish there occurs another contrast that has not been mentioned yet. In many macrosegments the syllable preceding the stressed syllable (provided that the two syllables belong to the same word) has a clear lengthening of the vowel and a pitch rise or fall in its second part; the glide may be missing in some cases, even if there is lengthening and possibilities of pitch contrast. The lengthening, together with the pitch change, is so clearly perceptible that it often seems as if there is vocalic gemination. The analysis of these contrasts raises several problems: in the first place, it is a complex contrast because it comprises quantity and height oppositions simultaneously; second, as regards the height, not only can there be pitch level contrast but also possibilities of glides; and, finally, when there are glides these can have different amplitudes and directions. For all these reasons it is necessary to represent, in each case, the presence of syllable lengthening as well as the initial height of the syllable and the permanence at the same level of the direction and amplitude of the glide. In this way, all the syllable lengthenings are represented by two pitch levels divided by a hyphen, which indicate at the same time the quantity difference with respect to the other syllables of the macrosegment and the pitch contrast:

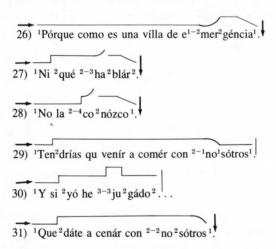

26) ^{1}Pórque como es una vílla de e$^{1-2}$mer^{2}géncia^1.

27) ^{1}Ni ^{2}qué $^{2-3}$ha^{2}blár^2.

28) ^{1}No la $^{2-4}$co^{2}nózco^1.

29) ^{1}Ten^{2}drías qu venír a comér con $^{2-1}$no^{1}sótros^1.

30) ^{1}Y si ^{2}yó he $^{3-3}$ju^{2}gádo^2...

31) ^{1}Que^{2}dáte a cenár con $^{2-2}$no^{2}sótros^1.

When the last word of the macrosegment begins with a stressed syllable, the lengthening, with or without a glide, can occur in the same stressed syllable[11]:

32) ^{2}Éran las diéz ménos cuárto de la $^{2-3}$nóche^2...

---

[11]The distribution of feature corroborates the existence of word juncture in Cordoba Spanish.

33) ¹Me²tí ónce matérias en primér ²⁻³áño². . .

However, in some intonational contours the lengthening can immediately precede a stressed syllable that is not the last of the macrosegment. The occurrence of this feature in this position is not very frequent and it seems to express emphasis in the affected word[12]:

34) ²Ni que me ²⁻³casára ²yó¹.

35) ¹Y ²yo que me hágo ²⁻³cualquiér ²cósa².

The occurrence of syllabic lengthening, with or without glide, is a prominence feature, since it brings out this syllable with respect to the others in the macrosegment.[13]

RHYTHM

Finally, it must be pointed out that rhythm is one of the aspects in which the three analyzed systems differ most clearly. In Tucuman Spanish the rhythm is stress-timed in spontaneous speech. There are marked differences in syllabic quantity that are correlated with stress: the stressed syllables are long, especially the first and the last ones of each macrosegment, whereas the unstressed ones are generally brief. In long macrosegments, there is a tendency to compress the part between the first and the last stressed syllables so that the duration of the different intonational contours is similar even if the number of syllables varies:

36) Péro resúlta que con castelláno no puéde.
37) Cómo   se   prepára.

Because of this compression of the central part of the macrosegment, its unstressed syllables are briefer than the initial and final ones. The quantity differences, together with the phonetic height differences between stressed and unstressed syllables at the same pitch level and with the occurrence of

---

[12]The role of this lengthening seems equivalent to the fifth possible pitch level of contrast in Buenos Aires Spanish (see footnote 8).

[13]In the analyzed corpus, there are lengthenings in more than half of the intonational contours. In the majority of the examples, the syllable where the lengthening appears has a rising glide; the cases in which there are level tones come next in frequency; and finally the falling glides, which are relatively few.

glides in the first and last stressed syllables, determine that in each intonational contour the stressed syllables stand out neatly, giving rise to a typical stress-timed rhythm.

As regards Cordoba Spanish, its rhythm is predominantly syllabic. There are no great differences in the quantity of stressed and unstressed syllables, although the stressed are slightly longer than the unstressed. However, this rhythm has a remarkable exception in certain macrosegment syllables in which there can be a lengthening with or without a glide.

Buenos Aires Spanish rhythm is definitely syllabic, and the differences of the provincial intonations in this respect are perhaps the ones that most attract attention from Buenos Aires speakers.

CONCLUSIONS

The analysis of the three intonational systems leads us to conclude that there are important differences among them, which are not limited to mere phonetic divergences but affect the phonological structure of each system. The following are some of the conclusions that can be extracted from the comparison of the three systems.

1. In general terms, the intonational system of Buenos Aires Spanish is less complex than the Tucuman and Cordoba ones, since, although the constituent elements of the first are limited to three terminal contours and three pitch levels that usually contrast in four positions (and exceptionally in five positions), in the Cordoba and Tucuman systems there are features of other kinds—the lengthening of the prestressed syllable, in the first case, and the secondary pitch level and the possibilities of a glide in the stressed syllable in the second one—that make their structure more complex.

2. The points at which the pitch levels contrast obligatorily are the same in Buenos Aires and Cordoba Spanish. In Tucuman Spanish they are similar, but not identical, since, although the first three contrast positions in the macrosegment are the same, the fourth contrast occurs in Tucuman Spanish only if there is an unstressed final syllable, whereas in Buenos Aires and Cordoba Spanish the final pitch of the macrosegment immediately before the terminal contour contrasts independently of whether the last syllable is stressed or unstressed.

3. With regard to the number of pitch levels, Buenos Aires and Tucuman Spanish have three pitch levels, and Cordoba Spanish has four. However, since the occurrence of the rising glide in Tucuman Spanish implies a one degree higher tonal rise, phonetically the intonational contours of Cor-

doba and Tucuman have more tonal amplitude than the Buenos Aires ones.

4. In the phonetic realization of stressed and unstressed syllables, Tucuman Spanish differs from the other two dialects in that the unstressed syllables are clearly shorter and lower than the stressed ones that correspond to the same pitch level, whereas in Cordoba and Buenos Aires Spanish the differences in height and quantity of stressed and unstressed syllables are much less marked.

5. With respect to the terminal contours, Buenos Aires and Cordoba Spanish coincide at the phonological level, since both systems present three terminal contours: falling /↓/, rising /↑/, and level /|/; however, phonetically the coincidence is not complete, because the fall in /↓/ is much more marked in Buenos Aires Spanish than in the Cordoba dialect. In Tucuman Spanish, on the other hand, there are only two terminal contours: rising /↑/ and level /|/. The absence of falling contours, together with the existence of glides that are always rising and the frequent occurrence of very high final unstressed syllables in statements,[14] cause certain sequences such as the following to appear as interrogative ones to Buenos Aires ears:

38) ²En pri²⁺mé³ro!

6. One of the factors that most clearly differentiate the three intonational systems under study is the rhythm, since, although the Buenos Aires Spanish has a definitely syllabic rhythm, in Tucuman Spanish there are height and quantity differences between stressed and unstressed syllables, a compression of the central part of the macrosegment, and glides in the stressed syllables that produce a typical stressed-time rhythm. With regard to Cordoba Spanish, the possibility of the occurrence of a marked lengthening in quantity, and a glide in the syllable preceding the last stressed one, in the last stressed syllable, or in an internal unstressed syllable, bring about a break in the syllabic rhythm of the macrosegment. The occurrence of this feature is the most outstanding characteristic of this intonational system and the one that differentiates it most markedly

---

[14]This rising character of the intonation of statements stands out from the "falling terminal frequency contour" of statements that Lieberman postulates as a "linguistic universal" (1967, p. 104), as I pointed out in my review of that book (Fontanella de Weinburg, 1968, pp. 107–111). This fact is not unique among Spanish intonational systems: the existence of rising intonational contours in statements was also noticed in the Extremadura Spanish by María Josefa Canellada (1941, pp. 86–88).

from the other intonational systems of Argentina, allowing the immediate identification of its speakers.

REFERENCES

Bolinger, D. L. 1949. Intonation and analysis. Word 5:248-254.
Bolinger, D. L. 1958. A theory of pitch accent in English. Word 14:109-149.
Bolinger, D. L. 1971. Generality, Gradiency, and the All-or-None. Mouton & Co., The Hague.
Conellada, M. J. 1941. Notas de entonación extremeña. RFE 25:70-91.
Crystal, D. 1969. Prosodic Systems and Intonation in English. MIT Press, Cambridge, Mass.
Fontanella, M. B. 1966. Comparación de dos entonaciones regionales argentinas. Thesaurus 21:17-29.
Fontanella de Weinberg, M. B. 1968. Review of Lieberman (1967). Thesaurus 23: 107-111.
Fontanella de Weinberg, M. B. 1971. La entonación del español de Córdoba (Argentina). Thesaurus 26:11-21.
Hadding-Koch, K. 1961. Acoustico-phonetic Studies in the Intonation of Southern Swedish. Gleerup Bokförlag, Lund.
Hockett, C. F. 1971. Curso de lingüística moderna, pp. 40-53. Traducido y adaptado al español por Emma Gregores y Jorge A. Suárez. Eudeba, Buenos Aies.
Lieberman, P. 1965. On the acoustic basis of the perception of intonation by linguistics. Word 21:40-55.
Lieberman, P. 1967. Intonation, Perception, and Language. MIT Press, Cambridge, Mass.
Lieberman, P., Sawashima, M., Harris, K. S., and Gay, T. 1900. The articulatory implementation of the breath-group and prominence. Language 46:312-328.

9/ Permissible and Impermissible Variations in Pitch Contours

Kerstin Hadding and Kerstin Nauclér

In a project still at a very preliminary stage, the various functions of intonation are being studied, among them the similarities and dissimilarities in pattern between languages and characteristic variations in pattern between the sexes, between generations, and between individuals. In one of the pilot studies within the project, data from a small group of speakers of southern Swedish have been analyzed.

Data collected from more than one subject often seem to point in different directions, much to the investigator's dismay. We had the same experience. It was obvious, however, that a certain amount of variation in pitch patterns[1] was not only tolerated by listeners but was felt to be perfectly acceptable.

PROCEDURE

A group of four students of phonetics, two male and two female, speaking roughly the same dialect and belonging to the same generation (ages 26 to 36) read the same sample piece of conversation, comprising statements and answers, questions (wh-questions, yes/no questions, and echo questions), exclamations, admonitions, and commands. The context did not invite strong emotional coloring, but a few utterances called for emphatic or contrastive stress.

Five students of phonetics listened to the recordings. The recordings were all of good quality and had been made in an anechoic chamber at our institute. A possible, although we believe in our case negligible, source of error is the fact that the listeners were acquainted with the speakers.

---

[1] "Pitch" is used here, somewhat loosely, instead of "voice fundamental frequency" (f_o).

Listeners were asked to judge whether the content of the utterances was transmitted satisfactorily or not by marking each utterance with either a plus or a minus. Zeroes were also permitted, if need be, to indicate that a particular utterance was neither quite satisfactory nor entirely unacceptable. After comparing the recorded speech and the listeners' responses, we drew the conclusion that zeroes in the majority of cases meant that listeners had reasoned like this: "Well, this does sound rather strange, but I can hear this particular person saying it just this way—so I will put a zero." When asked, listeners confirmed this interpretation of the zeroes. The zeroes are interesting, we believe, because they indicate that some variations are tolerated in connection with a particular speaker. However, since they would probably be unacceptable, or ambiguous, to people unacquainted with the speaker, they have been classed as minuses in this report. We intend to test this assumption in the future.

Data were also analyzed instrumentally by means of a pitch meter device (FONEMA 3-channel Phonetic Analysis Assembly and Siemens Mingograph 34T). Mingographic representations that were difficult to interpret were checked by means of narrowband sonagrams (Key Sonagraph 6061-A).

RESULTS AND DISCUSSION

In this report we only discuss pitch contours. We are, however, well aware of the fact that speech always involves a subtle interplay between features of pitch, duration, and intensity. We expected to find a few fairly clearly distinguishable pitch patterns: one pattern for statements (a moderately high or low precontour, a moderate rise on the stressed unit, and a fall in pitch at the end, accompanied by falling intensity); one for questions (a high, even precontour and a finally rising pitch); and one for echo questions (a continuous rise). Perhaps wh-questions would differ from yes/no questions by having a choice between a final rise and a fall. We assumed that exclamations and "commands" would show some similarities and would differ from other types of utterances by a finally sustained pitch and intensity (Hadding-Koch, 1961).

We found that, although these assumptions were on the whole borne out by our instrumental analysis, every speaker was, within limits, evaluated as a speaker "in his own right." The four speakers represent very different personality types. Listeners obviously made allowance for this fact, which also explains why different renderings of the same utterances were considered equally good. Since several utterances were nevertheless refused, our next step was to try to map out the limits for permissible variations.

In the following discussion, the female speakers are referred to as A1 and

A2 and the male speakers as B1 and B2. A few pertinent characteristic features can be mentioned. A1 is a woman with emminent common sense and great self-control. Her speech conforms well with the expected norms. A2 is a lively person and a bit of a bohemian. Very few of her utterances are entirely "neutral"—they are all said with "feeling." B1, on the other hand, is "neutral" in the extreme. His speech is said to be unacceptable much more often than that of anybody else. After all, every utterance demands an intonation that follows its content like a glove. If there is less pitch movement than called for, you get indifference, fatigue, or the like. B2 is a reasonable and amiable person—his intonation shows, by usually ending in a rise even in statements, that he is always willing to give the other person a chance to voice his/her opinion in the matter and to continue the conversation. In most conversational situations he is as strongly aware of the listener as most of us normally are only in "true" questions.[2] [We would like to add that we were conscious of the existence of this (universal?) listener-oriented pitch contour, but had expected to find it among the female speakers, if at all, in the age group in question (cf. Bolinger, 1964, 1972, 1973; Lakoff, 1972; Hadding and Studdert-Kennedy, 1974).]

Mingograms and sonagrams of the speech of our four subjects were analyzed and gave the following results.

Norm: Statements and Answers

These start on a medium or low pitch level, rise to a moderately high peak on the stress (or stresses, if several), and fall to the lowest pitch within the speaker's range of voice, accompanied by a slowly falling intensity. This was as expected:

> A2. Jag ska träffa 'John i'dag. (I'm meeting John today.) (Figure 1a)
> A2. Det är en 'hund. (It's a dog.) (Figure 1c)

Permissible Variations   *Emphasis* increases the height of the peak(s) and thus increases the size of the ups and downs of the utterance. Even a moderate extra emphasis or contrast may raise the pitch at the peak to very high (cf. Figures 1c and 1d):

> A1. En "katt. (A cat.) (Figure 1d)

Statements that expect or *invite a reaction* on the part of the listener may have a final rise. However, they show the medium or low initial pitch level of statements. This pattern is typical for B2. It occurs sometimes also in the

---

[2]By a "true" question is here meant a question to which the speaker truly wants to know the answer (cf. Lakoff, 1973).

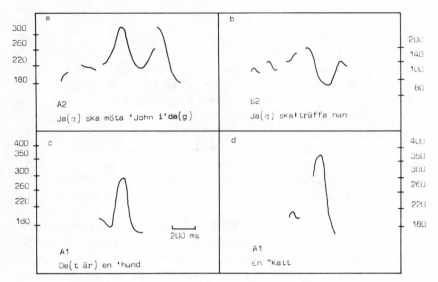

Figure 1. F_0 curves traced from mingograms. Statement contours.

speech of A1 and A2 in "introductory" statements (such as "I have got a cat," "I'm leaving now"), but is rare in responses to questions:

B2. Jag ska 'träffa nån. (I'm going to meet somebody.) (Figure 1b)

Even a slight coloring of some *attitude* or other, such as surprise, joy, indignation, or disgust, has an immediate and noticeable effect on the pitch pattern. These effects will be discussed in a later report.

Impermissible Variations   The few statements that were found to be unacceptable showed pitch contours affected either by attitudes not compatible with the context or by a deviating placement of the stress(es).

Norm: Wh-questions and Yes/No Questions

These differed from statements by having a raised even pitch in their initial part, followed by a fall and ending in a rise of varying size. The stressed syllable of a wh-question does not rise as much in pitch above the precontour as does that of a statement—it may even be realized by a fall in pitch. Wh-questions thus do not seem to point at any particular part of the utterance as more important than the rest. Instead, the utterance as a whole forms an interrogative unit. Yes/no questions, on the other hand, often have a very high stress peak:

A1. Vad har du 'där? (What have you got there?) (Figure 2a)

B2. Varför 'inte? (Why's that?) (Figure 2b)
A1. Har du 'också en katt? (Do you have a cat too?) (Figure 2c)
B2. Kommer du 'hit i'gen i'dag? (Will you be coming back today?) (Figure 2d)

Permissible Variations *A final fall* may occur in wh-questions instead of a rise, but in combination with a raised precontour. This variation is only

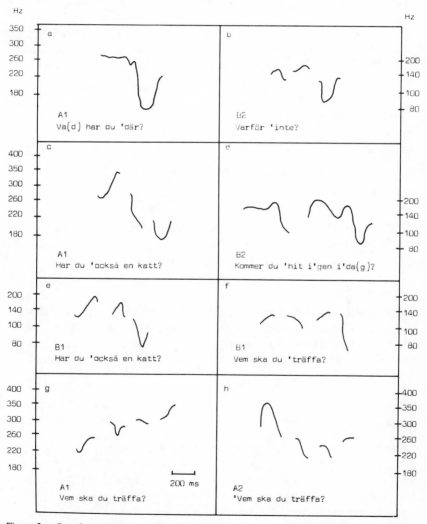

Figure 2. Question contours: a and b, wh-questions; c, d, and e, yes/no questions; f, unaccepted wh-question; g, echo question; h, unaccepted echo question.

used by B1. In his statements the fall usually ends in a "creak" and the intensity falls at the same time. In the questions, however, the pitch of the fall is measurable throughout and the intensity is comparatively sustained:

B1. Har du 'också en katt? (Do you have a cat too?) (Figure 2e)

The precontour may be *moderately high.* In that case the utterance must, in order to be accepted as a question, have a marked dip in pitch preceding a marked final rise.

Impermissible Variations   Utterances with a low or moderately high precontour and a low terminal fall are not accepted as questions—the speaker is not interested in the answer (cf. footnote 2):

B1. Vem ska du 'träffa? (Who are you meeting?) (Figure 2f)

Norm: Echo Questions

These show a continuous rise from low or medium pitch to high. The stress is usually evenly distributed:

A1. Vem ska du träffa? (literally: Who are you meeting?) (Figure 2f)

There are no permissible variations since no other type of contour conveys the echo effect. Figure 2h shows an utterance that was refused as an echo question—the pitch curve is that of the corresponding wh-question, but with emphatic stress on *vem:*

A2. 'Vem ska du träffa?

Norm: Exclamations

These usually lack the initially high pitch of questions. They may have the high peak of emphatic statements, but end on a finally sustained pitch. They are often combined with some strong emotion that affects the contour in some way and are therefore not included in the present report. Their most consistent feature is the finally sustained pitch.

CONCLUSIONS

A description of the pitch contour of statements as characterized by a final fall and, in contrast, of questions as characterized by a final rise, does not cover the data found in the present study. Instead, under certain conditions, statements may end in a final rise and questions may have a final fall.

Personal idiosyncrasies may, within limits, produce permissible variations. Permissible variations will be such as are caused by attitudes permissible within the semantic context of the utterance.

REFERENCES

Bolinger, D. 1964. Intonation as a universal. In: Proceedings of the 9th International Congress of Linguistics, 1962, Cambridge, Mass., pp. 833–848. Mouton & Co., The Hague.

Bolinger, D. 1972. Accent is predictable (if you are a mind-reader). Language 48:633–644.

Bolinger, D. 1973. Truth is a linguistic question. Language 49:539–550.

Hadding-Koch, K. 1961. Acoustico-phonetic Studies in the Intonation of Southern Swedish. Gleerup Bokförlag, Lund.

Hadding, K., and Studdert-Kennedy, M. 1974. Are you asking me, telling me or talking to yourself? J. Phonet. 2:7–14.

Lakoff, R. 1972. Language in context. Language 48:907–927.

Lakoff, R. 1973. Questionable answers and answerable questions. In: B. B. Kachre et al. (eds.), Papers in honor of Henry and Renée Kahane. University of Illinois Press, Urbana.

10/ Speaker-Independent Intonation Curves

Wiktor Jassem and Katarzyna Kudela-Dobrogowska

There are at present a number of both analog and digital methods of extracting from the speech signal fundamental frequency as a variable time function. There are also many different methods of analyzing and recording intonation. Basically, there are two types of pitch curves representing natural speech—impressionistic and instrumental. The vast majority of publications devoted to problems of intonation only use one of these, the well-known reason being that an impressionistic curve, if not incompatible with, is obviously different from an instrumental one, and no full-range attempt has yet been made to explain these differences, even though some of them are fairly well known. The two main origins of these are: 1) disturbances in the smoothness of the pitch curve caused by the effect of segmental articulation on the larynx as an excitatory system, and 2) the personal pitch and compass of the speaking voice.

The scarcity of correlative work that would produce comparisons between instrumental and impressionistic curves together with an analysis and explanation of the differences is unfortunate, at least for phonology as linguistic phonetics. The more work is done on the intonation of a language, the more the accounts tend to differ, both substructurally and functionally. Educated British English is a classical example. There are, of course, other methodological reasons for this as well, but one probably is that no attempt has been made to systematically describe data obtained instrumentally rather than impressionistic curves. The two excuses given almost invariably (if an excuse is made at all) are that an instrumental curve shows too much detail that is (probably) linguistically irrelevant, and that it has to be made on an absolute musical or physical scale and is therefore heavily dependent on the speaker's individual voice pitch and compass.

The present paper reports on the results of an initial experiment included in a project designed to correlate the perception of intonation with the results of automatic extraction of fundamental frequency from the speech signal. This experiment is essentially intended to produce a simple method of normalizing an F_0 trace so as to maximally reduce the effect of personal voice features. Apart from the linguistic implications, the project is directed toward automatic speech recognition and speech synthesis by rule.

"REPRODUCTION" OF TONAL PATTERNS

One speaker (WJ) uttered seven versions of the Polish phrase "dzień dobry" /dzeɲ'dobrɨ/ (good morning) so that at least some of them should be different in the tonal pattern. The utterances were recorded in one session and the tape was later edited by inserting lengths of leader tape so that there would be pauses between the utterances of approximately 5 seconds. Ten male and ten female voices were next selected at random. Each member of this team was requested to "reproduce" (or "repeat") each of the seven model utterances without any reflection and without attempting to mimic. The model tape was played back via a loudspeaker and the subjects were asked to use the breaks in the model tape to produce their versions, which were also recorded. It was assumed that the subjects—some of whom were naïve and some trained—would use their voices naturally, so that the experiment would involve psycholinguistic processes similar to those in first-language acquisition. By the same token, it was assumed that the "reproduced" versions would contain not only the linguistic (or paralinguistic) information contained in each of the model utterances, but also individual (personal) features. In order to verify whether, indeed, each of the reproductions was (para)linguistically equivalent to its respective model, a new tape was prepared on which each reproduction was preceded by a copy of the corresponding model.

The experiment was repeated with each subject four times: 1) in "zero" time, 2) directly after the first session, 3) one hour after the first session, and 4) the next day. On the final tape, the voices and sessions were randomized, but the order of the 7 models and the following reproductions in one session with one subject was preserved. This final tape, then, contained 7 (patterns) × 20 (voices) × 4 (replications) = 560 utterances excluding the models. This tape was played back to a listening panel of 20 subjects. Eleven of them had participated in the reproduction experiment. The listeners' task was merely to judge whether each of the reproductions was "the same" as the directly preceding model. No instructions were given as to what was meant by "the same," but all the listeners knew that they would hear the phrase "good morning" spoken in different ways by different voices who repeated the models without trying to mimic. The judgments were recorded by the listeners on prepared answer sheets in the form of pluses for "same" and minuses for "different." The choice was therefore binary. The total number of judgments was 7 × 20 × 4 × 20 (listeners) = 11,200.

The first finding, which was actually methodological, was that there was no statistically significant difference in the judgments whether they referred to the listener's own voice or a voice he or she knew well or an unknown voice. The results of the listening test are summarized in Table 1, which shows the number of *minuses* out of a total of 560 for each of the 20 voices.

In the table the voices are arranged according to the rank reflecting the evaluation of the performance. The first place was taken by the speaker whose voice was recorded for the models and who took part in the entire experiment. From the point of view of the ultimate aim of the investigation this fact was of no consequence, and it should be noted that the two next-ranking voices got only a few more negative marks. However, it was considered interesting to see whether there was any relation between the sex of the model voice (M) and the sex of the reproducing voices. The Whitney-Mann rank test was used to verify the null hypothesis of no difference between the sexes. The test values were $U_1 = 39.5$ and $U_2 = 60.5$ with critical values $U_{0.01} = 19$ and $U_{0.05} = 27$, so the null hypothesis of no difference cannot be rejected.

For the next stage of the study two males voices with the best scores and two female voices with the best scores, i.e., numbers 1, 2, 5, and 6 in Table

Table 1.   Results of listening tests

Voice number	Number of negative judgments	Sex	Rank
1	16	M	1
2	19	M	2
3	20	M	3
4	39	M	4
5	42	F	5 ½
6	42	F	5 ½
7	46	F	7
8	52	F	8 ½
9	52	F	8 ½
10	65	M	10
11	70	M	11
12	74	M	12
13	76	M	13 ½
14	76	F	13 ½
15	78	F	15
16	86	F	16
17	117	F	17
18	149	M	18
19	166	F	19
20	197	M	20

1, were selected. We henceforth refer to them by the subjects' initials: WJ (m) ZK (m), MB(f), and KD(f). Of these, WJ and MB have had considerable traditional phonetic training, KD some, and ZK no such training.

Instrumental pitch curves of the "reproductions" were obtained mainly with the aid of the pitch meter TM-1 designed and constructed by H. Kubzdela.[1] In some cases the Kay Electric Sona-Graph (narrowband) was used. The measurements that are now discussed were made on the F_0 traces of the reproductions by the selected four voices. One of the model intonations had a very low tone on the last syllable, degenerating into a creak. In some reproductions this syllable also showed a creak and in some the amplitude of the first harmonic was so low that a fully reliable F_0 trace could not be obtained. In this case (version 4) the measurements were only made as far as the end of the vowel /o/.

TIME NORMALIZATION

Mean values of the duration of the phrase for each of the speakers and for each tonal pattern showed that significant differences existed for both sources of variation (both factors). In order to make all the utterances directly comparable, a simple time normalization was performed. It consisted of dividing the entire length of each individual utterance into 20 equal time segments. Each time segment, therefore, represented 5% of the duration of the phrase. The fundamental frequency was first measured at equal absolute distances of $\Delta t = 20$ milliseconds and then at equal relative distances of $\Delta T_i = {}^1/_{20} T_i$ with $i = 1, 2, \ldots, 112$ and T being the duration of each of the 7 (patterns) $\times$ 4 (voices) $\times$ 4 (replications) $= 112$ utterances. For short phrases like the ones considered here (their total duration never exceeded about 1 second) each simple linear time normalization was found to be quite adequate.

FREQUENCY NORMALIZATION

After time normalization, when F_0, measured in hertz, was compared within replications by individual speakers and between the voices, it became evident that for a given pattern intraspeaker differences were very much smaller than interspeaker differences. The former were mostly about 5 to 15 Hz, whereas the latter quite often exceeded a 1:2 ratio in relative terms and about 100 Hz in absolute terms. Typical results of the comparisons are shown in Figure 1, which shows the pitch curves of the four replications of pattern 2 by each of the four speakers.

---

[1]See Kubzdela (1976).

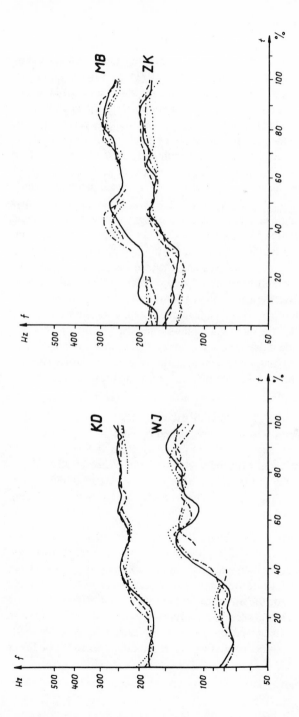

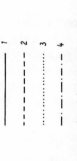

Figure 1. One tonal pattern reproduced four times by four subjects (normalized time scale).

Each voice was now characterized by examining the statistical distributions of instantaneous F_0 values (see Jassem, 1971). It was shown in Jassem, Batóg, and Czajka (1973) that when average (or instantaneous) F_0 values are measured in a sample of about 1 minute duration, the arithmetic mean ($\bar{x}$) and the standard deviation (sd) of the statistical distributions can be used to characterize the pitch and compass of the individual voices. Accordingly, each of the selected four subjects read an unemotional newspaper passage four times, again at "zero" time, directly after the first reading, 1 hour later, and approximately 24 hours later. Pitch curves were obtained using the pitch meter TM-1 and the instantaneous F_0 values were read from the F_0 envelopes at intervals of $\Delta t = 20$ milliseconds in the voiced segments of the first minute of each reading. Cumulative histograms showing the distribution of the random variable were prepared after 10, 20, 30, 40, 50, and 60 seconds. Figure 2 shows such histograms for the fourth reading of voice ZK. It can be seen that after 60 seconds the distribution becomes very regular and is approximately normal with slight positive skewness. Figure 3 shows F_0 distribution functions for three readings by the four voices with frequency on a log scale. They are the readings 1, 2, and 4—the one made 1 hour after "zero" time is left out. This is so because as the calculations progressed it became evident that no further information could be gained from the data on the intermediate sample. The following features of the distributions become apparent from the curves in Figure 3:

1. The approximation to a log-normal distribution is very good (in the ideal case, the distributions would be represented by straight lines).
2. Within speakers, the three distribution functions are almost identical in the case of WJ, ZK, and MB and very close in the case of KD.
3. Between speakers the curves differ both in the position along the frequency scale (indicating different means) and slope (indicating different dispersions).[2]

Although a comparison between the distribution functions prepared on a linear scale showed clearly that a log-normal distribution approximates the empirical distributions better than a normal one, it should be noted that we are working here within a range of values where the difference between a linear and a logarithmic scale for the empirical data is very small. The means and standard deviations for each of the three readings by each of the speakers were calculated both for the linear and the logarithmic frequency scale. The differences were found to be quite negligible. Corresponding means on the linear

---

[2]Similar distribution functions were prepared for a large number of speakers by Rappaport (1958).

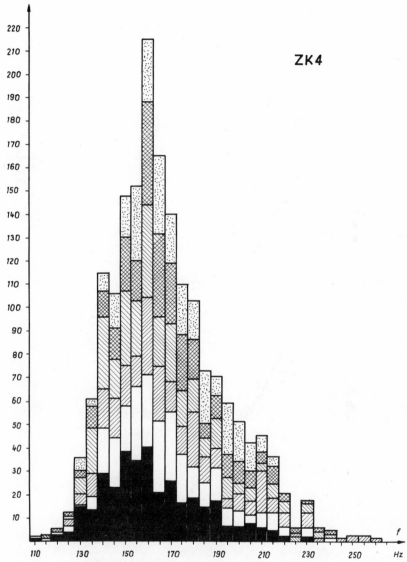

Figure 2.   A cumulative histogram showing the distribution of F_o values after 10, 20, 30, 40, 50, and 60 seconds of reading (subject ZK, session 4).

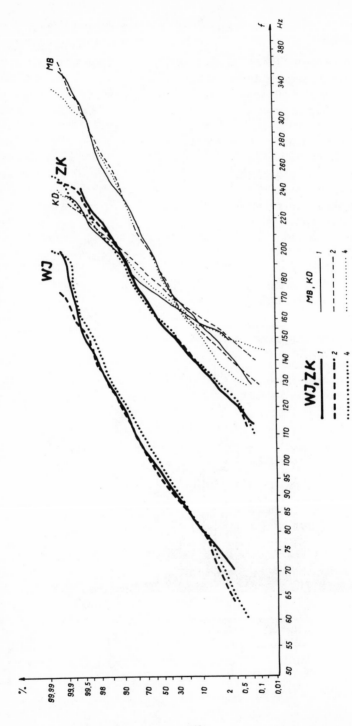

Figure 3. Distribution functions of F_o values.

and log scale never differed by more than 4 Hz and were in most cases around 1 Hz. When the standard deviations were compared it turned out that from the point of view of relating interspeaker variations to intraspeaker variations it made no difference which values were used. For instance, on the linear scale the standard deviations for ZK were 26.3, 25.3, and 23.7 Hz, respectively, for the three readings and for KD the corresponding figures were 16.5, 16.8, and 16.4 Hz. On the log scale the values were 0.116, 0.116, and 0.115 for ZK and 0.109, 0.109, and 0.109 for KD. Although a logarithmic frequency scale would thus have been slightly better, for the last part of the investigation linear means and deviations were used because they were found to be easier to manipulate in certain practical situations. Table 2 shows all these values.

Table 2 confirms the impression gained from Figure 3 that the four voices differ significantly in both pitch and compass. Considering the large number of data (given under N in Table 2), a comparison of the values of $\bar{x}$ and sd within speakers and between speakers shows the interspeaker differences so clearly that no further statistical testing was considered necessary.

FREQUENCY NORMALIZATION

Since the means and standard deviations were found to be strong differentiating factors between the voices, it was decided to use them for frequency normalization. Means of the three values of the means and deviations were calculated giving, for each speaker, $\bar{\bar{x}}$ (the mean of means) and $\bar{s}$ (the mean of

Table 2.   Linear means and standard deviations of instantaneous F_0 values

Voice reading	N	$\bar{x}$	sd
WJ_1	1885	103.3	17.8
WJ_2	1855	102.3	17.6
WJ_4	1990	105.4	19.3
ZK_1	1912	170.1	26.3
ZK_2	1768	169.5	25.3
ZK_4	1809	168.0	23.7
KD_1	1815	179.3	16.5
KD_2	1720	184.7	16.8
KD_4	1768	181.3	16.4
MB_1	1581	203.8	37.1
MB_2	1645	203.8	39.9
MB_4	1621	203.8	39.6

standard deviations), and the values of fundamental frequency were now expressed in relative standard units

$$\frac{x - \bar{\bar{x}}_i}{\bar{s}_i} \; (i = 1,2,3,4) \tag{1}$$

where $\bar{x}_i$ and $\bar{s}_i$ are the estimated parameters for each of the four voices.

Figure 4 shows one trace of each of the seven patterns for each voice, averaged over the four replications. Figure 5 shows these traces on a normalized frequency scale according to equation 1. The main observations that can be made on the basis of the figures are as follows:

1. Before normalization, the curves are systematically shifted in frequency between the voices.
2. After normalization, the curves largely overlap within each of the patterns, thus strongly reducing interspeaker differences.
3. The values of the normalized variable often exceed $\pm 3sd$ (three standard deviations).[3]
4. In most patterns, the normalized F_0 values in the voice KD tend to be the highest.

The following conclusions can be drawn from these observations: 1) the frequency normalization introducing the arithmetic mean and standard deviation for the individual voices works quite well generally, although better for some voices than for others; and 2) in some voices, the range of tones used in conversational speech is considerably greater than in unemotional reading. In view of the second point, it may in the future turn out to be better to use, for purposes of frequency normalization, a standard but more varied text including conversational passages.

How well frequency normalization based on the mean and standard deviation actually worked in this experiment is shown in Figure 6, which presents the ranking of the normalized F_0 values according to the four voices. This figure has been obtained by comparing, at each measuring point along the time normalized scale, the curves averaged over the four replications for each of the four voices in each of the seven patterns and stating the position, from low to high, on the normalized frequency scale.[4] The height of a bar indicates how often the value of normalized F_0 ranked first, second, third, and fourth for the given voice. Should there be no overlap between the voices at

---

[3]In an ideal normal distribution, over 99% of the values of the random variable are contained within ± 3 standard deviations.

[4]That is, at the measuring point X, WJ has, say, the lowest F_0 value, so he gets 1, ZK has the next higher value, so he gets 2, KD gets 3, and MB, who at that point has the highest normalized F_0, gets 4, and so on for all the 147 (7×21) measuring points.

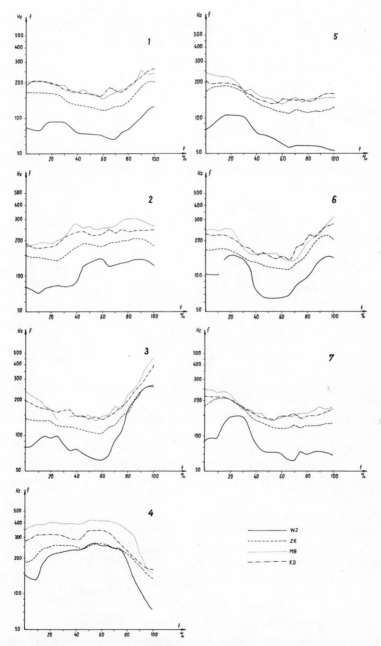

Figure 4.   Pitch curves of the reproductions of each of the seven patterns by four subjects, averaged over four replications (no frequency normalization).

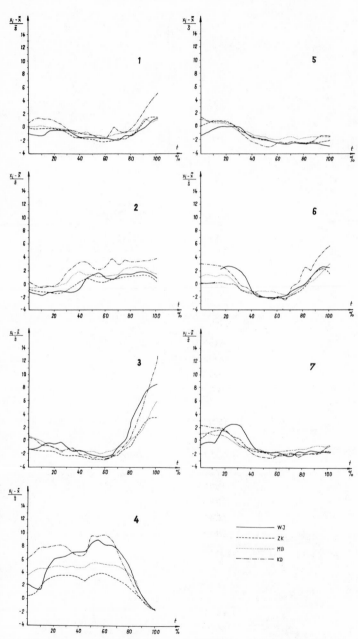

Figure 5. Pitch curves of the reproduction of each of the seven patterns by four subjects, averaged over four replications (normalized frequency scale).

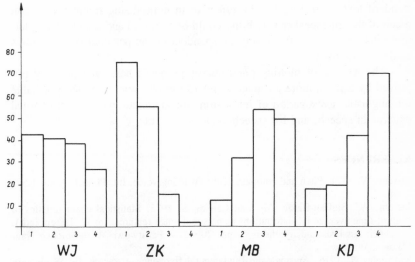

Figure 6.   Results of a rank test showing the effect of frequency normalization.

all, each voice would be represented by just one bar with a different number for each voice. This would indicate a perfect shift and separation between the voices. If the normalization were ideal, each voice would be represented by four bars of equal height. This would indicate perfect overlap and perfect removal of the personal effect. Figure 6 shows that the normalization works best for WJ and worst for KD.

In view of the fact that the range of tones (the "compass") was generally greater in the experimental patterns than in the readings of the newspaper text, another frequency normalization was performed that related the absolute F_0 value read from the pitch curves only to the individual values of $\bar{\bar{x}}$ (i.e., the variable was now $x/\bar{\bar{x}}_i$) and graphs similar to those in Figures 4 and 5 were prepared. An advantage of using a frequency scale normalized only for $\bar{\bar{x}}$ is that such a scale can be calibrated in musical intervals, e.g., semitones. However, a rank test corresponding to the one shown in Figure 6 indicated that such a frequency normalization is less effective.

SUMMARY AND CONCLUSIONS

(Para)linguistically equivalent utterances that are spoken several times by different voices show greater interspeaker than intraspeaker variability. The differences between voices are related to the statistical distribution of F_0 values. The parameters of such distributions, estimated from readings of a standard text, were found to be effective in normalizing frequency so that much of the interspeaker variability could be removed and a method of plotting pitch curves that are largely independent of the personal voice features could be proposed.

The method of plotting pitch curves proposed here, and possibly improved by using a more adequate standard sample, may be found profitable for linguistic investigation of intonation, for automatic recognition of tonal patterns in speech, and for speech synthesis by rule.

REFERENCES

Jassem, W. 1971. Pitch and compass of the speaking voice. Int. Phonet. Assn. 1:59–68.

Jassem, W., Steffen-Batóg, M., and Czajka, S. 1973. Statistical characteristics of short-time average F_0 distributions as personal voice features. In: W. Jassem (ed.), Speech Analysis and Synthesis 3, pp. 209–224. Państwowe Wydawnictwo Naukowe, Warsaw.

Kubzdela, H. 1976. An analogue fundamental frequency extractor. In: W. Jassem (ed.), Speech Analysis and Synthesis 4, pp. 269–279. Państwowe Wydawnictwo Naukowe, Warsaw.

Rappaport, W. 1958. Über Messungen der Tonhöhenverteilung in der deutschen Sprache. Acustica 8:200–225.

11/ Intonation, Main Clause Phenomena, and Point of View

D. R. Ladd, Jr.

MAIN CLAUSE PHENOMENA

In the last few years there has been a considerable amount of attention paid to what have been called Main Clause Phenomena (MCP). This term is Green's (1976), and has been adopted by Bolinger (1977); as Green points out, the term covers about the same ground as Emond's Root Transformation, which is also used by Hooper and Thompson (1973) and McCawley (1977). Green's article best presents the basic fact at issue in all these discussons: there are certain syntactic transformations, lexical items, and other grammatical phenomena whose occurrence is (largely) restricted to main clauses. Green gives numerous examples, including the following:

(1) Negative adverb preposing with inversion:
Never before have prices been so high.
* Nixon regrets that never before have prices been so high.
(2) Rhetorical questions:
Who can understand *Aspects?* (implying that no one can)
* It seems that who can understand *Aspects?*
(3) Participial phrase preposing with inversion:
Squatting in the corner was a spotted tree frog.
* I never enter the room when squatting in the corner is a spotted tree frog.

The acceptability judgments in these examples are Green's. As she points out, the stars are not categorical, but merely indicate that the sentence is at least somewhat peculiar. It is the more-or-less nature of these acceptability judgments—the fact that MCP are not absolutely restricted to main

Revised July, 1978. An earlier version of this paper was presented at the Annual Meeting of the Linguistic Society of America in Philadelphia, Dec. 29, 1976, under the title "Intonation is a MCP." Thanks to Noriko Akatsuka for comments and encouragement; responsibility for the speculations and such contained herein is mine.

clauses—that is the basis of Green's article. For every type of MCP, there seems to be a very restricted set of circumstances under which it can occur in subordinate clauses as well. Such conditions are extremely idiosyncratic, as can be seen from the following, also from Green:

(4)   I knew that never before had prices been so high.
(5)   We ought to assign Postal, because who can understand *Aspects?*
(6)   John knew that squatting in the corner was a spotted tree frog.

Bolinger (1977) provides further discussion of some of the conditions involved in the acceptability of embedded MCP.

Intonation Contours

Liberman and Sag (1974) describe an intonation pattern that they call the contradiction contour, which seems to behave like the "syntactic" MCP described by Green. Their illustration is the following:

(7)   Elephantiasis isn't incurable.

Let me add a few more examples that illustrate their suggested punctuation:

(8)   ¡You're not supposed to be here!
(9)   ¡I can't teach a class on Daniel Jones!

The meaning of this contour is something like contradiction, or, perhaps better, questioning of the addressee's assumptions. [Glenn (1977) provides additional discussion of the contour's meaning.] In any case, as Liberman and Sag point out, the contour cannot readily be embedded, that is, applied to an embedded clause. We cannot say:

(10)   * Medical science has demonstrated that ¡elephantiasis isn't incurable!
(11)   * John told me that ¡you weren't supposed to be here!

The sentences are acceptable, of course, if the intonation is spread out over the whole sentence:

(12)   ¡Medical science has demonstrated that elephantiasis isn't incurable!
(13)   ¡John told me that you weren't supposed to be here!

Making allowances, then, for the obviously different nature of a grammatical transformation and an intonation contour, what we have here is an intonation contour behaving like a MCP in that it cannot occur in a subordinate clause.

The similarity of the contradiction contour to MCP goes farther than that. We can find a few idiosyncratic environments where the contour *can* be embedded. Suppose you are teaching a course on the history of linguistics and invite me to give a guest lecture on the phonological theories of Daniel Jones. I accept, then reconsider and decline. Later, I tell the story to a friend:

(14)   He asked me to do the lecture on Daniel Jones for his history of linguistics
course. Well, at first I said OK, but then I got to thinking about it and I
realized that ¡I couldn't teach a class on Daniel Jones!, so I went and told
him I'd changed my mind.

Here the contradiction contour is applied only to the subordinate clause "I
couldn't teach a class on Daniel Jones" embedded under "I realized that . . . "

Now, in examples (7) through (14), when we have talked about embedding the contradiction contour, we have been referring to the placement of its
initial high-fall and terminal low-rise relative to the segmental part of the
sentence; the sense in which it "cannot be embedded" is that it must generally
begin at the beginning of the sentence [cf. Ladd (in press) for further discus-
sion]. The contradiction contour is relatively unusual among intonation contours, however, in being a kind of holistic unit with a recognizable beginning.
Nevertheless, by looking a little more closely at meaning rather than form, we
can find similar MCP-like effects with other intonation contours whose phonological shapes do not lend themselves as well to being identified as embedded
or unembedded.

For example, consider the contour that Sag and Liberman (1975) have
identified as the "surprise/redundancy tune." In the following dialogue, this
adds an implication something like "what else would you expect?"

(15)   A. What are you going to do with all that money?

B. Put it in the bank.

Unlike the contradiction contour, this contour does not have a well-defined
beginning, but is identified rather by the sequence of low-rising and high-
falling accented syllables. That is, in the same dialogue speaker B could have
said the following [using the British "tonetic" notation—see, e.g., Kingdon
(1958) and O'Connor and Arnold (1961)—to indicate the location of the
low-rise and high-fall]:

(16)   A. What are you going to do with all that money?
        B. I'm gonna ‚put it in the ˈbank.

That is, we would not expect:

(17)   B. ‚I'm gonna put it in the ˈbank.

In other words, the contour does not depend on the beginnings and ends of
sentences, but on the location of the major accented syllables. Because of this,
it can look as if the contour is embedded, as in:

(18)   A. What did John tell you to do with all that money?
        B. He said I should ‚put it in the ˈbank.

However, the intonation is not actually embedded here, because the what-else-would-you-expect implication *applies to the whole sentence*. The sentence suggests "what else would you have expected John to tell me?" It does not imply that *John's* attitude was "where else would you put it besides in the bank?" In fact, it says nothing at all about how John gave his advice; for all we can tell from the intonation, John may be a long-winded banker who took an hour to weigh all the pros and cons. The point is that even when the phonological locus of the intonation contour appears to be quite specifically on the embedded clause—as it does in example (18)—its implication never-theless applies to the whole sentence, and this is the sense in which it is not embedded.

The distinction is important, because here, too, there is a MCP-like effect at work. That is, in certain idiosyncratic environments, the implication of the intonation does apply only to the embedded clause. If we return to the original dialogue and change it slightly, we could get the following:

(19) A. What do you think you'll do with all that money?
      B. I guess I'll ,put it in the ˈbank.

Here the intonation is, in a sense, embedded. The implication is not "what else would you expect me to guess?"—this would be analogous to "what else would you have expected John to tell me?" in example (18)—but rather it is the same as in the original version in example (15)—"what else would you expect me to do with it."

Relationship between MCP and Intonation

It appears, then, that intonation, or at least certain intonation contours, behave in ways that are very similar to Green's MCP. At first glance, the similarity is very puzzling: there is no obvious connection between intonation and the stylistic devices like participial phrase preposing that Green discusses. Yet further investigation reveals other similarities that suggest some fundamental kinship.

Let us start by considering Green's observations about MCP. She reaches the tentative conclusion (p. 386) that "speaker's agreement" has something to do with the acceptability of MCP in subordinate clauses, i.e., that the speaker must agree with the proposition expressed in the clause containing a MCP. She further suggests (p. 394) that we need a theory of "assertion making": she concludes that MCP in some way affect what is being asserted, and suggests that what is common to all the idiosyncratic environments where MCP are acceptable in subordinate clauses is that they do not detract from the main assertion of the sentence, which is somehow signaled by the MCP.

These notions can be readily exemplified with the contradiction contour, which again hints at the similarity of MCP and intonation. The unembedded sentence "¡Elephantiasis isn't incurable!" questions the addressee's assumptions about elephantiasis, whereas "¡Medical science has demonstrated that elephantiasis isn't incurable!" is a claim about what medical science has done, not about the nature of elephantiasis. If, as in example (10), we put the contradiction contour on the embedded clause—"Medical science has demonstrated that ¡elephantiasis isn't incurable!"—our intonation seems to be saying something about elephantiasis, and then the purpose of the main clause "Medical science has demonstrated . . ." is unclear. That is, we seem to be making the assertion about elephantiasis in a special way—this meshes with Green's ideas about "assertion-making"—and yet we have embedded the assertion in a main clause that appears to contradict the special effect.

The idea that we can make assertions in particular ways suggests some sort of dichotomy between an assertion and the way it is made. Both intonation and MCP seem to bear out the existence of such a dichotomy. For example, suppose that, instead of accepting your offer to teach a class on Daniel Jones and then changing my mind, I had simply turned you down flat. When you asked why, I replied:

(9)   ¡I can't teach a class on Daniel Jones!

You could then have reported this as follows:

(20)   He pretty much told me I was crazy to expect him to teach a class on Daniel Jones.

My assertion was that I couldn't teach the class; the way I made the assertion is summed up by your paraphrase. There are all sorts of verbs like assert and exclaim, and an even greater variety of adverbial expressions like flatly, doubtfully, with surprise, and hesitantly, that are used in indirect discourse to summarize the force of the intonation of something being quoted.

Similar examples can be found with syntactic MCP. Suppose John tells the story of how he narrowly missed obtaining the only extant copy of an early Egyptian treatise on generative grammar:

(21)   I crept through the dark corridors toward the Pharaoh's library. My lantern cast flickery shadows and my footfalls echoed weirdly in the long halls. At last I reached the library, but at the crucial moment my attention was distracted by a treasure far greater than the Pharaoh's grammar. Squatting in the corner was a spotted tree frog.

Now, if someone subsequently reported the crucial moment as "Oh, he said he got distracted because there was a spotted tree frog squatting in the corner," an observer might report that John had told his story vividly or dramatically, but that the unvivid undramatic version was an accurate summary. John might complain that he was not being taken seriously, but he would certainly not claim to have been misrepresented.

What I am suggesting is that the function of the MCP is more a part of the way the assertion is made than a part of the assertion itself. The special force or effect signaled by the MCP is somehow an overlay on what we might call the propositional part of the message; that is, in speaking a sentence with a MCP the speaker is not just getting the facts across, but slanting them in a particular way—in the example just given, vividly or dramatically. In other words, there *is* an underlying similarity between MCP and intonation in that both are felt to contribute more to the "nonpropositional" part of the message—the way it is said. In the second half of the paper I explore the nature of this distinction between "propositional" and "nonpropositional," and its implications for the grammar of items like intonation and MCP.

PROPOSITIONAL AND NONPROPOSITIONAL

There can be no doubt that users of language are aware of the distinction between the propositional and nonpropositional aspects of utterances. The difference is summed up in everyday speech as "it wasn't what you said, it was the way you said it." This sentiment underlies such diverse nonlinguistic behavior as awarding Nobel literature prizes, administering spankings, hiring and firing employees, and being moved to tears, so we can assume that there is some reality to it, and I think that we can profit from taking it seriously.

At the outset, however, it is well to emphasize that there is no sharp formal division between the two aspects of utterances. In particular, I have argued elsewhere (Ladd, 1977b) that intonation is not to be separated off from the rest of language and treated as a peripheral phenomenon or as "the way a sentence is said." It is simply that intonation [along with various segmental phenomena, like German "modal particles" (cf. Schubiger, 1965, this volume) and English MCP] are *more* attitudinal or nonpropositional than many other lexical categories and syntactic devices. Thus the horns of the dichotomy are probably only two ends of a spectrum.

Suppose, for example, that at a critical point in an incident that led to Smith's trial for assault, Smith said to Jones:

(22)   One more step into this room, punk, and I'll beat the shit out of you.

Suppose, further, that Smith's lawyer represents this to the jury as follows:

(23)   My client merely advised the witness that he would be unwise to continue his progress into the room.

The lawyer's version is not the whole truth; Smith's words have been softened enough to distort their force. Smart lawyers, good writers, inspiring teachers, and clever con-men all know that the propositional and the nonpropositional are hopelessly intertwined.

Nevertheless, in the way that language is used the two are often treated separately. For example, if we add a hackneyed adverbial expression to the lawyer's slick phrase in example (23), the sentence comes out like a typical *New York Times* description of any sordid incident:

> (24) Mr. Smith told Mr. Jones in no uncertain terms that he would be unwise to continue his progress into the room.

This sounds like a parody of stodgy newspaper style, but not many would complain that the truth had been distorted. In other words, if the way that something is said is summed up in an adverb or a phrase, a bowdlerized version of the original language will pass as "what was said." Recall that both MCP and intonation can be summed up (or bowdlerized) in just this way.

Continuing with the courtroom example, we can discover further facets of the different treatment of the propositional and nonpropositional. The first thing worth noting is that the propositional is in some sense outside the speaker, whereas the manner of expression comes from the speaker and is taken to be the speaker's responsibility. Consider the way Jones is likely to phrase his testimony concerning Smith's threat in example (22). Naturally, he wants to communicate as effectively as he can the force of what Smith told him, yet he does not want to offend the judge by shattering the dignity of the courtroom with Smith's language. So he might say:

> (25) He told me if I took one more step into the room he'd beat me up.

Or perhaps:

> (26) He told me if I took one more step into the room he'd beat the shit out of me—and those were his exact words, your Honor.

In this second version, Jones uses Smith's words, but apologizes for them.

What this suggests is that, even when language is used to quote and to paraphrase, the way that something is said is often treated separately from what is said. The courtroom is an institution whose avowed purpose includes the public discussion of certain subjects that might otherwise remain unknown, so there are certain things that a speaker must talk about in that context that may for one reason or another be abhorrent to his audience. This is the sense in which the propositional is outside the speaker, beyond his control, externally verifiable. Yet the speaker still has control over the way the unpleasant subjects are expressed. Jones was specifically asked for his version of what happened, yet he felt compelled to apologize for quoting Smith's language. His reluctance can be explained by considering that he is in some way responsible for the way that his statements are phrased.[1]

Moreover, the distinction between external verifiability and speaker's responsibility has implications beyond the question of who may be charged with contempt of court: it goes right to the heart of semantic interpretation. Quang Phuc Dong (1969) notes that when epithets are embedded in indirect quotes, they are nevertheless taken to indicate the speaker's opinion, not that of the person quoted. His example is the following:

(27)   John says his landlord is a fucking scoutmaster.

The epithet is not taken to be part of what John said; in fact, John's opinion of scoutmasters may be wholly favorable. Rather, the epithet represents the point of view of the speaker. English has a wondrous variety of grammatical devices for inserting taboo lexical items into otherwise nontaboo utterances—in short, for changing the way something is said. The following list is merely illustrative:

(28)   Get the hell out of here.
       Shut the goddam door.
       Get your ass in here.
       That mattress sure is a lumpy son-of-a-bitch.

If it is true that the function of such taboo-insertions is mainly to change the nonpropositional aspect of the sentence, and if it is true that the nonpropositional aspect of the sentence is felt to be the speaker's responsibility, then Quang's observations about sentences like example (27) make sense. The converse of his observations, incidentally, is that if John said:

---

[1] The distinction between "externally verifiable" and "speaker's responsibility" is exemplified in the following intonational data from English. A certain type of exclamation—with the sentence accent on an interjection and the rest of the sentence deaccented (i.e., in this case on low pitch)—forces a "speaker's responsibility" reading, something like "This is my opinion and is not necessarily externally verifiable." Anomalous utterances can be made up by using this intonation on sentences that seem to have no such possible interpretation, and that can only be read as a report of an externally verifiable fact rather than an opinion. Thus:

Mán, it's hot!   * Mán, it's ninety-seven!
Jésus, Pete's in trouble!   * Jésus, Ithaca's in Tompkins County!
Gósh, Paris is a French city!   * Gósh, Paris is the French capital!
Bóy, I hate his guts!   * Bóy, I saw his dog!

[In all of these the intonation under consideration must be kept in mind. Any of the examples on the right would be perfectly normal with an additional accent on the main part of the sentence:

Jesus, Ithaca's in Tompkins County! (I'm surprised to learn that.)

(29)   My landlord is a fucking scoutmaster.

one could report this as

(30)   John says his landlord is a scoutmaster.

without being accused of misrepresenting John.

Point of View

The interpretation of inserted taboo words thus bears a remarkable similarity to the interpretation of deictic or indexical words, what Jakobson (1971) calls *shifters*. The most obvious examples are words like here, there, this, today, now, you, and I. If I say "here" it refers (or may refer) to somewhere different than if you say "here." If I say "today" on Wednesday, it refers to a different day than if I say it on Saturday. As is well known, these items are interpreted in any given context with reference to the speaker's point of view.

A corollary to this is that such deictic words do not preserve their original point of view when embedded in indirect quotes. If John tells me "I'll arrive tomorrow at ten," the next day I can report this as "John said he'd arrive today at ten" and obviously no one will suggest that I have misquoted him. Or again: suppose that John and I are fixing a car. I am having trouble finding the right size wrench for a certain bolt. John says, "Here, try this one." I cannot subsequently report this as "John told me to try this one" unless the very wrench under discussion is right there in front of me. This shifts its reference according to who says it—in this case, it shifts from John's point of view when he says it to my point of view when I say it, even though I am reporting what he said.

Recall the distinction that we noted in "Intonation Contours" between the contradiction contour and the surprise/redundancy contour. The former is excluded from subordinate clauses, whereas the latter occurs freely throughout the sentence but with an interpretation governed by the whole sentence, not by any subordinate clause. Green's MCP are thus like the contradiction contour—they are essentially excluded from subordinate clauses. Deictic words and inserted epithets, on the other hand, like the surprise/redundancy contour, are not themselves excluded from subordinate clauses, but their interpretation is in some sense governed by the whole sentence, controlled by the speaker's point of view.

It seems to me, then, that a notion of speaker's point of view is critical to an understanding of the sort of phenomena I have been discussing. When people speak, they convey two different sorts of information. The first is what I have been calling propositional—the message or assertion. The second is, broadly, point of view. Speakers convey a certain amount of information that locates them in space (here, that), in time (today, now), in society (ain't, goddam, French tu, vous), and in the speech event (I, you), or that locates their utterance in the discourse (look, indeed, moreover) or gives their attitude toward the utterance or its message (I guess, German doch, ja), and much more.

The point of view of items like here or that is often literally spatial: I am talking about how I see things from where I stand. Not all points of view are so easy to define, as the list just given suggests. If I tell you "Shut the goddam door," the goddam, as we saw, adds little or nothing to the propositional part of the message; you can comply with my request in exactly the same way as if I had said "Shut the door." Rather, the "goddam" conveys a whole complex of sociolinguistic point-of-view information about my relationship to you, my relationship to anyone else who may be listening, my current mood, perhaps my feeling about the door or the weather outside, and possibly even my attitude toward organized religion. However, just because the point of view is vague, diffuse, and hard to pin down, that doesn't mean it isn't there. If, say, Dwight Bolinger or Ilse Lehiste or Morris Halle walked in while I was giving a paper and I yelled "Shut the goddam door," the consternation and confusion would be just as great, albeit perhaps of a different sort, as if I started saying "that" when I meant "this." And the source of the uproar would just as surely be taken to be the speaker—myself.

Consistency in Point of View

All of the data discussed so far can be interpreted as exemplifying a principle that the point of view conveyed by a sentence must be relatively consistent. First, of course, it must be consistent with what the addressee can see or infer about the speaker's point of view—this is why it is confusing if I say "here" when I mean "there," or why it is scandalous if I yell "Shut the goddam door" at a respected scholar at a professional meeting. Second, however— and this bears much more directly on the question of MCP and related phenomena—the point of view of a sentence must be *internally* consistent. For example, the problem with embedding the contradiction contour is that it appears to convey two conflicting points of view. In example (10), *"Medical science has demonstrated that ¡elephantiasis isn't incurable!," the intonation says that the point of view about elephantiasis comes from the speaker, and the main clause says that the speaker says that it comes from medical science. Similarly, we can easily explain Green's observation (1976, p. 388) that main clauses with first person subjects, such as I know, I guess, or I realize, are consistently the best environments for embedding MCP of all sorts, because both the main clause and the MCP identify the point of view as being that of the speaker. Sociolinguistic points of view may produce anomalous sentences like MCP in subordinate clauses: sentences like the French

(31)   ??Qu'est-ce que tu fais, M. Dupont?

or the German

(32)   ??Wie geht's dir, Frau Schmidt?

with the familiar form of the pronoun and the formal title-plus-last-name address, strike native speakers as very odd.

If we take Green's principle of "speaker's agreement" (as discussed in "Relationship between MCP and Intonation") and change it so that it refers not to agreement with the assertion but rather to compatibility of point of view—that is, agreement with the way that the assertion is made—then we may have a general principle underlying the behavior of all of the phenomena we have been discussing, not just MCP. The point of view of a subordinate clause must be compatible with the point of view of the sentence.

It should be noted that the points of view do not necessarily have to be the same, they just have to be compatible (cf. Bolinger, 1977, p. 518: "To see whether 'slifting' can improve an exclamation, we must look for main verbs that are compatible"). I think that the question of what constitutes compatibility of point of view is central to an understanding of what is going on with the phenomena we have been discussing, and I have no clear idea of how to define such a concept. Some simple examples can illustrate the sort of thing I mean.

I just noted that spatially deictic words like this and that shift according to who says them. However, it is also relatively common for them to represent a point of view other than that of the speaker, provided the two do not conflict. Thus, if we have just described a set of favorable circumstances in which John once found himself, we could go on to say, "John could see that this was a golden opportunity." Here, unlike the case of the wrench that we cited above, we can use this in the embedded clause to refer to John's point of view, because somehow it does not conflict with ours. It seems to be relatively easy to shift to other spatial points of view this way—to put yourself in someone else's shoes, so to speak—whereas the shifting of sociolinguistic points of view does not seem to be so easy—hence the observation that the point of view in inserted taboo words remains that of the speaker.

If it is true that it is somehow easier to shift spatial points of view than sociolinguistic ones, then we may have an explanation of one of Green's most puzzling puzzles. She notes (1976, p. 393) that no principle of "speaker's agreement" will account for the fact that certain MCP are much more readily embeddable under third person subjects than most; her examples are

(33)   John knew that squatting in the corner was a spotted tree frog.

(34)   John realized that never before had prices been so high.

However, the preposed phrases in these examples—"squatting in the corner" and "never before"—refer to spatial or temporal location, as do many other such phrases that can readily be preposed even under third person subjects, such as "lurking in the bushes," "drooping sadly at half-mast," and "hard on the heels of the blizzard." When we foreground such items, we emphasize our relation to the time or place; this is the point of view, and it is spatially or temporally deictic in a way that the point of view in many of our other examples is not. Just as we found it relatively easy to shift to John's point of view in "John could see that this was a golden opportunity," similarly, when we say "John knew that squatting in the corner was a spotted tree frog," there is an added vividness that comes from the fact that we are seeing the situation through John's eyes, seeing from his point of view. However, other MCP do not involve spatial or temporal reference to as great an extent, and the speaker's point of view cannot so readily be identified with that of the third person subject; hence embedding is less acceptable.

The notion of point of view as it is often applied to literary narrative seems to be relevant here. In spite of the fact noted earlier that it is difficult to shift the point of view of inserted taboo words, we *can* do this in unambiguous situations. One such unambiguous situation is a novel written in the third person, but consistently maintaining the point of view of one character. In such a case, inserted taboo words (assuming the novel's style is sufficiently informal to include them) represent not the narrator's (i.e., speaker's) point of view, but the protagonist's. The following examples are from *Starting Over*, by Dan Wakefield. Potter is the character from whose point of view the story is told.

(35)   Potter took a deep drag, coughed, and passed the damn thing back to Arnie (p. 15).

(36)   Max was only three years older than Potter but seemed a lot more than that, maybe because he was so goddamn calm and in control all the time [goes on to describe Potter's feelings about Max's lack of emotionality] (p. 24).

(37)   [Describing Potter's reaction to the clean air after he moves from New York to Boston; he feels he might do less drinking] In New York you had to drink for your goddamn health (p. 34).

In all of these cases the attitudes underlying the inserted epithets are to be understood as Potter's, not the novelist's.

We can bring the discussion back to intonation with a final set of examples involving what has been called "semi-indirect discourse" (Gragg, 1972; see also Banfield, 1973, and McCawley, 1978). Semi-indirect discourse, like direct quotation, uses main clause word order and various other main clause features, but shifts pronouns and tenses according to the rules of indirect discourse. This is seen clearly with questions:

(38)   I asked him would he hurry.[2]

(Direct quotation would give something like "I asked him, 'Would you hurry?'," whereas indirect discourse would be "I asked him if/whether he would hurry.") Particles like well, yes, and so on, which are generally used to introduce main clauses, also find their way into semi-indirect discourse

(39)   They told me that yes, they would consider it.

as do exclamatory particles, with or without special exclamatory word order:

(40)   After six months she realized that boy, had *she* made a mistake!

Finally, intonation contours clearly belonging to the original main clause are also found in semi-indirect discourse, e.g.,

(41)   She asked me hadn't I ever read *Sound Pattern of English* and I said ,yeah, I ,had.

(The original reply was ",Yeah, I ,have.")

(42)   I told him "no, of "course I wouldn't.

(The semi-indirect quote preserves the intonational emphasis of the original ""No, of "course I won't.")

These intonational examples provide still another example of the notion of compatibility of point of view: when I am quoting myself, I can readily shift back to the point of view that I myself had at the time of the reported conversation, by directly reporting my own intonation. More difficult, but still possible, is to report directly the intonation of a third person participant in the dialogue:

(43)   ? I asked her hadn't she ever read *Sound Pattern of English* and she said ,yeah, she ,had.

This gives a vividness to the report as the speaker shifts back and forth between the two points of view. However, if one of the participants in the quoted dialogue is second person—i.e., the addressee in the present speech situation—the direct reporting of intonation sounds very odd:

(44)   ?? I asked you hadn't you ever read *Sound Pattern of English* and you said ,yeah, you ,had.

---

[2]From *Nathan LaFraneer*, by Joni Mitchell, copyright 1969 by Siquomb Music.

My intent in reiterating a dialogue between you and me is likely to be to make a point; given that, I am unlikely to express *your* point of view any more vividly than is necessary. Reporting your intonation in semi-indirect discourse thus involves incompatibility of points of view, and the effect of the whole sentence is rather strange.

SUMMARY

The arguments of the paper can be summarized very briefly. I have presented a variety of data that in one way or another involve the partial exclusion from subordinate clauses of certain constructions, intonation contours, and lexical items. Sometimes it is the item itself that is excluded; sometimes there is only a constraint on possible interpretations. This list of items so affected is not limited to the mysterious MCP, but includes intonation contours, inserted taboo words, and even simple deictics like this and that. I have argued that what these have in common is that in some way they convey a point of view, and that what we need to account for such phenomena is not a conglomeration of syntactic rules referring to specific transformations, but rather a principle that points of view in a sentence must be compatible.

In order to apply such a principle, of course, we need to determine what the points of view expressed by any given sentence *are*. This, it seems to me—and here I concur with Green and Bolinger—is a problem of fine lexical and pragmatic analysis. For intonation, such analysis is exemplified in recent work by the two Liberman and Sag papers already cited, and by my own work (Ladd, 1977a); the general ''lexical'' approach to intonation contours goes back at least to Pike (1945) (but see Cutler, 1977, for a critical review). Close analysis of other types of point-of-view items is presented in, for example, Gary, 1976 (a discussion of the use of certain preposing transformations), and Lakoff, 1972 (the discussion of the modals may, should, and must), as well as Green's and Bolinger's discussions of their various examples.

In any case, there is a limit to what syntax can tell us about MCP and intonation, and about point-of-view in general. Detailed explanations of these phenomena cannot be given in terms of general syntactic or logical principles alone, but only in conjunction with detailed knowledge about the meaning and function of the particular intonation contour, stylistic device, or lexical item whose behavior we are trying to account for. In Bolinger's words (1977, p. 511), "broad questions must be answered case by case."

REFERENCES

Banfield, A. 1973. Narrative style and the grammar of direct and indirect speech. Foundat. Lang. 10:10–40.

Bolinger, D. L. 1977. Another glance at main clause phenomena. Language 53:511–519.

Cutler, A. 1977. The context-dependence of "intonational meanings." In: Papers from the 13th Regional Meeting of the Chicago Linguistic Society, pp. 104–115. Department of Linguistics, University of Chicago.

Gary, N. 1976. A Discourse Analysis of Certain Root Transformations in English. Indiana University Linguistic Club Reprint, Bloomington.

Glenn, M. 1977. The pragmatic function of intonation. Paper presented at the Annual Meeting of the LSA, Chicago.

Gragg, G. 1972. Semi-indirect discourse and related nightmares. In: Papers from the 8th Regional Meeting of the Chicago Linguistic Society, pp. 75–82. Department of Linguistics, University of Chicago.

Green, G. 1976. Main clause phenomena in subordinate clauses. Language 52:382–397.

Hooper, J., and Thompson, S. 1973. On the applicability of root transformations. Ling. Inq. 4:469–498.

Jakobson, R. 1971. Shifters, verbal categories, and the Russian verb. In: R. Jakobson, Selected Writings, Vol. 2, Word & Language. Mouton & Co., The Hague.

Kingdon, R. 1958. The Groundwork of English Intonation. Longmans, London.

Ladd, D. R., Jr. 1977a. The Function of the A-Rise Accent in English. Indiana University Linguistics Club Reprint, Bloomington.

Ladd, D. R., Jr. 1977b. Intonation: Around the Edge of Language? Paper presented at the Annual Meeting of the LSA, Chicago.

Ladd, D. R., Jr. The Structure of Intonational Meaning: Evidence from English. Indiana University Press, Bloomington. In press.

Lakoff, R. 1972. Language in context. Language 48:907–927.

Liberman, M., and Sag, I. 1974. Prosodic form and discourse function. In: Papers from the 10th Regional Meeting of the Chicago Linguistic Society, pp. 416–427. Department of Linguistics, University of Chicago.

McCawley, N. A. 1977. What is the "emphatic root transformation" phenomenon? In: Papers from the 13th Regional Meeting of the Chicago Linguistic Society, pp. 384–400. Department of Linguistics, University of Chicago.

McCawley, N. A. 1978. Epistemology and Japanese syntax: Complementizer choice. In: Papers from the 14th Regional Meeting of the Chicago Linguistic Society. Department of Linguistics, University of Chicago.

O'Connor, J. D., and Arnold, J. F. 1961. Intonation of Colloquial English. Longmans, London.

Pike, K. 1945. The Intonation of American English. University of Michigan Press, Ann Arbor.

Quang Phuc Dong. 1969. Phrases Anglaises sans sujet grammatical apparent. Langages 14:41–55.

Sag, I., and Liberman, M. 1975. The intonational disambiguation of indirect speech acts. In: Papers from the 11th Regional Meeting of the Chicago Linguistic Society, pp. 487–497. Department of Linguistics, University of Chicago.

Schubiger, M. 1965. English intonation and German modal particles: A comparative study. Phonetica 12:65–84. Reprinted in D. L. Bolinger (ed.). 1972. Intonation, pp. 175–193. Penguin Books, Baltimore.

Wakefield, D. 1973. Starting Over. Delacorte Press, New York.

12/ A Point about the Rise-Endings and Fall-Endings of Yes-No Questions
W. R. Lee

It is now fairly generally recognized that yes-no questions in English (i.e., questions that can be answered by yes or no, although they can also be answered otherwise) do not necessarily end with an intonation rise (as in "Do you ‚know him?''), although considering all contexts of occurrence this may be the commonest ending for questions of this type. They can also end in other ways, not uncommonly in an intonation fall (as in "Do you ‚know him?'').[1]

It is not altogether clear in what circumstances a fall-ending is chosen rather than a rise-ending, and vice versa. Various suggestions have been made. Crystal (1969, pp. 3-4), for instance, believes that the difference lies in "the type of attitude involved,'' the rise-ending being "more friendly and interested,'' so long as other factors (such as stress, speed, and facial expression) are equal (see also Uldall, 1964). According to Lee (1956, p. 361, 1960, p.33), a fall-ending "tends to give a firmer and more insistent effect,'' resembling that of a command, whereas a rise-ending tends to suggest "sympathy and politeness.'' Schubiger (1958, p. 63), exemplifying various intonation patterns used in asking yes-no questions, describes questions such as "'Do you ‚know the prisoner?'' and "'Did you 'find my ‚camera?'' as "curt,'' having a "tone of cross-examination''; she includes among the examples the sort of questions that can follow one another in a guessing game—"'Is it ‚green?'' "Can we ‚eat it?'' and so on.

Does the choice between the two types of ending depend solely on the speaker's attitude? Does it depend on the kind of impression he wishes to make on others? Or are there perhaps other factors at work here that have little to do with attitude or feeling? For instance, could there be a connection

---

[1]C. C. Fries (1964), analyzing a large number of American broadcast panel-games containing only "yes-no'' questions, found that over 60% of these questions had a fall-ending.

between the frequency with which yes-no questions occur in stretches of speech (what one might call their "density") and the end intonations used? Fries, after all, confined his observations to television and radio programs of a kind in which "one may reasonably expect a large concentration of the type of expression that is to be the special subject of the investigation" (Fries, 1964, p. 245).

In order to make a preliminary investigation of this possibility, recordings were made of two distinct types of radio program: (A), in which yes-no questions occur frequently and with very little intervening material, and (B), in which there are few yes-no questions and these on the whole are widely separated by other forms of utterance, such as questions of another kind and lengthy answers.

A single long "Any Questions" program, that lasted over 20 minutes (BBC 4, 1 August, 1973) was recorded under (A), and under (B) were recorded extensive sections of a "Round Britain Quiz" that lasted a similar period of time (BBC 4, 1 August, 1973), an "Any Answers" program that lasted for about 10 minutes (BBC 4, 2 August, 1973), an "Any Questions" program of a different type that lasted more than 20 minutes, and a program called "It's Your Line" that lasted for about 10 minutes [BBC 4, 1973, (exact date not given)]. In the first "Any Questions" program a team of panelists had to guess a word or phrase of which the listeners were aware (e.g., "paddle-steamer," "a serenade," "Michael Flanders"); they did so by asking questions, almost exclusively of a yes-no type. The "Round Britain Quiz" consisted of the answering, again by a panel, of difficult general knowledge questions put by a question-master (e.g., "Can you tell me who were the Roman Emperors of whom these ladies were the wives?"). The questions in this broadcast came chiefly from the question-master, were usually separated by speculation on the part of the panelists, and were mainly of the "information" (wh-) type (e.g., "Where will you find this inscribed, and in memory of whom?"). In the second "Any Questions" program political and social questions (e.g., "What does the panel consider should be done to combat the ever-increasing problem of truancy in our schools today, and has the raising of the school leaving-age contributed to this problem?") were answered by a panel of well-known public figures; various types of questions occurred in this broadcast, the yes-no questions generally being separated considerably from one another. In "Any Answers" members of a panel expressed their opinions, at considerable length, on a variety of topical controversies mentioned by listeners; there were few questions and these were of various types. Finally, in "It's Your Line" listeners telephoned questions (about pension rights) to a small panel of experts; various question types occurred, but there was no close succession of yes-no questions.

The straightforward yes-no questions were extracted from this corpus of speech. All indistinct passages were ignored, and tag questions were not counted. Long yes-no questions were included as well as short, but only the end intonation (i.e., a fall on the last strongly stressed syllable or a rise starting from it) was taken into account. "Part sentences" (e.g., ",North of England?") were included. Questions taking the form of a statement (e.g., "It's actually a ,building?") were included when it was obvious that a reply was expected. A question repeated in identical words (e.g., ",Wales?"/ ",Wales?" or "A ,job?"/"A ,job?") was counted as two occurrences, whether or not the intonation was changed. "Repeated questions" (as in "Fancy it being a him."/",Is it a him?"), of which there was only one, were not included.

Separate counts were made of the occurrences of "yes-no" questions in (A) and (B). The results were as follows:

(A): 119 occurrences of "yes-no" questions
      69 ending with a rise intonation
      50 ending with a fall intonation
(B): 45 occurrences of "yes-no" questions
      25 ending with a rise intonation
      20 ending with a fall intonation

Thus where yes-no questions occurred very close together, forming the bulk of the material, about 42% of them ended in a fall intonation, while the rest (with the exception of two that had a fall-rise) ended in a rise intonation.[2] On the other hand, where yes-no questions did not occur close together, but were on the whole widely separated by other material, nearly half of the occurrences had a fall-ending.

The present investigator expected the opposite result, having assumed, although without much evidence to go on, that where questions of any given type were numerous and frequent there might be a tendency to vary the intonation ending in order to avoid a monotonous effect.[3] Of course, this factor may still be at work in both sets of material: only a fine analysis of *all* of the intonation patterns used in the whole material of the corpus could hope to indicate that. The first purpose of such an analysis might be to establish whether or not a given intonation pattern, no matter what the type of grammatical unit, tended to avoid *exact* recurrence in proportion to the

---

[2]These figures are very different from those arrived at by C. C. Fries (1964), who, analyzing a similar corpus, found that 61.7% of yes-no questions had a fall-ending.

[3]The investigation by Fries (1964) did perhaps suggest, even if not very definitely, that this may be so.

number of times it occurred, so that what might possibly be called an aesthetic factor was at work, as well as other factors that may help to give the stream of speech its intonational configuration. Such observations would, of course, have to be based on a very large corpus of material, and there would be considerable difficulty in carrying them out.

Admittedly, also, the present sample is a comparatively small one, the intention being only to make a preliminary probe. Possibly a larger corpus of (B) text would reveal a different ratio of rise-endings to fall-endings. A similar alternation is, of course, to be observed in "general" (wh-) questions, and it would doubtless be helpful to put that on a statistical basis too.

REFERENCES

Crystal, D. 1969. Prosodic Systems and Intonation in English. Cambridge University Press, Cambridge, England.
Fries, C. C. 1964. On the intonation of "yes-no" questions. In: D. Abercrombie et al. (eds.), In Honour of Daniel Jones, pp. 242–254. Longmans, London.
Lee, W. R. 1956. English intonation: A new approach. Lingua 4:361.
Lee, W. R. 1960. An English Intonation Reader. Macmillan, London.
Schubiger, M. 1958. English Intonation—Its Form and Function. Niemeyer Verlag, Tübingen.
Uldall, E. 1964. Dimensions of meaning in intonation. In: D. Abercrombie et al. (eds.), In Honour of Daniel Jones. Longmans, London.

13/ Interaction between Test Word Duration and Length of Utterance

Ilse Lehiste

The present paper is part of a general study of speech prosody in which I have been engaged for a number of years. The study concerns itself primarily with durational aspects of spoken English. The specific topic discussed below is the interaction between test word duration and length of utterance.

It has been found that, in Swedish and Dutch, the duration of a syllable nucleus decreases as the number of syllables that remain to be produced in the word at the beginning of the syllable concerned increases. Lindblom and Rapp (1972), analyzing nonsense words uttered in isolation by speakers of Swedish, found that the durations of stressed long vowels ranged from about 350 milliseconds in monosyllables to about 200 milliseconds when three syllables followed. Analyzing nonsense words spoken in isolation by Dutch informants, Nooteboom (1972) observed durations of long vowels ranging from more than 200 milliseconds in monosyllables to about 100 milliseconds in the first syllable of words with four syllables. The question naturally arises of whether the phenomenon is restricted to word level, or the principle might apply at the level of sentences. A further question that seems worthy of exploration is that of whether or not the results might conceivably be different if semantically acceptable words are used instead of nonsense words. Partial answers to both questions are presented in this paper.

Four sets of test words were used in the study. Two of the sets were similar to those used by Lindblom and Rapp and by Nooteboom. These lists consisted of monosyllabic, disyllabic, and trisyllabic words made up of the syllables *big* and *bag* in one list and *bick* and *back* in the other list. All

This study has been supported by the National Science Foundation under Grant GS-31494 #2. A preliminary version of this paper was presented at the 86th meeting of the Acoustical Society of America, October 30, 1973, Los Angeles.

possible stress placements were represented. The lists contained 34 words each. The third list contained 34 English words, selected to match the described nonsense words with regard to syllable length and stress placement. The fourth list (subdivided into 4a and 4b) contained 10 words in which the unstressed syllable *be* was combined with the stressed syllables *big* and *bag* in disyllabic and trisyllabic words, and 10 similar words in which the unstressed syllable *be* was combined with the stressed syllables *bick* and *back*. List 4 thus comprised 20 words; all four lists together contained 122 words.

These test words were placed in three frames: a short frame ("Say _____ instead"), and two long frames in which the test word appeared either near the beginning of the utterance or near its end. The first long frame was "Sometimes its useful to say the word _____ instead." The second long frame was "The word _____ is sometimes a useful example." In the short frame and the first long frame, the test words were thus at an equal distance from the end of the utterance. However, in the short frame they were preceded by one syllable, and in the long frame by nine syllables. In the second long frame, the test words were preceded by two syllables and followed by nine syllables.

The lists of words were read by three informants in the three given frames. Each informant produced 366 utterances, for a total of 1098 utterances. The informants were graduate students familiar with recording equipment and used to a laboratory environment. The recordings were made in an anechoic chamber, processed through a Frøkjaer-Jensen trans-pitch meter and intensity meter, and displayed on a Mingograf operated at a speed of 10 centimeters per second. Measurements were made from Mingograms using generally known techniques. The duplex oscillograms produced by the experimental setup served as the principal basis for segmentation.

Since the main concern of the present study is the interaction between word duration and length of utterance, the duration of syllable nuclei within the different syllables of the test words is not treated in this context. The basic units are frames and word lists. Average word durations are reported for each list; it should be kept in mind that words of one, two, and three syllables have been averaged together within each list, and the average word duration for a given list is thus a somewhat abstract concept.

Tables 1, 2, and 3 present the average durations of the test words in the four lists as a function of the length of the frame. (Figure 1 summarizes the information for the three speakers.) In the tables, List 4 is separated into 4a (containing stressed syllables with voiced final plosives) and 4b (containing stressed syllables with voiceless final plosives). A representative disyllabic word is given at the top of each column to illustrate the word types contained in each list.

Table 1.   Average durations, in milliseconds, of test words produced in three frames by speaker SG

	List 1 words	List 2 (bigbag)	List 3 (bickback)	List 4a (bebig)	List 4b (bebick)
Frame 1: Sometimes it's useful to say the word _____ instead	541	656	663	567	558
Frame 2: The word _____ is sometimes a useful example	551	668	701	563	528
Frame 3: Say _____ instead	586	755	761	607	601

A general observation may be made concerning the data for all three speakers: test words tended to be longest in the frame "Say _____ instead." For speakers SG and LS, this was the case for all lists; for speaker PM, the test words were longest in the frame "Say _____ instead" in two out of four instances. In this frame as well as in the frame "Sometimes it's useful to say the word _____ instead," the test words were followed by the same word, "instead." If the duration of the words depends on the number of syllables that remain to be produced in the utterance, test words should have the same duration in both frames. However, with only one exception (out of 12 instances), test words were found to be longer in the frame "Say _____ instead." It seems obvious that the number of syllables remaining to be produced in the utterance does not fully determine the duration of the test words.

Table 2.   Average durations, in milliseconds, of test words produced in three frames by speaker LS

	List 1 words	List 2 (bigbag)	List 3 (bickback)	List 4a (bebig)	List 4b (bebick)
Frame 1: Sometimes it's useful to say the word _____ instead	546	575	584	477	470
Frame 2: The word _____ is sometimes a useful example	537	565	571	463	496
Frame 3: Say _____ instead	562	658	615	534	532

Table 3.   Average durations, in milliseconds, of test words produced in three frames by speaker PM

	List 1 words	List 2 (bigbag)	List 3 (bickback)	List 4a (bebig)	List 4b (bebick)
Frame 1: Sometimes it's useful to say the word _____ instead	567	771	770	612	596
Frame 2: The word _____ is sometimes a useful example	599	862	806	624	614
Frame 3: Say _____ instead	539	842	831	663	639

The frame "The word _____ is sometimes a useful example" places the test words in a position in which nine syllables remain to be produced in the utterance. If the hypothesis to be tested holds, the test words should be shortest in this frame. This was true in one case out of four for speaker SG and in no instances for speaker PM. Only speaker LS had three cases out of four in which the test words were shortest in the frame in which the largest number of syllables follow the test word.

Individual variations are leveled off when all four lists and all three speakers are averaged together. Figure 1 shows the results graphically. The average durations, in milliseconds, are given inside the bars reproduced on the

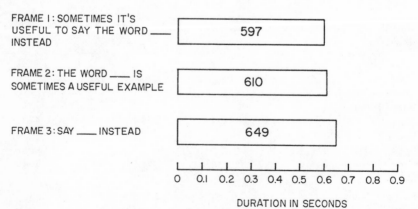

Figure 1.   Average duration of test words in different frames averaged for three speakers.

figure. The overall average duration of the test words was greatest in the frame "Say _____ instead," noticeably smaller in the frame "The word _____ is sometimes a useful example," and slightly smaller still in the frame "Sometimes it's useful to say the word _____ instead." This result appears somewhat paradoxical: if the hypothesis would hold, we would expect the words to have the same duration when only the word "instead" follows, and we would expect the words to be shortest in the frame in which nine syllables follow rather than two. Clearly the results cannot be explained in terms of the number of syllables that remain to be produced in the utterance.

Table 4.   Average durations, in milliseconds, of test words and frames in utterances produced by speaker SG

Frame and list	Duration of preceding part	Duration of word	Duration of following part	Total duration
Frame 1: Sometimes it's useful to say the word _____ instead				
words	1482	541	580	2603
bigbag	1470	656	509	2636
bickback	1460	663	506	2628
bebig	1467	567	559	2592
bebick	1478	558	540	2576
Overall average	1471	597	539	2607
Frame 2: The word _____ is sometimes a useful example				
words	233	551	1564	2348
bigbag	247	668	1545	2460
bickback	248	701	1566	2515
bebig	245	563	1598	2406
bebick	249	528	1603	2380
Overall average	244	602	1575	2421
Frame 3: Say _____ instead				
words	191	586	601	1379
bigbag	177	755	567	1499
bickback	197	761	606	1564
bebig	197	607	648	1452
bebick	197	601	611	1409
Overall average	192	662	607	1461

Table 5.   Average durations, in milliseconds, of test words and frames in utterances
produced by speaker LS

Frame and list	Duration of preceding part	Duration of word	Duration of following part	Total duration
Frame 1: Sometimes it's useful to say the word ____ instead				
words	1629	546	574	2750
bigbag	1576	575	549	2701
bickback	1578	584	534	2696
bebig	1566	477	558	2600
bebick	1572	470	540	2582
Overall average	1584	531	551	2666
Frame 2: The word ____ is sometimes a useful example				
words	268	537	1588	2393
bigbag	253	565	1540	2358
bickback	223	571	1504	2298
bebig	239	463	1546	2248
bebick	238	496	1528	2262
Overall average	244	526	1541	2311
Frame 3: Say ____ instead				
words	216	562	603	1381
bigbag	204	658	601	1463
bickback	170	615	576	1361
bebig	183	534	623	1340
bebick	166	532	594	1292
Overall average	188	580	599	1367

The apparent paradox can be solved by looking at the duration of complete utterances. Tables 4, 5, and 6 present average durations of the frame as a function of test word type and list for each of the three speakers; Figure 2 summarizes the information for all three speakers and four lists.

For all three speakers, the duration of the whole utterance (comprising the test word and the frame) was shortest for "Say ____ instead," followed by "The word ____ is sometimes a useful example." When the word durations are averaged over the different lists, the duration of the words is inversely correlated with the length of the total utterance, so that the test words appear longest in the shortest utterance ("Say ____ instead") and shortest in the longest utterance ("Sometimes it's useful to say the word _____ instead"). This observation is supported by the fact that the duration of the word "instead" is likewise inversely correlated with the length of the utterance: in the short utterance, the duration of "instead" is greater by approximately 50 milliseconds, which is a difference of the same order of magnitude as was found for the test words.

The results of the study thus indicate that the duration of test words depends on the total duration of the utterance rather than on the position of the test word within the utterance. A number of other conclusions may be drawn from these results.

Table 6.   Average durations, in milliseconds, of test words and frames in utterances produced by speaker PM

Frame and list	Duration of preceding part	Duration of word	Duration of following part	Total duration
Frame 1: Sometimes it's useful to say the word _____instead				
words	1760	567	529	2856
bigbag	1612	771	506	2889
bickback	1619	770	486	2875
bebig	1638	612	498	2748
bebick	1608	596	478	2682
Overall average	1647	663	499	2809
Frame 2: The word _____ is sometimes a useful example				
words	277	599	1647	2523
bigbag	301	862	1664	2827
bickback	298	806	1666	2770
bebig	312	624	1677	2613
bebick	298	614	1674	2586
Overall average	297	701	1665	2663
Frame 3: Say _____ instead				
words	181	539	549	1269
bigbag	194	842	525	1561
bickback	185	831	503	1519
bebig	175	663	544	1382
bebick	164	639	548	1351
Overall average	180	703	534	1417

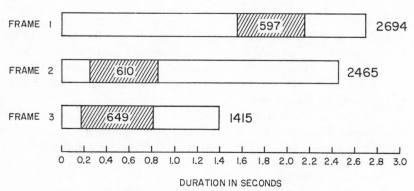

Figure 2.   Average duration of test utterances, averaged for three speakers.

I have often heard the comment that test words produced in a frame are really treated by the speakers as if they were produced in isolation, and that the use of frame sentences to simulate real utterances is at best a self-deception. I would have been convinced of that if the duration of the test words had turned out to be completely independent of the duration of the frames in which the test words were embedded. The way that the duration of the test words seems to interact with the duration of the frames shows clearly that the speakers integrate the test words into the utterance at the level at which the time program for the whole sentence is generated.

The test word lists used in this study contained both real English words and words made up of nonsense syllables. As far as interaction with the duration of the frames is concerned, there was no difference in the treatment of real words and nonsense words; both were integrated with the frame in the same way. Thus the study has also produced some evidence that, at least for the investigation of the durational aspects of speech, the use of frame sentences and nonsense words may be considered justified.

REFERENCES

Lindblom, B., and Rapp, K. 1972. Reexamining the compensatory adjustment of vowel duration in Swedish words. University of Essex Occasional Papers 13, pp. 204–224. University of Essex, Colchester, Eng.

Nooteboom, S. G. 1972. Production and Perception of Vowel Duration: A Study of Durational Properties of Vowels in Dutch. Utrecht, the Netherlands.

14/ Des Accents

P. R. Léon et Ph. Martin

Dwight Bolinger (1970), dans une remarquable étude, dégage le rôle de la hauteur mélodique dans le système prosodique de l'anglais, particulièrement dans la structuration des accents. Nous tentons ici, selon une démarche analogue, d'examiner en particulier pour le français, le fonctionnement et la distribution de trois types d'accents. Nous garderons, pour éviter de compliquer la terminologie, les appellations traditionnelles que l'on donne aux deux premiers de ces accents: 1) accent *tonique,* et 2) accent d'*insistance.* Nous conviendrons d'appeler le troisième type d'accent accent *émotif.*

Ces accents, en particulier les deux premiers, ont été étudiés par de nombreux chercheurs, parmi lesquels il faut citer, particulièrement pour le français, Paul Garde (1968), André Rigault (1962, 1970), Fernand Carton (1972) André Séguinot (1977), Ivan Fónagy et Pierre Léon (1979), Léon et Rossi (à paraître), et Philippe Martin (1979). Pour l'anglais, on trouvera, dans une optique voisine, une autre étude essentielle de la question par Bolinger (1965).

DÉFINITIONS

Le rôle de l'accent *tonique* est de permettre un découpage de l'énoncé en unités de sens. D'où la fonction *démarcative* attribuée par les linguistes à ce type d'accent (Martinet, 1960). La place de l'accent dans l'unité accentuable est déterminée dans le système de la langue. On peut montrer d'autre part (Martin, 1976) que la caractère d'accentuabilité d'une unité est lié aux relations de dépendance (i.e., de présupposition syntaxique) contractées par cette unité. Pour des langues comme le français, la réalisation effective de l'accent peut de plus faire l'objet d'un choix du locuteur, qui est libre d'accentuer ou non l'unité accentuable.

Quant à l'accent d'*insistance* il est presque toujours décrit en bloc avec l'accent *émotif.* C'est ainsi que Martinet (1960) englobe les deux accents dans une même définition fonctionnelle:

> Une autre fonction phonologique est la fonction expressive qui est celle qui renseigne l'auditeur sur l'état d'esprit du locuteur sans que celui-ci ait recours, pour cette fin, au schéma de la double articulation. C'est ainsi qu'en français, un

allongement et un renforcement du /p/ d'*impossible* dans *cet enfant est impossible* peut être interprété comme l'indication d'une irritation réele ou feint (p. 52).

Il est bien évident que dans l'exemple cité, la mise en relief du mot *impossible* n'implique pas forcément la manifestation d'une émotivité particulière. Il semble qu'on puisse opérer une distinction entre un accent d'*insistance* et un accent *émotif* en envisageant des critères à la fois fonctionnels et distributionnels.

CRITÈRES FONCTIONNELS ET DISTRIBUTIONNELS DES ACCENTS D'INSISTANCE ET DES ACCENTS ÉMOTIFS

L'accent d'*insistance* assure la mise en relief, sans expressivité speciale, d'un monème lexical ou grammatical. Il porte sur une unité inférieure ou égale au syntagme. Le locuteur dispose, dans le système de la langue, de plusieurs procédés parmi lesquels il effectue librement un choix.

L'accent émotif indique l'état affectif réel ou simulé du locuteur. Quant à sa place, Bolinger (1970) pour l'anglais, et Léon (1970) pour le français, arrivent aux mêmes conclusions: l'accent émotif n'est pas localisé mais s'étend à l'ensemble de l'énoncé.[1] On peut schématiser ainsi les unités sur lesquelles portent les trois types d'accent:

```
Enoncé   ##  _____  ##  accent émotif
Syntagme ##  _____ # _____ # _____ # _____ ## accent tonique
(i.e., unité
minimale
accentuable)
Monème   -----  -----  -----  -----  ##   accent d'instance
(syllabe)
```

Cette hiérarchie entre les trois types d'accents ressort clairement d'exemples d'analyses empruntées au français et semble également pouvoir être étendue à d'autres systèmes linguistiques. A un premier niveau, l'expressivité se manifeste sur la totalité de l'énoncé; c'est ainsi que le patron prosodique de la tristesse s'oppose en bloc au patron de la joie. A un second niveau, la démarcation s'effectue en groupes de sens, découpés par les accents *toniques*. A un troisième niveau, l'accent d'insistance peut se manifester pratiquement sur n'importe quel monème.

Si l'accent d'insistance paraît susceptible d'affecter n'importe quelle unité de l'énoncé, cependant sont exclues, en français, certaines catégories grammaticales comme les pronoms atones (M. Léon, 1972). Il faut toutefois

---

[1] Ce sont donc des paramètres globaux, concernant l'ensemble de l'énoncé, qui seront utilisés dans des systèmes de reconnaissance automatique des émotions, par exemple (cf. Martin, 1972b).

noter que des procédés d'insistance peuvent apparaître même dans ce cas. Il s'agit alors soit d'une insistance au niveau phrastique coïncidant, par hasard, avec le pronom atone, soit d'une fonction métalinguistique. L'auditeur qui répète son message, peut l'expliciter en soulignant un élément quelconque. Ainsi pourra-t-il dire: "Je n'ai pas dit elle va partir mais il va partir" en failsant ressortir emphatiquement un il, autrement atone, qu'il veut opposer à elle.

L'insistance peutêtre marquée également par la présence d'un contour mélodique spécifique qui ne fonctionne pas nécessairement toujours comme marque d'insistance.

Ainsi dans:

C'est Pierre qui est venu.

réponse à la question "Qui est venu?", et pourvue d'un contour mélodique long et descendant sur l'unité Pierre, l'insistance vient de la mise en opposition paradigmatique de cet énoncé avec, par exemple, "C'est Paul qui est venu." Il s'agit là en fait d'un cas de division de la phrase en propos ("c'est Pierre") et thème ("qui est venu"), division indiquée par la même marque prosodique que celle utilisée pour signaler le propos ("il est venu") et le thème ("Pierre") dans la phrase

Il est venu, Pierre.

qui est, elle, dépourvue d'insistance.

Si, en dehors de la fonction métalinguistique, certains outils grammaticaux ne portent jamais d'accent d'insistance, c'est sans doute parce que d'autres procédés de mise en relief existent dans le système. Le refus de la langue de permettre l'emploi de je, il, etc., avec insistance, vient probablement de l'existence de formes toniques correspondantes (moi, lui, etc.) et de constructions syntaxiques emphatiques du type "c'est moi qui," "c'est lui qui," etc.

Dans les cas où une forme emphatique grammaticale n'est pas disponible, l'accent d'insistance peut s'appliquer à des unités linguistiques a priori aussi peu accentuables que l'article défini, comme dans la femme dans: la femme éternelle et le pâté du chef.

DISTRIBUTION DES ACCENTS

L'accent émotif n'est évidemment pas susceptible d'une localisation particulière. En français standard, l'accent tonique est considéré comme placé sur la dernière voyelle prononcée. En réalité, de nombreaux facteurs de variation entrent en jeu: influences de substrats dialectaux, sociolectaux, et stylistiques.

Ainsi, la perception de l'accent tonique s'est révélée ambiguë dans 50% des cas pour un groupe de 34 locuteurs, représentant une douzaine de régions différentes; cela dans un groupe social relativement homogène et dans une même situation de communication, celle de l'interview (Léon et Léon, 1979). D'autre part, Fónagy (1979) a pu montrer, sur une période d'observation de 30 ans, les déplacements d'accents en cours et la formation de nouveaux schèmes accentuels en français.

Quant à l'accent d'insistance, la plupart des linguistes supposent qu'il affecte la *consonne initiale* de mot. En réalité, cet accent peut s'appliquer à une seule syllabe, comme dans:

for - midable

ou à toutes les syllabes du mot, comme dans:

i - ni - ma - gi - nable

où le locuteur détache chaque syllabe; d'autre part, lorsque l'accent ne concerne qu'une syllabe, la proéminence ne porte pas forcément sur la syllabe initiale. On relève ainsi, en français, des exemples tels que: ahurissant, immensément, etc., à côté de ahurissant, immensément. A l'intérieur d'un même monème, la variabilité de la place de l'accent d'insistance suggère qu'il s'agit là d'un procédé essentiellement intellectuel, contrôlé aux deux niveaux: 1) du *contenu* (n'importe quel monème peut être affecté), et 2) de l'*expression* (n'importe quel phonème peut être marqué). Il semble, à ce sujet, que la question de Jules Marouzeau (1924–1945) de savoir si l'accent d'insistance peut être affectif ou intellectuel est un faux problème, comme l'a bien montré Séguinot (1977).

Les trois types d'accents sont, à des degrés divers, des phénomènes de *nature* contrastive. Les uns comme les autres utilisent les mêmes paramètres (intensité, durée, hauteur, qualité), mais selon une combinatoire différente. L'accent tonique utilise surtout la *durée vocalique,* l'accent d'insistance l'*intensité* consonantique, et l'accent émotif le *registre* mélodique.

L'accent tonique, obéissant aux contraintes linguistiques du système, offre le moins de variétés de réalisations. On pourrait s'imaginer que l'accent émotif, parce que d'origine physiologique, présente des caractères communs dans toutes les langues. En réalité, il est semiconventionnalisé (Fónagy, 1971), et ses traits semblent fixés en un certain nombre de patrons prosodiques nettement déterminés (Léon, 1976). Ainsi les paramètres physiologiques de la colère, qui dénotent un manque de contrôle de la pression sousglottique résultant en sautes d'intensités et de hauteur—se retrouvent selon un patron stylisé dans l'expression de l'impatience, sentiment qu'on pourrait définir comme une colère socialisée (Léon, 1974). Quant à l'accent d'insistance, il peut être effectué par un accroissement des paramètres d'intensité, de durée, et de hauteur, en privilégiant l'un d'entre eux ou plusieurs à la fois. On constate en outre que cet accent se réalise souvent par un coup de glotte, lui-même précédé d'une pause, les deux formant une joncture démarcative, typique de ce procédé expressif (Léon, 1971). La pause de type théâtral peut également apparaître comme procédé d'insistance dans le style à suspense.

S'il arrive que l'accent d'insistance vienne à coïncider avec l'accent tonique, la réalisation de la proéminence demande un effort supplémentaire qui peut expliquer le faible rendement fonctionnel de l'insistance dans cette position.

La *répartition* des accents et de leur divers types de réalisation dépend non seulement de facteurs individuels mais plus encore semble-t-il de facteurs sociaux. Ainsi l'accent d'insistance marqué par un coup de glotte dénote-t-il presque toujours un *style* intellectuel alors que les contrastes intonatifs signalent le plus souvent une parlure snob. Dans une étude sur la répartition d'une variété d'accent d'insistance la joncture démarcative, considérée comme indice socioculturel, on aboutit au classement suivant (Léon, 1971):

1.	M.D.	Directeur de musée	17%
2.	G.M.	Peintre abstrait	16%
3.	H.B.	Romancier	10%
4.	A.T.	Romancier	10%
5.	G.C.	Romancier	10%
6.	G.B.	Peintre	4%
7.	M.X.	Commerçant	3%
8.	M.B.	Couturier	2%
9.	M.T.	Sportif	2%
10.	J.V.	Chanteur	0%

(Dans ce tableau, les chiffres indiquent le pourcentage des mots du discours affectés d'un accent d'insistance à l'initiale).

Des schèmes accentuels caractéristiques du parler de sociolectes particuliers ou de situations de communication se constituent sous l'influence de facteurs expressifs comme ceux qu'on vient de signaler. L'accent tonique peut alors disparaître et se confondre avec l'accent d'insistance. Plusieurs systèmes peuvent se superposer où il est bien difficile de démêler les fonctions démarcatives, culminatives, et expressives. On en a montré plusieurs cas particulièrement probants (Léon et Léon, 1979). Il est fort probable que le cas n'est pas spécial au français, qui se comporte alors comme une langue à accent libre.

Y A-T-IL DES UNIVERSAUX DE L'ACCENTUATION?

Une expérience à caractère très limité, a été tentée, en prenant pour corpus plusieurs langues différentes (anglais, français, polonais, et ukrainien).

On a demandé à un petit groupe d'étudiants de l'Université de Toronto de lire trois fois une liste de phrases dans chacune des langues précitées: une première lecture d'une manière naturelle et aussi neutre que possible; une deuxième lecture mettant en relief un monème particulier, une troisième lecture signalant l'impatience. On a enfin procédé à l'analyse instrumentale avec l'analyseur de mélodie du laboratoire de phonétique de Toronto (Martin, 1972a).

Nous n'entrerons pas ici dans le détail des résultats que nous résumons brièvement:

1. Pour l'accent d'insistance, bien que les exemples aient été proposés volontairement sous forme d'une lecture paradigmatique, nous avons constaté qu'un même locuteur n'utilise pas constamment un même procédé de mise en relief expressive.

2. L'accent émotif se réalise dans le cas précis de l'impatience, par une augmentation d'intensité, de fréquence du registre de la voix, et parfois d'une diminution de la durée de l'énoncé. Les variations d'intensité et de hauteur présentent, chaque fois et pour des langues différentes, un patron saccadé conforme au modèle attendu. Nous donnons ci-dessous (Figures 1 à 3) à titre d'illustration les patrons prosodiques d'une phrase "neutre" comparée à une même réalisation "impatiente" dans trois langues différentes.

Le nombre limité de nos exemples ne nous permet pas de tirer de conclusions définitives de cette comparaison entre des langues de structures aussi différentes. Toutefois, il semble bien, (ainsi que paraissent l'indiquer des

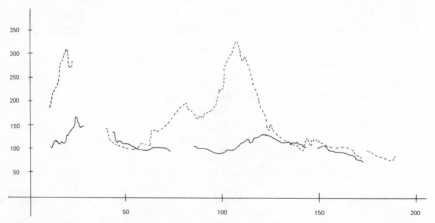

Figure 1.   Patrons prosodiques de l'énoncé anglais "neutre" (—) et "impatient" (---): "This dog was remarkably intelligent."

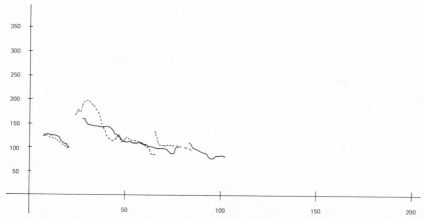

Figure 2.   Patrons prosodiques de l'énoncé gujarati "neutre" (—) et "impatient" (---): "ūtjadʒaūtʃū".

expériences plus complètes en cours de dépouillement), lorsqu'on compare des systèmes linguistiques différents, qu'il s'établisse une hiérarchie des structures selon le modèle suivant:

1. Les accents *toniques* se réalisent dans des limites de variations relativement étroites, structurées différemment selon chaque code linguistique (éventuellement de sous-codes discursifs).
2. Les accents d'*insistance* se réalisent dans des limites de variations beaucoup plus larges, qui dépendent de sous-codes sociaux et individuels,

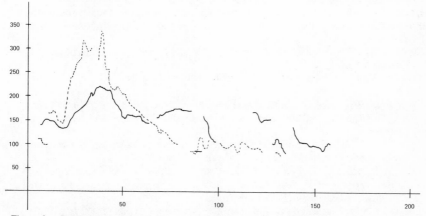

Figure 3.   Patrons prosodiques de l'énoncé polonais "neutre" (—) et "impatient" (---): "wiedzała że on jusz poszedł."

mais restent cependant tributaires des contraintes de chaque code linguistique.

3. Les accents *émotifs*, sans doute parce qu'ils restent motivés, présentent des patrons offrant de grandes similitudes d'une langue à l'autre.

Ces conclusions, toutes provisoires, rejoignent cependant celles d'un grand nombre de linguistes qui ont apporté une contribution à la question des universaux de la prosodie particulièrement, Dwight Bolinger (1964).

BIBLIOGRAPHIE

Bolinger, D. L. 1964. Intonation as a universal. Dans: H. Lunt (éd.), Proceedings of the 9th International Congress on Linguistics, Cambridge, Mass., 1962, pp. 833–949. Mouton & Co., The Hague.

Bolinger, D. 1965. Forms of English. Harvard University Press, Cambridge, Mass.

Bolinger, D. 1970. Relative height. Dans: Prosodic Feature Analysis, pp. 109–125. Studia Phonetica 3. Didier, Montréal-Paris-Bruxelles.

Carton, F. 1972. Recherches sur l'accentuation des parlers populaires dans la région de Lille. Service de reproduction des thèses, Université de Lille.

Fónagy, I. 1971. Le signe conventionnel motivé. La Linguistique 7:55–80.

Fónagy, I. 1979. L'accent français, accent probabilitaire. Dans: I. Fónagy et P. Léon (éds.), L'accent en Français Contemporain. Studia Phonetica. Didier, Montréal-Paris-Bruxelles.

Fónagy, I., et Léon, P. (éd.). 1979. L'accent en Français Contemporain. Studia Phonetica. Didier, Montréal-Paris-Bruxelles.

Fónagy, I., et Magdic, K. 1963. Emotional pattern in intonation and music. Z. Phonet. 16:293–326.

Garde, P. 1968. L'accent. Presses Universitaires de France, Paris.

Léon, M. 1972. L'accentuation des pronoms personnels en français standard. Studia Phonetica 5. Didier, Montréal-Paris-Bruxelles.

Léon, P. R. 1970. Systématique des fonctions expressives de l'intonation. Dans: Prosodic Feature Analysis. Studia Phonetica 3, pp. 57–74. Didier, Montréal-Paris-Bruxelles.

Léon, P. R. 1971. Essais de Phonostylistique. Studia Phonetica 4. Didier, Montréal-Paris-Bruxelles.

Léon, P. R. 1972. Patrons expressifs de l'intonation. Acta Univ. Carol. [Philolog.] 1:149–156.

Léon, P. R. 1974. Modalité impérative et intonation. Dans: World Papers in Phonetics: Festschrift for Dr. Onishi's Kiju, pp. 253–280. The Phonetics Society of Japan, Tokyo.

Léon, P. R. 1976. De l'analyse psychologique à la caractérisation auditive et acoustique des émotions dans la parole. J. Psychol. 3-4: 305–324.

Léon, P. R., et Léon, M. 1979. Observation sur l'accentuation des français régionaux. Dans: I. Fónagy et P. Léon (éds.), L'accent en Français Contemporain. Studia Phonetica. Didier, Montréal-Paris-Bruxelles.

Lucci, V. 1979. L'accent didactique. Dans: I. Fónagy et P. Léon (éds.), L'accent en Français Contemporain. Studia Phonetica. Didier, Montréal-Paris-Bruxelles.

Marouzeau, J. 1924–1925. Accent affectif et accent intellectuel. Bull. Soc. Ling. Paris XXV:80–86.

Martin, Ph. 1972a. L'analyseur de mélodie du laboratoire de phonétique expérimentale de l'Université de Toronto. Dans: Proceedings of the VIIth International Congress of Phonetic Sciences, pp. 1246–1248. Mouton & Co., The Hague.

Martin, Ph. 1972b. Reconnaissance automatique de patrons intonatifs. Acta Univ. Carol. [Philolog.] 1 [Phonetica Pragensia III, Prague 1972]: 77–81.

Martin, Ph. 1976. L'accentuation en français: Théorie présuppositionnelle. Rapport d'Activités de l'Institut de Phonétique ULB, Bruxelles 10/1, 1976, pp. 75–82. L'institut de Phonétique ULB, Bruxelles.

Martin, Ph. 1979. Une théorie syntaxique de l'accentuation en français. Dans: I. Fónagy et P. Léon (éds.), L'accent en Français Contemporain. Studia Phonetica. Didier, Montréal-Paris-Bruxelles.

Martinet, A. 1960. Eléments de linguistique générale. A. Colin, Paris.

Rigault, A. 1962. Rôle de la fréquence, de l'intensité et de la durée vocaliques dans la perception de l'accent en français. Dans: Proceedings of the 4th International Congress of Phonetic Sciences, Helsinki, pp. 735–748.

Rigault, A. 1970. L'accent dans deux langues à accent fixe: le français et le tchèque. Dans: Prosodic Feature Analysis. Studia Phonetica 3, pp. 1–12. Didier, Montréal-Paris-Bruxelles.

Séguinot, A. (éd.). 1977. L'accent d'insistance. Studia Phonetica 12. Didier, Montréal-Paris-Bruxelles.

15/ The Innate, Central Aspect of Intonation

Philip Lieberman

Intonation is a difficult aspect of human communication to study. The complex signals that involve the interplay of modulations of fundamental frequency, amplitude, the duration of various segments of the acoustic signal, and its spectral balance are difficult to quantify. Complex electronic instruments are necessary and their output is again difficult to interpret. Linguists have had almost as much difficulty at the syntactic and semantic levels. Traditional orthography records only part of the intonational signal and linguists differ among themselves regarding the particular intonations that should be ascribed to various utterances. The temptation naturally arises to ignore the role of intonation in human communication and to instead concentrate on the segmental elements. Intonation thus is relegated to the dim and shadowy area of "paralinguistics" or the "expression of emotion." The linguist need not pay very serious attention to intonation since it is not part of language. Intonation according to this view is supposed to be a chancy, variable element that is subject to the whims of uncontrolled "stylistic" variation. Different dialects and different speakers supposedly have different styles of intonation that are a function of the speakers' varying backgrounds and the effects of chance. The factors that structure intonation supposedly are part of the study of sociolinguistic variation or the as yet undefined study of performative variations. The factors that structure intonation thus have no relation to the "competence" that reflects innately determined language-specific neural mechanisms that are part of the endowment of all humans. The focus of this paper is that this view of the linguistic status of intonation is completely wrong.

I instead propose that intonation is a central, innately determined, and innately structured element of human language. I draw on a number of different studies that involve different experimental techniques. What all of these studies have in common is that they explore the physiology of intonation and thus involve functional approaches to the role of respiratory and muscular mechanisms in the control and production of intonation. These studies lead to the view that intonation is a central and basic element of human language in that it is structured in terms of some of the most basic vegetative constraints of human physiology. That is, intonational signals are structured to take advantage of the respiratory maneuvers that humans *must* effect in order to sustain life. At the phonetic level intonational signals are thus truly "unmarked," i.e., basic communicative signals. At the syntactic level the basic functions of intionational signals also appear to be tied to one of the most essential aspects of communication—segmentation—signaling the beginning and end of distinct messages that must be analyzed as syntactic units. Intonation segments the sentence-like sequences of words that form the data base for the sentences of formal grammar.

The physiologic mechanisms that structure intonation are determined in part by vegetative constraints. They thus are clearly not "language-specific" in the restricted sense that many linguists, psychologists, and philosophers view the structure of the hypothetical innately determined linguistic "competence" of *Homo sapiens*. I have argued elsewhere (Lieberman, 1973, 1975) that human language is not disjoint from other aspects of human behavior and the behavior of other animals. Human language, like all other aspects of human behavior, must be viewed as the result of a Darwinian process of natural selection that gradually developed from simpler communications systems. Intonation can be viewed as a basic and "primitive" element in human language in that the laryngeal and respiratory mechanisms that structure the segmenting aspects of human intonation are to be found in many other animals.

THE PHYSIOLOGY OF INTONATION

A short discussion of the larynx and the mechanism of phonation is essential to any discussion of the physiology of intonation. The activity of the larynx was first described by Ferrein (1741), who, however, made an incorrect assessment of the nature of the mechanism of phonation. Johannes Müller (1848) first correctly described the mechanism of phonation. Müller performed a number of experiments in which he induced phonation in excised human larynges by blowing air through them while he systematically adjusted the position and tension of the vocal cords. The larynx consists of a number of cartilages and muscles that support in a complex manner two "flaps" that themselves consist of cartilage, muscles, and ligaments. The term "vocal cords," which was first used by Ferrein, is really inappropriate, but so is the term "vocal folds," which is often used in medical texts. The vocal "cords" or "folds" can be pulled against the side of the ringlike thyroid and cricoid cartilages, leaving a relatively unobstructed air passage to the lungs through the larynx. This is the situation that is typical of quiet respiration. The vocal cords are opened as wide as they can be opened by a set of muscles called the posterior cricoarytenoids. These muscles are positioned in the back (posterior) part of the larynx and they go from the cricoid cartilage to the arytenoid cartilages. When they contract they swing the arytenoid cartilages that form part of each vocal cord backward and outward, opening the air passage between the two vocal cords. The open air passage between the vocal cords is called the glottis. The numerous muscles that can apply tension to the two vocal cords in their closed position all relax during this opening gesture, which is an essential aspect of respiration. The glottis obviously must open during respiration in order to admit air into and out of the lungs. This simple fact plays a crucial role in structuring the primary phonetic and syntactic aspects of intonation. The maximum size of the glottal opening during inspiration is also of interest since it bears on the fact that the human larynx, as well as those of many other animals, has adapted specifically for communication. (I return to discuss some of the evolutionary aspects of intonation later.)

Phonation is effected by swinging the two vocal cords together so that they obstruct or partially obstruct the air passage through the larynx. Muscles like the interarytenoids, which pull the arytenoid cartilages together as they contract, or the lateral cricoarytenoids are involved in adducting or closing the vocal cords. These muscles and others, such as the vocalis muscles (which form part of the body of each vocal cord), also apply a tension to each vocal cord. The vocal cords are thus positioned so that they obstruct the flow of air through the larynx and tensioned so that they resist movements from this "phonation neutral position." In other words, if a vocal cord is pushed away from this neutral position it will tend to return to the neutral position because of the tensions applied by the various muscles. The muscles of the larynx can apply greater or lesser tension to the vocal cords so that they will either be lax and relatively nonresistent to forces that perturb them from the neutral position or tense and resistent to perturbing forces. Müller noticed this in his investigations in the early part of the 19th century. The muscle that he paid most attention to was the cricothyroid muscle, which applies tension to the vocal cords by moving the cricoid and thyroid cartilages apart. Müller explored the activity of this muscle in great detail since it was most accessible with his experimental techniques. The vocal cords, however, are tensioned by a number of muscles that act either independently or in concert (Van den Berg, 1960; Atkinson, 1973). The net effect of these muscular maneuvers is the following process.

In order to achieve phonation the speaker closes the vocal cords and tensions them with some given degree of muscular force. The vocal cords are usually adducted after the speaker's lungs are full of air, i.e., after inspiration. The speaker then commences expiration and air flows out of the lungs through the larynx to the nose and mouth. The vocal cords are, however, obstructing the air passage through the larynx. The impeded flow of air thus exerts a force against the adducted vocal cords as the air pressure builds up against the obstruction. The vocal cords swing open as the force exerted by the air against the obstruction mounts and overcomes the tension applied by the laryngeal muscles. The glottal opening thus increases and air flows outward through the larynx. As the air flows outward through the glottis the static tension applied by the laryngeal muscles tends to restore the vocal cords to their closed "phonation neutral position." The closing force of the muscles is augmented by the Bernoulli force as air flows through the glottis. The Bernoulli force, which is essentially a consequence of the physical principle of the conservation of energy, generates an aerodynamic force that sucks the two vocal cords together (Lieberman, 1967). The Bernoulli force can be seen in action in everyday situations when newspapers accumulate between two closely sited buildings as the wind blows through the narrow passage between them. The Bernoulli force and the laryngeal muscles close the glottis. The cycle then repeats itself, since the opening force of the obstructed airstream is at its maximum when the glottis is closed. The Bernoulli force is, moreover, reduced to zero since no air is flowing through the closed larynx. Phonation thus is the result of a rapid alternation of opposing forces. One force, the aerostatic force of the obstructed airflow, tends to open and the other, the aerodynamic force generated by the airflow through the glottis, to close the glottis. The force exerted by the laryngeal muscles tends to augment the closing force. The net result is a series of "puffs of air" that issue from the larynx as the glottis rapidly opens and closes. The rate at which these puffs occur is the fundamental frequency of phonation. The perceptual correlate of the fundamental frequency of phonation is perceived pitch. The fundamental frequency of adult human males typically varies from about 70 to 200 Hz, i.e., 70 to 200 puffs of air per second. The fundamental frequencies of children and adult females can range to as high as 1500 Hz.

The lower average fundamental frequency of phonation of adult males is a consequence of secondary sexual dimorphism in *Homo sapiens*. The larynges of males usually grow disproportionately large during puberty. The vocal cords thus become larger and heavier and they therefore move more slowly, since the aerodynamic and aerostatic forces don't increase proportionately. The reason for the slower activity of the heavier vocal cords follows from Newton's laws of motion; since force = mass × acceleration, the acceleration of the vocal cords will be lower if the mass increases. Since velocity is equal to the integral of acceleration with respect to time, the velocity of the vocal cords will also be slower and they will open and close at slower rates, thereby yielding lower fundamental frequencies of phonation.

A given speaker can obviously vary the fundamental frequency of phonation by changing either the moving mass of vocal cords or the forces exerted on the vocal cords during phonation. The vibrating mass of the vocal cords can be changed by adjusting the laryngeal muscles that determine the vocal cords' phonation neutral position (Van den Berg, 1960). The fundamental frequency of phonation can also be adjusted by changing the magnitude of the forces and the balance of the forces that move the vocal cords during phonation. An increase in the air pressure exerted by the flow of air outward from the lungs obviously will increase the speed with which the vocal cords move open and shut, thereby raising the fundamental frequency of phonation. A decrease in this air pressure, the alveolar (the term refers to the lungs) air pressure, obviously will cause the fundamental frequency to fall. The human respiratory system readily allows adjustments in alveolar air pressure and speakers typically change fundamental frequency by this physiologic mechanism (Van den Berg, 1960; Lieberman, 1967; Atkinson, 1973). The other physiologic mechanism that permits fundamental frequency to be varied is the tension exerted by the laryngeal muscles. Higher tensions generally result in increases in fundamental frequency (Atkinson, 1973). The details of the physiology of phonation are fairly complex and certain muscular adjustments are necessary to position and tension the vocal cords to get the process started. The shape and tension of the vocal cords also affects the details of the phonatory cycle by making the Bernoulli force more or less important in relation to the force exerted by the muscles of the larynx. This changes the inherent sensitivity of the larynx to changes in subglottal air pressure (Atkinson, 1973), but the essential aspects of the physiology of phonation are quite simple. The fundamental frequency of phonation is a function of both the tension of certain laryngeal muscles and the alveolar air pressure. These facts, which were first noted by Müller (1848), in conjunction with the necessity to breathe structure the basic phonetic properties of intonation in human language.

THE BREATH GROUP

Phoneticians have long noted that the intonational pattern of speech is structured in terms of the breathing pattern of the speaker (Armstrong and Ward, 1926; Jones, 1932). The breathing pattern is manifested by the pattern of fundamental frequency and tempo, which plays a major role in signaling the end of a sentence in most, if not all, human language (Lieberman, 1967). Both traditional and generative grammars (Chomsky, 1957, 1968) regard a sentence as the minimal unit from which a complete semantic interpretation can be made. The traditional functional description of a sentence, that it expresses a complete thought, has real validity. It is easy to perform a small experiment that tests this statement. All that one has to do is read a short passage after moving the sentence-final period punctuation one word over. The resulting sequences of words will for the most part be unintelligible. The primary function of orthographic punctuation is to indicate the ends of sentences. The sentence-final "period" symbol is essential. Question marks can be optionally replaced by special words in most language, English being a special case insofar as some of the options have fallen out of use in comparatively recent times (Lieberman, 1967). Commas are usually optional insofar as the reader would have been able to derive the sentence's meaning if they were omitted.

During normal speech the prosodic content of the message, which is largely determined by the perceived pitch as a function of time, signals the ends of sentences. The phonetic feature that speakers make use of to segment the train of words into sentences is the *breath group*. The breath group is the phonetic feature that enables a listener to group words into meaningful sentences. It probably is one of the most central, basic aspects of language and it, or some equivalent phonetic feature, would have had to have been present in the earliest forms of hominid language. It is not a question of language being more difficult without signaling the boundaries of sentences. Language would be impossible without this information, because we would be reduced to one-word utterances each of which would have a fixed, immutable meaning. Language is not a code in which particular signals have fixed meanings. It is impossible to transmit a message in a code if the message is not already in the code book. Language has the potential of transmitting new, unanticipated information. Syntax and the sentence are necessary factors for the presence of language and the breath group is one of the basic, primitive phonetic features that must be present in all languages.

This view of the basic, primitive status of the breath group is consistent with the physiologic mechanisms that structure and constrain its form. In the production of normal speech the acoustic cues that characterize the normal breath group are a consequence of minimal deviation from the respiratory activity that is necessary to sustain life. The primary function of the human respiratory system is *not* to provide air for speech production. Oxygen transfer to the bloodstream is the primary vegetative function of the respiratory system. Speech production is a secondary function. Constant respiratory activity is necessary to sustain life, and in the absence of speech there is an ongoing cyclic pattern in which inspiration is followed by expiration as the lungs alternately expand and deflate, forcing air in and out through the nose, mouth, pharynx, and trachea. In Figure 1 a graph of the volume of the lungs during quiet respiration is plotted. The graph represents a quiet passive state when the subject is at rest. Note that the durations of the inspiratory and

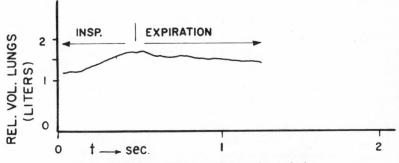

Figure 1.   Volume of the lungs during quiet respiration.

expiratory phases are almost equal. If the subject were running or performing some more strenuous physical activity, the quantity of air that went in and out of the lungs would increase, but the basic pattern in which almost equal time was allotted to the inspiratory and the expiratory phases would remain unchanged (Mead and Agostoni, 1964). If we were to measure the pressure of the air in the human subject's lungs during this respiratory activity we would find that the alveolar air pressure was higher than the atmospheric air pressure outside of the subject's nose and lips during the expiratory phases when air was being pushed out of the lungs. The alveolar air pressure would have to be lower than the atmospheric air pressure in the inspiratory phases in order to get air to flow into the lungs.

The anatomical mechanism that has evolved to carry out the constant pattern of alveolar activity is both complex and efficient. The major amount of work involved in respiration occurs when the lungs expand during inspiration. The lungs are rather like rubber balloons in that they are elastic. The inspiratory muscles expand the rib cage and effectively store energy as the lungs expand. During expiration much of the force that pushes air out from the lungs comes from the elastic recoil. Human speech almost always takes place during expiration because the speaker is able to control the rate at which the lungs deflate by working against the elastic recoil force. During the production of speech the speaker can vary the duration of an expiration over broad limits. Whereas the duration of an expiration is about 2 seconds during quiet respiration, it can vary between 300 milliseconds and 40 seconds during the production of speech. In Figure 2 a graph that shows respiratory activity during speech is plotted.

If we consider the alveolar air pressure during the respiratory activity plotted in Figure 2, one thing is certain—the air pressure during the expiratory phase must be greater than the atmospheric air pressure. During the inspira-

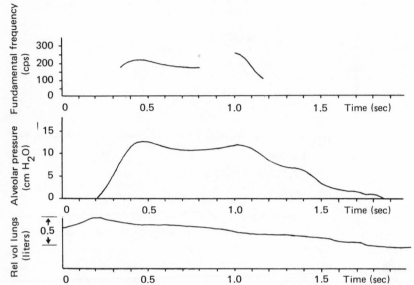

Figure 2.   Respiratory activity during speech: volume of the lungs, alveolar air pressure, and fundamental frequency.

tory phase it must, in contrast, be lower than the atmospheric air pressure. At the end of the expiratory phase of the breath group plotted in Figure 2 there must be an abrupt transition in the alveolar air pressure from the higher (positive) air pressure necessary for expiration to the lower (negative) air pressure necessary for inspiration. If a speaker moves his larynx into the phonation position during an expiration and does nothing to change the tensions of the various laryngeal muscles, then the fundamental frequency of phonation will be determined by the transglottal air pressure drop (Lieberman, 1967; Ohala, 1970; Atkinson, 1973). If a speaker maintains a relatively unobstructed supralaryngeal airway and keeps his larynx in a fixed phonation position, then the fundamental frequency will be determined by the alveolar air pressure. These conditions are met in the cries of newborn humans (Truby, Bosma, and Lind, 1965) where the supralaryngeal vocal tract's configuration is maintained throughout the cry and where phonation occurs until the very end of the breath group. The fundamental frequency at the end of the breath group in these cries always falls; it must, because, in the absence of increased activity of the laryngeal muscles, the alveolar air pressure goes from a positive to a negative value at the end of the breath group. The transition in alveolar air pressure is a consequence of the act of breathing. The falling fundamental frequency contour at the end of the breath group is a consequence of a state of minimal departure from the vegetative state of the organism. In other words, the easiest way of producing sound over the course of an expiration will necessarily produce a fundamental frequency contour that falls at the end of the breath group.

The normal breath groups used by adult speakers are modeled on the state of minimal control in that the fundamental frequency contour always falls at the end of the breath group. In Figure 2 alveolar air pressure and fundamental frequency are also plotted above the lung volume function. Note that the alveolar air pressure was maintained at a relatively steady level for the nonterminal portions of expiration. This is typical for unemphasized sentences in American English (Lieberman, 1967; Atkinson, 1973). In a sense the steady alveolar air pressure is the simplest way of maintaining phonation at or near the same fundamental frequency. At the end of the expiration the alveolar air pressure abruptly falls. The fundamental frequency follows the air pressure function because the speaker does not tension laryngeal muscles that could offset the falling air pressure. The feature of the normal breath group that appears to be universal for human languages is the terminal falling fundamental frequency contour that follows from this condition of minimal departure from the vegetative aspects of respiration. Human speakers have the ability to produce virtually any sort of terminal fundamental frequency contour, but they usually don't. The falling fundamental frequency contour, which is structured by the vegetative aspects of respiration, is the universal language signal signifying the end of an ''ordinary'' sentence.

Many sentences, like English yes-no questions, however, end with a terminal rising fundamental frequency contour. These sentences are produced by means of a *marked breath group* (Lieberman, 1967). The notation +breath group can be used for the marked, and −breath group for the normal breath group. The rising fundamental frequency contour of the marked breath group is the consequence of maneuvers of laryngeal muscles like the thyroarytenoids, lateral cricoarytenoid, and cricothyroid. The muscles are tensed at the end of the breath group, thus counteracting the falling air pressure. The configuration of the larynx throughout the entire +breath group is, however, different from its state in a −breath group. The shape and tension of the vocal cords are adjusted from the very start of a +breath group in a manner that makes their motion less dependent on air pressure. The internal muscles of the larynx as well as muscles like the sternohyoid, which affects the position of the larynx relative to the rest of the body, change the ''mode'' of phonation (Atkinson, 1973). The larynx thus behaves in a different way throughout the entire +breath group. Atkinson's experiments involved monitoring the air pressures below and above a speaker's larynx while the activity of specific laryngeal muscles was measured by means of inserted electrodes. His data demonstrate that, at the start of a +breath group, a speaker of English adjusts his larynx to a mode of phonation that minimizes the effects of the falling air pressure. The rise in fundamental frequency at the end of a +breath group is in a sense the simplest perceptual contrast with the falling fundamental frequency contour of the −breath group. The −breath group's defining characteristic is the terminal fall in fundamental frequency. The simplest and clearest contrast with this acoustic cue is a rising (or nonfalling) terminal fundamental frequency contour. The breath group thus can be viewed as a binary phonetic feature that is structured by the physiology of the respiratory system and perceptual simplicity.

PHYSIOLOGIC STRUCTURING PRINCIPLES AND PHONETIC FEATURES

I have been careful to discuss the structuring properties of the constraints of physiology. The physiologic principles that I have discussed *structure* the actual implementation of particular prosodic patterns by particular speakers. They do not *determine* the particular articulatory maneuvers that a speaker employs to generate a particular prosodic pattern. Individual speakers in fact deviate from the "archetypal" patterns of muscular activity that I have discussed (Lieberman, 1967). However, the basic archetypal patterns structure the acoustic patterns of human language. The falling fundamental frequency patterns of the −breath group can obviously be generated by all sorts of complementary patterns involving different laryngeal muscles and the respiratory system. A speaker can, for example, effect a falling fundamental frequency pattern by simply relaxing all the laryngeal muscles well before the end of expiration. However, the crucial factor is that the basic pattern of respiratory activity places a special status on the role of a −breath group final falling intonation contour. I propose that there exist neural mechanisms in the human brain that are "tuned" to the acoustic patterns of the breath group. These neural mechanisms embody the "acoustic correlates" of the phonetic feature breath group. They would have evolved by the same process of mutation and natural selection that yields neural mechanisms that respond to the acoustic correlates of mating croaks in bullfrogs (Capranica, 1965). Electrophysiologic evidence shows that the primate brain can form neural units that respond to acoustic signals that are of interest to the organism (Lieberman, 1975). The argument is essentially that the constraints of the respiratory system made certain fundamental frequency patterns "natural" or "basic" signals for communication, and that neural mechanisms responsive to these patterns evolved through the process of natural selection. The breath group thus is an innately determined phonetic feature because there exist physiologic mechanisms that make it easy to produce and there exist neural mechanisms that are "tuned" to its acoustic properties.

LANGUAGE-SPECIFIC MECHANISMS
AND ANIMAL COMMUNICATIONS

The physiologic constraints that structure the breath group probably would apply with equal force to the intonational signals of a number of other animals. The larynges of dogs and wolves, for example, are not substantially different from human larynges, nor are their respiratory systems fundamentally different. Negus (1949) showed that the larynges of these animals, like those of humans, are not optimal for efficient respiration but are instead adapted for phonation. The cries of wolves and dogs in particular, have many of the phonetic qualities of the −breath group. It's likely that there is no sharp boundary between the analysis of the intonation of the cries of these animals and human speech. This does not make intonation less of a "linguistic" element than, for example, vowel quality. It simply demonstrates the continuity of evolution that must apply to human language with the same force that it applies to, for example, human hunting. Although all of the elements that structure human hunting are not evident in the behavior of animals like chimpanzees, there are parallels (Goodall, 1971) that probably reflect the common elements in the ancestry of humans and chimpanzees. There is a great gulf between the behavior of the chimpanzee when hunting and the behavior of human hunters. Chimpanzees, for example, cannot effectively throw stones (Beck, 1975). If we were to take stone throwing as an absolute mark of human hunting, we might be tempted to postulate an abrupt nonlinear model for the evolution of human hunting where the stone-throwing activity of *Homo sapiens* was disjoint with the stone-throwing activity of all other living animals. Only man among all other living animals can accurately throw stones. We therefore would postulate a model in which some hominids abruptly acquired the ability to throw stones and thus began to hunt in the same manner as modern humans. This probably was not the case, since we can find evidence that some early hominids, e.g., *Australopithecus africanus,* made round stone projectiles (Leakey, 1972), although they did not have the same cultural accomplishments as later hominids and probably did not hunt in the same manner as modern humans. The seemingly "abrupt" nature of stone-throwing ability is an artifact of the limited data sample that we have when we consider only living animals. All of the intermediate stages that intercede between modern *Homo sapiens* and our most primitive ancestors are now extinct.

The situation for the evolution of language is probably similar. The "classic" Neanderthals who inhabited Western Europe some 70,000 years ago did not have the same phonetic abilities as modern *Homo sapiens* (Lieberman and Crelin, 1971; Lieberman, Crelin, and Klatt, 1972; Lieberman, 1973,

1975). They could not produce many of the segmental phonetic elements that typify modern languages; sounds like the vowels /a/, /i/, and /u/, as well as consonants like /g/ and /k/ were not possible. There are serious consequences that derive from the absence of these sounds, since they include some of the most effective auditory signals of human language. Classic Neanderthal hominids, however, surely had a form of language (Lieberman, 1975). The relative importance of intonation in the phonetic repertoires of these earlier hominids probably was greater than is the case for modern *Homo sapiens*. Livingstone (1973) has proposed that *Australopithecus africanus* probably placed even greater reliance on intonational signals. Intonational signals are still with us as a basic and central part of language.

OTHER INTONATIONAL FEATURES

The breath group obviously is not the single phonetic feature that can account for all aspects of intonation. We are using the term *feature* in the sense of a signaling unit that has clear articulatory and acoustic correlates that reflect the presence of neural mechanisms that govern its production and perception (Lieberman, 1970). There is some evidence that supports this view for a number of phonetic features (Eimas and Corbit, 1973; Lieberman, 1975). There are good reasons for supposing that a number of intonational phenomena that have been described involve other features, and much work yet remains. The point that I want to stress here, however, is not the total range of features that may define intonation, but what seems to be the basic segmenting aspect of intonation. This aspect of intonation seems to be a central element of language and it is in all likelihood structured by innately determined physiologic mechanisms.

REFERENCES

Armstrong, L. E., and Ward, I. C. 1926. Handbook of English Intonation. B. G. Teubner, Leipzig and Berlin.

Atkinson, J. R. 1973. Aspects of intonation in speech: Implications from an experimental study of fundamental frequency. Unpublished Ph.D. dissertation, University of Connecticut.

Beck, B. B. 1975. Primate tool behavior. In: S. Tax (ed.), Proceedings of the IXth International Congress of Anthropological and Ethnological Science, Chicago, Ill. Mouton & Co., The Hague.

Capranica, R. R. 1965. The Evoked Vocal Response of the Bullfrog. MIT Press, Cambridge, Mass.

Chomsky, N. 1957. Syntactic Structures. Mouton & Co., The Hague.

Chomsky, N. 1968. Language and Mind. Harcourt, Brace, Jovanovich, Inc., New York.

Eimas, P. D., and Corbit, J. D. 1973. Selective adaptation of linguistic feature detectors. Cog. Psychol. 4:99–109.

Ferrein, C. J. 1741. Mem. Acad. Paris, pp. 409–432 (Nov. 15).

Goodall, J. 1971. In the Shadow of Man. Dell Publishing Company, Inc., New York.

Jones, D. 1932. An Outline of English Phonetics, 3rd ed. Dutton, New York.

Leakey, M. D. (ed.). 1972. Olduvai Gorge, Vol. 3. Cambridge University Press, Cambridge, England.

Lieberman, P. 1967. Intonation, Perception, and Language. MIT Press, Cambridge, Mass.

Liberman, P. 1970. Towards a unified phonetic theory. Ling. Inquiry 1:307–322.

Lieberman, P. 1973. On the evolution of human language: A unified view. Cognition 2:59–94.

Lieberman, P. 1975. On the Origins of Language: An Introduction to the Evolution of Speech. Macmillan Publishing Company, Inc., New York.

Lieberman, P., and Crelin, E. S. 1971. On the speech of Neanderthal man. Ling. Inquiry 2:203–222.

Lieberman, P., Crelin, E. S., and Klatt, D. H. 1972. Phonetic ability and related anatomy of the newborn adult human, Neanderthal man, and the chimpanzee. Am. Anthropol. 74:287–307.

Livingstone, F. B. 1973. Did the Australopithecines sing? Curr. Anthropol. 14:25–29.

Mead, J., and Agostoni, E. 1964. Dynamics of breathing. In: I. W. O. Fenn and H. Rahn (eds.), Handbook of Physiology, Part 1: Respiration. American Physiological Society.

Müller, J. 1848. The Physiology of the Senses, Voice and Muscular Motion with the Mental Faculties. Translated by W. Baly. Walton and Maberly, London.

Negus, V. E. 1949. The Comparative Anatomy and Physiology of the Larynx. Hafner Press, New York.

Ohala, J. 1970. Aspects of the Control and Production of Speech. Working Papers in Phonetics, No. 15. University of California, Los Angeles.

Truby, H. M., Bosma, J. F., and Lind, J. 1965. Newborn Infant Cry. Almqvist and Wiksell, Uppsala.

Van den Berg, J. M. 1960. Vocal ligaments versus registers. Curr. Probl. Phoniat. Logoped. 1:19–34.

16/ Western Scottish Intonation: A Preliminary Study

J. Derrick McClure

In view of the fact that the world's most widely spoken language exhibits, as a matter of course, an enormous number of regionally and socially marked forms, it is somewhat surprising that only two out of the total range of accents have been at all extensively described. It is even more surprising that linguists seem to have accepted the designation of those two forms by, respectively, the dubious term "American English" and the even more erroneous term "British English," a nomenclature that almost overtly suggests that in each of the two politically defined territories of America and Britain only one form of the language, or at any rate only one worthy of notice, is to be found.

Considering that some recent Presidents of the United States have spoken with accents strikingly different from the educated Midwestern speech miscalled "American English," it can hardly be true now, if it ever was, that this is the only prestige-bearing accent of America; and in any case such factors are, as we would all admit, irrelevant to the science of descriptive linguistics. It would also be very difficult or impossible to find, on the level at which differences between accents exist, any features common and exclusive to all the accents of the United States. There is in fact no sense in which the phrase "American English" could be used, with reference to the phonetic or phonological levels of anlaysis, as an adequate and accurate descriptive term.

As far as the other side of the Atlantic is concerned, a brief initial summary of the linguistic situation in Britain (that is, the British archipelago exclusive of Ireland and the small islands surrounding it, the Isle of Man, and the Channel Islands) may not be out of place. Four languages besides English are spoken within this area: Scots (which is entitled by its long, distinguished, and continuing independent literary tradition to be classed as a language, and is in any case not a dialect, as it has itself in its spoken form several dialects), Scottish Gaelic, Welsh, and Cornish (which has never been fully extinct, and is now apparently undergoing something of a revival). Very few inhabitants, however, are not either monolingual or bilingual (or bi-dialectal, since several

English dialects still exist) in the language based on a Southeast Midland dialect of England—the official tongue of Britain and many other parts of the world. The numerous different forms that this language takes in Highland and Lowland Scotland, Orkney and Shetland, North and West England, Wales, and Cornwall are the results of its adoption (centuries ago in some cases) by speakers of other languages or dialects; and it is a matter of elementary observation that there is *no* form that is native to the whole of Britain, nor any shared features that distinguish the various British accents from those found in the rest of the English-speaking world.

It is certainly true that in England one particular accent carries a considerable, though probably a diminishing, social and educational prestige as compared to the other accents, and the dialects, of England. "England" and "Britain," however, are not synonymous terms, any more than "Prussia" and "Germany" are, though English imperialism, Scottish pusillanimity, and universal ignorance have combined through several generations in causing them to be used as if they were. In Scotland and Wales, this form of the language is thought of simply as "an English accent," carrying no particular prestige and indicative of nothing except the place of origin of the speaker. No native-born Scot or Welshman grows up with this accent as his first form of speech, and the few who acquire it later, by education in England or some other source of English influence, are considered to be speaking in a manner foreign to their countries of origin. There is no question of its having the same social status in Scotland and Wales as it has in England, or of its being regarded there as a marker of a certain degree of educational achievement. To refer to this accent as "British English" is therefore totally without justification: it is an accent of England, with roughly the same status in the rest of Britain as it has in, say, the United States. ["Received Pronunciation" (R.P.), though increasingly anachronistic, is perhaps the least unsatisfactory label currently applied to it. "General English," said with the same intonation pattern as "General American," would also be a possible term. "Educated English English" would be much more accurate than either, but not very satisfactory on aesthetic grounds—of course, the polysemy of the word "English" is the cause of the difficulty in naming a form of the language spoken in that particular country: even among Englishmen, however, there are speakers of the highest academic calibre who neither attempt nor wish to exchange their native accents for this one.]

Among the many accents of English other than R.P. that are to be heard in Britain, those native to Lowland Scotland form a fairly well defined group. ("Lowland Scotland" may be defined linguistically as the area where Gaelic either was never spoken or was superseded by Scots no later, and in most areas much earlier, than the eighteenth century; in "Highland Scotland" Gaelic either is still in active use or has been superseded by English, rather than Scots, within the last two or three generations. That is, the substratum of the various forms of English heard in the Lowlands is Scots; in the Highlands it is Gaelic.) The most general and fundamental characteristic of this group of accents, on the phonological level, is the loss of the almost universal Germanic distinction between long and short vowels: in any given phonetically or morphonemically defined environment, the differences in actual duration between vowels are in most cases negligible.[1] Related to this is the use of monophthongal [i e o u] corresponding to the diphthongs found in most other forms of English, and of identical vowels in such word-pairs as good-food, cot-caught, and Sam-psalm (though in the case of the last pair, some degree of differentiation between the vowels, by length or quality or both, is not infrequently made). Vowel distinctions before postvocalic /r/ (which, incidentally, is realized as a fricative or an approximant much more commonly than as a trill) are also retained to a greater extent in Lowland Scottish English than in other /r/-pronouncing forms of the language: except in Edinburgh (this is a notable shibboleth of that particular accent), the vowel of pert is invariably kept distinct from those of dirt and hurt; and (with the same exception) those of the latter two words are usually distinguished also from each other. Regional differences between the accents of Lowland Scotland can readily be found, particularly in intonation; and, though no single accent has the status in Scotland that R.P. has in England, socially marked variations also exist: however, the various forms of English spoken in this particular area resemble each other, and differ from any accents of England or Wales, enough to make generalizations about "Lowland Scottish English" possibly meaningful, and generalizations about "British English" invariably meaningless. (This statement is as true of idiom and vocabulary as it is of phonology, though it is only with the latter that I am at present concerned.)

Compared to R.P. and Midwestern American English, there is a lamentable paucity of descriptive material on any of the other accents; and of all their distinguishing features that on which least work has appeared is their intonation. As far as Scottish English is concerned, apart from an admirable but unpublished Edinburgh University dissertation (Garlick, 1961) little exists except a short and largely misleading passage in Jones (1963) and some very odd descriptions in Grant (1914) and Grant and Robson (1925). [I know of no Scottish accent in which

[hi z 'nɛvɪr bin tu 'ɛdnbʌrʌ bɪ'for]

---

[1]An instrumental investigation conducted since this paper was written (McClure, 1977) has shown this statement to be inaccurate.

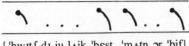

['hwɪtʃ dɪ ju lʌik 'bɛst, 'mʌtn ɔr 'bif]

with all the peaks being apparently of equal height and the unstressed syllables said on a monotone, would sound natural; though Jones's observation that "a succession of high falling tones is characteristic of the speech of Edinburgh and the East of Scotland generally" (1963, p. 162) is partly true, and, as will be shown, not only of the East. In

wɔt'du:juminbaɪ'ðat

(sic: the first symbol should be ʍ)

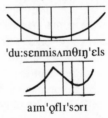

'du:sɛnmisʌmθɪŋ'ɛls

aɪm'ɒflɪ'sɔrɪ

not only the intonation patterns but also the idioms are about as typical of Scottish usage as another of Grant's examples: "If it were so, it was a grievous fault" (1914, pp. 90–92)]. The following descriptive study of a few grammatically functioning intonation patterns in the English of the Western Lowlands is an attempted first step toward filling this gap. The data are drawn from the accents of college- or university-educated speakers belonging to the towns of Ayr, Paisley, and West Kilbride. The accents of these towns, which are within a 16-mile radius, are by no means identical, but are sufficiently similar to provide a basis for some general observations on Western Lowland intonation. The accent of each utterance cited will be identified by the initial letter of the name of the town. Throughout the description, the term *stress* will refer to phonetic stress as defined by Abercrombie (1967, pp. 35–36) and Ladefoged (1967), and the term *pitch prominence* to intonational prominence as defined by Bolinger (1958); the features thus designated are mutually independent.

A set of hand-drawn copies of displays obtained on the pitch meter at the University of Toronto (see Léon and Martin, 1972), with the kind cooperation of the Linguistics Department, will first be presented and discussed. These displays represent model sentences, including forms of utterance that might be expected to differ in their intonation patterns, spoken by the investigator (A accent) in as close a simulation as possible of the manner in which they would be pronounced in normal conversation. In all the displays, the pitches represented by the horizontal lines are constant. The positioning of the letters is impressionistic and necessarily approximate.

(1)   He'll be arriving on Monday.

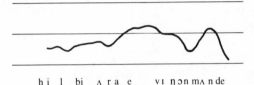

h i l bi ʌ ra e   vɪ ŋ ɔn mʌ n de

The jump in pitch on the last stressed syllable, clearly shown on this tracing, is a prominent feature. The two peaks, which coincide fairly closely with the nuclei of the stressed syllables, have their turning points at roughly equal pitches (but if there were an intervening pitch-prominent syllable it would not be said on the same pitch, as Jones seems to suggest, but on a somewhat lower one: this will be demonstrated later). The prehead shows a fairly level pitch with only a slight upward-sloping gradient: the syllables -ving on, by contrast, show a steady fall to a point somewhat lower than that reached by the initial unstressed syllables. Finally, the pitch drops suddenly and considerably at the end of the utterance. The effect of this pattern is to give considerable pitch prominence to the final stressed syllable and to impart a "spiky" form to the contour of the entire sentence.

(2)   Yes, he will be arriving on Monday.

j ɛ   s   i   wɪ l   bi ʌ ra e vɪ ŋ   ɔn mʌ n de

An emphasizing of one syllable at the expense of the rest of the utterance results, in this confirmatory (not contradictory) statement, in a pattern very different from that of the simple assertion. Here the <u>Mon-</u> is said on a lower pitch than the neighboring unstressed syllables: indeed, on the lowest pitch reached during the utterance. Following the peak on the emphasized syllable, an abrupt fall gives way to a level section imparting a degree of pitch prominence to the second syllable of <u>arriving;</u> after this a steady downdrift gives place to a slight rise, which brings the pitch of the voice at the end of the utterance to approximately the same level as at the beginning.

(3)   Why will he be arriving on Monday?

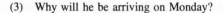

ʍ a e wɪ l i bi ʌ ra e   vɪ ŋ ɔ n mʌ n de

(4)   When will he be arriving?

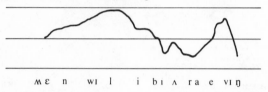

ʍ ɛ   n   wɪ l   i   bɪ ʌ ra e   vɪ ŋ

The typical pattern for wh-questions is shown by these very similar tracings. The relation of the curve to the word divisions should be noted here: in both questions the initial rise in pitch extends through and beyond the interrogative word and continues onto the following syllable, so that the peak occurs not on a stressed syllable but on an unstressed one. From the peak, the curve descends more or less steadily (with, in the case of sentence 3, a level section corresponding to the stressed syllable of arriving) until the last stressed syllable, when a sudden rise occurs and is followed by an equally sudden drop. As in many other types of English, the pattern for wh-questions is noticeably similar to that for simple statements: however, the two kinds of utterance can be seen to differ intonationally in two important respects. First, whereas in statements the initial and final peaks are almost equal in height, in wh-questions the pitch attained during the final rise-fall is decidedly lower than that reached at the beginning of the utterance. Second, and a more striking difference still, the coincidence of pitch peaks with stressed syllables is less exact in the question than in the statement pattern. Whereas in sentence 1 the turning points of the curves occur close to the nuclei of the syllables -riv- and Mon-, in sentences 3 and 4 the pitch of the voice continues to rise after the utterance of the question words, and the movement toward the final peak, rather than the peak itself, occurs on the last stressed syllable. (Observe that the distance along the time dimension from peak to end of utterance is much less in sentence 3 than in sentence 1.)

(5)   *Why* will he be arriving on Monday?

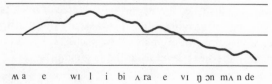

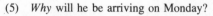

ʍ a   e   wɪ l i bi ʌ ra e   vɪ ŋ ɔn mʌ n de

The implication of this sentence is "I know he *will* be arriving on Monday, but I want to know the reason for it." Why is therefore the part of the sentence that requires the greatest degree of emphasis. It is not (noticeably) the part on which the main peak occurs: as in the other wh-questions, the rising curve continues past the question word itself onto the following unstressed syllables. The shape of this curve is much the simplest yet considered, and the slight perturbations do not occur in places where they could readily be interpreted as imparting pitch prominence to any particular syllable. The descending part of the curve is smoother and less steep than the corresponding part of the tracing for sentence 3, and the pitch on which the utterance ends is slightly lower than the lowest pitch reached during that sentence. The peak, too, is less high than the first of those in sentence 3. This intonation pattern seems to function specifically as a means of avoiding prominence on any word after the first, which, in view of the content presupposed by the utterance, is precisely what is required.

(6)   Will he be arriving on Monday?

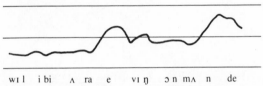

wɪl   i bi   ʌ   ra   e   vɪ ŋ   ɔn mʌ   n   de

A fair degree of resemblance between the patterns associated with simple statements and with wh-questions is not unexpected: this form of Scottish English differs strikingly from some other accents in having a somewhat similar pattern for yes-no questions. The curve for this sentence has three conspicuous features in common with those for sentences 1, 3, and 4: the familiar jump at the end of the utterance, the falling tendency on unstressed syllables between the peaks, and the final fall. A major difference, however, is also visible between this pattern and those of the other three sentences mentioned: a general hint of updrift contrasted with the downdrift that those exhibit. The medial unstressed syllables in this utterance are uniformly higher in pitch than the prehead, and their downward gradient is very slight indeed; the second pitch peak is also decidedly higher than the first. The terminal fall in pitch is only to a level scarcely lower than that of the first peak. The fact that there *is* a final fall makes it impossible to describe this particular intonation pattern as "rising": it is noteworthy that there is no unambiguous final rise in any of the sentences here described, but the general upward direction of the curve as contrasted with the general downward directions of the statement and wh-question patterns is unmistakable. (True rising intonations are very rare in this form of English, and at least in the A accent seem to occur not with a grammatical function but only as indications of certain types of emotional

loading, such as sarcasm or ridicule. It may be that they are not in fact native
to this accent: this question, however, is beyond the scope of the present
study.)

(7)   *When* will he be arriving??

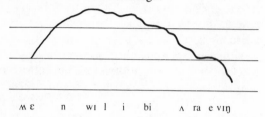

     ʍ ɛ   n   wɪ l   i   bi   ʌ ra e vɪŋ

(8)   *Why* will he be arriving on Monday??

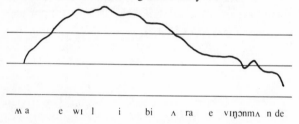

    ʍ a   e wɪ l   i   bi ʌ ra e vɪŋɔnmʌ n de

    These are repeat questions ("Did you ask *when* he would be arriving?")
and both show very similar patterns, which may be compared to that of sentence 5. As in the simple sentence, the pitch rises throughout the articulation
of the interrogative word, reaches a peak during the following unstressed syllables, and then falls fairly steadily until the end of the utterance. The difference between "*Why* will he be arriving on Monday?" and "(Did you say:)
'*Why* will he be arriving on Monday?'?" is expressed intonationally not by any
change in the general shape of the curve, but by the employment of a much
wider range of pitch in the repeat question. Although the starting and finishing
pitches of the two utterances are virtually the same, the peak is considerably
higher in sentence 8 than in sentence 5, so that the rising and falling
gradients—particularly the former—are steeper. Both sentences 7 and 8 show
a more or less level stretch that breaks the steady descent of the curve: this
coincides with the syllable -riv- and imparts to it a slight pitch prominence.
Following this syllable, the pitch of the voice drops sharply in sentence 7, but
in sentence 8 it momentarily holds an almost level pitch, lower than that on
-riv-, to give a hint of pitch prominence to Mon- before the terminal fall.
(Though this is not an intonational feature, it may be observed that sentences
5 and 8 also differ strikingly from each other in the relative durations of the
words.)

(9)   Why will he be arriving on *Monday*??

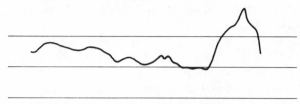

ʍ a   e   wɪ l i bi ʌ ra   e vɪ ŋ ɔnmʌ n de

This is another repeat question, to which the corresponding simple question is sentence 3. The degree of similarity between the curves for sentences 3 and 9 is, however, much less than that between sentences 5 and 8. In sentence 9 the syllable Mon- is by far the most pitch prominent part of the utterance, the extremely abrupt and rapid rise that occurs on that syllable being emphasized still further by the restricted range of pitch employed until then. The initial rise on the Why does not continue onto the following unstressed syllables as in sentence 3, but gives place to an unevenly descending curve, broken by a jump, which does not reach the height of the first peak, on the stressed syllable of arriving. The final peak, which occurs not on the nucleus but on the [n] of Mon-, is followed by a sharp drop to a pitch virtually equal to that on which the utterance began: a much higher point than that on which sentence 3 ended. It is noteworthy that, whereas in that sentence both the interrogative word and the word that carried the focus of attention were highlighted by the intonation, in the repeated version only the Mon- receives pitch prominence, and intonational emphasizing of the Why is minimal. This, however, is almost a necessity: the meaning of Why is presupposed and therefore the information content of the word is low. A repeat question in which both words were emphasized, giving a pattern that would bear the same relation to that of sentence 3 as the pattern of sentence 8 does to that of sentence 5, would presumably mean something like "Did you ask why he would be arriving and also why it would be on Monday?"—which is, if not impossible, certainly most unlikely.

(10)   When will he be arriving?

ʍ ɛ   n   wi l i bi ʌ ra e vɪ ŋ

This is the intonation of a recapitulation question: the speaker is asking to be reminded of something that he already knows. The very rapid rise in the interrogative word and the rising tendency toward the end of the curve are the most conspicuous features of the pattern. The peak occurs earlier than in sentence 4, thus emphasizing the interrogative word itself more than is done in that utterance: this shows that the intonational marking of straightforward wh-questions does not consist of a simple highlighting of the question word. After the peak, the zigzag shape of the next section does not conceal a downdrifting tendency that continues until the curve begins to head upward on the first syllable, rather than the second, of arriving. The voice reaches a high pitch, holds it, and then turns momentarily downward on the last syllable: even in this "uncertainty" pattern, despite a general updrift the final direction of the voice is downward.

(11)   He'll be arriving when?

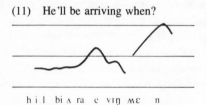

h i l   bi ʌ ra   e   vɪŋ ʍɛ   n

This is an echo question, the interrogative word being thrown into relief by a rapid rise leading to a peak much higher than the one that occurs (squarely) on the previous stressed syllable. The pitch of the first three syllables is low and almost steady (this type of question, like the yes-no question and unlike the wh-question, begins on the same pitch as the simple statement), and the pitch to which the voice falls after the first peak is lower still. Once again, a final downward curve is noticeable.

(12)   He'll be arriving *when*?

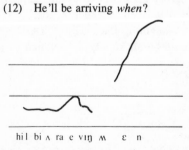

hi l bi ʌ ra e vɪŋ ʍ   ɛ   n

This pattern, suggestive of incredulity, provides an interesting comparison with that of the previous sentence. Several differences are visible, all with the function of heightening the emphasis given to the last word: the much higher pitch reached toward the end of the utterance, the extreme compression both in pitch range and in time of the first words, and the greater duration of the initial (voiceless) segment of <u>when</u>. Even in a sentence of this type, the only example of an emotionally charged utterance in the present corpus, there is a tendency for the curve to flatten and turn downward in the last fraction of a second.

These pitch tracings illustrate three of what appear to be the most characteristic features of Western Lowland Scottish intonation: the imparting of pitch prominence by "jumps" in the curve; the lack of exact coincidence, in utterances of types other than the simple statement, between stressed syllables and intonation peaks; and the absence of a final rising tone.

The examples now to be discussed are taken from tape recordings of spontaneous conversation. Impressionistic transcriptions rather than mechanically obtained tracings are given, not because of any theoretical preference but simply because it is difficult, to say the least, to obtain from informal domestic visits tape recordings of a quality sufficiently high for pitch meter analysis. The relative pitches of the syllables are indicated as precisely as possible: on the time axis, however, nothing is indicated but the sequential order of the pitch changes—no attempt is made to suggest their actual rate beyond, in the only extended passage, marking pauses by a double space between the printed words of the discourse.

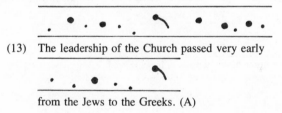

(13)   The leadership of the Church passed very early

from the Jews to the Greeks. (A)

A somewhat more elaborate example of statement intonation than that provided by sentence 1 is visible in this extract. The subject noun phrase is seen to begin on a fairly low pitch, which rises sharply to the first stressed syllable and again to the second, which, however, is lower than the first. The intonation curve on the unstressed syllable(s) following these two peaks shows a downward tendency. <u>Church</u> begins on the highest pitch reached during the noun phrase, and includes a sharp fall. The same pattern—stressed syllables relatively high and following unstressed syllables that descend, with each successive stress coinciding with a lower peak than its predecessor—is clearly demonstrated by the phrases <u>passed very</u>, <u>early from the</u>, and <u>Jews to the</u>. (The first syllable of <u>very</u> receives no pitch prominence because the semantic force of the word here is nil: it has no intensifying function, but merely serves as a space-filler to avoid <u>passed early</u>, which would be unusual in colloquial speech.) Finally, a considerable jump in the curve brings the pitch on the final stressed syllable to a level equal to the highest previously reached in the utterance, after which a fall to roughly the middle of the voice range occurs: a statement-final intonation does not necessitate a fall to anything like the lowest register of the voice. Characteristically, therefore, a peak occurs on the stressed syllable of each semantically important word, the two highest peaks being near the beginning and near the end of the utterance. [Compare Jones's transcription of "He's never been to Edinburgh before," (1963).] That the word in the subject noun phrase with the greatest pitch prominence is Church and not leadership is explained by the context of the sentence: the previous part of the discourse had centered on a difference in emphasis between the Judaic and the Greek (more correctly Graeco-Roman) ethical systems without reference to the history of the Church. Church is thus the most informative word in the phrase. The pitch prominence of Greeks cannot be so explained, since the word in its context is no more informative than Jews.

On the evidence of this, we may expect to find in a "normal" or unmarked statement the features of maximally high pitch at or near the beginning and the end of the utterance, "long-term" downdrift on all the pitch-prominent syllables up to the last and "short-term" downdrift on the syllable sequences between two pitch-prominent syllables, and a final fall to the mid rather than a low pitch.

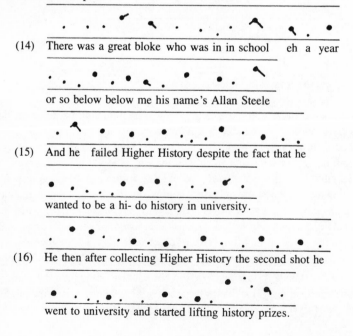

(14)   There was a great bloke who was in in school   eh a year

or so below below me his name's Allan Steele

(15)   And he   failed Higher History despite the fact that he

wanted to be a hi- do history in university.

(16)   He then after collecting Higher History the second shot he

went to university and started lifting history prizes.

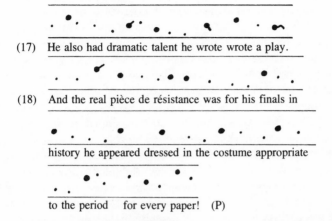

(17) He also had dramatic talent he wrote wrote a play.

(18) And the real pièce de résistance was for his finals in

history he appeared dressed in the costume appropriate

to the period   for every paper!   (P)

In the continuous monologue that these five sentences form, some apparent cases of departure from this pattern are visible. However, all the variations can be explained. In sentence 14, the low information content of bloke (if the word has any emotional overtones they are minimal: it is merely a style-marked synonym for person) can be cited as the cause of its being lower in pitch, rather than higher, than the following stressed syllable. The pitch of the second in, which reverses the usual downward tendency of unstressed syllable sequences, suggests the explanation that the speaker had at this point decided what to say next, and was thus beginning a new section of the discourse: it is observable that this word was said on a pitch very close to that of the unstressed syllables at the opening of the utterance. (This explanation is supported by the fact that the duration of the first in was much greater than that of the second.) During the following hesitation, the pitch of the voice drops, and a year or so below displays a pattern that suggests that the speaker intended to conclude that part of the utterance with below me: the peak on the first below is equal in height to that on school, which initiates the section. A change of mind is signaled by the repetition of below with a pitch pattern that no longer suggests finality, and the use of a high pitch, indicating a resumption of the phrase, for name's. Steele reaches the same height as great, thus unifying intonationally the entire passage.

In sentence 15, after the initial hesitation on he the expected pattern is at first departed from only by the absence of pitch prominence on Higher. This is simply explained on semantic grounds: a Higher is a school-leaving examination, and in a discourse on school matters in collocation with failed the word is almost predictable. Its information value is therefore very low. Despite begins a new section of the discourse; hence its pitch prominence is greater than that of history, although less than that of the first stressed syllable of the sentence. The peak on university, the last in the utterance, does reach the same height as that on he. (It occurs not on the nucleus of -ver- but on its arresting consonant: in the P accent the tendency for pitch peaks not to coincide with stressed syllable nuclei appears to be more general than in the A accent. This does not obscure the considerable similarity between the intonation patterns of the two accents.) It is likely that if the speaker had, in accordance with what appears to have been his original intention, ended the sentence with "... wanted to be a history teacher," the rise to hi- would have continued onto the following -sto- or -st'ry, bringing the final peak to the required height.

After the beginning of sentence 16, a section occurs in which the information content is slight and, as a consequence, the pitch is low and varies little throughout. The liveliness of the intonation, evidently, is directly related to the interest value of the utterance. A sudden and extreme rise in pitch on the stressed syllable of the penultimate word likewise highlights the unexpected nature of the information conveyed in the last part of the sentence.

In sentence 17, the repetition of wrote, the second time on a higher pitch than the first, suggests that the speaker decided that the information carried by wrote a play deserved more intonational underlining than he had at first intended to give it. The patterns of dramatic talent and play are unusual, and by being pointedly unlike the regular final pattern they convey a sense of preparation and anticipation. This is perhaps an emotionally rather than a grammatically marked contour. Finally, the updrift that appears instead of the expected downdrift on the peaks of the costume appropriate to the period is a departure from the norm for the clear purpose of emphasizing the oddity of the situation being described. Throughout this discourse, therefore, evidence is presented for a basic statement intonation pattern that perturbations of the contours, for emotional, grammatical, or other reasons, do not completely obscure.

The patterns that characterize three types of question are illustrated by the remaining transcriptions:

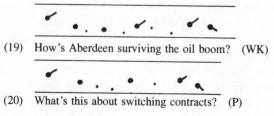

(19)   How's Aberdeen surviving the oil boom?   (WK)

(20)   What's this about switching contracts?   (P)

These two sentences bear obvious resemblances in their intonation patterns to sentence 3: the initial rise, subsequent fall to a much lower pitch, and final rise-fall that attains neither the height nor the depth reached during the rest of the utterance are readily comparable to the corresponding parts of that sentence. Sentences 19 and 20 differ intonationally from sentence 3 in two respects: the failure of the initial rise to continue beyond the interrogative word, and the much slower final descent of the pitch curve. This is most probably conditioned by the distribution of stressed and unstressed syllables. The rising pitch on <u>surviving</u> in sentence 19, which is absent on <u>switching</u> in sentence 20, is explainable by the context: sentence 19 had no reference to any topic previously discussed (it was in fact prefixed by "To change the subject . . ."), so that both <u>surviving</u> and <u>oil boom</u> have a high information content and require pitch prominence. Sentence 20 occurred in the course of a discussion of malpractice among American oil firms operating in Scotland, during which the specific subject of falsifying contracts had been briefly mentioned, so that <u>switching contracts</u> was a predictable collocation and both elements did not require emphasis.

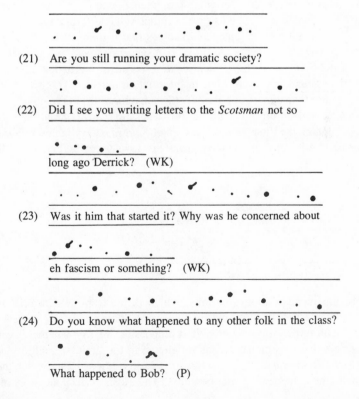

(21) Are you still running your dramatic society?

(22) Did I see you writing letters to the *Scotsman* not so

long ago Derrick?   (WK)

(23) Was it him that started it? Why was he concerned about

eh fascism or something?   (WK)

(24) Do you know what happened to any other folk in the class?

What happened to Bob?   (P)

(25)   But what would they have done then? Given the Africans the vote?   (A)

Sentence 21 closely resembles sentence 6 in showing a general updrift, a rising pitch on the first stressed syllable, and a final fall to a pitch considerably higher than that on which the utterance began. Sentence 22 shows, however, that, if a relatively uninformative section follows the last pitch-prominent syllable in a yes-no question, the final fall continues unchecked to a very low pitch. (The *Scotsman* is a daily newspaper.) That this is also true of wh-questions is demonstrated by the last section of sentence 23. Sentences 23, 24, and 25 consist of successive wh- and yes-no questions (or vice-versa), and confirm the nature of the intonation contours that mark those types of utterance. Within the basic patterns the behavior of the curve is visibly subject to minor variations, depending frequently on the semantic importance of lexical items (either absolutely or as conditioned by the context): happened, in sentence 24, for example, receives no pitch prominence, and the rise to the peak on dramatic in sentence 21 begins on the initial syllable, although it is un-stressed. The second part of sentence 25 shows that if more than two words must be emphasized in a yes-no question each successive peak is higher than the last: as the first part of the sentence suggests, all of the lexical items— given, Africans, and vote—are high in information content. This situation, however, is rarer than that exemplified by the behavior of the curve on writing in sentence 22 and on any in sentence 24—when no word coming between those that contain the first and the last pitch-prominent syllables requires particular emphasis, any intervening peaks are lower, not higher, than the first.

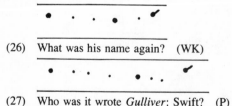

(26)   What was his name again?   (WK)

(27)   Who was it wrote *Gulliver*: Swift?   (P)

These are recapitulation questions, which differ from sentence 10 in showing neither a rise on the interrogative word nor a final fall, however slight. Without further investigation it is impossible to say whether these differences are due to regional accent variations, to the limits of auditory as opposed to machine sensitivity, or to the artificial conditions under which the corpus including sentence 10 was obtained. The close correspondences already noted between the patterns of the sentences in that corpus and those of the ones extracted from real conversation cast doubt on the last of these possibilities, and the fact that the features referred to would seem from the curve of sentence 10 to be prominent enough to be heard does likewise regarding the second: the differences may, therefore, be described with some plausibility as variations between the A accent on the one hand and the accents of WK and P on the other. If this is correct, it is the only instance so far discovered of a case where accent differences include the use of actual different "tunes" for the same grammatical function.

Disregarding the recapitulation question and other types of utterance for which the present study does not provide sufficient data, the sentence classes of statement, wh-question, and yes-no question have been shown to be marked, in this form of English, by distinctive intonation patterns. These patterns may be labeled with reference to the behavior of the curve at or near the first and the last stressed pitch-prominent syllable: that for statements as *high-fall: high-fall,* that for wh-questions as *high-fall: mid-fall,* and that for yes-no questions as *mid-fall: high-fall.* Pitch-prominent syllables intervening between the beginning and the end of the utterance impart considerable elaboration to the basic patterns. In such cases ad hoc descriptions and explanations rather than attempts at general rules have been given here, but such generalizations will no doubt be made possible by further research. In the meantime, the distinctive nature of Western Lowland Scottish intonation has, it is hoped, been demonstrated clearly enough to suggest the desirability of more extensive examination, not only of it but of others among the many underinvestigated forms of English.

REFERENCES

Abercrombie, D. 1967. Elements of General Phonetics. Edinburgh University Press, Edinburgh.

Bolinger, D. L. 1958. A theory of pitch accent in English. Word 14:109–149.

Garlick, I. F. 1961. Some observations on the intonation of a West Fife accent. Unpublished diploma dissertation, Edinburgh University.

Grant, W. 1914. The Pronunciation of English in Scotland. Cambridge University Press, Cambridge, Eng.

Grant, W., and Robson, E. H. A. 1925. Speech Training for Scottish Students. Cambridge University Press, Cambridge, Eng.

Jones, D. 1963. The Pronunciation of English, 4th ed. Cambridge University Press, Cambridge, Eng.

Ladefoged, P. 1967. Stress and respiratory activity. In: P. Ladefoged (ed.), Three Areas of Experimental Phonetics. Oxford University Press, Oxford.

Léon, P. R., and Martin, P. 1972. Machines and measurements. In: D. L. Bolinger (ed.), Intonation. Penguin Education, New York.

McClure, J. D. 1977. Vowel duration in a Scottish accent. J. Int. Phonet. Assn. 7:10–16.

17/The Intonation of Verifiability

Rose Nash and Anthony Mulac

THE PROBLEM

Nonverifiable Events

One of the functions of language is to enable human beings to verbalize their interpretations of physical and mental events that flash unexpectedly on the consciousness and compete for attention with previously identified events. In its simplest form, the process may be schematized as follows:

$$\text{Event} \rightarrow \frac{\text{Sensory}}{\text{impressions}} \rightarrow \text{Interpretation} \rightarrow \text{Report}$$

Interpretations are possible only when the sensory impressions are sufficient to identify the event, as in:

(1) I saw a shooting star.
     I felt a cold clammy hand on my neck.
     I tasted garlic in the soup.
     I heard the rattling of chains.
     I smelled gasoline leaking from the tank.

In reporting on the interpretation of such physical events, the speaker may imply, rather than express, the particular sense involved, as in:

(2) There was a shooting star.
     (I know; I saw it)
     There was a cold clammy hand on my neck.
     (I know; I felt it)
     There was garlic in the soup.
     (I know; I tasted it)
     There was a rattling of chains.
     (I know; I heard it)
     There was gasoline leaking from the tank.
     (I know; I smelled it)

This research was conducted at the University of California at Santa Barbara, utilizing the facilities of the Department of Electrical Engineering Signals Processing Laboratory, and the Department of Speech Laboratory for Quantitative Research in Speech. It was supported by grants from the National Endowment for the Humanities and from the Academic Senate of the University of California at Santa Barbara.

If the sensory impressions are insufficient in number or clarity to positively identify the event, speakers have two choices. They may bypass the identification and merely report the presence of sensory information, as in:

(3) I saw something.
     I felt something.
     I tasted something.
     I heard something.
     I smelled something.

or they may attempt a provisional interpretation on the basis of insufficient information and include this element of doubt in their report:

(4) I thought I saw a shooting star.
     I thought I felt a cold clammy hand on my neck.
     I thought I tasted garlic in the soup.
     I thought I heard the rattling of chains.
     I thought I smelled gasoline leaking from the tank.

In the extreme cases, the event may be so difficult to identify that even the presence of sensory information is doubted, as in:

(5) I thought I saw something.
     I thought I felt something.
     I thought I tasted something.
     I thought I heard something.
     I thought I smelled something.

This element of doubt may also be expressed in the present tense:

(6) I think I saw . . .
     I think I felt . . .
     I think I tasted . . .
     I think I heard . . .
     I think I smelled . . .

If, however, the event is ongoing rather than completed at the time of reporting, present tense for the doubt-expressing verb is obligatory:

(7) I think I see . . .
     *I thought I see . . .
     I think I feel . . .
     *I thought I feel . . .

and so on. This paper is concerned only with completed events.

There are many ways to express provisional interpretations other than I think and I thought, using various lexical paraphrases such as:

(8) I thought I saw a shooting star.
     A shooting star caught my eye.
     I believe I saw a shooting star.
     I saw what looked like a shooting star.
     That must have been a shooting star I saw.
     Didn't I just see a shooting star?
     I'll be a monkey's uncle if that isn't a shooting star.

All of these semantic variants are encompassed in range and degree of uncertainty by "I thought . . .".

The initial schematic process, revised to include the possibility of provisional interpretations and unidentified events, is as follows:

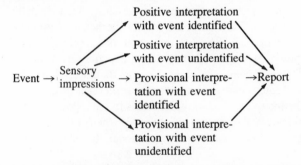

Thus, four different reports may be triggered by the same completed event, depending on the strength of the received sensory impressions and the ability of the speaker to make an interpretation:

(9) I saw a shooting star.
     I saw something.
     I thought I saw a shooting star.
     I thought I saw something.

     I felt a cold clammy hand on my neck.
     I felt something cold and clammy.
     I thought I felt a cold clammy hand on my neck.
     I thought I felt something cold and clammy.

Up to this point we have been discussing reports based exclusively on actual physical events, that is, events that might be experienced by more than one person, although the interpretations of each are not necessarily identical. Sensory impressions, however, are also a product of mental events, which makes them no less real to the individual experiencer. In dreams, fantasy, hallucinations, poetic invention, and other kinds of imagination, the mental event is the image that clamors, like the physical event, for attention and identification. We must therefore include in this category of sentence types such reports as the following:

(10) (I thought) I saw a purple gnu.
(I thought) I felt the wrath of God.
(I thought) I tasted the inside of a morpheme.
(I thought) I heard Ghandi talking to Christ.
(I thought) I smelled the River Styx.

It should be pointed out that the dividing line between mental and physical events is indistinct and, in the strictest sense, even nonexistent. This is because reports of this kind are interpretations based not on factual evidence, but on sensory impressions. The person who claims to have "seen" a purple gnu or any other bizarre image cannot be disproved. Similarly, the person who says "(I thought) I saw a shooting star" may have had his senses stimulated by an object classified in the external world as a satellite, a swiftly moving jet plane, a firecracker, a blow on the head, or nothing at all. The reality of the event, either physical or mental, is never in question because the sensory impressions are always real to the experiencer. The report is thus a *true* report. It accurately describes a chain of associations leading to one logically valid interpretation. Expressing the element of uncertainty does not invalidate the interpretation—it merely adds to the report the information that the associational links were somewhat weak. Whether the interpretation of the sensory impressions is positive or provisional, the event is NOT VERIFIABLE.

Finally, there is a tight time link between the nonverifiable event and the report, which is necessary if no additional external information is to intervene that may affect the interpretation of the sensory information. Reports of nonverifiable events frequently include a time adverb expressing immediacy, as in:

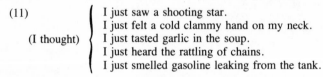

(11)

(I thought)

I just saw a shooting star.
I just felt a cold clammy hand on my neck.
I just tasted garlic in the soup.
I just heard the rattling of chains.
I just smelled gasoline leaking from the tank.

Verifiable Events

A verifiable event leads to a report that has sharply restricted characteristics. To illustrate, let us go back to our star-gazer, who saw, or thought he saw, a shooting star. Let us suppose that, the next morning, while lingering over his second cup of coffee as he reads the newspaper, he comes across an item about an unusually bright meteor that was sighted briefly at precisely the time of his own observation. He recalls the event, and, by means of the additional factual evidence in the newspaper, can now confirm his original interpretation. His report of the nonverifiable event, based only on sensory impressions, was "I thought I saw a shooting star." His later verified report, based on sensory impressions PLUS factual evidence, is:

(12)   I thought I saw a shooting star, and (as it turns out) I was right.

However, suppose the newspaper item is about a UFO sighting rather than a meteor. If he connects this fact with his experience of the previous night, he has also verified his interpretation of the event, but found it to be contrary to fact. His later report, based again on sensory impressions PLUS factual evidence, will be:

(13)   I thought I saw a shooting star, but (as it turns out) I was wrong.

Not all events can be treated to such fortuitous verification. Mental events must be eliminated; there is no way to check on the presence or absence of a purple gnu somewhere in the brain. This includes the figurative use of the senses, as in "I thought I smelled a rat."

Only identified events can be confirmed or denied; a report of the kind

(14)   I thought I saw something, and (as it turns out) I was right.

makes little sense unless either something is at least provisionally identified, so that it can be verified by the speaker with later factual evidence, or many other witnesses also "saw something," and confirmation of the event is based on the weight of shared observations.

Only completed events can be verified:

(15)   *I think I see a shooting star $\begin{cases} \text{and I'm right.} \\ \text{but I was wrong.} \end{cases}$

Only events given a provisional interpretation can be verified:

(16)   *I saw a shooting star, $\begin{cases} \text{and I was right.} \\ \text{but I was wrong.} \end{cases}$

Reports of verified events never follow immediately after the event, since there must be time for the additional factual evidence to appear. Such reports frequently include a time adverb pointing backward to the event:

(17)   I thought I saw a shooting star last night,
          $\begin{cases} \text{and (as it turns out) I was right.} \\ \text{but (as it turns out) I was wrong.} \end{cases}$

The time lapse between the event and the verified report forces the doubt-expressing element to be viewed as part of the completed event and therefore also past tense. Compare example (17) with:

(18)   I think I saw a shooting star last night
          (but I'm not positive).

To put the temporal relationship of event-to-report differently, we may say that a nonverifiable report occurs at Time 1, and a verifiable report occurs at Time 2:

$$\text{Event} \rightarrow \begin{matrix} \text{Sensory} \\ \text{impressions} \end{matrix} \rightarrow \begin{matrix} \text{Inter-} \\ \text{pretation} \end{matrix} \rightarrow \overset{\text{Time 1}}{\text{Report}} \rightarrow \begin{matrix} \text{Factual} \\ \text{evidence} \end{matrix} \rightarrow \begin{matrix} \text{Reinter-} \\ \text{pretation} \end{matrix} \rightarrow \overset{\text{Time 2}}{\text{Report}}$$

In summary, the differences between Time 1 reports and Time 2 reports are as follows:

Time 1	*Time 2*
The event is not verified	The event is verified as confirmed or denied
The event may be physical or mental	The event is physical
The event may be on-going or completed	The event is completed
The event may be identified or unidentified	The event is identified
The interpretation is based only on sensory information	The reinterpretation is based on earlier sensory information plus later factual evidence
The interpretation may be positive or provisional	The reinterpretation follows only a provisional interpretation
There is no time lapse between the event and the report	There is a time lapse between the event and the report

The Semantic Opposition Manifested in Prosody

We come now to the main topic of this paper, the intonation patterns of the sentence types described. Time 1 reports of nonverified events have intonations similar to those of other declarative sentences, with no special prominence given to the element expressing uncertainty. Compare these two sentences:

(19) Amanda is a pretty girl.
      I thought I saw a shooting star.

In the absence of emphasis or contrast, both sentences have the same contour, with the main sentence accent on the last lexical item.[1]

Time 2 reports of verified events carry obligatory pitch accent on the element expressing uncertainty. All such reports will have either form (a) or (b):

(a) I *thought* X (X confirmed).
(b) I *thought* X (X denied).

---

[1]The effect of emphasis or contrast on reports of nonverified events is easier to observe in a longer utterance. In

I thought I just saw AMANDA crossing the street.

the presupposition is that someone performed the action. The identity of the performer is not certain, but the act is. Movability of accents can, of course, produce contrast at various points in the utterance, implying answers to various questions (see Gunter, 1966).

where X represents all possible verifiable events. This can be replaced as a cover symbol in actual speech by the lexical item <u>so</u>, enabling us to economically describe the confirmation/denial opposition of the simple utterance "I thought so, . . ." (and implied verification). Let us now look at the possible accent intonation patterns.

An A accent is characterized by an abrupt fall, either within the accented syllable or in the immediately following syllable (Bolinger, 1958).[2] The approach to the accent may be above, below, or on a level with the accented syllable. If the fall begins in the accented syllable <u>thought</u>, and an upglide is used on <u>so</u> before the pause, the utterance may take the following forms:

(20) I
          \
      I→t h o u g h t
      /   so-o
      I

Bolinger calls Accent A <u>assertive</u>: "it is used with items that are separately important, contrastive and/or new to the discourse" (p. 52). The hypothesis here is that Accent A with falling pitch signals a Time 2 report that CONFIRMS the event.

Accent C is characterized by a skip down to the accented syllable, which then levels off or rises. If the pitch rises on the accented syllable, the utterance has the following form:

(21) I
          \ t h o u g h t
                  so-o

Bolinger calls Accent C *anti-assertive:* "this is a kind of anti-Accent A, both in form and in meaning" (p. 50). The hypothesis here is that Accent C with rising pitch signals a Time 2 report that DENIES the event.

However, rising <u>thought</u> may also be approached from below or on a level:[3]

(22) I
          \
      I→ t h o u g h t
      /   so-o
      I

---

[2]Page numbers ci·ed refer to the reprinted version.

[3]In Bolinger's description, this would be a B Accent in form, like the pitch movement on <u>so</u> before the pause. However, in this case, going directly from <u>I</u> to <u>thought</u>, it does not carry quite the same meaning of "connectedness" or "incompleteness."

If we eliminate the level approaches, in which the pitch movements are less definitive, the contrasting patterns can be reduced to two with rising thought and two with falling thought:

(23)   I↘

     I↗ $^{t\,h}o\,^{u}\,{}_{g}\,{}_{h}\,{}_{t}$

            so-^{o} (and I was right)

(24)   I↘ ${}_{t}\,{}_{h}\,{}_{o}\,{}_{u}\,{}_{g}\,{}^{h}\,{}^{t}$

     I↗   so-^{o} (but I was wrong)

The semantic contrast thus has two elements: rising versus falling pitch on thought, and approach from above versus approach from below on I. If pitch direction rather than accent alone is the more essential factor in the semantic opposition, we might expect that the unbroken lines (high-pitched I with falling thought and low-pitched I with rising thought) intensify the implied confirmation or denial, and the broken lines (a jump up to falling thought and a jump down to rising thought) increase ambiguity.[4]

To eliminate the possible effect of other factors present in natural speech (timing, intensity, voice quality, and so on) on the interpretation of various patterns, a speech synthesis experiment was designed in which the only variable was pitch.

THE EXPERIMENT

Experimental Objectives

The experiment was designed to answer the following specific questions:

1. Is the information required for a listener to make semantic interpretations of intonation patterns actually present in the acoustic signal? That is, can

---

[4]What counts is the proportion of uninterrupted upmotion or downmotion in the utterance, not the pitch movement on thought alone. If there are enough extra unstressed syllables to indicate a general upward or downward line, the same overall effect can be produced with a level thought. Bolinger (personal communication) supplied the following example for the interpretation "... but I must have been mistaken":

                   re

               I

        thought

     I

                              u

                            o

     ceived a letter from y   .

In other words, thought is lengthened and given gradient pitch to compensate for the lack of extra syllables that might otherwise carry the tune.

subjects make interpretative distinctions between synthesized versions of utterances presented out of context and differing only in fundamental frequency patterns?

2. Are intonation patterns perceived differently by males and females, or by monolinguals and bilinguals? That is, can a listener interpret with equal facility a pattern he might or might not use himself?

3. What is the effect on interpretation of rising versus falling thought? That is, does gradient intonation intensify the semantic function of the pitch accent?

4. What is the effect on interpretation of approach to thought from above versus approach to thought from below? That is, does pitch accent or overall pitch direction play the more decisive role in semantic decisions?

5. How well do listeners "remember" their interpretations of specific patterns? That is, how consistent are interpretations on repetitions of the same pattern at different times?

6. Are listeners aware of potential ambiguity? That is, how often do they impose interpretations rather than admit their inability to do so, and to what extent do they disagree with other listeners and with themselves on the "meaning" of an utterance?

Preparation of Tape

To obtain pitch range and timing information, a male speaker recorded the utterance "I thought so . . ." several times, using a variety of tempos and degrees of emphasis. The taped samples of the natural voice were processed on a Kay Sonograph Model # 6061B and a Frøkjar-Jensen Transpitchmeter, and the displays were divided into phonetic segments. Measurements were made of the duration of each segment, which were then averaged and used as constant values for the synthesized versions. Maximum and minimum fundamental frequencies of vowel segments were used to set the pitch range of the synthesized versions. The intervening fundamental frequency movements were then plotted to create mirror images on combinations of I and thought, with the pattern for so remaining constant throughout.

A Glace-Holmes Jaword synthesizer, in connection with an IBM 1800 computer, was utilized to prepare the test versions, using the Mattingly Synthesis by Rule Program to obtain vowel formant and amplitude values (Holmes, Mattingly, and Shearme, 1964). Seven versions of "I thought so" were made. The first three were monotones at 85 Hz, 180 Hz, and 260 Hz, respectively, outlining the total pitch range used in the synthesis. This was done to accustom the listeners to the sound of the synthesized speech. A spectrogram of the synthesized monotone version at 180 Hz is given in Figure 1.

The other four versions, comprising the actual test patterns, varied the pitch direction movement on thought and the pitch level on I relative to the

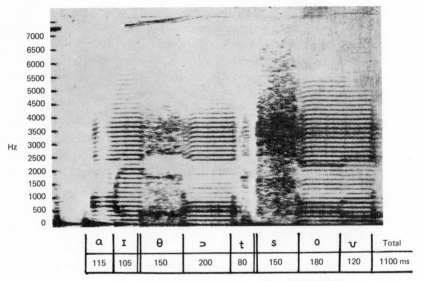

Figure 1.   Narrowband spectrogram of monotone version of I thought so at 180 Hz.

starting pitch of thought. Thus, falling thought was approached by a higher I in pattern I, and a lower I in pattern II. Similarly, rising thought was approached by a higher I in pattern III, and a lower I in pattern IV. The complete schema of intonation patterns imposed on the utterance is shown in Figure 2.

The test tape was prepared as follows: the three monotone versions were recorded first, followed by the four intonation patterns in four orders determined by a Latin square to eliminate order effects, making a total of 16 stimuli. Each pattern was immediately followed by its repetition after a 2-second silence. Between patterns there was a 10-second silence. Halfway through, between the eighth and ninth stimuli, there was a pause of 1 minute. In order that listeners not be distracted by a change of voice during the experiment, nothing was recorded on the tape other than the synthesized versions. Total playing time was approximately 5 minutes.

Response Form

Subjects were asked to choose one of two interpretations for each pattern, with a "can't tell" option if they could not decide. The response form is shown in Figure 3.

Subjects

Subjects were 67 students enrolled in five sections of Fundamentals of Speech at the University of California, Santa Barbara. The students were predomi-

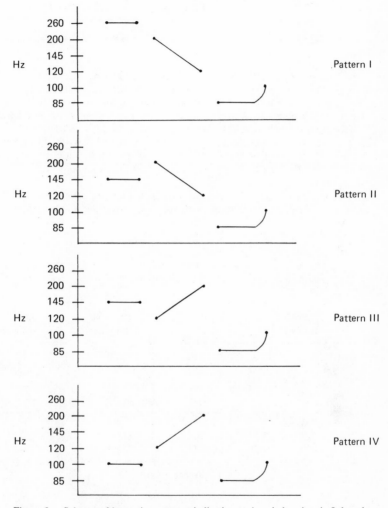

Figure 2.   Schema of intonation patterns indicating major pitch points in I thought so.

nantly freshmen, averaging 19 years in age. Fifty-five percent were males, forty-five percent females. Nearly one-third of the subjects indicated on the test form that they were bilingual, with Spanish the predominant second language.

Administration of Listening Test

Data collection took place as part of the regularly scheduled course lecture titled "Speech Delivery: Voice and Bodily Action," given by one of the

LISTENING TEST

Listener's 2nd language: _____   Listener's sex: _____
(if bilingual)

Instructions: You are asked to listen to the phrase, "I thought so," spoken in several different ways. For each example, try to determine whether the speaker is trying to convey the idea that he later found he had been right, or that he was later proven wrong; i.e. (a) "I thought so. And I was right." or (b) "I thought so. But I was wrong." If you can't decide which the speaker means, mark (c) Can't tell.

You will hear 16 examples in all, with a brief rest period halfway through the testing session. (If the speaker sounds inhuman to you, it is because all of these examples were "uttered" by a speech synthesizer, used in conjunction with a computer and tape recorder.)

Each example will be repeated immediately. You will then have 10 seconds to mark your test sheet next to that example's number with one of the following letters:

Test:

a (= "And I was right.")
b (= "But I was wrong.")
c (= Can't tell which the speaker meant.)

Example number	Inferred meaning	Example number	Inferred meaning
1.	_____	9.	_____
2.	_____	10.	_____
3.	_____	11.	_____
4.	_____	12.	_____
5.	_____	13.	_____
6.	_____	14.	_____
7.	_____	15.	_____
8.	_____	16.	_____

Figure 3.   Response form.

investigators. Students were asked to participate in a brief "listening test," conducted as part of the research program of the Laboratory for Quantitative Research in Speech. They were told that this task would help to introduce one aspect of speech delivery—the use of voice to express ideas. The lecturer wrote the phrase I thought so on the board, stating that a speaker might wish to convey two different ideas with this statement: "a. And I was right," or "b. But I was wrong." At no time did the lecturer-investigator say the phrase I thought so out loud. Test forms were then distributed and the subjects asked to read all instructions carefully, asking questions if necessary.

To familiarize the listeners with the sound of the synthesized speech and with the test procedure, the training portion of the tape was played separately. This consisted of the three monotone versions of "I thought so." The lecturer then played the test examples of "I thought so" with the different intonation patterns. At the 1-minute pause halfway through the test, the lecturer told the listeners to relax, say something to their neighbor, and so on. The subjects displayed no difficulty or hesitancy in completing the assigned task.

RESULTS

Overall Effect of Patterns on Interpretation

The effect of intonation pattern on listener response was clearly substantiated by a chi-square analysis of responses to the four intonation patterns ($\chi^2 = 173.94$, $df = 6$, $p < 0.001$).[5] This means that listener responses to some patterns differed substantially from their responses to other patterns. Table 1 displays combined responses to these four patterns. All chi-square values for responses to each intonation pattern were significant ($p < 0.001$). Thus it is clear that each pattern had a distinct effect on listener interpretation.

Lack of Effect of Listener Sex and Language Background

To determine whether listener sex or bilingualism affected responses to the four intonation patterns presented, a separate chi-square test was conducted for differences in subgroup responses to each pattern. These tests failed to show any differences in responses among the four groups on any of the four patterns: pattern I ($\chi^2 = 5.90$, $df = 6$, $p > 0.25$), pattern II ($\chi^2 = 10.64$, $df = 6$, $p > 0.05$), pattern III ($\chi^2 = 7.61$, $df = 6$, $p > 0.25$), or pattern IV ($\chi^2 = 3.06$, $df = 6$, $p > 0.50$). Therefore, the data from these subgroups were combined, and the remaining analyses were conducted using these combined-group data.

Effect of Pitch Direction on thought

Analysis of this study's data clearly supports the basic research hypothesis regarding the effect of rising or falling pitch movement of the word thought on listener interpretation. As Table 2 indicates, a falling inflection on thought led to the interpretation "and I was right," whereas a rising inflection on thought led to the interpretation "but I was wrong" ($\chi^2 = 137.53$, $\chi^2 = 1$, $p < 0.001$).

---

[5]The two-way classification chi-square test employed here established the likelihood that any apparent differences among group responses occurred by chance. The differences tested here were so slight that sampling error could easily have caused them. For a complete description of the chi-square procedure, see Siegel, 1956.

Table 1. Combined data: responses to four intonation patterns[a] of I thought so

Intonation pattern	Response alternative[b]	Percentage of responses[c]	
		For each alternative	Combined (χ^2)[d]
I	a	78	
	b	19	92.79
	c	4	
II	a	54	
	b	32	24.33
	c	14	
III	a	27	
	b	58	29.85
	c	15	
IV	a	34	
	b	54	26.75
	c	12	

[a] As shown in Figure 2.
[b] a. "And I was right."
    b. "But I was wrong."
    c. Can't tell.
[c] Total number of subjects = 67; total number of responses = 1072.
[d] $df = 2$; $p < 0.001$.

Table 2. Comparison of responses to two pitch pattern directions on the word thought

Pitch pattern direction	Response alternative[a]	Percentage of responses for each alternative
Falling	a	66
(patterns I and II)	b	25
	c	9
Rising	a	30
(patterns III and IV)	b	56
	c	13

[a] a. "And I was right."
    b. "But I was wrong."
    c. Can't tell.

Effect of Pitch Level on I

When the data were analyzed to determine whether the pitch level of <u>I</u> (above or below the initial pitch of <u>thought</u>) had an effect on listener response, it was found that the interpretation depended on the pitch direction of thought. As Table 3 shows, pattern I with <u>I</u> above the initial pitch of the falling <u>thought</u> more consistently evoked the response "and I was right," than did pattern II where <u>I</u> was below the initial pitch of the falling <u>thought</u>, ($\chi^2 = 35.44$, $df = 2$, $p < 0.001$).

On the other hand, whether <u>I</u> approached a rising <u>thought</u> from above or below had no effect on listener reaction ($\chi^2 = 4.16$, $df = 2$, $p > 0.10$). Both of these patterns were interpreted equally as "but I was wrong."

Order Effects

The four intonation patterns were presented in groups of four, each time in a different order (determined by Latin Square to control for order effects in judging). Therefore, the judges heard each pattern four times during the 16-example listening session. Since each intonation pattern was preceded by every other pattern at some time during the session, the effect of hearing a given pattern immediately after another pattern can be analyzed. To determine whether such an effect due to order of presentation did occur (whether, for example, the response to pattern I was different when it was preceded by pattern II than when preceded by pattern III or pattern IV) a series of chi-square tests was conducted. The differences among responses to the four presentations of each pattern are clearly indicated by the results of these tests: pattern I ($\chi^2 = 34.48$, $df = 6$, $p < 0.001$); pattern II ($\chi^2 = 24.11$, $df = 6$, $p < 0.001$); pattern III ($\chi^2 = 41.11$, $df = 6$, $p < 0.001$); and pattern IV ($\chi^2 = 28.71$, $df = 6$, $p < 0.001$). These suggest that the preceding pattern did in fact make a difference in the listener's response to a particular pattern. Response differences due to order effect may be studied in Table 4.

Table 3.   Chi-square values for comparisons of each of the four intonation patterns with every other pattern

	Pattern I	Pattern II	Pattern III	Pattern IV
Pattern I		35.44[a]	138.68[a]	101.89[a]
Pattern II			45.74[a]	28.43[a]
Pattern III				4.16[b]
Pattern IV				

[a] $df = 2$, $p < 0.001$.
[b] $df = 2$, $p > 0.10$.

Table 4.   Responses to sixteen examples of I thought so in order presented

			Percentage of responses	
Order of presentation	Intonation pattern[a]	Response alternative[b]	For each alternative	Combined $(\chi^2)^c$
1	I	a b c	76 22 1	90.73
2	II	a b c	39 55 6	37.85
3	III	a b c	15 75 10	79.30
4	IV	a b c	33 57 10	33.48
5	II	a b c	61 21 18	34.94
6	IV	a b c	25 52 22	16.54
7	I	a b c	92 6 1	158.61
8	III	a b c	12 67 21	52.76
One minute pause				
9	III	a b c	30 60 10	38.39

(continued)

Pattern I (falling thought approached from above) responses seem to have been least affected by the patterns preceding them. In all four presentations, the primary response was "and I was right." The fact that only 55% of the listeners gave this response the fourth time the pattern was presented, as opposed to 76%, 92%, and 87% for the other three presentations, appears to be more the result of listener fatigue than order effect.

Pattern II (falling thought approached from below), on the other hand, received different interpretations depending on which pattern preceded it. Although the majority of students responded "and I was right" three of the

Table 4. (continued)

Order of presentation	Intonation pattern[a]	Response alternative[b]	Percentage of responses	
			For each alternative	Combined (χ^2)[c]
10	I	a	87	
		b	12	132.76
		c	1	
11	IV	a	24	
		b	70	66.03
		c	6	
12	II	a	60	
		b	25	33.85
		c	15	
13	IV	a	55	
		b	37	35.64
		c	8	
14	III	a	51	
		b	30	16.03
		c	19	
15	II	a	58	
		b	25	29.64
		c	16	
16	I	a	55	
		b	34	30.73
		c	10	

[a] As shown in Figure 2.
[b] a. "And I was right."
 b. "But I was wrong."
 c. Can't tell.
[c] $df = 2$, $p < 0.001$.

times they heard the pattern, they responded "but I was wrong" when this pattern was preceded by pattern I. This may have occurred because these were the first two patterns heard, and, as the other analyses show, the effect of pattern I was the most pronounced and consistent of all the patterns. Many of the listeners may therefore have felt that pattern II, in comparison to pattern I, meant "but I was wrong." Only after hearing the two falling thought patterns did the listeners begin responding to pattern II as "and I was right."

Pattern III (rising thought approached from above) led to the response "but I was wrong" the first three times it was presented. However, when it was preceded by pattern IV on the fourth hearing, it was marked "and I was right" by 51% of the listeners. An analysis of subject responses to the final presentation of the four patterns (the 13th through 16th examples presented), suggests that fatigue and/or disinterest may have set in by this time. These last four presentations were all judged by a slight majority to indicate "and I was right" (55%, 51%, 58%, and 55%), even though the first two utilized rising intonation on thought. It is of course possible that the presence of pattern IV immediately before pattern III caused the observed result.

Pattern IV (rising thought approached from below) was also marked "but I was wrong" by the majority of listeners (57%, 52%, and 70%) the first three times it was presented. However, when it was presented the final time, after pattern II, 55% of the listeners indicated "and I was right." As in the case of pattern III, the most likely cause of this change in response is listener fatigue. Further evidence for this explanation is given by the fact that responses to the last four presentations failed to differ. That is, the four different intonation patterns resulted in the same responses ($\chi^2 = 6.51$, $df = 6$, $p > 0.25$). By this time in the listening task, it appears that all patterns sounded alike, even though the listeners had been able to consistently differentiate between them during their earlier presentations.

It is clear from the above results that further study is needed to determine the effect of a preceding intonation pattern on the interpretation of the following pattern. The Latin Square design employed here controlled for order effects in the overall results. However, a separate investigation would be required to study the specific effects of order of presentation, controlling for possible learning and fatigue effects.

Ambiguity Effects

A question of great interest in this study was the relative extent to which the four intonation patterns were ambiguous to the listeners; that is, the extent to which each was "admitting of more than one interpretation..." (Neilson, 1966, p. 81). The data may be analyzed in several different ways to answer this question. First, although each of the four patterns consistently led to the response "and I was right" or "but I was wrong" for the majority of listeners, a substantial minority indicated a different interpretation for each pattern. These minority response groups ranged from 39% to 6% of the listeners, depending on the pattern and presentation. The average percentage of subjects disagreeing with the majority interpretation was 24%. By this measure, the intonation patterns can be seen as moderately ambiguous.

Another index of ambiguity is provided by the extent to which each listener agreed with himself on the interpretation of each pattern during its several presentations. This measure was computed as the percentage of intralistener agreement for each intonation pattern. Since each subject heard

Table 5.   Percentages of intralistener agreement for
four presentations of each pattern

Intonation pattern[a]	Number of agreements	Percentage of listeners
I	3	58
	2	31
	1	10
II	3	9
	2	51
	1	40
III	3	19
	2	36
	1	45
IV	3	25
	2	46
	1	28

[a]As shown in Figure 2.

each pattern four times, it was possible for him to agree with himself three times, twice, or once for each intonation pattern. Combined intralistener percentages of agreement for each pattern are presented in Table 5. These range from a high for pattern I of 58% of the listeners showing complete internal consistency in their responses to a low of 9% showing complete consistency for pattern II. Table 6 displays the specific responses of those subjects who were completely consistent in their response to a given pattern.

The average across all patterns was only 29% of the listeners who consistently responded to a given pattern.[6] On the other hand, an average of 31% of the listeners found the patterns so ambiguous that they averaged only one agreement out of three chances. By this measure, the intonation patterns clearly led to "more than one interpretation," even within any individual listener.[7]

One final means of assessing ambiguity is to analyze the percentages of listener-perceived ambiguity embodied in the "c. Can't tell" responses. Whereas 48% of all responses were "a. And I was right," and 41% were "b.

[6]Of the 67 subjects, only one showed complete consistency of response for all four presentations for all four patterns.

[7]For a discussion of the causes of perceptual differences in the interpretation of ambiguous sentences, see Nash, 1970.

Table 6. Responses of subjects demonstrating
complete intralistener agreement on a given
intonation pattern

Intonation pattern[a]	Response alternative[b]	Number of subjects
	a	39
I	b	0
	c	0
	a	5
II	b	1
	c	0
	a	0
III	b	13
	c	0
	a	2
IV	b	14
	c	1

[a] As shown in Figure 2.
[b] a. "And I was right."
   b. "But I was wrong."
   c. Can't tell.

But I was wrong," only 11% of all responses were "c. Can't tell.'"[8] In fact,
22 of the 67 subjects failed to mark "c. Can't tell" for any of the 16 examples, and only one listener marked that response as many as seven times.
Although the other two indexes had shown the intonation patterns to be
moderately to highly ambiguous, listeners admitted their inability to discern
the intended meaning of a particular pattern only 11% of the time.

Summary of Results

The results of the experiment provide the following answers to the specific
questions posed:

1. Listeners are able to make statistically significant differences in semantic
    interpretations of synthesized intonation patterns.

---

[8] Although the response "a. And I was right" appeared before "b. But I was wrong" on the
test form, a chi-square test on percentage of total responses marked for each of these categories
failed to uncover a significant difference ($\chi^2 = 0.55$, $df = 1$, $p > 0.75$). Apparently, the order of
presentation of response choices "a" and "b" had no effect on the subjects' marking them for a
given intonation pattern. The fact that for seven of the 16 presentations, the majority of subjects
marked "b. But I was wrong" also argues against any possible order effect for response alternatives.

2. Semantic interpretations remain consistent regardless of listener sex or language background.
3. Falling thought (patterns I and II) evokes the interpretation ''and I was right''; rising thought (patterns III and IV) evokes ''but I was wrong.''
4. I approaching thought from above versus from below produces a more noticeable effect on the certainty of interpretations for falling thought than for rising thought. By far the most powerful effect was created by pattern I, in which the pitch descended in an unbroken line.
5. Listeners are not completely consistent in their responses to specific patterns repeated later. This may be due to order of presentation, fatigue, or other psychological effects of the test situation.
6. Utterances are in fact more ambiguous than they appear to the listener to be. That is, listeners prefer to impose definite, albeit contradictory, interpretations, rather than to recognize inherent ambiguity.

DISCUSSION

Let us return to the hypothesis stated at the close of the first section (''The Problem'') with regard to verbal reports of events that are interpreted provisionally on the basis of sensory impressions alone, then later verified as confirmed or denied by additional factual information: that, in the portion of his final report referring to his initial uncertainty (I thought . . .), a speaker will make a prosodic contrast between implied confirmation (I was right) and implied denial (I was wrong); and that a listener will be able to determine which of the two types of verification is intended without the expressed lexical information. It is predicted that Accent A with falling intonation will most clearly signal confirmation, whereas Accent B or Accent C with rising intonation will signal denial.

What do the results of the experiment show? Statistically, it is obvious that gross pitch movements alone, without the quality improvements of finely distributed gradations of timing and intensity present in the human voice, can carry a considerable amount of semantic information. Falling or rising intonation appears to be the more decisive factor; accent intensifies, but does not change, the favored interpretation.

Accent A, with falling intonation, clearly elicited the predicted interpretation. In this experiment it was confirmation, and in Bolinger's description it was assertion; it is fairly easy to supply a whole cluster of related semantic labels that have been used by scholars from time to time for describing various linguistic functions of falling pitch: completeness, unmarkedness, presentation, basic contour, and Tune 1. What all of these have in common from a physiological point of view is relaxation of muscle tension. It is simply easier to descend the pitch ladder.

Accents B and C, with rising intonation, on the other hand, force the muscles to tighten up. This physiological tension is reflected in an opposing cluster of labels: denial, anti-assertion, discontinuity, markedness, and Tune 2. There is little doubt that the overall reactions to pitch movement are universal, and that they apply to music as well as speech. In both, melody always rises to its emotional climax, and falls to its denouement.

Thus, we may conclude that, in general, the hypothesis about verifiable reports is supported by the experimental evidence. Is this phenomenon limited to sensory events? If we look at other types of sentences in which verifiability is reported, we find that confirmation versus denial is similarly associated with the falling versus rising pitch opposition. First, there are verifiable non-sensory events reported with falling or rising thought:

(25) I thought [you'd get drunk at the party,   and I was right.
                  class started at 8:30,
                  the weather would be nice today,
                  I'd flunk the exam,
    I thought   this new girdle would fit me,   but I was wrong.

Second, there are verifiable conditions with rising or falling thought, such as:

(26) I thought [all men were male chauvinist pigs,   and I was right.
                  Harry was a con-man,
                  I had you all figured out,
                  there was a skeleton in the closet,
    I thought   this was the train to Poughkeepsie,   but I was wrong.

Finally, there are verifiable events and conditions in which the report uses doubt-expressing elements other than thought that have the same characteristic intonational opposition of confirmation versus denial:

(27)

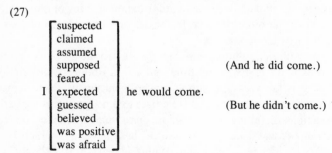

    [suspected
      claimed
      assumed
      supposed   (And he did come.)
      feared
   I expected   he would come.
      guessed   (But he didn't come.)
      believed
      was positive
      was afraid]

These data strongly suggest that English may have something like a lexical tone distinction in some parts of its intonational system. If so, then we have barely begun to realize the linguistic potentialities of the most expressive part of language.

REFERENCES

Bolinger, D. L. 1958. A theory of pitch accent in English. Word 14:109–149. Reprinted in I. Abe and T. Kanekiyo (eds.), Forms of English, pp. 17–56. Harvard University Press, Cambridge, Mass.

Gunter, R. 1966. On the placement of accent in dialogue: A feature of context grammar. J. Ling. 2:159–179.

Holmes, J. N., Mattingly, I. G., and Shearme, J. N. 1964. Speech synthesis by rule. Lang. Speech 7:127–143.

Nash, R. 1970. John likes Mary more than Bill: An experiment in disambiguation using synthesized intonation contours. Phonetica 22:170–188.

Neilson, W. A. (ed.). 1966. Webster's New International Dictionary of the English Language, 2d ed., (unabridged). G. & C. Merriam Company, Cambridge, Mass.

Siegel, S. 1965. Nonparimetric Statistics for the Behavioral Sciences, pp. 175–179. McGraw-Hill Book Company, New York.

18/ Intonation in Discourse

Emily Rando

In this article I point out and suggest derivations for the intonational patterns characteristic of questions and certain related constructions. I attempt to characterize the semantic and functional uses of such basic patterns as "rising" and "falling," and discuss the rules that assign them. It can be seen that, in general, falling intonation correlates with assertiveness, new information, and finality, and rising intonation correlates with lack of assertiveness, old information, and nonfinality. It can also be seen that, if yes-no questions are derived from a disjunctive source, "question intonation" can be derived simply and naturally if intonation assignment is ordered before conjunct deletion.

THE PROBLEMS

In this section, I describe the normal intonation pattern of various sentence types, mentioning a few of the exceptions in each case. I restrict my attention at first to the coda or cadence of the patterns.

Declarative sentences generally have falling cadences, for example:[1]

(1) It's probably raining in Vancouver.

(2) Montana has a unique beauty.

(3) Moe was bitten by a Samoyed.

Sentences with the syntactic form of statements may end with rising intonation, as in example (4), but the effect is that of a question with the expectation of a positive answer expressed:

From *Questions and Answers in English*, by Emily Pope. Copyright © 1976 by Mouton & Co., The Hague. Reprinted by permission.

[1]I will indicate intonation with wavy lines, where "up" means high pitch, and "down" means low pitch.

(4)   He rarely mentions it?

There are other counterexamples—a special type is discussed in "Rising and Falling Intonation," below—but in the vast majority of cases (the normal, usual, uninteresting cases), statements have a falling cadence.

Yes-no questions normally end with a rise in intonation, for example:

(5)   Is it snowing again?

(6)   Does Steve have a car?

(7)   Can you touch your nose with your tongue?

(8)   Aren't you tired?

Under special circumstances, as in example (9), a question may end with falling intonation:

(9)   A.   Steve's car ran out of gas.

      B.   Oh, does Steve have a car?

Here B had not known that Steve had a car, but realizes that the answer to his question must be "yes." In effect, he is merely registering the fact that this information is news to him.

Again under special circumstances, as in example (10), the rise may occur in some position other than the end, in which case the tone remains high until the end, where there may optionally be a further rise.[2,3]

(10)   Did Penny impart that information to you?

Here "Penny," rather than any of the constituents ending in "you," is the focus of the question.

There are many other sorts of counterexamples, but, again, in the usual cases yes-no questions have a rising cadence.

---

[2]Such examples, along with many other variations in question intonation, are discussed in Chafe, 1968.

[3]The contour of example (10) suggests that there is a low-level rule that distributes the last functionally assigned pitch rightward to the end of the sentence or to the next assigned accent.

Tag questions appear from their form to be part statement and part question, and, indeed, they may have either a falling cadence or a rising cadence. The two types have different uses and, probably, different presuppositions. I call the first type—the one with a falling cadence—an S tag, and the type with rising cadence I call a Q tag. The S tag is used in nearly the same way as a statement, except that a response is more specifically asked for. There is a strong expectation on the part of the speaker that the response will confirm his pseudostatement. He is not so. much imparting or requesting information as he is seeking acknowledgment that his interlocutor shares the belief expressed in the statement part of the sentence.

This use of the tag question has a falling cadence. In particular, the pitch of the pronoun in the tag is lower than the pitch of the auxiliary or modal. (To many people, it seems wrong to write a question mark after such a sentence, so I use a period.)

(11)   It's raining, isn't it.

(12)   It isn't raining, is it.

The second type of tag questions—Q tags—are more nearly questions than statements. The speaker still expresses his own belief in the statement part of the sentence, and in the question part he still calls for a response, expecting confirmation. However, some doubt as to the correctness of his belief has entered his mind, and disconfirmation would not surprise him as much as in the previous case.

This use of the tag question has a rising cadence. In particular, the pitch of the pronoun in the tag is higher than the pitch of the auxiliary or modal:

(13)   It's raining, isn't it?

(14)   It isn't raining, is it?

S tags and Q tags are not the only possible types. A third very common use of the tag question is as a rhetorical question. This is discussed in Pope, 1976 (Ch. 2). Then there are the belligerent tag sentences, where the statement and question halves of the sentence are either both positive or (in some dialects) both negative. Belligerent tags are discussed below.

S tags and Q tags share more properties with statements and questions, respectively, than just intonation. For instance, consider the sorts of responses that are appropriate for each. In example (15), speaker B, questioning the motivation for A's speech act, uses the verb "say":

(15)   A.   It's raining, isn't it.

     B.   No. [pitch drops sharply indicating surprise] What makes you say so?

In example (16), speaker B, again questioning the motivation for A's speech act, uses the verb "ask":

(16)   A.   It's raining, isn't it?

     B.   No. [with the milder pitch drop of matter-of-fact question answering] Why do you ask?

Examples (15B) and (16B) are still possible, but much less appropriate, in response to examples (16A) and (15A), respectively. Since there is no performative verb corresponding uniquely to tag questions, one is forced to choose between the two that correspond to their component parts. As we have seen, the choice is usually not arbitrary.

Another example is provided by the grammatical restrictions on S tags and Q tags. S tags have many of the same restrictions as statements, whereas Q tags pattern like questions in certain respects. For instance, it is grammatical to question people, but not to inform them, on their suppositions. The S tag in example (17), like the statement in example (18), is ungrammatical, whereas the Q tag in example (19), like the question in example (20), is grammatical. (However, I do not mean to imply that the members of the pairs are paraphrases of each other.[4])

(17)   *You don't suppose he'll come, do you.
(18)   *You don't suppose he'll come.

(19)   You don't suppose he'll come, do you?
(20)   Do you suppose he'll come?

Conversely, adverbs like "certainly" are grammatical in statements, but not in questions. The S tag in example (21), like the statement in example

---

[4]Also, of course, the parallelism of S tags and statements does not always hold, as examples (i) and (ii) show (see R. Lakoff's discussion of these constructions in Lakoff, 1969):

(i)   *I don't suppose he'll come, do I.
(ii)   I don't suppose he'll come.

(22), is grammatical, whereas the Q tag in example (23), like the question in example (24), is ungrammatical:

(21) Bob certainly is a stone, isn't he.
(22) Bob certainly is a stone.

(23) *Bob certainly is a stone, isn't he?
(24) *Isn't Bob certainly a stone?

Another kind of example is provided by positive polarity items. "Already" is a positive polarity item. Hence example (25) is grammatical, but example (26) is not, except as a denial of a sentence like example (25):

(25) It's already raining.
(26) *It isn't already raining.

The S tag in example (27), like that in example (26), is ungrammatical:

(27) *It isn't already raining, is it.

However, examples (28) and (29) are grammatical:

(28) It isn't already raining, is it?
(29) Is it already raining?

What we have seen so far is that yes-no questions and sentences that function and pattern similarly have rising cadences, whereas statements and sentences that function and pattern similarly have falling cadences. Now let us examine the intonations of wh-questions[5] to see where they fit into this scheme.

Ordinary wh-questions have falling cadences. They may contain more than one wh-word, but the extra ones do not affect the cadence, nor do they occasion special rises or falls of their own:

(30) Who did what to who?

(31) How do you do?

---

[5]Although yes-no questions are technically wh-questions, I have been using and will continue to use the term to designate questions with a wh-word other than "whether."

(32)   What time is it?

(33)   What are you going to do when you grow up?

(34)   Why don't we talk about your mother?

There are a few types of wh-questions that have rising cadences. One is exemplified by the question in example (35B):

(35)   A.   What's the matter with Barbara?

       B.   What's the matter with Barbara?
       A.   That's right. What's the matter with Barbara?

Here B thinks he has heard correctly, but is not quite sure and wants to check. Example (35B) is probably derived from something like example (36), in which case it is not surprising that it has the intonation of a yes-no question:

(36)   Did you $\left\{ \begin{array}{l} \text{say} \\ \text{utter} \\ \text{ask} \end{array} \right\}$ "What's the matter with Barbara?"?

This derivation does not, however, work for example (37B):

(37)   A.   What's the matter with Barbara?

       B.   What's the matter with who?
       A.   Barbara. What's the matter with her?

I do not think such questions are derived from any sort of yes-no question, so their intonation cannot be explained in that way. Besides, the rise is not really associated with the cadence, as it is in example (35B), and in yes-no questions generally. In example (38), the rise is on "who," and high tone is maintained to the end, where a further rise is only optional:

(38)   How did who find out where we live?

In fact, such questions are not even especially associated with wh-questions. They are quite a general phenomenon called echo questions, and may be formed from any type of sentence, as the following examples show:

(39)   Did who eat all his grainies?

(40)   Rita married who?

(41)   Wash who?

In statements and imperatives, but not sentences that are already questions, the wh-word may be moved to the front:

(42)   Who did Rita marry?

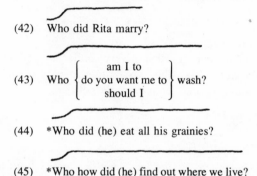

(43)   Who $\left\{ \begin{array}{c} \text{am I to} \\ \text{do you want me to} \\ \text{should I} \end{array} \right\}$ wash?

(44)   *Who did (he) eat all his grainies?

(45)   *Who how did (he) find out where we live?

These questions are used either when the word in question was not heard, or when the word replaced by the wh-word occasions amazement. For statements and imperatives, sentences like those in examples (40) and (41) are preferred for the amazement version, and sentences like those in examples (42) and (43) for the unheard version.

"Whether" is never used in echo questions. Instead, one of the possibilities in example (46B) may be used:

(46)   A.   John put it away.

       B1. John what?

       B2. John did what?

       B3. John did (or didn't) put it away?

       B4. John did put it away (or didn't)?

Example (47B) must be considered an echo question, although it does not echo any of the preceding sentence:

(47)   A.   Prices slumped.

       B.   What did you say?

What is going on here is that "What" has replaced the entire surface sentence in example (47A). The rest of the sentence, "did you say," echoes either the performative sentence that dominated example (47A) in deep structure, or the utterance situation that is "in the air." I am hesitant to claim this as a good argument for the performative analysis because of the possibility of echo questions like example (48B):

(48)   A.   Doomsday is coming! Doomsday is coming!

B.   What are you shouting about?

"Shout" is not a performative verb.

There is another type of wh-question that is very similar to echo questions, but with the opposite intonation. This type is used mostly when the referent of a pronoun is not understood, as in example (49):

(49)   A.   Where did he hit Ken?

B.   Where did who hit Ken?

Again, like echo questions, these questions may be formed from any kind of sentence (as long as it contains a pronoun), and the two types of question have much the same restrictions. For both, as mentioned before, the wh-word may not move left past another Q, but otherwise may usually go to the beginning of the sentence. Also, both must avoid certain constructions. That is, strict echo is not always possible. This is true whenever the questioned element is something that, in the original sentence, had been preposed without causing subject-auxiliary inversion:

(50)   A.   There it is!

B1. $\left\{ \begin{array}{c} *\text{Where} \\ *\text{Where} \end{array} \right\}$ it is?

B2. $\left\{ \begin{array}{c} \text{Where} \\ \text{Where} \end{array} \right\}$ is it?

The same problem arises with sentences like "Him, I like" and "Then, we knew the truth."

The big difference between these two types of wh-questions, aside from their functions, is that echo questions have rising intonation on the wh-word, whereas the questions under discussion, which I call REF-questions, have falling intonation on the wh-word.

The last group of intonations I discuss in this section is the intonation of answers. Answers to questions and tag questions have falling intonation, except in certain cases, such as where the reply is being offered hesitantly or as a guess. However, the fall in intonation may be either relatively slight or relatively steep. I refer to a slight fall as an instance of "mild" intonation and to a steep fall as an instance of "sharp" intonation.[6]

Usually, when it is obvious what answer is expected (as with tag questions) an answer that agrees with the expected answer will have mild intonation, and a disagreeing answer will have sharp intonation. This is illustrated in examples (51A1, 2):

(51) Q.   You're Wally, aren't you?

A1.   Yes. [agreeing]

A2.   No. [disagreeing, surprised]

A3.   Yes. [agreeing, surprised]

A4.   No. [disagreeing]

However, the other combinations, examples (51A3, 4), are also possible. In example (51A3), sharp intonation is used to agree. This happens when the answerer must admit the truth of the questioner's assumptions, but is surprised either that this should be so or that the questioner should possess this information. In example (51A4), mild intonation is used to disagree. This happens when the answerer knows that the questioner's assumptions are wrong, but is not surprised at his taking such a position.

The basic intonational distinction here, then, is not one of agreeing versus disagreeing intonation, but rather mild versus sharp. Mild intonation, whether used to agree or to disagree, is appropriate when the speaker is calm and sure of himself. The speaker could be said to be secure in his position, unsurprised, unobjecting. Sharp intonation, whether used to agree or to disagree, is appropriate when the speaker is surprised either at the questioner's position or at the position he himself is forced to take. He is insecure, surprised, or protesting.

Echo questions provide another instance of the mild versus sharp distinction. Consider the following four dialogues:

---

[6] James McCawley once told me that one of his students had shown that pitch falls that corresponded to a musical fourth served, as in music, as nonfinal cadences, indicating some doubt or leaving the conversation open. Pitch falls corresponding to a musical fifth served, again as in music, as final cadences, indicating strong assertion and closing conversations. This may be one more concrete way of regarding the mild-sharp distinction.

(52) A. The mayor has arrived.

B. {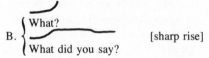
What?
What did you say?   [sharp rise]

A. That's right.

B. Oh, my God!

(53) A. The mayor has arrived.

B. {
What?
What did you say?   [mild rise]

A. The mayor has arrived.   [enunciated clearly]

B. Oh. I thought you said "The *mare* has arrived" or
something like that.

(54) A. The mayor has arrived.

B. What? [with median rise]

A. The mayor has arrived. [enunciated clearly]

B. No, no. I heard you the first time. But I didn't know he was coming!
I'm not ready!

(55) A. The mayor has arrived.

B. What? [with median rise]

A. That's right.

B. No, no. I just didn't hear what you said.

In examples (54) and (55), it is not clear whether B's intonation is supposed to
be mild or sharp. A has incorrectly interpreted the ambiguity, and consequently thrown the dialogue off course. In examples (52) and (53), B has
made his meaning clear by using more extreme intonation.

Here again sharp intonation correlates with surprise and agitation, and
mild intonation with cases where these elements are less evident, but here,
"mild" refers to a slight rise, rather than a slight fall, and "sharp" to a steep
rise, rather than a steep fall.

We might surmise, then, that there is a feature distinguishing mild and
sharp, and a feature distinguishing rise and fall, and that the two combine to
yield four possibilities. The rise-fall distinction usually correlates with syntactic distinctions, whereas the mild-sharp distinction does not. For instance,

there is a difference in usage and meaning between mild "What?" and sharp "What?", but I know of no syntactic difference between them, so we would want to say that the mild-sharp distinction is attitudinal and peripheral.

RISING AND FALLING INTONATION

In the last section, I made a suggestion that questions and sentences that function and pattern like questions have rising cadences, whereas statements and sentences that function and pattern like statements have falling cadences. It became obvious that this could not be correct when wh-questions were taken into consideration. These have falling cadences, so here the correlation of rising intonation with questions and falling intonation with statements breaks down.[7]

---

[7]Lieberman (1967) concerns himself with this problem. The solution he proposes is that if a question has a special question morpheme (WH in English) in surface structure, the pitch falls at the end; otherwise, it rises. In other words, there is a trading relationship. A question must have some signal of its questionhood. The signal may be either rising intonation or a question morpheme appearing on the surface.

This is a very attractive hypothesis. Nevertheless, there are a few problems with it. First, as Kim (1968) asked in his review of Lieberman's book, why is inverted word order not as good a signal of questionhood as WH in English? There are not many types of sentences other than yes-no questions that begin with tensed AUX in English. One type that does invert is exclamatory sentences, as in example (i):

    (i)   Is he ever zealous!

A second, rather spurious sort of counterexample is repeated questions, as in example (iiA2):

    (ii)   A1.   Is he annoying you?

           B.   Is he annoying me?

          A2.   Yes. Is he annoying you.

Example (iiA2) is not really a question, but rather a statement of what A's previous question said. It has falling intonation, as does example (i).

There are other types of sentences with inverted word order, but, with the exceptions mentioned above, yes-no questions are the only type that begin with an indicative tensed AUX in surface structure. This should, then, be a pretty strong signal of questionhood. Why is rising intonation needed in addition?

Now consider the distribution of wh-words. Wh-words are used not only for questions, but also for relative clauses, and for embedded questions, which are quite different in function from questions proper. Limiting ourselves to sentence-initial position doesn't help to limit the scope of the problem, first because relative pronouns may be sentence-initial, as in example (iii):

    (iii)   What really finished him off was the piano.

Example (iii) is not a question, and so we cannot say that a sentence-initial wh-word is a reliable question signal. One could argue that the hearer knows, after he hears "was," that "what" in

What I would suggest instead is that the difference in intonation between yes-no and wh-questions is an automatic consequence of a difference between their underlying structures. Yes-no questions are derived from disjunctions; wh-questions are not. The first halves of disjunctions receive rising intonation; the second halves receive falling intonation. During the derivation of single-term questions, first intonation is assigned, then the second terms are deleted, leaving a single term that has rising intonation. The rising-falling distinction serves to set off other types of oppositions, too. To see this, a bit of background is needed.

Many people have previously talked about the opposition between rising and falling intonation. In Lieberman's book (1967), rising intonation is correlated with the feature [+BG] and falling intonation with the feature [−BG] (BG = breath group). Dwight Bolinger (1965) has A and B pitch accents. His A accent corresponds to falling intonation. His B accent corresponds to a fall-rise pattern, which is a variant of rising intonation. Ray Jackendoff (1972) discusses these two accents in great detail. He says, "The two pitch accents we are interested in are called A and B accents by Bolinger. In both accents,

---

example (iii) is not immediately dominated by the topmost S, as a question signal would be, but this additional condition makes for a rather weak and complicated signal.

In the second place, REF-questions must be considered a special type of wh-question. That is, although the wh-words in REF-questions occur more freely, since they need not move, they are generated in the same way as and have the same forms as the wh-words of wh-questions. REF-questions, like wh-questions, have falling intonation, so that the wh-word is again the only signal of questionhood. Yet the wh-word need not be in sentence-initial position, as it is not in example (ivB).

    (iv)   A.   Romy did it!

           B.   Romy did what?

For these two reasons, it is hard to argue that Q-WHs are easy to distinguish positionally from other WHs. This weakens the theory that they are sufficient signals to obviate the necessity for rising intonation.

Neither do wh-questions necessarily exclude rising intonation. In fact, they often do, optionally, have rising cadences, as in example (v):

    (v)   Why is grass green?

Furthermore, echo questions, which are, again, a special type of wh-question, *always* having rising intonation.

In summary, I think the theory that rising intonation and wh-words enjoy a trading relationship as question signals is inadequate for the following reasons: 1) inverted word order seems as good a question signal, at least for yes-no questions, as WH is for wh-questions, but yes-no questions still have rising intonation; 2) wh-words, qua morphemes or qua morphemes in certain positions, do not uniquely signal questions—rather, one must consider in addition the abstract structures in which they participate; and 3) wh-words, even when signaling normal wh-questions, do not preclude rising intonation.

the focus syllable has a high pitch. By the onset of the next vowel there is an abrupt drop to low pitch. The two accents differ in that the A accent concludes with a fall in pitch, and the B accent concludes with a rise in pitch.''

He shows that when a sentence has only one focus, it normally gets an A accent. When a sentence has two foci, invariably one will receive an A pitch accent (falling) and one will receive a B pitch accent (rising). This shows that the two are not independent of each other, but rather perform an oppositional function. The opposition—the difference in meaning between the two—is approximately that between topic and comment. An A accent is assigned to a focus syllable when the focus provides new information or makes an assertion or comment or answers a question. Jackendoff calls this the dependent variable, since its value must be chosen so as to make the sentence true. A B accent is assigned to a focus syllable when the focus is old information—a topic or idea mentioned or presupposed in previous discourse. This he calls the independent variable. In Pope, 1976, this difference is represented in terms of TH. (TH is a marker indicating a presupposition of anaphoricity. It is attached to definite and generic NPs and to factive Ss.) B accents are assigned to things with TH attached to them (things with B accents must be anaphoric), and A accents are assigned to things without TH (things without A accents need not be anaphoric—they provide new information). The following two discourses (Jackendoff's examples) illustrate the A and B accents. Suppose there were a number of people and a number of things to eat. Various people ate various things, and I am asking about how they paired up:

(56) Q. What about FRED? What did HE eat?
           ＼／ B   ＼ A
      A. FRED ate the BEANS.

Here Fred is the topic and refers back to the question, and beans provides the answer:

(57) Q. What about the BEANS? Who ate THEM?
           ＼ A   ＼／ B
      A. FRED ate the BEANS.

Here beans comes from the question, and Fred is the answer. Examples (56A) and (57A) are identical, except for the placement of the A and B accents, but their meanings, and the questions they answer, are quite different.

This opposition is the same as that between echo questions and REF-questions. Observe the three-way contrast below:

(58) Where did who go? [echo question]

(59)   Where did who go? [REF-question]

(60)   Where did who go? [wh-question]

Katz and Postal (1964) rightly contend that the reason the intonation of "who" is dynamic in example (58) but level in example (60) is that "who" receives emphasis in example (58). They do not discuss questions like example (59), but the same thing is true in such cases. The only problem, then, lies in determining why emphasis occasions a rise in pitch in example (58) but a fall in pitch in example (59). Example (60) is merely a wh-question with two wh-words.

The difference between examples (58) and (59) lies in the nature of the information being sought. Example (58) asks for a repetition of information previously given (and therefore anaphoric), and has rising intonation. Example (59) asks for new information—specifically, the referent of a pronoun (which has failed to meet its presupposition of being anaphoric)[8]—and has

---

[8]As I said, REF-questions ask for the referent of a *pronoun*, and not just that of a NP whose referent is not clear. Thus example (iA) cannot give rise to example (iB), although examples (iiA) and (iiB) are good:

   (i)   A.   John went somewhere.

         B.   *John went where?
   (ii)   A.   John went there.

         B.   John went where?

Notice what is gotten in response to "one":

   (iii)   A.   John ate one.

         B.   John ate one what?

Also, REF-questions *can* ask for the referents of deletions, at least certain kinds of deletions:

   (iv)   A.   John knows.

         B.   John knows what?

   (v)   A.   John knows.

         B.   *John knows what?

I think that, here again, it will turn out that deletion of material that is presupposed to be anaphoric can be questioned by a REF-question, but deletion of, for example, unspecified NPs cannot be.

falling intonation. Example (58) would be asked in reply to "Where did John go?", and example (59) in reply to "Where did he go?"

I can now explain the echo-REF distinction in the same way as the A-B distinction. In Jackendoff's notation, examples (61) and (62) would have the following presuppositions (λ = "the class of"):

(61) John hit who?
      +emph
      Presupposition: $\lambda(x)$ [John hit x] is well formed; x is an independent variable

(62) John hit who?
      +emph
      Presupposition: $\lambda(x)$ [John hit x] is well formed; x is a dependent variable

Wh-movement is obligatory for [−emph] wh-words, but optional for [+emph] wh-words. Movement is blocked if the COMP node is already filled, as explained by Chomsky (1971).

Jackendoff points out another type of case where the only accent in a sentence is a B accent. This occurs when the function of the other focus is filled by the affirmation-negation distinction, but the AUX is not actually accented. In such sentences, the affirmative or negative is taken out of the presupposition and associated with the focus. This explains the difference between examples (63) and (64):

        A
(63) All of the men didn't go.
      Presupposition: $\lambda(x)$ [x of the men didn't go] is well formed; x is a
                             dependent variable
      Assertion: All $\in \lambda(x)$ [x of the men didn't go]
        B
(64) All of the men didn't go.
      Presupposition: $\lambda(x)$ [x of the men went] is well formed; x is an
                             independent variable
      Assertion: All $\notin \lambda(x)$ [x of the men went]

In such sentences, there may be a focused syllable that is emphasized, as "all" is in these examples. Then the B accent goes on the focused syllable. However, it is also possible for the entire sentence to be focused. When this is the case, and the variable is dependent, an A accent is placed on the last stress peak, so that the sentence is ambiguous as to how much of it is the focus. When the entire sentence is the focus *and* the negative is associated with the focus, so that a B accent can be gotten, it is not placed on the last stress peak. Instead, it is placed on a stressless syllable, as in example (65).

(65)   John didn't break it.
      Presupposition: $\lambda(x)$ [x is the case] is well formed; x is an independent variable
      Assertion: John broke it $\notin \lambda(x)$ [x is the case]

X's being an independent variable means that "John broke it" is presupposed not in *this* sentence but in previous discourse ("John broke it" is anaphoric). When the whole sentence is the focus, the presupposition of that sentence is rather vacuous, except that the type of variable is specified.

It is possible to be more exact about where the B accent is placed in these sentences. When there are two stress peaks, as there usually are, the B accent goes on the first stressless syllable after the first stress peak. This situation seems contrived to make example (66) unambiguous—to alleviate the possibility that any particular word will be understood to be the focus. It also shows that intonation assignment must follow the operation of the Nuclear Stress Rule:

(66)   The man from Pennsylvania didn't break it.

Sentences like those in examples (65) and (66) have about them a certain lack of assertion, or feeling of protest. In some cases, assertiveness or its lack is a more important factor in choosing between A and B accents than the dependence or independence of the variables. To illustrate this, consider disagreeing replies to statements. Such replies have what I call nonstop intonation. In replies to questions of the form [no/yes] + tag, there is always a break, at least potentially, between [no/yes] and the tag. In nonstop intonation, such a break is impossible. Nonstop intonation replies may have either an A accent or a B accent:

(67)   S.   It's hot out.

     R1.   No it isn't.

     R2.   No it isn't.

In isolation, example (67R1) sounds as if the speaker is quite sure of what he is saying, and example (67R2) as if he were less so. Example (67R1) is a stronger contradiction than example (67R2). In example (67R1), the

speaker seems secure, assertive, perhaps even threatening. In example
(67R2), the speaker seems surprised, less assertive, more polite. Notice the
behavior of tags after the two sorts of replies:

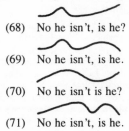

(68)   No he isn't, is he?

(69)   No he isn't, is he.

(70)   No he isn't is he?

(71)   No he isn't, is he.

A falling tag is used when the speaker expects confirmation from his
addressee. Since it is strange to expect someone you are contradicting to
confirm your contradiction, examples (69) and (71) are best if the first part is
addressed to the contradictee and the tag to someone else. A rising tag makes
a statement more like a yes-no question, and introduces an element of uncertainty as to what the reply will be. So example (68) [example (67R2) + rising
tag] is much better than example (70) [example (67R1) + rising tag], since it
is a bit schizophrenic to make a very strong contradiction [example (67R1)]
and then to immediately express doubt about its correctness. In example
(67R2), there is already some doubt in the contradiction.

As replies, examples (67R1) and (67R2) are both better following
nonhesitant statements and S tags than following hesitant statements and Q
tags. This is because nonstop intonation is a device specifically intended for
use in contradicting assertions. There are many degrees of assertiveness in
between completely neutral questions that are not biased toward any particular
answer, and emphatic declaratives. The less assertive the sentence, the more
inappropriate nonstop intonation is in the reply.

However, interestingly enough, when nonstop intonation *is* used in reply
to a hesitant statement or Q tag, example (67R1) (the stronger form) is better
than example (67R2), whereas in reply to nonhesitant statements and S tags,
example (67R2) is better than example (67R1):

(72)   Q.   He's not going, is he? S. He's not going... ?

       R1.   Yes he is. [is better than] R2. Yes he is.

(73)   Q.   He's not going, is he. S. He's not going.

       R2.   Yes he is. [is better than] R1. Yes he is.

It can be seen here that a less assertive sentence invites a more assertive sentence, and vice versa, when their assertions are opposite.[9] This is another example of the correlation of the falling-rising distinction with oppositeness.

---

[9]When their assertions are the *same,* on the other hand, it's better if their intonations *match.* Thus there is a difference in the intonation of answers like "That's right" and "You're right" used in reply to S tags on the one hand, and to Q tags and negative questions, on the other. In reply to Q tags and negative questions "That's right" is stressed on "that." More accurately, the sentence has a B accent. ("You're right" for some reason may not have this intonation pattern, and so it is not very good as a reply to Q tags and negative questions.) In replies to S tags, "That's right" may have this pattern, but it is better if "right" is stressed, or, again more accurately, if the sentence has an A accent. "You're right" may have this pattern, so it is good as a reply to an S tag.

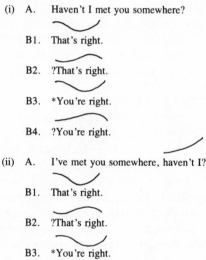

(i)   A.   Haven't I met you somewhere?

    B1.   That's right.

    B2.   ?That's right.

    B3.   *You're right.

    B4.   ?You're right.

(ii) A.   I've met you somewhere, haven't I?

    B1.   That's right.

    B2.   ?That's right.

    B3.   *You're right.

    B4.   ?You're right.

(iii) A.   I've met you somewhere, haven't I.

    B1.   ?That's right.

    B2.   That's right.

    B3.   *You're right.

    B4.   You're right.

In the text I have shown that S tags have A accents and Q tags have B accents, and that, when such sentences receive disagreeing replies, the reply with the opposite accent is the preferred one. Here it can be seen that when such sentences receive *agreeing* replies, the reply with the *same* accent is the preferred one.

The first example showed that the rising-falling distinction correlated with the distinction between old information and new information, i.e., TH and $\emptyset$. This second example has shown that replies that contradict tend to have intonation opposite (B or A) to the intonation (A or B, respectively) of the statement they are contradicting.

Many sentences have the intonation pattern of example (67R2). For example:

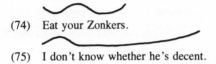

(74)   Eat your Zonkers.

(75)   I don't know whether he's decent.

The final rise here is not intrinsically associated with the coda, but is a deferred rise associated with the earlier fall. Many sentential patterns affect the last word of the sentence without in any way reflecting its intrinsic function. For instance, "who" at the end of a sentence may have rising intonation without marking an echo question, and the stressless pronoun "him," unfocused in example (77), can have a rise:

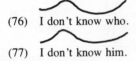

(76)   I don't know who.

(77)   I don't know him.

It is possible that the intonation of Q tags can be explained as a variant of the pattern illustrated in examples (74) to (77). As in those examples, Q tags have a high point in the first part of the sentence, and a rise at the end:

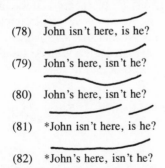

(78)   John isn't here, is he?

(79)   John's here, isn't he?

(80)   John's here, isn't he?

(81)   *John isn't here, is he?

(82)   *John's here, isn't he?

The statement part may not have level intonation and may not end in a rise. The only important difference between the intonation of Q tags and the patterns in examples (74) to (77) is that the final rise of the Q tags may terminate at a somewhat higher level. From a semantic point of view, it seems to be true that these sentences all have the same mood or attitude. There is about them the same feeling of protest and lack of assertiveness that was mentioned in connection with "No he isn't."

I have argued elsewhere (Pope, 1976) against trying to derive tag questions in a way parallel to questions, i.e., from structures like that underlying example (83):

(83)   John is here, isn't John here or is John here?

As I pointed out, there is the very upsetting fact that, when disjunctions do occur with tags, they do not always conform to what is expected from a source like example (83):

(84)   John's here, isn't he? Or IS he.

(85)   John isn't here, is he? Or IS he.

Both the positive and the negative tag may disjoin with a positive term. Since we cannot then derive Q tags from disjunctions, their rising intonation must be otherwise explained. The protest intonation pattern provides such an explanation. Thus the rising cadence of Q tags is actually only the deferred rise of a fall-rise B accent on the whole sentence. These rising cadences are thus derived quite differently from those on yes-no questions.

So far I have discussed two uses of the rising-falling distinction. It correlates with the topic-comment distinction and with the nonassertive-assertive distinction. A third use of the rising-falling distinction is in positional opposition. This is the well-known phenomenon of comma intonation, where nonfinal clauses and terms of conjunctions get B accents, and the final term gets an A accent. I use disjunctions with exclusive "or" as examples. These are disjunctions where, of the two terms, we must choose one and we cannot choose both. Such disjunctions generally have a B accent on the first term and an A accent on the second, as in examples (86) to (88):

(86)   Either the butler did it with a hammer in the den,

       or somebody's lying.

(87)   Do the dishes or scrub the floor; I don't care which.

(88)   Do it quickly or not at all.

Before proceeding further, I should explain the variants of the B accent. The A accent, or falling intonation, assumes everywhere the same shape, as far as I am here concerned, but the B accent has at least two quite different shapes. One is the plain rise found at the end of yes-no questions, and the other is the fall-rise pattern discussed by Bolinger and Jackendoff. The fall-rise is the form that occurs more freely. The rise of the fall-rise may optionally (and preferably) be deferred to the end of the sentence if no other focus follows it. Thus examples (89) and (90), which are synonymous, are obtained, but example (91) cannot become example (92).

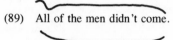

(89)   All of the men didn't come.

(90)   All of the men didn't come.

(91)   Fred ate the beans.

(92)   Fred ate the beans.

When and only when there *is* another accent before the end of the sentence, the B accent may optionally become a plain rise. Thus example (93) [the same as example (91)] *can* become example (94), but example (95) cannot become example (96):

(93)   Fred ate the beans.

(94)   Fred ate the beans.

(95)   Fred ate the beans.

(96)   Fred ate the beans.

A second factor, which influences the shape of the B accents in disjunctions in particular, is that, the more nearly true opposites the two terms are, the more likely it is that the B accent will take the form of a plain rise:

(97)   Is this dog female or does it just *look* pregnant?

(98)   *Is this dog female or male?

(99)   Is this dog female or male?

(100)   Either it was done by John or we have the wrong man.

(101)   *It was done either by John or by someone else.

(102)   It was done either by John or by someone else.

(103)   I want to know whether this dog is

a Pekinese or whether he's some other weird breed.

(104)   *I want to know whether this dog is a Pekinese or not.

(105)   I want to know whether this dog is a Pekinese or not.

(Sometimes the starred sentences are acceptable if there is special emphasis on the second disjunct.)

This leads back to the original problem of why wh-questions have falling cadences whereas yes-no questions have rising cadences. What I would like to propose is that it is not wh-questions but yes-no questions that are exceptional in this regard. There is an important distinction between yes-no questions and wh-questions that has many consequences—"whether" is binary-valued, whereas other wh-words are many-valued. A yes-no question asks us to choose one of two answers; a wh-question asks us to supply one of many possible NPs.

I argue that yes-no questions are, in fact, derived from disjunctions.[11,11] This is shown by their intonation. Most yes-no questions have the underlying form "whether S or not S" (or "whether not S or S"). There are no truer opposites than S and not S: there is no third possibility. So yes-no questions, when both terms survive, always have a plain rise on the first term, as in example (106), rather than a fall-rise, as in example (107).[12]

---

[10]This is not a new idea. Lieberman (1967) adopts this analysis. Katz and Postal (1964) recognized the connection between yes-no questions and disjunctions, but consigned the association to the semantic, rather than the syntactic, component. Hasegawa (1968), Langacker (1969), 1970), and Moravcsik (1971) derive yes-no questions from disjunctions and argue for the derivation of yes-no question intonation that I give here.

[11]The main drawback of a syntactic association between disjunctions and yes-no questions is that it apparently doesn't work as well for negative yes-no questions as it does for positive ones. I contend that it is always the second half of the disjunction that is deleted to form yes-no questions, rather than sometimes the first half and sometimes the second half. This means that we must postulate underlying disjunctions of the form neg-or-pos as well as the more natural and grammatical pos-or-neg. I gave some semantic and syntactic arguments for this analysis of negative questions in Pope, 1976 (Ch. 3).

[12]If the "not" receives special emphasis, so that the first term may receive a fall-rise, the "not" can't be deleted, since the presence of [+emph] will not fit into the structural description of the deletion transformation.

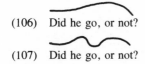

(106)   Did he go, or not?

(107)   Did he go, or not?

If yes-no questions are derived from such disjunctions, and if intonation is assigned to the questions before the second half is deleted, then the first half will have a rising cadence. The second half, with its balancing fall in intonation, is then deleted. The result is the so-called question intonation. The fact that a B accent may not take the form of a plain rise unless an A accent follows explains why a plain rise can occur at the end of a sentence only if the sentence is a reduced disjunction (as in yes-no questions) or if the rise is the deferred rise of an earlier fall-rise pattern (as in Q tags).

The rule that deletes ''or not'' is an example of a syntactic deletion rule that must operate after the phonological process of intonation assignment. Another such example is discussed in Pope (1971).

Under this hypothesis, wh-questions are in no way exceptional. They have falling cadences like any other normal English sentence type. Yes-no questions are not exceptional, either. Part of their intonational pattern has been deleted along with part of their structure, but their pattern as a whole has a function independent of sentence type.

There is one important piece of evidence supporting the disjunction hypothesis that is based on intonation alone. That is the fact that, when the second term of the disjunction is *not* deleted, the intonation pattern of the question is that of a disjunction, not that of a yes-no question. In particular, the second term may not have a rising cadence:

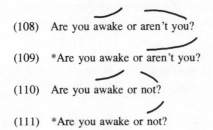

(108)   Are you awake or aren't you?

(109)   *Are you awake or aren't you?

(110)   Are you awake or not?

(111)   *Are you awake or not?

This cannot be explained by saying that questions with two terms that are opposed always have opposing intonation, because conjunctions do not have the same pattern here, even though they do elsewhere:

(112)   Did you laugh and cry?

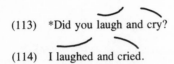

(113)   *Did you laugh and cry?

(114)   I laughed and cried.

The derivation of question intonation from disjunction intonation explains why, in English and many other languages, yes-no questions have rising cadences but wh-questions do not. It is because wh-questions are not derived from disjunctions, unless, as some have proposed, the disjunctions are infinite.[13] In that case, however, the question would be derived not by deleting all but one term, but rather by collapsing them all, so the situation is not at all parallel, intonationally.

One problem that remains but is rather peripheral is that of intonational placeholders. John Ross has pointed out to me that "hunh" and "hm" are not mere bestial grunts. They serve a linguistic function as intonational placeholders, rather like zeros in the number system. Each has a distinct function, and there are restrictions on their use. (For many people, they tend to merge phonetically. Thus their one grunt allows anything allowed by either of our two distinct grunts.)

"Hm" is a placeholder for rising intonation. It may not be used after statements—that is, it may not replace tags:

(115)   *He's coming, hm?

(116)   *He's coming, hm?

It may be used redundantly after yes-no questions, which already have rising intonation, but because it is redundant it sounds rather insistent here:

(117)   Is he coming, hm?

It has two primary uses. First, it is used following wh-questions, where the rising intonation on "hm" is not redundant:

---

[13]Langacker (1969) proposes that all questions are derived from disjunctions, but that in all cases other than yes-no questions, the disjunction is infinite. This has some semantic, but little syntactic, plausibility. However, even in terms of semantics alone, the situation is more complicated than he has indicated, as I show in Pope, 1976 (Ch. 2). At any rate, an infinite disjunction would certainly defy intonation assignment, so either intonation would simply not be assigned to infinite structures, or intonation assignment would follow the collapse of the disjunction. In either case, the intonational pattern of wh-questions would still be different from that of yes-no questions.

(118)   Who's coming, hm?

Its other primary use is as a complete reply in itself. It may be used in response to one's name or some other attention-getter to signal receptivity, or it may be used in response to any sentence to mean "What did you say?", either as a request for repetition or, with a sharper rise, to register incredulity:

(119)   A.   John?

        B.   Hm?
(120)   A.   Aardvarks have wings.

        B1.   Hm? (request for repetition)

        B2.   Hm? (incredulity)

"Hunh" is a placeholder for other intonations. It may not be used after any sentence that ends in a rise:

(121)   *He's coming, hunh.

(122)   *Is he coming, hunh.

It may not be used with redundant falling intonation following a wh-question:

(123)   *Who ate all the cookies, hunh.

"Hunh" is used to replace two sorts of tags. One is the negativity-switching tag, which is a request for confirmation and has falling intonation (the tag of S tags):

(124)   He's coming, hunh. (cf. He's coming, isn't he.)

The other is the sarcastic or belligerent tag, which does not switch negativity:

(125)   So I'm stupid, hunh? (cf. So I'm stupid, am I?)

These tags have rising intonation, but it is not the questioning intonation, which starts high and rises. Rather it starts quite low and rises to normal speaking level.

"Hunh" is used in a similar way following belligerent or accusing questions. Its intonation here differs from that which it has in example (125) only in that there is a sudden sharp rise at the very end. (Here it is particularly common to use "hunh" and "hm" interchangeably.) Again, this usage sounds redundant after yes-no questions:

(126)   Did you do it, hunh?

(127)   What's the matter, hunh?

Perhaps the confounding of "hunh" and "hm" here is due to the fact that this intonation is a combination of the belligerent intonation of "hunh" in example (125) and the rising intonation of "hm" in example (118).

"Hunh" may also be used as a complete reply in itself, usually, again, to register incredulity or bewilderment. "Hm" indicates puzzled incredulity; "hunh" indicates that B is pretty certain A is wrong:

(128)   A.   Aardvarks have wings.

        B1.   Hm? I thought they were some sort of mammal.

        B2.   Hunh? You're crazy!

I can suggest sources for most of these uses of "hm" and "hunh." The ones requesting repetition or registering incredulity are derived, by deletion of everything but the intonation, from

"What?"

which in turn is derived from the echo question

"What did you say?"

Two uses of "hunh" were shown to be related to tags earlier. In fact, they are probably derived from these tags. Neither "hm" nor "hunh" may replace the tag of a Q tag, however. This may be because, although a belligerent tag sentence without its tag still sounds belligerent and an S tag without its tag is still a statement, a Q tag without its tag cannot stand alone as a question. In other words, an intonational placeholder can only replace segments and support intonations that are more or less redundant anyway. (The "What?" above may seem to be a counterexample to this, but I think it is not, because the slightest gesture of surprise or puzzlement, such as a widening of the eyes or a raising of the eyebrows, achieves exactly the same effect. "What did you say?" as an expression of amazement is a case of verbal overkill.)

"Hm" and "hunh" following yes-no questions are probably derived
from tags also. Tags and placeholders sound about equally redundant in this
position. Many people will not accept either one:

(129)   Is it too late, ⎰ hm? ⎱
                         ⎱ is it? ⎰

(130)   Are you going to step over the line, ⎰ hunh? ⎱
                                             ⎱ are you? ⎰

Only after wh-questions do placeholders lack for a source. The only
morphologically specified substitute I can think of that has the same intonation is "do you know?":

(131)   Why did he do that, hm?

        hunh?

        *did he?

        *why did?

        *why? (cf. why?)

        *yes?

        *no?

        *I ask you? (cf. I ask you?)

        *tell me? (cf. tell me?)

        do you know?

        do you know?

However, I do not think "do you know" is a likely source for the placeholders, because it has too much semantic content. For instance, example (132)
is a strange sentence, semantically. But example (133) has none of this
strangeness.

(132)   Why do you think he did that, do you know?

(133)   Why do you think he did that, hm?

What I am rejecting here is the idea that placeholder formation could improve a semantically difficult situation. It is, however, quite possible for placeholder formation to improve a grammatically difficult situation. In fact, "hunh" as a tag replacer is especially popular in sentences where the full tag would be awkward or ungrammatical. It is well known that the tags that do not have negativity opposite to that of the first part of the sentence—i.e., the belligerent tags—are fully grammatical only if both statement and tag are positive, as in example (134). If both are negative, as in example (135), some speakers get the sentences marginally, others not at all:

(134)   So I'm a sap, am I?

(135)   ??So you can't do it, can't you?

However, example (135) with "hunh" replacing the tag and taking over its intonation, is fully acceptable:

(136)   So you can't do it, hunh?

If example (136) is indeed derived from example (135), this situation is reminiscent of rules like Sluicing, which can convert ungrammatical sentences into grammatical ones.

This suggests another source for placeholders after wh-questions. Since there seems to be no good morphological source for these placeholders, perhaps what is going on is that tag formation applies to wh-questions, producing, of course, some monstrosity. However, if the monstrosity were then immediately wiped out by placeholder formation, nobody would be the wiser. I know of no good argument for such a source, however, so I leave this as an unsolved problem.

This completes my analysis of basic intonation patterns. The last section deals with a remaining problem—the intonation of embedded "whether" questions—and concludes with a summary and discussion of the rules that have been postulated.

EMBEDDED YES-NO QUESTIONS

In the light of the generalizations discovered so far, the intonation of embedded yes-no questions is somewhat strange. They never end in a rise, even when the second term has been deleted. Langacker (1969) says about this "It is reasonable to suppose that the declarative intonation of the main clause overrides that of the embedded question when the former is truncated so that only one clause remains." I think a more plausible solution is that examples (137) to (139) are related, and examples (140) and (141) are not related to the first three:

(137)   I wonder whether she likes me or not.

(138)   I wonder whether or not she likes me.

(139)   I wonder whether she likes me.

(140)   I wonder whether she likes me or not.

(141)   I wonder whether she likes me or not.

I have already suggested that example (141) has special emphasis on "not," and so cannot be reduced. The difference between examples (140) and (137) is that in example (140) "not" is part of the focus, but in example (137) it isn't. In embedded questions, then, unlike topmost questions, "or not" can be moved or deleted only if it is not part of the focus.

I can think of two ways in which "or not" might come to be outside the focus. The first method derives example (137) from example (138); the second does the reverse. I think the second is closer to the truth.

The first method works as follows: "or not" is unaccented just in case the whole disjunction as a unit is focused, rather than each term separately, and the first S, instead of the second, deletes. The A accent comes on the last stress peak of the second S, and that is the only accent. "Or not," being unaccented, may either move to the end of the sentence or delete. This means that example (142) is the source of examples (143) to (145):

(142)   I don't know [whether I like him or not I like him]. focus

(143)   I don't know whether Ø or not I like him.

(144)   I don't know whether Ø Ø I like him <u>or not</u>.

(145)   I don't know whether Ø Ø I like him Ø.

The second method works as follows: "or not" is unaccented just in case it is considered an unimportant possibility, in a manner completely parallel to examples (146) and (147):

(146)   Give it to Donna or somebody.

(147)   Why don't you complain or something.

When the sentence following "or not" is deleted, and "or not" is unaccented, "or not" may either be attracted to "whether" or may delete. This means that example (148) is the source of examples (149) to (151):

(148)   I don't know [whether I like him] $_{focus}$ or not <u>I like him</u>.

(149)   I don't know whether I like him or not Ø.

(150)   I don't know whether or not I like him Ø Ø.

(151)   I don't know whether Ø I like him Ø Ø.

Both methods have the virtue that they relate examples (137) to (139) as opposed to examples (140) and (141). That this is a virtue is shown by the fact that the two groups pattern differently in other environments. For instance, the first group but not the second is ungrammatical in adverbial clauses, as in examples (152) to (156):

(152)   *I'm leaving, whether you like it or not.

(153)   *I'm leaving, whether or not you like it.

(154)   *I'm leaving, whether you like it.

(155)   I'm leaving, whether you like it or not.

(156)   I'm leaving, whether you like it or not.

In topmost questions, too, the first group, but not the second, is only marginally acceptable in special usages. Thus examples (157) to (159) could only be used in answer to something like "What did you ask?":

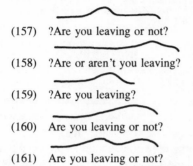

(157) ?Are you leaving or not?

(158) ?Are or aren't you leaving?

(159) ?Are you leaving?

(160) Are you leaving or not?

(161) Are you leaving or not?

However, although the first method shares this one virtue with the second, it also has many disadvantages that the second does not. First, the first method, but not the second, requires us to move a complementizer ("not") rightward out of its sentence. I think complementizers may move rightward into their own sentences. The placement of sentential negatives on the auxiliary may be such a rule. Others are discussed in Pope, 1976 (Ch. 1). Complementizers may also move leftward and upward out of their sentences. Chomsky (1973) argues that WH-Movement is such a rule. In the cases we are considering, where a complementizer moves out of its own sentence but not upward, we add less power to the grammar if this movement is leftward than if it is rightward. The left restrictions already allow complementizers to move out of their own sentences so long as they do not move down. The rightward restrictions do not allow complementizers to move out of their own sentences. The two proposed movements are illustrated again in examples (162) and (163):

(162) I wonder whether [or not it's true] (first method)

(163) I wonder whether it's true [or not] (second method)

The second problem with the first method is that it requires backward deletion in a conjoined structure. Jorge Hankamer (1971) argues that backward deletion is never possible in conjoined structures. He explains backward gapping, the best argument for the existence of such deletions, as a result of node raising and scrambling. If Hankamer is right, our first method, which allows either the first or the second term of a questioned disjunction to be deleted, requires a more powerful grammar than would otherwise be needed.

The second method requires only forward deletion, which is quite well motivated. The two proposed deletions are illustrated in examples (164) and (165):

(164)   I wonder whether $\emptyset$ or not it's true. (first method)

(165)   I wonder whether it's true or not $\emptyset$. (second method)

For these reasons I adopt the second method of deriving the irregular intonational patterns of embedded questions. The conditions on the rules affecting "or not," then, must include the following: "or not" may delete only when it is the second term of a disjunction to which WH is attached, and, in embedded position, only when it is outside the focus; "or not" may be attracted to "whether" only wnen it is outside the focus; and "or not" may be outside the focus only when it is the second term of a disjunction in a complement sentence (thus excluding topmost sentences and adverbials) to which WH is attached.

CONCLUSIONS

I now formulate a few of the rules most relevant to intonation for questions, indicate their approximate ordering within a generative grammar, and make some predictions about intonational possibilities in other languages. Many of the rules I propose have been previously formulated by others.

1. $\left\{\begin{array}{c} N \\ TH \\ WH \end{array}\right\}$ [either or] $\rightarrow$ [$\left\{\begin{array}{c} N \\ TH \\ WH \end{array}\right\}$ + either $\left\{\begin{array}{c} N \\ TH \\ WH \end{array}\right\}$ + or]

WH + or is later realized simply as "or" (sometimes "or whether"). TH + either is realized as "both," and TH + or as "and."

2. $\left[(\left\{\begin{array}{c} N \\ TH \\ WH \end{array}\right\}) + \text{either}, (\left\{\begin{array}{c} N \\ TH \\ WH \end{array}\right\}) + \text{or}, A, A \right]_A \rightarrow 1\ 3\ 2\ 4$

$\qquad$ 1 $\qquad\qquad\qquad$ 2 3 4

3. WH + either S WH + or not S $\rightarrow$ 1 2 3 4 $\emptyset$ [Optional]

$\quad$ 1 $\qquad$ 2 $\qquad$ 3 $\qquad$ 4 5

Condition: 2 = 5

4. Assign B accents to focus syllables that are independent variables, or nonfinal terms of disjunctions (etc.). When the entire sentence is the focus and the sentence has two stress peaks, assign a B accent to the first stressless syllable after the first stress peak. Otherwise, assign it to the highest stress peak.

5. Assign A accents to focus syllables that are dependent variables or final terms of conjunctions (etc.). When the entire sentence is the focus, assign an A accent to the last stress peak.
6. A accents are realized as falls (start higher than normal and fall to lower than normal).
7. B accents are realized as fall-rises (start higher than normal, fall to lower than normal, then rise, but not as high as the first high). When the B accent is nonfinal and no other focus syllable follows it, the final rise is (preferably) deferred to the end of the sentence. When the B accent is nonfinal and another focus syllable follows it, the B accent may take the form of a rise (rising higher than the normal B accent's final rise) with no preceding fall. This rule is optional except that in disjunctions, the more nearly true opposites the two terms are, the more obligatory this rule becomes.
8. X [Whether S or not] Z → 1 2 3 ∅ 5 [Optional]
        1   2   3 4   5

    In embedded sentences, "or not" must be unaccented.
9. Whether S Y → ∅ 2 3 [Obligatory] Applies only in topmost S's.
           1   2 3
10. X [Whether S or not] Y → 1 2 4 3 5 [Optional]
      1   2   3   4   5

    Applies only in embedded Ss. "Or not" must be unaccented.
11. Negative Incorporation (see Klima, 1964)

Intonation assignment is ordered quite late in the syntactic component, following most transformations. This includes some root transformations, such as Adverb-Preposing and Topicalization. Furthermore, intonation assignment must follow the operation of the Nuclear Stress Rule, since rule 4 refers to the stress peaks of a sentence, and these are determined by the Nuclear Stress Rule.

However, there are some syntactic rules that have to follow intonation assignment. In Pope, 1971, I show that Answer Deletion—the rule or rules reducing answers from full sentences to fragments—must follow intonation assignment. Now I have shown that the rules that delete and move "or not" (rules 8 and 10) must also follow intonation assignment. (I would like to do away with the rule that moves "or not," and claim that only deletion rules may follow intonation assignment, but so far I have been unable to do so.) The differing conditions on deletion of "or not" in embedded and main clauses explain the differing intonational patterns of embedded and main sentence questions with only one term. (Embedded questions always have falling cadences, whereas most single-term main sentence questions have rising cadences.)

The fact that certain aspects of intonation assignment depend on the prior operation of the Nuclear Stress Rule, and the fact that some syntactic rules follow intonation assignment, taken together, lend support to Bresnan's argument that the Nuclear Stress Rule (NSR) must operate within the syntactic component (Bresnan, 1971).

Furthermore, from the facts that Adverb-Preposing, a last-cyclic rule, must precede intonation assignment, and "or not" deletion in embedded questions, a cyclic rule, must follow intonation assignment, we may surmise that intonation assignment, like Bresnan's NSR, applies cyclically. This also means that the rules that follow intonation assignment on the regular cycle have to follow last-cyclic rules on the final cycle. Since I am offering an analysis of only a very small subset of English intonational phenomena, I cannot defend this ordering hypothesis. Rather, I merely suggest it as one way in which the phenomena I have studied could fit within the generative framework. If the hypothesis is correct, it means that not all last-cyclic rules can be ordered after all cyclic rules on the final cycle. I leave open the questions of whether all intonation assignment and realization rules come together in the ordering, or whether other types of rules may be interspersed among them. The former situation, however, would seem to be the more natural, i.e., the less marked or "expensive."

I do not wish to claim that there is anything universal about the rules or ordering I have proposed, since the analysis is based only on English. It is possible that in other languages no syntactic rules follow intonation assignment. However, I would venture to make some contingency predictions about the relationship between question type and intonation pattern for language in general.

First, I think that in most, if not all, languages yes-no questions or their equivalents are derived from disjunctions. This is evidenced by facts such as the following: 1) the disjunction, with both terms intact, sometimes appears on the surface; 2) single term questions are interpreted to mean the same as a disjunction of that question and its negation; 3) if single-term questions have rising cadences, so do first terms of disjunctions of S and not S; and 4) the question word for yes-no questions, if there is one, bears some relationship to the word for "either" or the word for "or." Of course, not all of these facts show up in every language, but all of the languages I have investigated exhibit one or more of them.[14]

---

[14]See Moravcsik (1971) for further discussion.

Second, I think that in no language are (non-whether) wh-questions derived from disjunctions. This is evidenced by facts such as the following: 1) such questions are not able to show up as disjunctions analogous to those possible for yes-no questions on the surface; 2) single-term questions are not interpreted as meaning the same as a disjunction of that question and its negation; and 3) wh-questions do not have rising cadences unless there is some intonational pattern in the language, other than that of disjunctions, that applies to wh-questions as a subcase.[15]

In summary, we have seen that the falling-rising intonational distinction serves in English to set off opposites, whether they be functional opposites, semantic opposites, or positional opposites. The intonations and their variants are assigned by rule at a position in the syntax before the operation of at least one movement and at least one deletion rule. Question intonation, echo and reference questions, and sundry other anomalies can be explained by more general intonational processes.

REFERENCES

Bolinger, D. 1965. Forms of English: Accent, Morpheme, Order. Harvard University Press, Cambridge, Mass.

Bresnan, J. 1971. Sentence stress and syntactic transformations. Language 47:2.

Chafe, W. 1968. English questions. PEGS Paper #26. Center for Applied Linguistics, Washington, D.C.

Chomsky, N. 1973. Conditions on transformations. In: Anderson and Kiparsky (eds.), A Festschrift for Morris Halle. Holt, Rinehart and Winston, New York.

Hankamer, J. 1971. Constraints on deletion in syntax. Unpublished Ph.D. dissertation, Yale University.

Hasegawa, K. 1968. An Aspect of English Question Formation. Unpublished paper.

Jackendoff, R. 1972. Semantic Interpretation in Generative Grammar. MIT Press, Cambridge, Mass.

Katz, J., and Postal, P. 1964. An Integrated Theory of Lingusitic Descriptions. MIT Press, Cambridge, Mass.

Kaufman, E. 1971. Whether or Not, or Not. Unpublished paper, Massachusetts Institute of Technology.

Kim, C.-W. 1967. Review of Intonation, Perception, and Language. Language 44:4.

Klima, E. 1964. Negation in English. In: Fodor and J. Katz (eds.), The Structure of Language. Prentice-Hall, Inc., Englewood Cliffs, N.J.

---

[15]Several problems related to intonation assignment still need to be more fully explicated, but cannot be dealt with here. For one thing, the reduction possibilities in embedded "whether" clauses need further study, as do the stress and intonation of adverbial "whether" clauses (see Kaufman, 1971). Intonational placeholders pose some problems for the analysis I have proposed, and the notion of independent and dependent variables needs refinement and explicit reformulation in terms of TH.

Lakoff, R. 1969. A syntactic argument for negative transportation. In: Papers from the Fifth Regional Meeting of the Chicago Linguistic Society. Department of Linguistics, University of Chicago.

Langacker, R. 1969. An Analysis of English Questions. Unpublished paper, University of California at San Diego.

Langacker, R. 1970. English question intonation. In: Sadock and Vanek (eds.), Studies Presented to Robert B. Lees by his Students. Papers in Linguistics, Monograph Series 1. Linguistic Research, Inc., Edmonton.

Lieberman, P. 1967. Intonation, Perception, and Language, MIT Press, Cambridge, Mass.

Moravcsik, E. 1971. Some cross-linguistic generalizations about yes-no questions and their answers. In: Working Papers on Language Universals, #1. Stanford University, Stanford, Ca.

Pope, E. 1971. Answers to yes-no questions. Ling. Inquiry 2:1.

Pope, E. 1976. Questions and Answers in English. Mouton & Co., The Hague.

19/ English Intonation and German Modal Particles II: A Comparative Study

M. Schubiger

PRELIMINARY REMARKS

In a former study of this subject (Schubiger, 1965b), a specific type of modal coloring of an utterance, expressed in German mainly by the particle doch, formed the starting point of the analysis. The possible intonation patterns of the corresponding English utterances, which in most cases do not express the modal coloring locutionally, were described. In this paper the procedure moves in the opposite direction. An English nuclear glide, the rise-fall (RF), forms the starting point. The various German particles that in many instances correspond to this complex glide are passed in review. The sources of information are of the same type as in the former article. They are mainly of two kinds: 1) tonetically transcribed English texts (quite a number of the RFs occurring in them suggest a German particle), and 2) English translations of German plays. Not a few of the modal particles untranslated in the English version suggest an RF nuclear glide.[1]

The English RF

Contrary to the fall-rise (FR), the RF is not an indispensable glide of Received Pronunciation (RP) English intonation. It is an emotional variant of the fall (F), just as the rise-fall-rise (RFR), which is also dispensable, is an emotional variant of the FR. Many speakers do not use the RF at all, others very rarely. Yet it is surprising that this glide has been noted relatively late by phoneticians. Robert Kingdon describes it in an article of "Le maître phonétique" (1939, pp. 61–62), and then deals with it in great detail in *The Groundwork of*

[1]The tonetically transcribed English version was submitted to several native speakers of RP English for corroboration. I also owe thanks to Mr. J. D. O'Connor for discussing some controversial points with me.

English Intonation (1958a). Since then all treatises and even many hand-books for foreign students have taken it into account, and have tried to assign a function, or rather a variety of functions, to it.

In America the RF was noted even later. Pike in his detailed analysis of American intonation (1945) does not deal with it (see, however, NOTE below), nor does Rulon S. Wells in his "Language" article (1945). Trager and Smith's elaborate system of four pitch levels plus three contours (1951) has no room for the RF. It was not until 1956 that James Sledd, in an article on "Superfixes and Intonational Patterns," pointed to this glide, exemplified with words like "$_2$won^{3}der$_1$ful." Subsequently it was described by Dwight Bolinger (1958) in "A Theory of Pitch Accent in English," by Stockwell (1962) in "On the Analysis of English Intonation," and by Richard Gunter, who calls it the humped descent, in *Intonation and Relevance* (1972).

Some of the authors who analyze the RF distinguish between a high and a low variety, just as they distinguish a high and a low F or R. Jassem does (1952, pp. 64, 80), and so does Halliday (1967, p. 16, 1970, p. 18); O'Connor and Arnold (1961) do not. Halliday makes a remark about the slightly different emotional involvement of low or high RF (1970, p. 113); so does Jassem (1952, p. 80). This difference is not taken into account in the present paper.

> NOTE: The formal characteristic of the RF here dealt with (the RF proper) is that the center of dynamic force is at the beginning, so that the actual rise + fall follows on this point of maximum energy, and is sometimes spread over more than one syllable. The other type of RF has a rise, often very slight, *up to* the center of dynamic force, and a fall after it. It was described much earlier than the RF proper (see Armstrong and Ward, 1926; Jones, 1956). It is also the RF of Harold Palmer's books, although Palmer does occasionally describe the RF proper as a variant (1922, pp. 13, 52). Jones, who otherwise does not treat the RF proper, exemplifies the two types of RF with the sentence word no, the RF proper being appropriate in rejoinders (1956, Sec. 1016). Considering the low pitch of the glide, Pike's single specimen of an RF, $_4^{3}_4$no (1945, p. 56), is most probably a RF proper. The frequent RF on the sentence word no (also on oh and yes) must have struck the ears of phoneticians long ago. In Henry Sweet's *Primer of Spoken English* (1890), the RF, no doubt an RF proper, is quite frequent on no and oh (see "Emotions in Answers or Retorts: aber").
>
> The most detailed description of the various RF glides is by Crystal (1969, pp. 214, 218). I disagree with Crystal, however, when he calls the pattern with an extensive rise up to the center of dynamic force a complex tone 2, i.e., an RF proper. The center of dynamic energy at the top of the curve does not qualify it as such, no matter how extensive the on-glide may be. Jones has on-glides of the same extent, although the glides in question are not RF's proper.

German Modal Particles Corresponding to the RF

A variety of German modal particles can correspond to the English RF. That which most frequently suggests itself to the translator is doch, with its near synonyms ja, eben, and the corresponding interrogative denn. (This group was treated in the preceding article, but it is here viewed again in a wider context.) Then there is aber or mal, which, like doch, come in the body of the sentence, and initial aber, with another function. There is a ja that is irreplaceable by doch, and yet another ja that can introduce questions. It is also shown that the emotive RF can, in favorable circumstances, also express certain notional concepts—those rendered by sogar and auch (English even and also). Other German particles touched on here are überhaupt, schon, bloss, and nur.

Modal Particles and Emotional Intonation Patterns

No mention was made in my former article of the German emotional intonation pattern likely to underline, or, in some cases, even determine the function of the particle. In this paper the most likely intonation of utterances comprising modal particles can only be touched on in the broadest outlines. Contrary to English (Uldall, 1964) and French (Fónagy and Bérard, 1972), German has not been made the subject of a detailed analysis of emotive connotations.[2] Such an analysis would be a prerequisite of a detailed tonetic transcription of German utterances with modal particles, so I can only give a few hints about how the particle behaves in the tone pattern of the utterance.[3] It normally follows the stressed finite verb and forms a melodic unit with it. The full stress is on the verb, often with raised pitch, and the following unstressed particle is approximately on the same tone level:

$_2$Du ^{4}bist ^{4}ja $_1$blau.
$_2$Du ^{4}hast ^{4}ja $_1$recht.
$_2$Er ^{4}wird ^{4}wohl $_1$zustimmen.
$_2$Er ^{4}liest ^{4}doch ^{4}die $_1$Zeitung.[4]

If the predicative item or the object is a pronoun, which is normally unstressed, it comes between verb and particle, so that the three form a melodic unit on the same pitch level:

---

[2]A short paper on results obtained by means of synthetic speech was submitted to the 7th Congress of Phonetic Sciences by Jens-Peter Köster (1972). It is, however, of no help within the framework of this article.

[3]I am indebted to A. Krivonosov, who has made a special study (auditive) of intonation and modal particles in German, (1965/1966) and also to O. von Essen (1956a, 1956b) in whose textbook (1956a) there are a great many sentences with modal particles. Yet von Essen does not touch on the problem of their possible influence on intonation. Like Krivonosov, from whose papers I quote some examples in this paragraph, I make use of the 5 4 3 2 1 marking system. The British tonetic stress marks, which will be used with the English specimen sentences, are unsuitable for German. In "Analysis of Texts" the German sentences will not be marked tonetically. What is said here should suffice, considering the lack of precise knowledge we have of German intonation, and the main point of interest being the choice of particle.

[4]The second possible German falling nuclear tone, a high fall, would be, for example, $_2$Er ^{3}liest^{3}doch ^{3}die ^{4}Zeitung$_1$. There is no consensus among scholars as to the different function of the two patterns.

$_2$Ich ^{4}hab ^{4}es ^{4}ja $_1$gleich ge$_1$sagt.
$_2$Sie ^{4}wissen ^{4}es ^{4}ja $_1$besser.

If there is no fully stressed element after the verb, i.e., if the verb is the nucleus, the following particle, or pronoun and particle, cooperates with the verb to bring about the nuclear fall. In the latter case the voice drops either on the pronoun or only on the particle:

$_2$Er ^{4}kommt $_1$ja.
$_2$Ich ^{4}komme $_1$schon.
^{4}Lass $_1$das $_1$doch.
$_2$Nun ^{4}reicht's $_1$mir $_1$aber.
$_3$Was ^{5}fehlt ^{5}ihm $_1$denn?
$_2$Sie ^{4}sind ^{4}es $_1$doch.
$_3$Wie ^{5}hiess ^{5}sie $_2$denn?

Here is a comparison of two otherwise identical sentences, one with a particle (Krivonosov, 1965, p. 577):

$_2$Was ^{3}ist $_1$das?
$_3$Was ^{5}ist ^{5}denn $_2$das?

An initial unstressed aber or ja is pitched relatively high if the voice drops on the nuclear fall, and low before a rise up to the beginning of the nuclear fall:

^{4}Aber $_1$nein.
$_2$Aber ge^{4}wiss$_1$.
$_2$Ja ^{4}frei$_1$lich.
$_2$Ja $_2$wo ^{5}ist $_1$er $_1$denn?

Use of the RF and the Modal Particle

It has been said that some speakers make use of the English RF very sparingly, or not at all. The same cannot be said of the corresponding German particles. Everybody uses them, although with different frequency. In writing, moderation in this respect is said to be a sign of good style. When comparing corresponding utterances of the two languages, we see that there are many cases where an English RF nucleus does not allow any particle to be inserted in the German sentence, whereas there are others where a German particle cannot without stretching a point be rendered by an RF. It stands to reason that the emotive connotation of the utterances to be considered here is not expressed exclusively by the RF in English or the particle in German. In both languages the bearer of the connotation is an emotive tone pattern—comprising in English a possible RF—plus the voice quality, facial expression, gestures, and so on brought to bear on the words and the context of the utterance. What the English RF and most of the German particles here treated do is to underline the implication expressed by those other means (Crystal,

1969, pp. 283–286). Here English is at a certain disadvantage. One nuclear tone pattern has to make do for the expression or underlining of the most various implications. In German there is that variety mentioned briefly above in "German Modal Particles Corresponding to the RF," which is passed in review in the next section.

ANALYSIS OF TEXTS

Noncorresponding RFs and Modal Particles

Here, by way of introduction, are a few specimens of emotive RF's in exclamations where no German particle is appropriate in the corresponding utterance, so that the effect is produced by other means, mainly increased—or reduced—pitch range:

> ^Wonderful i₁dea! or ₍Wonderful i₁dea! (Halliday, 1967, p. 46, 1970, p. 29)
> Grossartiger Gedanke!
> ' Most ef˘fective! (Jassem, 1952, p. 64)
> Höchst wirkungsvoll!
> Im˘possible! (Arnold and Tooley, 1972, p. 60)
> Unmöglich!
> ₍What a ₍nuisance! (Kingdon, 1958a, p. 243)
> Wie lästig!

There are also a few cases where a German particle cannot be rendered by an RF, but may correspond to an emphatic high rise (see Kingdon, 1958a, p. 211):

> Ist es <u>auch</u> wahr?
> Is it ″true?
>
> Hörst du <u>auch</u> zu?
> Are you ″listening?
>
> Schläfst du <u>etwa</u>?
> Are you a″sleep?

Various turns of English syntax can sometimes correspond to a German particle:

> Vergiss es <u>auch</u> nicht.
> Mind you don't forget it. (Or: You won't forget it, will you?)
> Du wirst es <u>doch</u> nicht verloren haben.
> Don't tell me you've lost it.
> Was hat er <u>wohl</u> getan?
> I wonder what he has done.

Exclamatory Statements: mal or aber

When emotive utterances like those quoted at the beginning of the preceding section are complete sentences (exclamatory statements), a particle easily slips into the German sentence: mal or aber. A tail of a certain length often ends in a rise. Marked tonicity is an essential element of the effect. The speaker is *impressed*—*favorably* or *unfavorably* (in the latter case only aber occurs).

A. I've finished painting the kitchen.
B. ^Have you, now? You ^have got a ,move on. (O'Connor and Arnold, 1961, p. 151)
Du hast dich mal (aber) beeilt.

A. You can keep it if you want to.
B. You ^are ,kind. (O'Connor and Arnold, 1961, p. 155)
Das ist mal (aber) lieb von dir.

A. They can have a week off.
B. They ^will be ,pleased. (O'Connor and Arnold, 1961, p. 155)
Werden die sich aber (mal) freuen.

Those ^chocolates are ,good. (Halliday, 1970, p. 112)
Diese Pralinen sind mal (aber) gut.

It ^was nice of you to think of ,calling. (Halliday, 1970, p. 112)
Das war mal (aber) lieb von dir, mich zu besuchen.

^That's a thing you don't see ,every ,day.
Das ist mal (aber) etwas, das man nicht jeden Tag sieht.

^That's a surprise for ,you.
Das ist mal (aber) eine Überraschung für dich.

^That's a disap,pointment for ,you.
Das ist aber eine Enttäuschung für dich.

¯That ˏwill be a ,nuisance. (Kingdon, 1958a, p. 221).
Das wird aber lästig sein.

Exclamatory commands also belong here; mal is the appropriate particle:

(About somebody giving vent to his feeling of superiority)
'Listen who's ^talking. (mockery) (Arnold and Tooley, 1972, p. 90)
Hör mal wie der redet.
'Look at the 'way he is ^swimming. (impressed)

Exclamations proper can comprise schon or auch:

'What 'queer i^deas this ,fellow ,has!
Was der Kerl auch für Einfälle hat!
'What a 'marvellous ^language ,Schiller ,wrote! (Frisch, 1969, p. 66)
Was die schon für eine Sprache haben, diese Klassiker! (Frisch, 1955, p. 124)

Statements of Fact and Antiphrasis: <u>ja</u>

In statements <u>ja</u> implies that the person addressed is aware of the fact mentioned. Therefore the mentioning of it mainly gives vent to the speaker's feelings:

,Juan, you are ˆlimping. (concern) (Frisch, 1969, p. 116)
Juan, du hinkst <u>ja</u>. (Frisch, 1962, p. 65)

He can 'scarcely ˆstand any more. (mockery or contempt) (Frisch, 1969, p. 117)
Der kann <u>ja</u> kaum mehr auf seinen Beinen gehen. (Frisch, 1962, p. 66)

Husband to wife: You ˆdon't seem to have been neˆglected in my ,absence. (mockery) (Schubiger, 1958, p. 51)
Du scheinst <u>ja</u> in meiner Abwesenheit nicht vernachlässigt worden zu sein.

Why not read something about ancient Rome. After ,all, you were ˆfounded by the ,Romans. (playful superiority) (Schubiger, 1958, p. 51)
Ihr seid <u>ja</u> schliesslich von den Römern gegründet worden.

Why should he be dumb? Why just him? We shall ˆsee. We have ways of making him speak. (menacing) (Frisch, 1969, pp. 38-39)
Es wird sich <u>ja</u> zeigen. Wir haben ein Mittel, ihn zum Sprechen zu bringen. (Frisch, 1955, p. 71)

Nobody took notice of me. I was ˆalways just a ,servant at ,home. (grudging resignation)
Ich war <u>ja</u> immer nur das Dienstmädchen zu Hause.

When, as with the last example above, there is a cause/effect relation between the two sentences, <u>eben</u> (or Southern German and Swiss <u>halt</u>) is also possible: Ich war <u>eben</u> (<u>halt</u>) immer nur . . . Here are two more examples:

Chaplain: The milk is good. As far as quantity goes, we may have to reduce our Swedish appetites somewhat. We are deˆfeated. (Brecht, 1972, p. 2)
Wir sind <u>eben</u> besiegt. (grudging resignation) (Brecht, 1957a, p. 110)

Mother Courage: Here you sit, one with his religion, the other with his cash box, I don't know which is more dangerous.
Chaplain: We're in ˆGod's hands now. (grudging resignation) (Brecht, 1972, p. 2)
Wir sind <u>eben</u> jetzt in Gottes Hand. (Brecht, 1957a, p. 109)

<u>Ja</u> also occurs in reverse phrases (antiphrasis), which are always emotionally tinged, expressing irony and sarcasm:

That ˆwould have ,helped him.
Das hätte ihm <u>ja</u> viel genützt.

,Love? A 'lot ˆyou know about it.
Liebe? Du verstehst <u>ja</u> viel davon.

A.   The trouble with you is you're lazy.
B.   ˆYou can ,talk. (O'Connor and Arnold, 1961, p. 149)
Du bist <u>ja</u> der Rechte, mir das zu sagen.

Retorts: doch and eben

Doch, often replaceable by a less pointed ja, occurs in responses that have the character of a retort. The connotation, especially of doch, is of complacent superiority or challenge: by the way you talk (or act) one would think you didn't know (or were ignorant of the facts). Other English tone patterns can convey this connotation. They were treated in detail by Schubiger (1965b), where some variants with the RF were also quoted. Some new specimen sentences have been gleaned since then:

Bishop: Have you seen the play in Seville?
Don Juan: I 'never ˆgo to ˌSeville. (Frisch, 1969, p. 151)
Ich komme ja nicht nach Sevilla. (Frisch, 1962, p. 131)

Chaplain: You think she can work it?
Mother Courage: It's in her 'own ˆinterest. I pay the two hundred and she gets the wagon. (Brecht, 1972, p. 37)
Sie hat doch ein Interesse daran, dass. . . . (Brecht, 1957a, p. 124)

A.   Why don't they open these places in spring?
B.   ˆSummer's the ˌonly ˌtime to ˌgo ˌmountain climbing. (Halliday, 1970, p. 92)
Nur im Sommer unternimmt man doch (ja) Bergtouren.

(A has expressed dissatisfaction.)
B.   The ˆothers ˌall seemed ˌsatisfied. (Halliday, 1970, p. 92)
Alle anderen waren doch befriedigt.

(A has expressed a hope that he will be released.)
B.   ˆObviously they ˌwon't reˌlease you. You are too valuable. You ought to know that. (Halliday, 1970, p. 91)
Ist doch klar, dass sie dich nicht auf freien Fuss setzen werden.

A man needs to be understood. 'So does a ˆwoman, said ˌEmma. (O'Connor, 1971, p. 19)
Eine Frau doch auch, sagte Emma.

As in the preceding paragraph, eben (halt) points more explicitly than doch to the obvious cause or consequences of what precedes:

A.   I don't think he will invite you to his concert.
B.   Then I shall ˆbuy a ˌticket.
Dann kaufe ich mir eben eine Karte.[5]

If you 'want the 'luxuries of ˌlife, you must 'have the 'money ˆfor them. (see Schubiger, 1963, p. 275)
. . . . dann musst de eben das Geld dafür haben.

NOTE: There is also a friendly type of statement with doch, corresponding to an English RF (marked tonicity) + rise in the tail:

(To a child afraid of ants) ˆThey won't ˌhurt you.
Die tun dir doch nichts an. (Schubiger, 1958, p. 52)

[5]Here the RF and German eben underline what is expressed by English then and German dann, and signal greater personal involvement.

(To somebody wondering where to get information)
^John could ,tell you. (Halliday, 1967, p. 42)
John könnte es dir <u>doch</u> sagen.

Commands: <u>doch</u> and <u>eben</u>

In commands, <u>doch</u> (to the exclusion of <u>ja</u>) and <u>eben</u> (<u>halt</u>) are appropriate. Both point to the obvious conclusion to be drawn. <u>Doch</u> (to the exclusion of <u>eben</u>) comes in sentences that are reactions to the interlocutor's attitude, whereas <u>eben</u> (or the more pointed <u>doch</u>) is a reaction to a remark of his. The connotation is of complacent superiority, and possibly impatience. I quote a few examples from Schubiger, 1965b (75-76), using the RF throughout:

> (To somebody laughing at our ignorance): You'd 'better ex^plain it to me.
> So erklär er mir <u>doch</u>.
>
> (To somebody out of breath): 'Don't be in 'such a ^hurry.
> Haben Sie <u>doch</u> nicht solche Eile.
>
> A. This pen is useless.
> B. Well, 'try a ^different one.
> Versuch es <u>eben</u> mit einer anderen.
>
> A. I ought to invite her.
> B. Well then in^vite her.
> So lade sie <u>eben</u> (<u>doch</u>) ein.[6]

Here is a specimen that has come to hand since:

> Mee Lan: The eighth prince! . . . . He's dying for me, that's what they all say.
> Then ^let them. (Frisch, 1969, p. 24)
> Dann sollen sie <u>doch</u>. (Frisch, 1955, p. 44)
>
> NOTE: There is also a friendly type of command with German <u>doch</u>. As with statements, it corresponds to an English RF (marked tonicity) + rise in the tail:
>
> A. What's behind the door, Mummy?
> B. ^Open it a ,little.
> Oeffne sie <u>doch</u> ein wenig.
>
> A. This cake looks good.
> B.   ^Taste a ,piece of it.
> So koste <u>doch</u> ein Stück.

Emotion in Answers or Retorts: <u>aber</u>

Affirmative and negative answers or retorts are often emotionally colored. In German, initial <u>aber</u> (in affirmations also <u>ja</u>) somewhat complacently implies: how can you ask? . . . doubt it? . . . be surprised?

---

[6]In French <u>donc</u> corresponds to this <u>doch</u>, <u>eh bien</u> to <u>eben</u>: "Aidez-moi donc," "Eh bien invite-là."

A. You won't tell a soul, will you, John?
B. ˆNo, Mr. Harris. (O'Connor and Arnold, 1961, p. 148)
<u>Aber</u> nein, Mr. Harris.[7]
A. You've won again.
B. ˆNaturally. I'm ˆgood at ˌdarts. (O'Connor and Arnold, 1961, p. 149)[8]
<u>Aber</u> (<u>ja</u>) natürlich. Ich bin <u>doch</u> geschickt im Pfeilwerfen.
A. Must she type it out again?
B. ˆObviously she ˌmust. It's ˆfull of misˌtakeś. (O'Connor and Arnold, 1961, p. 149)[8]
<u>Aber</u> natürlich (<u>ja</u> freilich, <u>ja</u> gewiss). Ist <u>doch</u> voller Fehler.
A. It's a silly business, all this giving of presents.
B. ˉOhˏno. It's ˌjust that it 'takes a lot of time ˆfinding things and there is 'so much to ˆdo.[9] (Kingdon, 1958b, p. 149)
<u>Aber</u> nein. Bloss dass es sehr viel Zeit erfordert . . . , Geeignetes zu finden, und man so viel zu tun hat.

Questions

Ja and Denn   Initial <u>ja</u> adds a querulous or a challenging note to the question, which in addition sometimes comprises the particle <u>denn</u>:

A. You'd better say you're sorry.
B. ˈI'd better ˌsay I am ˌsorry! 'What about ˆFrank((O'Connor and Arnold, 1961, p. 149)
<u>Ja</u> und Frank?
A. Freddy is neither in the house nor in the garden.
B. Where ˆis he then?
<u>Ja</u> wo ist der <u>denn</u>?

The RF occasionally comes on a preposition (marked tonicity):

You say this isn't an honest business. Then 'why did you 'stay ˆin it?
<u>Ja</u> warum bist du <u>denn</u> dabeigeblieben? (Schubiger, 1963, p. 275)

A. I am going to found a new party.
B. 'What are you 'going to 'do ˆwith the ˌparty?
<u>Ja</u> (<u>ja</u> und) was tust du <u>denn</u> mit dieser Partei? (Schubiger, 1963, p. 275)

Denn, Eigentlich, and Etwa   <u>Denn</u>, <u>eigentlich</u>, <u>denn eigentlich</u>, and in general questions also <u>etwa</u> add the same complacent or challenging note to a question as <u>doch</u> does to a statement. Many of these questions are rhetorical:

A. I've had this pain for days.
B. 'Why don't you ˆdo something aˌbout it? (O'Connor and Arnold, 1961, p. 165)

---

[7]French <u>mais</u> would be appropriate here: "Mais non, Monsieur Harris."

[8]For the second RF, corresponding to <u>doch</u>, see "Retorts," above.

[9]With the last two RF's no German particle can render the note of casual superiority expressed by this pattern.

Tu doch etwas dagegen. (Or: Warum tust du denn nichts dagegen?)

A. I've never seen you so angry.
B. 'How would ^you have ˌliked it? (O'Connor and Arnold, 1961, p. 165)
Hätte das etwa (denn) dir gepasst?

A. You seem very happy about your success.
B. 'Wouldn't ^you be ˌhappy? (O'Connor and Arnold, 1961, p. 165)
Wärst du etwa (denn) nicht glücklich?

'What do you ^take me for? (Frisch, 1969, p. 239)
Wofür halten Sie mich eigentlich? (Frisch, 1967, p. 52)

‾What ´are you ˌtalking about? (Jassem, 1952, p. 64)
Von was redest du eigentlich?

‾What ´are you ˌup to here? (Frisch, 1959)
Was machen Sie da eigentlich?

Bloss and Nur Bloss or nur characterizes the question as puzzled. Tonicity is often marked (nucleus on the auxiliary). Many of these questions are addressed to oneself:

‾Where ˌhave I dropped it?
Wo hab ich's bloss fallen lassen?

Now 'what ˌhad he ˌmeant by ˌthat? (Schubiger, 1935, p. 50)
Was hat er bloss (nur) damit sagen wollen?

‾What ˌis his name? (Schubiger, 1935, p. 50)
Wie heisst er doch bloss![10]

'Where ˌdo you ˌget your ˌlingo? (Schubiger, 1935, p. 50)
Woher hast du bloss dieses Kauderwelsch?

Who ˌever ˌtold you to ˌwrite to them? (Kingdon, 1958a, p. 218)
Wer hat dir bloss (denn, see above) gesagt, du sollst ihm schreiben?

Schon A question comprising schon practically amounts to a disdainful negative statement. It characterizes the matter as one of small concern:

A. I can't understand her.
B. 'Who ^can? (O'Connor and Arnold, 1961, p. 165)
Wer versteht die schon?

A. The children who obey are no problem for the caretaker.
B. 'Who ^does oˌbey him?
Wer gehorcht ihm schon?

The first God: Very well, we strike him (the swindler) out. But 'what does it ^matter if ˌone ˌman is corˌrupted? We shall 'soon find ^plenty who fulˌfill the conˌditions. (Brecht, 1970, p. 6)
Schön, er fällt weg. Aber was ist das schon, wenn einer angefault ist? Wir werden schon[11] genug finden, die den Bedingungen genügen. (Brecht, 1957b, p. 222)

---

[10]Familiar French déjà is suitable here: "Qu'est-ce qu'il a déjà voulu dire?" "Comment s'appelle-t-il déjà?"

[11]This schon, in a statement, conveys reassurance, here self-assurance.

Frontier Guard (pushing Galileo's Discorsi with his foot): There 'can't be much
^in them.[12] (Brecht, 1971, p. 122)
Na was kann schon viel drin stehen? (Brecht, 1957c, p. 194)

Expansion: sogar and noch

Here are listed responses expanding something previously mentioned. The
notional concept of expansion is usually expressed by English even, and
German sogar, noch, or sogar noch. The tone of such responses is often one of
pride, of self-satisfaction. Even, contrary to German sogar and so on, is
sometimes suppressed, the RF then having both an emotional and a notional
function.[13]

A.   How soon do you want them? By Tuesday?
B.   ^Sooner, if you can ,manage it. (O'Connor and Arnold, 1961, p. 150)
Noch früher, wenn du es einrichten kannst.

A.   Is he as tall as his father?
B.   ^Taller ,even. (O'Connor and Arnold, 1961, p. 150)
Sogar noch grösser.

A.   There will be about ten, I suppose.
B.   There'll be ^more. (Schubiger, 1965a, p. 518)
Sogar noch mehr.

A.   You should at least have drawn the game.
B.   I should have ^won. (O'Connor and Arnold, 1961, p. 157)
Ich hätte sogar gewinnen sollen.

A.   Is Rita intelligent?
B.   She is ^brilliant. (Cf. is `stupid.[14])
Sie ist sogar hochintelligent.

If the RF comes on a word expressing the extreme limit of what is
possible, auch is sometimes the most appropriate particle:

It's useless writing him a letter. A ^telegram wouldn't ,reach him in ,time.
(Schubiger, 1965a, p. 519)
Auch (sogar) ein Telegramm würde ihn nicht zeitig genug erreichen.

You 'couldn't ^look at a ,girl in this ,district. (Schubiger, 1935, p. 29)
Auch nur anblicken darf man ein Mädchen nicht in diesem Quartier.

(Begging has been mentioned.) I'd do ^that to ,get the ,children ,bread.
(Schubiger, 1935, p. 29)

---

[12]This is my own version, since the translation is not correct.

[13]For this function of the RF see Schubiger, 1965a.

[14]The RF would be out of place here. It is only appropriate if the word bearing this glide is
an expansion of what precedes it, in number, speed, excellency, and so on, not contrasting with
it. Intelligent is included in brilliant, stupid is not. In the preceding example a draw stands
midway between losing and winning (see Smith, 1972, p. 280).

Auch (sogar) das würde ich tun, um Brot für die Kinder zu bekommen.
I 'wouldn't 'have it as a ^gift. (Schubiger, 1935, p. 29)
Auch als Geschenk wollte ich es nicht haben. Nicht einmal als. . . .

Generalization: überhaupt

Contrary to sogar, which points to an expansion of what precedes, überhaupt, which is often stressed, introduces a more or less emphatic statement that generalizes what precedes it. In English this emphasis can easily result in marked or unmarked tonicity with an RF nuclear glide:

> Water-seller Wang (who in order to be the first to meet the Gods is waiting at the city gates): There will hardly be a chance for me later; they will be surrounded by important people, and there will be ^far too many de,mands on them. (Brecht, 1970, p. 3)
> Sie (die Götter) werden von Hochgestellten umgeben sein, und überhaupt stark überlaufen werden. (Brecht, 1957b, pp. 217-18)

> Woman (to two poor women who have been taken in by Shen Teh): Thank her... (to Shen Teh) They would ^never have ,known where to ,go (or... to ^go). Just as well you have got this shop. (Brecht, 1970, p. 17)
> Die hätten überhaupt nicht gewusst wohin. (Brecht, 1957b, p. 242).

> Shui Ta: My cousin regrets being unable to make unbounded concessions to the laws of hospitality.
> Man: Our 'Shen 'Teh could ^never ,bring herself to ,say such ,things. (Brecht, 1970, p. 23)
> Unsere Shen Te würde so etwas überhaupt nicht über die Lippen bringen. (Brecht, 1957b, p. 253)

> Officer (to Mother Courage, who hesitates to buy bullets from him): You can resell them for five gilders, maybe eight, to the Ordinance Office.... He 'hasn't a ^bullet left. (Brecht, 1972, p. 20)
> Der hat überhaupt keine Munition mehr. (Brecht, 1957a, p. 94)

> Are they always so enthusiastic? I've 'never seen 'anything ^like it.
> Ich habe überhaupt noch nie so was gesehen. (Halliday, 1970, p. 92)

The corresponding direct or indirect question is a basic query, a negative answer to which would make further discussion pointless:

> (Some subtle grammatical distinctions have been pointed out): The 'question ,is whether 'this is of ^interest in a ,school ,grammar.
> Es fragt sich, ob dies in einer Schulgrammatik überhaupt von Interesse ist.

> A. Shall I mention it to Freda?
> B. Is it 'worth^while d'you ,think? (O'Connor and Arnold, 1961, p. 166)
> Lohnt sich das überhaupt?

> A. What do you think, Terry?
> B. 'Does it matter ^what I think? (O'Connor and Arnold, 1961, p. 166)
> Ist meine Meinung überhaupt von Belang?

Connective Relations: auch

In the body of the sentence auch can express a causal relation with what precedes, or a similar connective relation, such as expectation/realization. In English tonicity is often marked and then is the decisive element of the pattern. The RF adds a personal note:

A.   You seem to know London very well.
B.   I've ˆlived here for a ˌlong ˌtime.
Ich wohne auch schon lange hier.

A.   You look exhausted.
B.   I ˆam exhausted.
Ich bin auch erschöpft.

A.   This is a lovely piece of embroidery.
B.   I've ˆworked at it for a ˌlong ˌtime.
Ich habe auch lange daran gearbeitet.

A.   Henry got a first in math.
B.   'That's what I exˆpected.
Das habe ich auch erwartet.

"It's my first time in England," she keeps saying, "and perhaps my last. So I want to see everything." And she ˆwill. (Arnold and Tooley, 1972, p. 80)
... und sie wird es auch durchführen.

Well, they'll have to stay, won't they? If 'only for the 'Christmas ˆpudding. (Arnold and Tooley, 1972, p. 82)
.... wenn auch nur wegen des Christmas Pudding.

A.   I suppose you're honest men.
B.   I 'hope we ˆare, ˌsir. (Kingdon, 1958b, p. 170)
Hoffentlich sind wir das auch.

A.   You look as if you wanted to leave before the end.
B.   'That's what I was ˆthinking of ˌdoing.
Daran habe ich auch gedacht.

The first three of the above examples lend themselves to a comparison with ja. Ja instead of auch would suggest that the cause of what A has stated was known to him, too (cf. "Statements of Fact and Antiphrasis," above).

Here is, for comparison, an example of an unemotional German auch of this type, where the RF would be inappropriate in English:

He 'looked like a ˌlawyer, which he ˌwas.
Er sah wie ein Jurist aus, was er auch war.

Additives: auch, auch nicht

Another German auch, at the beginning or in the body of the utterance, is additive. In matter-of-fact English speech, also or too correspond to it. Yet in favorable circumstances—some sort of personal involvement—an RF coupled with marked tonicity can imply the notional concept of addition. The emotive connotation depends on the lexical content and the context:

A.   Fancy taking a taxi for so short a distance.
B.   ^You'd ‚take a ‚taxi if you ‚had all ‚this to carry. (reproachful) (Halliday, 1970, p. 92)
Du nähmest <u>auch</u> ein Taxi, wenn du all das zu tragen hättest.

A.   I was absolutely flabbergasted.
B.   ^I would have been. (Or: ^I˙would have been, ^too.) (impressed) (O'Connor and Arnold, 1961, p. 148)
Ich wär's <u>auch</u> gewesen.

^John sees that you are a ‚liar. (Bolinger, 1971)
Auch John sieht dass du ein Lügner bist. (censure)

(To a girl) What about Alfred Porter? ^He's at your ‚feet now. (Viëtor, 1918, p. 71)
<u>Auch</u> der liegt dir jetzt zu Füssen. (playful banter, mockery)

.... And this idea of Soames's, building a house.
^That would ‚have to be ‚looked into. (Schubiger, 1935, p. 30)
<u>Auch</u> das erforderte ein wachsames Auge. (superiority)

In narrative prose the F is more appropriate than the RF. Also can be implied by marked tonicity alone:

George said it was absurd to put only potatoes, peas, and cabbage in the stew. So we overhauled both the hampers, and picked out all the odds and ends and the remnants, and 'added 'them to the ‚stew. There were... left, and we 'put 'them in. Then George found... and we 'emptied 'that into the ‚pot. (Jerome, 1934, p. 179)

Examples of German <u>auch</u> <u>nicht</u>:

Ivette (scrutinizing the cook): You're fat.
Cook: For 'that 'matter, ^you're no ‚beanpole. (mockery) (Brecht, 1972, pp. 61–62)
Du gehörst <u>auch nicht</u> mehr zu den Schlanken. (Brecht, 1957a, p. 70)

Milly: What's the matter with you, Jane? Are you frightened?
Jane: ^You don't ‚look ‚too ‚bright, ‚Milly.
<u>Auch</u> du schaust <u>nicht</u> eben gut gelaunt drein. (Schubiger, 1958, p. 82)

A.   You are too inexperienced to understand that.
B.   ^You haven't ‚seen any ‚life, ‚have you? (Schubiger, 1935, p. 30)
<u>Auch</u> du, glaub ich, hast das Leben noch <u>nicht</u> kennengelernt. (Or: Kennst <u>etwa</u> du das Leben?)

NOTE: In general questions, corresponding to this additive function of German <u>auch</u>, the implication is sometimes expressed by an emphatic high rise:

Have "you got sisters-in-law?
Hast <u>auch</u> du Schwägerinnen? (Viëtor, 1918, p. 71)

CONCLUSION

Although only a small selection of English RF utterances corresponding to German unstressed modal particles have been examined, a few remarks about a possible classification suggest themselves. One thing is certain: sentence type is no satisfactory means of classification. Whether the sentence is a statement, an exclamation, a command, or a question is of little concern. Besides, the grammatical form does not always correspond to what is meant. Rhetorical questions are frequent. Tag questions often make a statement into an exclamation.[15] In the works of literature examined, the translator often chooses another sentence type, in order to render the original text more convincingly. I tentatively suggest the following classification:

1. Utterances primarily giving vent to the speaker's emotions, i.e., exclamatory utterances in a narrow as well as in a broad sense of the word. They are either verbless (see "Noncorresponding RFs and Modal Particles"), or exclamatory sentences (see "Exclamatory Statements"). Some of the sentences imply that the hearer, too, is aware of what is mentioned (see "Statements of Fact and Antiphrasis"). Some of the questions quoted in the sections on "Bloss and Nur," and "Schon" belong here.

    Connotation: the speaker is impressed, favorably or unfavorably, which in the latter case can mean concern, mockery, or in reverse phrases also sarcasm.

2. Utterances with a distinct appeal to the interlocutor, in most cases letting him know that there is something thoughtless or even objectionable in what he has just said or been doing. The speaker appeals to him to give an answer ("Ja and Denn," "Denn, Eigentlich, and Etwa," and partly also "Bloss and Nur") or to do something ("Commands"); or his utterance is a retort ("Retorts" and "Emotions in Answers or Retorts").

    Connotation: the speaker feels superior, complacent, and often censorious or challenging. Lack of sympathy is common to all of these attitudes.

3. Utterances where the German particle expresses a notional concept. In English the RF hints at this notional concept more or less distinctly. In "Expansion" and "Additives" the concepts of expansion and addition are expressed quite distinctly, together with pride or self-satisfaction and lack of sympathy. In "Connective Relations" the causal relation is mostly in the foreground; the RF adds a personal note. In "Generaliza-

---

[15]O'Connor and Arnold (1961) list all sentences with interrogation mark under "Questions," which blurs the issue, since attitudes are here allocated according to sentence type.

tion'' the generalizing effect of <u>überhaupt</u> is barely hinted at by the emotive English tone pattern.[16]

In German the particles vary according to the type of sentence, although there are not quite enough of them to go round, so that some occur in different types of sentences, either at the beginning or in the body of the utterance, either alone or in combination with another particle. Within one and the same sentence type the choice of particle is in some cases conditioned by the lexical content and the context, underlining what is suggested by the words (see <u>mal</u> and <u>aber</u> in "Statements of Fact and Antiphrasis"; <u>denn</u>, <u>bloss</u>, and <u>schon</u> in "Questions"; <u>doch</u>, <u>ja</u>, and <u>eben</u> in "Retorts").

Can the results of this analysis contribute in any way to elucidating some controversial problems of English intonation? One point can perhaps be made, although it is no more than a hint at what would be worth investigating more closely. It concerns the function of the rise in the tail (r.t.) of the RF tone pattern.[17] Consider utterances where in German one particle is appropriate to the exclusion of another, which sometimes occurs in the same type of sentence. <u>Doch</u> in the NOTE in "Commands" is an instance in point. It connotes sympathy, and <u>eben</u> is not appropriate. However, if in English I omit the r.t., the tone changes, and the less friendly <u>eben</u> is then a possible variant of <u>doch</u>. The command loses its sympathetic undertone. <u>Doch</u> in the NOTE in "Retorts" conveys a similar connotation to a statement, and so does the RF + r.t. in the corresponding English statement. In "Exclamatory Statements" the r.t. is more appropriate where <u>mal</u> is possible in German, less so where only <u>aber</u> occurs. All this points to a possible emotive function of the r.t., in addition to its notional function of marking "a minor information point" (Halliday, 1967). Halliday, who otherwise only mentions the notional function, once made a remark about this aspect of the r.t. (1967, p. 42). He said that the RF + r.t. (5 3 in his notation) "tends to imply eagerness to help rather than the superiority or even censure that are often associated with the RF (5)." The comparison with German particles corroborates this view.

NOTE 1:   The connotation "eagerness to help" corresponds to that of Kingdon's RFR, both divided and undivided: "expressing enthusiasm at conveying pleasant news or welcome advice" (1958a, p. 227). To all intents and

---

[16]The above classification suggests a comparison with Karl Bühler's model of what human speech achieves: a) <u>Ausdruck</u> (expression of the speaker's emotions); b) <u>Appell</u> (appeal to the interlocutor); c) <u>Darstellung</u> (presentation of facts) (1934, p. 2).

[17]O'Connor, Halliday, and Crystal speak of compound tone groups when there is a rise in the tail of an F or RF nuclear glide. Kingdon calls F + R a combined tune.

purposes Kingdon's RFR, divided up, is identical with the RF + r.t. here discussed. In Kingdon (1958a) there is no room for the RF + r.t. marking only secondary prominence, but it occurs in the Reader, e.g., I've ˆspoken to him ˌonce or ˌtwice. There ˌhasn't been much ˆhappiness in her ˌlife (1958b, pp. 141, 162).

NOTE 2:   Halliday says that with the F + r.t. (1 3), as compared with the F (1), there is no change of connotation—the r.t. just marks a minor information point. This view contrasts with that of Bolinger, who in his review of Schubiger (1958) objects to a rising tail where the text suggests no emotional connotation. He says that in sentences of the type ˌFather is ˌcoming, The ˌpost has ˌcome, The ˌwater's ˌrunning, or My ˌboots want ˌmending, the r.t. would be unconvincing in the last two instances. He goes on to say that a gradual, but almost imperceptible rise instead of a level pitch is also normal in unemotive utterances, but not an r.t. going up quite noticeably. He ends with the question of whether or not anything to match this degree of rise is to be found in Received Pronunciation[18] (Bolinger, 1958, p. 200, Note 5).

REFERENCES

Armstrong, L. E., and Ward, I. C. 1926. Handbook of English Intonation, pp. 71–73. B. G. Teubner, Leipzig and Berlin.
Arnold, G. F., and Tooley, O. M. 1972. Say It with Rhythm 3. Longmans, London.
Bierwisch, M. 1966. Regeln für die Intonation deutscher Sätze. In: Studia Grammatica 7. Akademieverlag, Berlin.
Bolinger, D. L. 1958. A theory of pitch accent in English. Word 14:109–149.
Bolinger, D. L. 1959. Review of Schubiger (1958). Am. Speech 34:197–201.
Bolinger, D. L. 1971. Semantic overloading: A restudy of the verb remind. Language 47:522–547.
Brecht, B. 1957a. Mutter Courage und ihre Kinder. Stücke VII. Suhrkamp Verlag KG., Frankfort.
Brecht, B. 1957b. Der gute Mensch von Sezuan. Stücke VII. Suhrkamp Verlag KG., Frankfort.
Brecht, B. 1957c. Leben des Galilei. Stücke VIII. Suhrkamp Verlag KG., Frankfort.
Brecht, B. 1970. The Good Person of Szechuan. Transl. by J. Willett. Methuen Paperback, New York.
Brecht, B. 1971. The Life of Galileo. Transl. by D. I. Vesey. Methuen Paperback, New York.
Brecht, B. 1972. Mother Courage and Her Children. Transl. by Eric Bentley. Methuen Paperback, New York.
Bühler, K. 1934. Sprachtheorie: Die Darstellungsfunktion der Sprache. Fischer-Verlag, Jena.
Crystal, D. 1969. Prosodic Systems and Intonation in British English. Cambridge University Press, Cambridge, England.

---

[18]Crystal (1969, p. 150) states that the endpoint of a nuclear glide carries no linguistic contrast. His only mention of the width of the rise in an F + R compound tone group comes when he says in passing that this rise is frequently narrowed (p. 220).

Fónagy, I., and Bérard, E. 1972. "Il est huit heures." Contribution à l'analyse de la vive voix. Phonetica 26:157–192.

Frisch, M. 1955. Die chinesische Mauer. Suhrkamp Verlag KG., Frankfort.

Frisch, M. 1959. Biedermann und die Brandstifter. Suhrkamp Verlag KG, Frankfort.

Frisch, M. 1962. Don Juan oder: Die Liebe zur geometrie. Suhrkamp Verlag KG., Frankfort.

Frisch, M. 1967. Biografie, ein Spiel. Suhrkamp Verlag KG, Frankfort.

Frisch, M. 1969. Four Plays. Transl. by M. Bullock. Methuen Paperback, New York.

Gunter, R. 1972. Intonation and Relevance, p. 207. Penguin Modern Linguistic Readings, New York.

Halliday, M. A. K. 1967. Intonation and Grammar in British English. Mouton & Co., the Hague.

Halliday, M. A. K. 1970. A Course in Spoken English: Intonation. Oxford University Press, Oxford, England.

Jassem, W. 1952. Intonation of Conversational English. Wrocławska Drukarnia Naukowa, Wrocław, Poland.

Jerome, J. K. 1934. Three Men in a Boat. F. A. Brockhaus, Leipzig.

Jones, D. 1956. Outline of English Phonetics. 8th ed. Section 1060–1061. Heffer, Cambridge, England.

Kingdon, R. 1939. Tonetic stress marks for English. Le maître phonétique 68:60–64.

Kingdon, R. 1958a. The Groundwork of English Intonation. Longmans, London.

Kingdon, R. 1958b. English Intonation Practice. Longmans, London.

Köster, J.-P. 1972. Role de l'intonation dans l'information émotionelle des phrases allemandes synthétisées. In: A. Rigault and P. Charbonneau (eds.), Proceedings of the Seventh International Congress of Phonetic Sciences, pp. 914–921. Mouton & Co., The Hague.

Krivonosov. A. 1965. Die Wechselbeziehung zwischen den modalen Partikeln und der Satzintonation im Deutschen. Z. Phonet. Sprachwiss. Kommunikationsforsch. 18:573–589.

Krivonosov, A. 1965/1966. Die Rolle der modalen Partikeln in der kommunikativen Gliederung der Sätze in bezug auf die Nebensatzglieder. Z. Phonet. Sprachwiss. Kommunikationsforsch. 18:487–503/19:137–140.

O'Connor, J. D. 1971. Advanced Phonetic Reader. Cambridge University Press, Cambridge, England.

O'Connor, J. D., and Arnold, G. F. 1961. Intonation of Colloquial English. Longmans, London.

Palmer, H. 1922. English Intonation. With Systematic Exercises. Heffer & Sons Ltd., Cambridge, England.

Pike, K. L. 1945. The Intonation of American English. University of Michigan Press, Ann Arbor.

Priebsch, R., and Collinson, W. E. 1958. The German Language, 4th ed. Faber & Faber Ltd., London.

Schubiger, M. 1935. The Role of Intonation in Spoken English. Heffer & Sons Ltd., Cambridge, England; Fehr'sche Buchhandlung, St. Gallen.

Schubiger, M. 1958. English Intonation: Its Form and Function. Niemeyer Verlag, Max, Tübingen.

Schubiger, M. 1963. Again: The stressing of prepositions. Engl. Stud. 44:275–277.

Schubiger, M. 1965a. A note on the rise-fall nuclear glide in English intonation. In: H. Zwirner and W. Bethge (eds.), Proceedings of the Fifth International Congress of Phonetic Sciences, pp. 517–520. Karger AG., S., Basel.

Schubiger, M. 1965b. English intonation and German modal particles. Phonetica 12:65-84. [Reprinted in D. L. Bolinger (ed.), Intonation, pp. 175-193. Penguin Modern Linguistics Readings, New York.]

Sledd, J. 1956. Superfixes and intonational patterns. Litera 3:35-41.

Smith, S. B. 1972. Relations of inclusion. Language 48:276-284.

Stockwell, R. 1962. On the analysis of English intonation. In: E. A. Hill (ed.), Second Texas Conference on Problems of Linguistic Analysis in English, pp. 39-55. University of Texas, Austin.

Stopp, F. J. 1957. A Manual of Modern German. University Tutorial Press Ltd., London.

Sweet, J. 1890. Primer of Spoken English. Clarendon Press, Oxford, England.

Trager, G. L., and Smith, H. L. 1951. An Outline of English Structure. Battenburg Press, Norman, Okla.

von Essen, O. 1956a. Grundzüge der neuhochdeutschen Satzintonation. A. Henn Verlag, Ratingen.

von Essen, O. 1956b. Hochdeutsche Satzmelodie. Z. Phonet. Allg. Sprachwiss. 9:75-85.

Uldall, E. 1964. Dimensions of meaning in intonation. In: D. Abercrombie et al. (eds.), In Honour of Daniel Jones, pp. 271-279. Longmans, London.

Viëtor, W. 1918. Sprachliche Randbemerkungen zu Pinero und Shaw. Neuer. Sprach. 26:70-72.

Wells, R. S. 1945. The pitch phonemes of English. Language 21:27-39.

Weydt, H. 1969. Abtönungspartikel. Die deutschen Modalwörter und ihre französischen Entsprechungen. Linguistica et Litteraria 4. Max Gehlen, Bad Homburg.

20/ Sidelights on Tag Questions

Berthe Siertsema

In the recent discussions on the syntax of English tag questions[1] there have so far remained a number of obscurities and unexplained facts. The present paper tries to cast a few sidelights on these areas from three different angles: from the wider *contexts* of tag questions, from their *intonation* patterns, and from their *equivalents* in a related language, Dutch. The first two aspects are dealt with together in the first part, and the third in the second part, of the paper.

The following terms and tone indications are used; they are partly taken from the writers mentioned in footnote 1, and from O'Connor and Arnold's book (1961):

Main sentence: The whole sentence up to the tag question.
Host clause: The clause on which the tag question is formed.
Tag (question): (roughly) The repetition of the expressed or implied subject and verb of the host clause in the shape of pronoun and auxiliary, respectively, in inverted order, at the end of a sentence.[2]
Matching tag: A positive tag after a positive host clause; a negative tag after a negative host clause.
Contrasting tag: A positive tag after a negative host clause; a negative tag after a positive host clause.

Intonation will be marked in three levels: ò, low tone; o or ō, midtone; ó, high tone. This is with the implication that the succession of levels makes a contour, as follows: ǒ, low-high rise; ̄ó, mid-high rise; ˎō, low-mid rise; ô,

---

[1]See Lakoff (1969), Jackendoff (1971), and Cattell (1973). There is some confusion in the use of the term *tag question*. Lakoff, following Klima, uses it for the whole sentence ending in a tag, and "tag" for this last part, whereas Cattell, following Kingdon (1958, e.g., p. 249), uses "tag question" for the tag only, as Jackendoff does, too. Kingdon also uses O'Connor and Arnold's nonambiguous term "question tag" (1961, e.g., p. 253).

[2]From this definition it is clear that I have left out of the account similar question constructions in which there is a change of speaker (A: "You've got a lot done today"—B: "Yes, haven't I?), or an emphatic change of subject ("I don't like it; do you?"; "John hasn't read it; has Peter?"), as well as comparable cases of wholly different phatic construction ("It's too late, I assume?"; "It's too late, no doubt?") (see Bolinger, 1957, p. 10).

high-low fall; ˉò, mid-low fall; 'ō, high-mid fall. A doubling of ' or ˋ marks a widening of the tone range, e.g., in emotional speech: "ò, fall from extra high to low; ō̄ marks lowered mid. The frame within which these terms apply is the range of speaking tones of the speaker.

This rough indication by means of relative tone levels should not be confused with that in three or four nonoverlapping pitches used in some intonation studies. On this point Dwight Bolinger's criticisms (1951) are as valid as ever.

The levels marked here are meant as mere direction indicators in a continuous contour; the endpoints marked are not necessarily reached in all cases (just as on the phatic side, diphthongs are marked [ɑi] and [ɔi], whereas the tongue hardly ever actually reaches the [i] position). Similarly, in the *marked* (parts of) sample sentences nonmarked syllables are somewhere halfway between high and low; if there is a succession of them each may be a little higher or lower than the one preceding it, depending on whether the next marked tone is high or low, respectively. It is the patterns that matter; "... pitch range plays a role secondary to that of pitch pattern. The range is a sort of quantifier of the configuration ... : we find different magnitudes of intonation patterns" (Bolinger, 1951, p. 208). This also means that in performance the intervals may become so small as to be hardly audible, which may cause an overlap between patterns. However, the hearer will always select one of them for his interpretation (Bolinger, 1961), as he does with overlapping realizations of phonemes.

Each of the three aspects of tag questions dealt with in this paper has received some attention from previous writers; the intonation patterns have even had a great deal of attention. The intonation handbooks of R. Kingdon (1958) and of O'Connor and Arnold (1961), for instance, give a wealth of examples of many different patterns together with their meanings.

As a rule such intonation studies pay little attention to the rest of syntactic structure. Thus O'Connor and Arnold present without further comment a contrasting and a matching tag question as two examples of presenting an imperative as an invitation: "Cóme and sit do͞wn, wòn't you?"; "Cóme over he̅re à minùte, wìll you?" (1961, p. 52). Similarly, a compound main sentence in which the second clause is host clause is listed together with simple main sentences in examples of low rising tags: "It's about tén o'clo͞ck, ìsn't it?"; I dón't think you could have do͞ne ìt, còuld you?" (1961, p. 51). Conversely, recent studies of the syntax of tag questions might have profited by taking more of their intonation and context into account, as well as by using more imagination in thinking up possible contexts. As it is, too many printed tag question sentences in the latter studies are declared to be "impossible" or "meaningless" that seem to be quite all right with a different intonation and/or in a different context from the ones the authors must have tacitly selected for their analysis.[3] The same applies to many so-called ambiguous sentences that look alike in present-day ordinary print, but are in fact distinguished by different intonation patterns.[4] Not that this makes sentence description any easier when it is to be made within a frame designed to do without intonational data, but it might help to place the problems where they belong.

Besides the possibilities of other intonations and other contexts, there is a third aspect that would seem to deserve more attention in the syntactic analysis of tag questions—their translation into other languages. The fact that they are often best rendered by one or more modal particles (in Dutch, for instance) seems to lend support to the suspicion that many English tag question constructions are on their way out of syntax, are in fact halfway toward the lexicon, growing into an unpredictable whole, an idiom. We find several hints in this direction in Cattell's study (1973). As an example—and at the same time as an illustration of what has just been said about further possibilities of context and intonation—I follow part of his argument below.

INTONATION PATTERNS AND EXTERNAL SYNTACTIC RELATIONS

Cattell on Tag Questions with not

Starting from an ordinary negative yes-no question, "Didn't Aunt Eliza get married?", Cattell notes that one of its interpretations is the positive "base sentence" "Aunt Eliza got married," for which the speaker asks the hearer's

---

[3]Cf. D. L. Bolinger: "Too often we find asterisks caused by a subject's unawareness of what he might do or say given the right conditions" (1971, p. 524). For instance, if John says, "Claude is rich," Harry may indeed answer: "Claude *is* rich, is he", but Cattell says that Harry "cannot reasonably utter as a response 'Claude is rich, isn't he?'," for "if he did, John would think Harry hadn't been listening" (Cattell, 1973, p. 615). This is only true, however, under the assumption that John's information was new to Harry and that Harry's remark would have a low-mid or low-high rising tone on the tag. If John's remark concerned a mutual friend whose financial position had become apparent to both from the amount of money he spent, Harry could very well utter the condemned sentence, with a falling tone on the tag, in answer to it. Again, if John says: "I have translated that Russian sentence for you. It means: . . . ," Harry may indeed answer: "It means '. . .' does it?" However, Cattell says that Harry could not use the tag "doesn't it?", since if he did, "John could justly be annoyed here, because it seems that Harry is claiming as his own translation what he has surely just heard from John, . . . he is putting forward the translation as his own view" (1973, p. 616). This is only true, however, under the assumption that Harry has not in the meantime asked someone else, who has said the same as John says now. But what if he has? In that case the negative tag would be perfectly acceptable, certainly if it had a falling tone. Some further explanation would probably follow, such as "Peter told me already."

[4]For a fine illustration of the variety of interpretations possible for one and the same phatic construction according to the intonation patterns it will take and the contexts in which it may occur, see D. L. Bolinger, 1972b.

confirmation.[5] Under this interpretation "*the negative seems to be associated with the questioning device,* rather than with the original sentence. It is as though NEG-Q were a type of question rather different from plain Q, and as though the polarity of the questioning element were in contrast with that of the base sentence" (p. 618, italics mine).

Apart from the interesting general conclusion that this fact removes the ground for any assumption "that there will be a one-to-one systematic relationship between statements and questions" (p. 617), Cattell draws an equally interesting special conclusion with regard to comparable tag question constructions such as "Sally isn't pregnant, is she?" This sentence, too, allows a positive interpretation: "It isn't correct, by any chance, that Sally is pregnant, is it?" [Cattell: ". . . the speaker may be hinting that he thinks Sally IS pregnant" (p. 617)]. So here again we would have a positive base sentence, and the author concludes that with this interpretation again "*the negative is to be taken as part of the question,*" i.e., "*the negative is grammatically linked to the question device*" (p. 619, italics mine). For ". . . 'Sally is not pregnant . . .' does not contain a positive reading, but . . . 'Sally isn't pregnant, is she?' does. *Thus an extra meaning seems to be imported along with the tag question*" (p. 619, italics mine).

From here it is but one step to the conception of the tag question as an idiom. Cattell does consider this step toward "idiomhood" for a number of modal clauses that cause trouble in tag formation, but not for the tags themselves. Yet there is one significant sentence in his paper: "(It is quite possible, and perhaps even probable, . . . that tags are not fashioned by a tag formation rule)" (p. 624). This is the line of thought that I follow.

Special Lexical Items

Among the modal clauses considered by Cattell are "I'm not sure/certain/ aware (that) . . . , I don't know (that) . . . , I can't see (that) . . . , I find it difficult to believe (that) . . . , Don't tell me (that) . . . ," in which that is a conjunction. All of these take a positive tag question on their positive object clause: "I'm not sure that's right, is it?" This cannot be explained by Robin Lakoff's "neg-transportation" (= neg-raising), because in her view neg-transportation, like tag formation, "occurs only if a performative verb with

---

[5]It seems to me that there would be a different intonation here whenever context or situation failed to "disambiguate," for example, "márrièd," "màrrièd," or "márrièd" in the positive interpretation (c), or "marrièd" or "màrrièd" in the negative one of (a), all after a steady high-mid fall in the preceding part of the sentence; whereas the less confident negative interpretation (b) would probably have "márriéd," after a mid-low fall or a low-mid rise during the preceding part. Cattell only says the intonation is "rising" in (b) and (c) and "falling" in (a) (1973, p. 617).

the meaning of <u>suppose</u> is present—abstract or real" (1969, p. 144).[6] Cattell's examples show that this is too strict a condition, but even if we do assume neg-transportation for these sentences also, there remains the problem pointed out by Bolinger (cf. Lakoff, 1969, pp. 140, 141), that these sentences do not mean the same as their "basic" counterparts without neg-transportation: "I'm not sure it's right" is not equal to "I'm sure it's not right."

Cattell now concludes: ". . . it is possible that 'be not sure' and 'not know' are *special complex lexical items, having meanings of their own,*" viz. "tend to believe that . . . not"; thus also "Don't tell me that Max has gone again, has he?" would mean something like "Surely Max hasn't gone again, has he?" (p. 624, 625, italics mine).

I believe this is a correct interpretation. Cattell enumerates a number of objections to be made to his "special lexical item" proposal, but they in fact only lend more support to it, such as the objection that the set of "environments" for these items would be restricted more than for any other lexical verb since they can only be in the first person singular present tense (p. 625). These are features of the item itself, however, not of its environment; they are the very features that make up the idioms formed from these common verbs, just as "my goodness" at one time was an idiom and "your goodness" never was.

However, even the restriction "first person singular present tense" as such seems to be too narrowly formulated. "Harry doesn't know that it is very important" and "I didn't know that it was (is) very important" do not necessarily lead to the nonspecial interpretation only, as Cattell holds (p. 625), nor do they consequently allow only the tags "does he?" and "did I?" respectively, with tags on the head clauses. They can have either interpretation, special or nonspecial, in the right contexts, although in the complete absence of any context or situation the nonspecial meaning does seem to come up first. However, no language ever functions under such circumstances, so let us follow Bolinger's example of always providing his data sentences with sufficient contextual setting to function in, and try to find a background for the above two expressions to lead to their interpretation as "special lexical items":

---

[6]Contrary to what she says, Lakoff's "performatives" are not "performatives" in Austin's sense. Neither "I think," "I suppose," or "I am surprised" are "an action that is performed in the act of description" (1969, p. 143) as, for example, "I promise" and "I apologize" (Austin's examples) are. In fact, none of Lakoff's three very common verbs is to be found in any of Austin's five classes (Austin, 1955, pp. 152–162) and this means much, since his lists do actually include verbs such as "believe" (with Austin's own question mark) that do not fit his own three criteria of "saying the verb is doing the thing" *and vice versa,* plus impossibility of negation.

Two brothers of Harry's are discussing whether or not to reserve seats on the train for a planned journey, off-season, for Harry and themselves. One of them goes up to Harry's study to ask what he thinks should be done. This brother may well return with the message: "Harry doesn't know that it is very important at this time of the year," meaning "Harry doubts that. . . ." Afterwards, Harry comes down for dinner and the subject is brought up again, and Harry is questioned about his making so light of the matter. He could defend his earlier answer saying: "Well, I didn't know that it was (is?) very important to book in advance in the off-season, is it, so I left it to you."

If this seems to be stretching the construction a bit too far, see also Jackendoff's counterexample with subject you: "You don't suppose they'll win, will they?" (incredulously) (1971, p. 295).

Repetitive Questions

After Indirect Questions   In any case it does not seem correct to put the sentence "I don't know that it's very important, is it?" on a line with the corresponding sentences with if or whether instead of that, as Cattell does (1973, p. 626): "I don't know if/whether it is very important, is it?" To me these latter sentences do not seem to contain a tag question, but rather a more independent and purposeful question in a new sentence, arising from the lack of knowledge admitted in the preceding main sentence. This preceding sentence has itself a somewhat interrogative flavor; it contains what some grammarians have called a "dependent" (Zandvoort, 1950) or "indirect" (Kruisinga, 1941) *question*. Perhaps this is why the tag has more weight here and sounds more insistent, whereas in the construction with that this interrogative flavor is absent from the main sentence and the function of the tag is less that of a real question and more that of a mere appeal for confirmation. Hence the different term *repetitive question*, used for the tag after the sentences with if and whether; a term that receives stronger support in the next section.[7] Hence, too, my suggestion to bring out this difference in writing: "I don't know if/whether it is very important. Is it?" The question here may follow without a break, but also after quite a pause, and it may take intonations like is 'it or is it, with rather heavy stress on is. The sentence with "I don't know that . . . ," on the contrary, does normally seem to end in a proper tag, which would follow without a pause and be more likely to remain within the tone range of the main sentence without any noticeable new stress.

Those are subtle differences to measure; besides—owing to the great many variants that intonation patterns show and to the lack of statistical

---

[7]Bolinger uses this term for "*Ditto Questions,* in which the speaker repeats his own question" (1957, p. 8). In the present cases only part of the question is repeated, but the function of the repetition is the same.

data—their characterizations are inevitably impressionistic and can only be given in relative terms.[8] The omission of the word very from the examples seems to help to show the difference more clearly:

I don't know that it is important, 'ıs it/is 'ıt?
I don't know if/whether it is important, 'ıs it/is ıt/is 'ıt/ıs 'ıt?

After Direct Questions   The difference suggested just now between real tag questions and reduced repetitive questions is more evident after direct questions. In this position the tag certainly is a repetition and thus even more of a new question in its own right. It may be preceded by a pause, and its semantic function is more clearly that of a certain insistence: "Does he drink much, does he?", "Did John drink beer, did he?" Therefore, after direct questions, just as after indirect questions, these constructions would perhaps better be represented in writing as weightier than mere tags, viz., as new sentences: "Does he drink much? Does he?"; "Did John drink beer? Did he?" But . . . who am I, to think I notice such subtle differences in a foreign language when native speakers never mention them? I may be quite mistaken.

Two Further Restrictions Refuted

Incidentally, there are two other more general statements in Cattell's paper that seem to call for some comment because to my mind they put too great a restriction on the occurrence of tag questions. The first is his characterization of matching tags as occurring when the host clause expresses a point of view that is not the speaker's own but someone else's (1973, p. 615). This would wrongly exclude cases like:

A: "What a lovely dress!"
B: "You lĭke ĭt, dò you?"
A: "I slapped John's face today."
B: "You've quárrèled wĭth hìm, hàve you?" (O'Connor and Arnold, 1961, p. 52)
A: "I haven't bêen."
B: "You've played trúànt, hàve you?"

By the time speaker B utters these sentences he does express his own opinion in the headclause, as a *conclusion* drawn from previous information, verbal or

---

[8]Not impressionistic but based on sound experiments are statements to this effect by J. 't Hart and A. Cohen (1973). Their findings prove clearly "that alternations of the contour do not inevitably and consistently result in changes of interpretation, as seems to be the generally adopted view." For instance, as to Bolinger's two different interpretations of the same sentence according to whether it has a steady rise or a rise-fall-rise before the comma ("If he returned bôth of thém/bóth òf thĕm/ . . ."), they conclude: "Unless it is completely impossible to compare two different languages with respect to these phenomena, our findings clearly contradict Bolinger's position" (p. 326) (Cf. Bolinger, 1972a, p. 155).

nonverbal. Cf., for example, "You have to go, do you?" (Bolinger, 1957, p. 29), said to a visitor rising from his seat to leave. Such "direct tags," as O'Connor and Arnold call them, "refer back to something already established and accepted by both parties" (1961).

The second restriction to be questioned in Cattell's paper is his apparent acceptance of Lakoff's rule that in the case of "performatives" it is always the next clause down from the headclause that is made host clause for the tag: "I suppose *John* thinks the war is ending, doesn't *he*?" (Cattell, 1973, p. 613, italics mine). I am not sure that this is a rule; to me the following sentences sound all right, but it is up to native speakers of English to decide: "I think/John thinks/you ought to buy one because you will need one, won't you?"; "Sheila believes John married the girl in order to tease his brother, who was in love with her, wasn't he?" Cf. Bolinger's examples of a confusion of tags, such as "It was John who did it, did he?", and his conclusion that "part of the mixing . . . is due to the proximity of the subordinate verb" (1957, p. 29). Cf. also Kruisinga on reported words or thoughts of a person, in longer passages (1941, p. 141).

Tag Questions as Appeals

I do not follow Cattell any further in his brave but unsuccessful enterprise to find a "satisfactory underlying structure" for these and similar tag question sentences. What matters for the present argument is his suggestion that some of their modal headclauses are "special lexical items," a kind of idiom, therefore. This is unobtrusively illustrated by the fact that at least one of them is paraphrased by means of a modal adverb—"Don't tell me that . . ." equals "Surely . . . not . . ." (Cattell, 1973, p. 624; see above, p. 303).

I would suggest not only that these headclauses are idioms, but that the tag questions, too, are well on their way to "idiomhood." Tag questions do not really form full-grown questions—they merely reduce the assertiveness of statements and the peremptoriness of orders to some milder form by lending them a modal quality. The modality takes the form of an *appeal* to the hearer for confirmation or negation of an opinion tentatively posited by the speaker as a truth, or of an order tentatively given. This tentativeness is probably what Lakoff tries to express when she states as the condition for tag formation the real or "abstract" presence of a "verb with the meaning of *suppose*" (1969, p. 144).

The degree of tentativeness may vary; it ranges from near certainty in exclamations and the above-mentioned conclusions to complete unbelief in sentences like the "Sally isn't pregnant" example in its positive interpretation (p. 302) and in ironical remarks like B's in the following conversation:

A: "You can't catch me!"
B: I can't, can't I?" (Zandvoort, 1950, p. 254)

Indeed, the said appeal has the phatic form of a question and the term *tag question* is therefore quite in order for that part of the sentence; however, the whole sentence would be better characterized by some term such as Bolinger's *tentation* (1957, p. 10) (which he seems to use for tentative assertions only), *suggestion,* or *conclusion* rather than as a *question*. Probably a vague term like *appeal* would do best as a general technical label for all proper tag question sentences, even though we are well aware that plain questions, as well as many plain statements and imperatives, may contain no less of an appeal in the ordinary nontechnical sense of the word.

Thus we would have to distinguish three categories of sentences instead of two in English, apart from *imperatives* and *exclamations:* 1) *statements;* 2) *questions* (direct and indirect, both with or without a *repetitive question*); and 3) *appeals* (ending in a *tag question*).

Tag Questions as Half-Idioms

I have so far found support for the idea that tag questions may be considered as half-idioms in the following phenomena:

1.   Their fairly great freedom in the choice of a host clause. Tag questions are not necessarily formed on the headclause or the first subclause of a sentence. They can occur on "lower" subclauses as well, especially in longer sentences, although traditional school-teaching will try to counteract this.
2.   Their difference in form (stress, intonation, and/or pause allowed before they set in) from truncated real questions that repeat a preceding direct or indirect *question* and that should be called *repetitive questions*.
3.   Their difference in function from repetitive questions. As we saw, repetitive questions repeat and insist—they may be viewed as "intensifiers"; tag questions appeal and make tentative—they may be viewed as "down-toners."

Apart from these differences in form and function, a repetitive question also differs from tag questions proper by its complete phatic predictability: "Did John drink beer? Did he?"; "Will you do this? Will you?" Like repetitive questions, tag questions proper have the form Aux (+ not) + Pron. Subj, in which Pron. Subj is usually predictable from the host clause.[9] Contrary to

---

[9]Note, however, cases like "Nothing wrong, is there?", "I went Thursday, wasn't it?" "They had gone, was it?", and "Get there, will they?" (Bolinger, 1957, p. 29).

repetitive questions, however, the Aux of a tag question is only partly predictable; it is not, for example, in "Let's go, shall we?"; "Let me have a look, may I?"; "Push harder, can you?"; "Tell him the truth, dare you?"[10]

This only partial predictability makes it difficult to find a place for tag questions in a transformational grammar. They would probably belong somewhere halfway between lexicon and syntax, in a component of the grammar to be called, for example, "idioms and word formation." No such component has as yet been developed, but—to quote a remark of the kind that is becoming increasingly frequent in present-day linguistic studies—"I will assume that formal machinery could be devised to reflect what seems to be a clear enough notion . . ." (Cattell, 1973, p. 619).

EQUIVALENTS IN DUTCH

Tag Questions as Modal Particles

The second part of this paper highlights the character of tag questions as half-idioms through their equivalents in another language, Dutch. The modal function of tag questions comes out clearly when we try to translate them into this language. Usually we need one or more of the subtle modal particles in which Dutch, like German, abounds. For German, some of these particles and their English equivalents have been investigated and described, notably by Collinson (1954)[11] and Schubiger (1965).[12] Neither author establishes any general relation between German modal particles and English tag questions. In her comparative study Schubiger instead looks for English equivalents among intonation patterns, as the title of her paper shows. Only once in this study does she use an English tag question to render German "doch," with the remark that in some cases of this word "the English counterpart is a turn of syntax, e.g., the doch which makes a statement into a request for confirmation; e.g., Du hast doch die Fenster geschlossen? You have shút thē wìndòws, háveǹ't yòu?" (1965, p. 191; tone marking mine).

Schubiger does mention the fact that English "locutional equivalents can be found in most cases," but notes that "in the spoken language there is a strong tendency to do without them" (1965, p. 175, Note 1). An exception should have been made here for tag questions, however, common as they are, especially in spoken English. It is true, they can be left out and an appealing or disapproving or some other emotional intonation can do the job, but this

---

[10]Most of these and many more examples of unpredictable auxiliaries are to be found in J. D. O'Connor (1955) and in D. L. Bolinger (1957).

[11]Mentioned by Schubiger (1965). I have only had access to Priebsch and Collinson (1954).

[12]I have not had access to W. E. Collinson's paper (1938), mentioned in Schubiger's paper.

is also true in German and in Dutch. Intonation, that "half-tamed servant of language" (Bolinger, 1964, p. 29), is indeed of itself already capable of expressing infinitesimal nuances of meaning, but its combination with the said "turns of syntax" or with modal particles multiplies its possibilities.

Modal Particles in Dutch Syntactic Statement Constructions

Few tag questions are used in Dutch nowadays.[13] Some (older) people might use "is 't niet (zo)?" [is it not (like that)?], "(is 't niet) waar?" [(isn't it) true?], "niet?" (not?), or "(is 't) wel?" (is it?), and they might add "wil je?" (will you?) to soften down an imperative into a request, as in English. However, most of the present generation, certainly the younger ones, consider these phrases to be stilted, old-fashioned, or dialectal. Instead, Dutch has a great number of modal particles, which consist of the unstressed forms of words that also occur stressed and may then have a completely different meaning, occasionally modal as well. Cattell's "Sally isn't pregnant" example (p. 302, above) will serve for an illustration (tone indications mine, interpreting Cattell's rough directions):

"Sally isn't pregnant, is she?"
Interpretation A.   The speaker is confident that Sally is not pregnant and expects agreement:
Sally ísń't pregnànt, is shè?
(Sally is zeker níet zwàngèr?)
[Sally is "certainly" not pregnant?]

Interpretation B.   Like A, but more tentative:
Sally ísń't pregnànt, ìs she?
(Sally ìs tòch níet zwàngèr, hě?)
[Sally is "after all" not pregnant, eh?]

Interpretation C.   The speaker thinks it quite possible that Sally is pregnant and may be hinting that he thinks she is:
Sally isn't prégnànt, ìs shé?
(Sally ìs tòch nìet zwángěr?) (or ... zwàngér?)
[Sally is "after all" not pregnant?]

What is of interest for the idea of the tag question as "special lexical item" is that both in English and in Dutch the main sentences have the syntactic form of statements, including falling intonation in most of them. Cattell relates the different interpretations with different intonation patterns in the tag questions only: mid-low, low-mid, and low-high respectively, in my

---

[13] A frequent interjection-like tag is hě? (eh?). Highly fashionable among young people right now in explaining their ideas is a slightly paternalizing Ja? (Yes?), as a tag meaning "Have you been able to follow my argument so far?" L. Geschiere drew my attention to this.

marking. What does not come out in his description is that the "positive" interpretation, C, is usually also marked by a difference in the intonation pattern of the main sentence, which would have a high or extra low tone on stressed preg- (higher or lower than the tone of the preceding unstressed syllables), whereas in A and B this high tone would come on is and the tone would fall from there onward (still will stress on mid- or low-toned preg-).[14] The same difference (high-low or not on married) may disambiguate his Aunt Eliza example (see footnote 5).

Here are two more examples of the Dutch particles zeker and toch— sample sentences are either my own or borrowed from the various authors quoted earlier. In the English interlinear translation the meaning of the words functioning as modal particles is given as the one they have in their stressed form (as modal adverbs or other parts of speech); it is therefore underscored: Zeker (particle):

> Jè bent zekèr zîek!   [(I'm sure) you are îll, aren't yòu?]
> You are certainly ill.
>
> Je hebt het zekèr vèrgétèn!   (You've forgóttèn ìt, haveń't yòu?)
> You have it certainly forgotten.

Toch (particle):

> Je hebt het toch níet vérgètèn?   (You háveń't fórgòttèn ìt, have yòu?)
> You have it after all not forgotten.
>
> Je hebt het tòch nìet vèrgétěn? (You haven't forgóttèn ìt, hàve you?)
> You have it after all not forgotten.
> (The difference in meaning is the same as in the Sally example above)
> Ján ís toch 'n̄ zèurpìet'.   (John ìs à b̌ore, isǹ't hè!)
> John is after all a bore.
>
> Wat is Ján toch 'n̄ zèurpìet'. (Whát a b̌ore Jóhn îs, isǹ't hè!)
> What is John after all a bore.

To illustrate the difference of meaning, here follow some of these sentences with the same words as modal adverbs (usually stressed):

> Sally is zékér niet zwàngèr.   (Sally certainly is not pregnant.)
> Sally is certainly not pregant.
>
> Sally is tóch niet zwàngèr.   { (Sally is not pregnant, after all.)
> Sally is after all not pregnant.   { (Still, Sally is not pregnant.)
>
> Je hebt het tóch niet vergèten.   { (You háven't forgòtten ìt, àftèr àll.)
> You have it after all not forgotten.   { (Still, you haven't forgotten it.)

Similar behavior is found with other Dutch modal particles such as dus (so), even (for a moment), hoor (hear), immers [as you (ought to) know],

---

[14] Abundant proof of the importance of the intonation of unstressed syllables is given in D. Bolinger (1972b).

<u>maar</u> (but), and <u>wel</u> (really or indeed). The list shows that in their stressed form these words may be either modal adverbs or other adverbs (of time, for instance), conjunctions, and even an imperative (hoor). It is only in their unstressed (particle) form that they can be rendered by English tag questions:

<u>Dus</u> (particle):

A: Wat 'n mooie jurk! (What a nice dress!)
B: Dùs jè vìndt 'm̀ well lèuk/lék? (You lîke ìt, dò you?)
   <u>So</u> you find it indeed nice.

A: Ik heb Jan vandaag in z'n gezicht geslagen. (I slapped John's face today.)
B: (Zô) dùs jè hebt rúzìe mèt hèm gèmăăkt! (You've quárrèled with him, hàve you?); *lit.* [(I see) <u>so</u> you have quarrel with him made.]

A: Ik ben er niet geweest. (I haven't been.)
B: (Zô) dùs jìj hèbt gèspíjbèld! (You have played trúànt, hàve you?)
   (I see) <u>so</u> you have played truant.

Stressed <u>dus</u> (conjunction, often unstressed too):

Het régent nìet, dús we gaân.   (It isn't raining, so $\begin{cases} \text{off we go!)} \\ \text{we're going.)} \end{cases}$
It rains not, <u>so</u> we go.

<u>Eens</u> (particle); <u>even</u> (particle):

Kóm eens even hìer/hĭer.   (Júst come hère/hĕre, will yóu?/won't yóu?)
Come <u>once a moment</u> here.
Jîj bènt èvèn èlègănt!   (Yóu âre èlègànt, aren't yòu!)
You are <u>for-a-moment</u> elegant.

Ben jîj èvèn èlègănt! (question form)   (Àren't you élègànt! Aren't yòu)
Are you <u>for-a-moment</u> elegant.

Stressed <u>eens</u> (adverb of time):

Eéns wās zī͞j mòoi.   (<u>At one time</u> she was beautiful.)
Ik heb haar eéns geinvite'erd.   (I have invited her <u>once</u>.)

Stressed <u>even</u> (adverb of time):

Kom eens éven hĭer.   [Just come here for a moment (wŏn't yòu?)]
Come once <u>for a moment</u> here.
Éven wàchtèn.   (Wait a minute).
<u>For a moment</u> wait.
Het duurt maar èvèn.   ⌠(It only takes a short time.)
It lasts (takes) but <u>a moment</u>. ⌡(It won't take a minute.)

<u>Hoor</u> (particle):

Hìj ìs lâat hŏor!   (He's lâte, ìsh't hè!/He îs làte, . . .)
He is late <u>hear</u>.
Kom nĭet té lâat, hŏor!   (Dón't be làte, wìll you?/mìnd you.)
Come not too late, <u>hear</u>.

Stressed <u>hoor</u> (imperative):

> Hoor! De klokken luiden.   (Listen! The bells are tolling.)
> <u>Hear</u>! The bells toll.

<u>Immers</u> (particle):

> Jan kan niet komen, hij is immers zîek/zîék?   (Jóhn cǎnnǒt còme: he's ˋill, ish't hè?)
> John can not come, he is <u>as you know</u> ill.

Stressed <u>immers</u> occurs at the beginning of a sentence in public speech and writing style with the same meaning: "as you know/as we all know or ought to know."

<u>Maar</u> (particle):

> Kóm maar eens hǐer (!)   [Cóme hère, will yòu? (if you dare!)]
> Come <u>but</u> once here.
>
> Ga maar zitten.   { (Sit dòwn, will yóu/sit dòwn, wòn't you?)
> Go <u>but</u> sit.   { (Dô sìt dǒwn.)

Stressed <u>maar</u> (conjunction, often unstressed too):

> Màar ìk wîl nìet.   (But I dǒn't wânt tò.)
> <u>But</u> I want not.

<u>Wel</u> (particle):

> Het zǎl wèl láng dûrèn.   { (It'll take ā lóng tīme, wòn't ìt?)
> It will <u>indeed</u> long last. { (It'll probably take a long time.)
>
> Heb je 't wēl gèlêzèn?   { (You have not réad ìt, have yòu?)
> Have you it <u>indeed</u> read. { (Are you sure you've réad ìt?)

Stressed <u>wel</u> (adverb of modality):

> Het zal wêl lang dúrèn.   (but it will take a long time.)
> It will <u>indeed</u> long last.   (It can be done), (it will take a long time, however.)
>
> Het zal wêl làng dùrèn.   (It wîll tàke à lòng tìme.)
> (contradicting a statement to the contrary)

All of these particles occur in what syntactically are Dutch statement, exclamation, and imperative constructions. Some of them (<u>even</u>, <u>wel</u>), and a number of other ones, also occur in syntactic questions, as is shown below.

Modal Particles in Dutch Syntactic Question Constructions

<u>Soms</u> (particle):

> Ben je sòms zîek? (You ãreñ't îll, àre yóu?)
> Are you <u>sometimes</u> ill.
>
> Heb je het sōms vērgétèn? (Yōu haveñ't forgótten ìt, hàve you?)
> Have you it <u>sometimes</u> forgotten.
>
> Ben ik soms te laat?   { (I'm not lâte, àm I?)
> Am I <u>sometimes</u> too late. { (Am I lâte? Am I?)

O, moet îk hèm dàt sòms zèggèn?
(sarcastic remark)   (You mean Î hàve tò tèll hìm, $\begin{cases} \text{dò you?} \\ \text{hàve I?} \end{cases}$
Oh, must I him that <u>sometimes</u> say?

Stressed <u>soms</u> (adverb of indefinite time):

Sóms drînkt hìj tè vèel.   (He wĩll sometimes drînk tòo mùch.)
<u>Sometimes</u> drinks he too much.

Ook (particle):

Jǎ, dat zegt Jân, màar ìs hèt òok wâar?   (Yĕs, thàt's whāt Jôhn sàys, but it
ĩsñ't trûe, ìs ít?)
Yes, that says John, but is it <u>also</u> true?

Heb jîj hèt òok gèzĭen/gèzĭen? $\begin{cases} \text{(Yóu hàveǹ't sèen ĩt, have yóu?)} \\ \text{(Have yóu sèen ĩt, by any chánce?)} \end{cases}$
Have you it <u>also</u> seen.

Stressed <u>ook</u> (also, too):

Heb jij het óók gèzĭen?   (Have yóu seen it, tŏo?)
(Have you also seen it?)

Conclusion

These are some of the most frequent Dutch particles with their English equivalents, with a mere selection of possible intonations of the sentences containing
them, each intonation lending its own particular flavor to the whole. Indeed,
intonation can do in English what in German and Dutch is done by modal
particles, as Schubiger said. If we left it at this, however, there would arise a
serious problem for translators, because intonations are hardly ever indicated
in print, and, if they are, most people find them hard to read. It is not
necessary to leave it at this, however, nor is it necessary to thus put a heavier
load of responsibility on the shoulders of intonation in English than it has to
carry in the other two languages: "het Engels heeft <u>immers</u> 'tag questions'?"
(English has tag questions, <u>hasn't it</u>?).

REFERENCES

Austin, J. L. 1955. How To Do Things with Words. Harvard University Press,
Cambridge, Mass.
Bolinger, D. L. 1951. Intonation: Levels versus configurations. Word 7:199-210.
Bolinger, D. L. 1957. Interrogative Structures of American English. University of
Alabama Press, University, Alabama.
Bolinger, D. L. 1961. Generality, Gradience, and the All-or-None. Mouton & Co.,
the Hague.
Bolinger, D. L. 1964. Around the edge of language: Intonation. Reprinted in D. L.
Bolinger (ed.), 1972, Intonation. Penguin Books, Inc., New York.
Bolinger, D. L. 1971. Semantic overloading: A restudy of the verb remind. Language
47:522-547.

Bolinger, D. L. 1972a. Intonation and grammar. In: D. L. Bolinger (ed.), 1972, Intonation. Penguin Books, Inc., New York.

Bolinger, D. L. 1972b. Relative height. In: D. L. Bolinger (ed.), 1972, Intonation. Penguin Books, Inc., New York.

Cattell, R. 1973. Negative transportation and tag questions. Language 49:612–639.

Collinson, W. E. 1938. Some German particles and their English equivalents. A study in the technique of conversation. In: German Studies Presented to Professor H. G. Fiedler, pp. 106–124. Oxford University Press, Oxford, England.

Collinson, W. E. 1954. The German Language Today: Its Pattern and Historical Background. Hutchinson Univ. Library (Humanities Press, Inc.), Atlantic Highlands, New Jersey.

't Hart, J., and Cohen, A. 1973. Intonation by rule: A perceptual quest. J. Phonet. 1:309–327.

Jackendoff, R. 1971. On some questionable arguments about quantifiers and negatives. Language 47:282–297.

Kingdon, R. 1958. The Groundwork of English Intonation. Longmans, London.

Kruisinga, E. 1941. An English Grammar, 6th ed., Vol. 1, part 1. Noordhof, Groningen.

Lakoff, R. 1969. A syntactic argument for negative transportation. In: Papers from the 5th Regional Meeting of the Chicago Linguistic Society, pp. 140–147. Department of Linguistics, University of Chicago.

O'Connor, J. D. 1955. The intonation of tag questions in English. Engl. Stud. 36:97–105.

O'Connor, J. D., and Arnold, G. F. 1961. Intonation of Colloquial English. Longmans, London.

Priebsch, R., and Collinson, W. E. 1954. The German Language. Faber & Faber Ltd., London.

Schubiger, M. 1965. English intonation and German modal particles: A comparative study. Reprinted in D. L. Bolinger (ed.), 1972, Intonation, pp. 175–193. Penguin Books, Inc., New York.

Zandvoort, R. W. 1950. A Handbook of English Grammar. Noordhof, Groningen.

21/ Intonation in Glottogenesis

Henri Wittmann

INTONATION "IN THE WIDER SENSE"

It has become somewhat commonplace to consider the superficial structure of "distal" communicative performance on a two-level basis: linguistic and extralinguistic. On the linguistic level, according to Hockett (1963, p. 19), "a speaker transmits, simultaneously, a nonintonational and an intonational message." The extralinguistic contribution to communication seems to correspond again, according to Trager (1958), to a two-level discrimination between "paralanguage" and "kinesics." The linguistic level is integrated by Sebeok (1968b, pp. 8–9) into "anthroposemiotics," whereas the extralinguistic side is equated to what he calls "zoosemiotics." In other words, we have on one hand a two-level macrostructure and on the other hand an underlying four-level structure consisting of linguistic segmental, linguistic suprasegmental, paralinguistic, and kinesic.

The interaction of linguistic segmental and kinesic levels constitutes a well-known dichotomy. In terms of Hockett's design feature 1, linguistic segmental messages are conveyed on the vocal-auditory channel, whereas kinesic messages travel the gestural-visual (haptic-optic) channel of communication. Man's "congenital"[1] predisposition toward dominance of vocal-auditory over gestural-visual can be explained as an evolutionary outcome of recent standing (Hewes, 1973). In between the two extremes of linguistic segmental and kinesic, the intermediary levels of linguistic suprasegmental and paralinguistic are far less well defined as to their nature and genesis.

The most common assumptions define intonational features of language as propositional or distinctive in nature and relegate paralanguage either to the emotional or the subliminal. Bolinger (1964, p. 841) introduces, for the meaningful nontonemic uses of fundamental pitch, the rather ingenious notion of the convertibility of intonational formatives into grammatical formatives.

---

[1]Following R. W. Wescott's suggestion (in Hewes, 1973, p. 19), I substitute "congenital" for the rather ambiguous "innate."

For example, "interrogative particles may take over for interrogative intonations." However, Bolinger never loses track of the obvious fact that paralinguistic formatives (those characterized by Trager as vocal characterizers, qualifiers, and segregates) convert equally well into lexical formatives or paraphrases of some sort.[2] His conclusions should therefore not surprise us at all (1964, pp. 843–844):

> Finding comparable meanings in intonation therefore requires us to put them in the most general terms, away from the polarity of likes and dislikes. And generalizing forces us back to emotion. The very thing that was ruled out of the system comes back at the heart of it; . . . *It is impossible to separate the linguistically arbitrary from the psychologically expressive.* (Italics are mine.)

The typology of intonation, then, Bolinger would add "in the wider sense," has to "start at the central theme and trace its metamorphoses." The central theme includes both the "linguistic suprasegmental" as well as the "paralinguistic." As a universal pivot, it inserts into the dichotomy of the linguistic segmental versus the kinesic; it seems to be "vocal-auditory," but also (Bolinger, 1964, p. 844) "is like gesture," and as such it is "suprasegmental" to both.

INTONATION AND LINGUISTIC PHYLOGENESIS

Little can be said about the intonation of languages such as Proto-Indo-European or Sumerian, removed both in time and accessibility. Since linguistic phylogenesis is, practically speaking, synonymous with the history of writing, it is understandably difficult to go beyond mere guesswork, based on comparative materials from modern languages, such as Hermann's (1942) assumption that the universality of high pitch in questions constitutes proof for a "genetic" kinship of all languages.[3] There is possibly more to be said on the subject of tonic suprasegmentals (intonation in the wider sense) in a glottogonic perspective.

---

[2] Cf. also Lakoff, 1972, on problems relating to phenomena of a kind such as the German particle *doch* or Stockwell, 1971, and Wittmann, 1970, on aspects of correlation between deep structure and intonation.

[3] I was first introduced to Hermann back in 1961 while working as assistant to Bolinger, a fact that Bolinger generiously acknowledged in his paper in 1964 (p. 836, fn. 24). In a subsequent letter he writes: "I have of course acknowledged your translation, but don't expect your reputation to be permanently established by a footnote. In other words, bear down on the scholarship, my lad, and the best of luck to you, and thanks from your friend." It is with this personal note in mind that I dedicate the conclusions of this paper to a great friend whose qualities of perception and vision took him beyond the narrow constraints of a single discipline to conclusions not always understood by Hall, Hockett, and Messing (1973).

There is, first of all, Hewes' (1973, p. 6) observation that the universality of individual language features may be the outcome of cultural diffusion rather than of congenital human propensities.[4] This argument is quite useful when we wish to distinguish the social uses of individual signata from the full range of possible signantia that are species-specific to man. On the particular subject of intonation universals, Bolinger (1964, pp. 840-843) feels that:

> The similarities among languages without apparent genealogical ties can hardly be the result of chance; but the differences that we find argue against heredity as the all-pervasive influence, powerful as it may be in the short run.[5] On the one hand intonation seems to cling even when a community adopts a new language; on the other, it does not cling tenaciously enough to prevent dialects of the same language from diverging. . . . The paradox is resolved if we see intonation as tied with other forms of behavior such that it will change with a change in community manners as much as with a change in language. . . . This leads me to propose that in addition to heredity, certain underlying physiological or psychological traits are at work.

It is Bolinger's basic assumption that fundamental pitch, as it turns up in natural languages, reflects a natural condition of human speakers. He is therefore able to take into account evidence from developmental psycholinguistics such as the acquisitional primitive of the child's response to "melody" in general and to "suprasegmentals" in particular, or the observation that intonational contours are deep-structure related. He concludes quite simply:

> A tension-relaxation dichotomy lies back of fluctuations in fundamental pitch, and its universality rests on our psychophysical makeup. It is extended by outreaching metaphors, likewise shared among languages to the extent that they are obvious but are less shared, and differ from language to language, as they become more occult. The primary, transparent metaphor is the simulation of tension, still part of the physiological given: on the one hand nervous excitement, on the other, unfinished business. At a first remove, excitement, besides pitching high the entire length of an agitated utterance, gives us the rudiments of an accent system in which the pitch goes up only on the items that are exciting. Unfinished business, besides telling us that we are in the middle of an utterance, next transfers the high pitch of the middle to the end, enabling us to leave things like questions deliberately unfinished for the interlocutor to finish them. . . . Metaphors are overlaid on metaphors: a speaker reins himself in and holds down a high-pitched accent the way he controls his temper; this too is simulated and we get the reversed accents that are so common in Indo-European languages to signal restraint. At yet another remove a language using accents for the exciting of

---

[4]Cf. also Gelb's hypothesis (1952, pp. 212-220, 303-304) for monogenesis of writing through stimulus diffusion.

[5]"Heredity," as used by linguists, refers to the uninterrupted extragenetic transmission of code fixations and traditions through learning and teaching. The same is true of "genetic."

important items of discourse may exploit differences in order to show degrees of importance: a scheme of relative heights among accentual peaks. Meanwhile, much of this gets partially grammaticized. An accent language employing relative heights may distinguish old from new or topic from comment, with intonating getting a foothold in the syntax. But the foothold is with one foot; the other one is back there doing its primitive dance (Bolinger, 1964, p. 843).

If we are to take considerations of this kind seriously, the quest for universals of intonation and the genesis of tonic suprasegmentals must go beyond the phylogenetic reconstructions of traditional historical linguistics. Since, in Bolinger's own words (1964, p. 844), "the universality of intonation in the wider sense is hardly to be doubted," we must extend our interest in the matter to the question as to whether suprasegmentals as a level of communicative performance are species-specific to man or shared by a larger phylum of biological evolution.

GLOTTOGONIC ASSUMPTIONS: STATE OF THE ART[6]

Glottogonic research has been marred to this day by three basic assumptions, all closely related to subsisting negative attitudes of containment toward so-called anti-intellectual trends.

1. Glottogonic statements, because of the very nature of the enquiry, cannot be shown as either true or false.
2. No complex communicative skills exist below the level of man. Language therefore cannot be compared to animal systems of communication.
3. Intonation and paralanguage are incidental to human communication.

The first assumption led to the 1868 ban by the Société de linguistique de Paris against all papers dealing with language origins.[7] The ban proved quite ineffectual against the proliferation of new ideas on the subject, particularly in the area of comparative psychology. The second assumption is clearly directed toward confining efforts to compare the propensity for language in humans and nonhumans:[8]

"In the beginning was the Word," the Logos, reason, the creative idea. Human existence begins with language. As Wilhelm von Humboldt says: man is only man because of language; he had to be human to invent language. The formula: *no language without man, no man without language,* lends a special interest to

---

[6]I cannot consider here all the varieties of far-fetched ideas on the subject. For a bibliography, see Hewes, 1971.

[7]Mémoires de la Société de linguistique de Paris 1: III.

[8]See Nehring's review (1964) of relevant literature, where he denounces the anthropocentric attitudes of most authors.

the question of the origins of language, and furnishes a clearly-defined starting-point for research (Révész, 1956, pp. 6–7).

These arguments rule out the possibility that our presumed ancestors at any time in human prehistory adopted from animals of any sort either the initiative for linguistic communication or the material for it. The same may be said of music. In view of all this we are entitled to eliminate the animal-psychology hypothesis once and for all from the question of origins, or for that matter from comparative and genetic linguistic science as a whole. We can consequently declare that the misleading expression "language," which has given rise to so many misunderstandings, is inappropriate for use in animal psychology (Révész, 1956, pp. 36–37).

It just does not belong to the nature of the beast to speak, or want to speak. . . . The chimpanzee has simply no built-in mechanism which leads it to translate the sounds that it hears into the basis around which to unite its own ideas or into a complex mode of behavior (Wiener, 1954, pp. 82–84).

No living animal represents a direct primitive ancestor of our own kind and, therefore, there is no reason to believe that any one of *their* traits is a primitive form of any one of *our* traits (Lenneberg, 1967, pp. 234–235; cf. also Lenneberg, 1971).

Anyone concerned with the study of human nature and human capacities must somehow come to grips with the fact that all normal humans acquire language, whereas acquisition of even its barest rudiments is quite beyond the capacities of an otherwise intelligent ape: a fact that was emphasized, quite correctly, in Cartesian philosophy. It is widely thought that the extensive modern studies of animal communication challenge this classical view; and it is almost universally taken for granted that there exists a problem of explaining the "evolution" of human language from systems of animal communication. However, a careful look at recent studies of animal communication seems to me to provide little support for these assumptions. Rather, these studies simply bring out even more clearly the extent to which human language appears to be a unique phenomenon, without significant analogue in the animal world. If this is so, it is quite senseless to raise the problem of explaining the evolution of human language from more primitive systems of communication that appear at lower levels of intellectual capacity (Chomsky, 1968, p. 59).

The third assumption is a direct corollary to the second. Narrowing down the definition of language so as to exclude paralanguage or kinesics from consideration is essential to establishing animal systems of communication as mere "finite behavioral repertoires" or "closed repertoires of calls," where every repertoire consists of a fixed, finite number of signals, and where each signal is associated with a specific range of behavior or emotional state:

The noise-making aspect of language, at least today, is only one incidental feature of our form of communication (the deaf have language without noise-receiving or making) (Lenneberg, 1967, p. 235).

... expressive gestures and sounds do not constitute a means of communication as such. . . . Very few words in human language can be derived from expressive sounds. . . . It is therefore much more likely that it is not the expressive sounds that have played a constructive role in the origin of language, but rather the reverse: the linguistic function has transformed some expressive sounds into a means of communication (Révész, 1956, p. 24).

Expressive gestures only become language when the natural eloquence of the human body is developed and transformed into a system of symbols on the model of an evolved language, as in the gestural language of the deaf-mutes (Bühler, 1934, p. 70; translated from the German).

As indications of the evolutionary priority of gesture language, [the communicative gestures of the chimpanzee] are irrelevant, simply because the chimpanzee has also expressive sounds, and makes use of them to a greater extent than gestures. Hence there is no proof that among anthropoid apes gestures preceded expressive sounds (Révész, 1956, p. 52).

Et il ne doit pas confondre les paroles avec les mouvements naturels qui témoignent les passions, et peuvent être imités par des machines aussi bien que par les animaux; ni penser, comme quelques anciens, que les bêtes parlent, bien que nous n'entendions pas leur langage (Descartes, 1637, p. 58).

Aprioristic attitudes of this kind, Fouts (1973, pp. 1–8) shows, have gained such wide acceptance that positive proof in the area is no longer considered a necessary prerequisite to the debate. The underlying anathema, in fact, comes through loud and clear: Extra ecclesiam, nulla salus. However, it shouldn't seem strange to us that fundamentalists would be hostile to apes and robots alike.

GLOTTOGONIC RESEARCH: RECENT DEVELOPMENTS

It is Hockett's basic merit to have shown that "human language as a whole can be compared with the communicative systems of other animals, especially the other hominoids, man's closest living relatives, the gibbons and great apes." Although his concept of a design feature framework was an unstable and evolving one [seven in 1958 (pp. 574–585), 13 in 1960, 16 in 1963, and 26 in 1968 (Hockett and Stuart)], he was bold enough to suggest that a comparative method modeled on that of the zoologist would further the investigation into the origin of language. However original this point of view may have been, many did not share it, and some rejected it outright (see Lenneberg, 1967, pp. 232–234).

The debate around the topic has been considerably enlivened through recent successful attempts to teach chimpanzees the rudiments of human language. Since the use of the vocal-auditory mode of communication seemed inappropriate when dealing with apes [cf. the discussions by Kortlandt (1968, 1973) and Fouts (1973, pp. 8–9), as well as Bryan's (1970) intelligent reply to

Carini, 1970], Gardner and Gardner (1969) and Premack (1970) independently came to base hominoid language acquisition on a gestural-visual model (see report on progress along these lines in Fouts, 1973). Obviously, the underlying language ability in these apes must be "homeomorphic" to the basic human ability under consideration, which is exactly Lenneberg's (1971) prerequisite to comparison of animal communication with language. It should therefore be useful to see how homeomorphic mapping for the two systems could be conceived in terms of an adapted set of design features.

Design features of communicative capacity, as understood here, are logical assumptions that we can make about congenital "hardware" propensities that favor and shape the development of communicative behavior in man and chimp.[9] The inherent capacities of the two systems may be projected from a descriptive perspective correlating two frameworks of interpretation:

A. Features characterizing the capacity of the channels of transmission relative to the sensory and modulating capacities of the receiving and emitting apparatus.
B. Features characterizing the power of code flexibility.

These frameworks of comparison characterize, in fact, the biophysical and the biosemiotic aspects of the systems under discussion. Although the two are logically interdependent, relative characterizations of each and both of them can be obtained whenever mutually exclusive perspectives are implied.

A1. Channel Capacities for Distal Communication

The first question we might ask is whether distal or proximal modes of communicative linkage are involved. If we decide, as in the case here, that the privileged channel of complex communication is distal, we must presuppose the existence of proximal communication on a lower level.[10] Distal communication, as observable on planet Earth, necessarily implies modulating and demodulating capacities of the following kinds:

A1a. Visual decoding
A1b. Auditory decoding
A1c. Gestural encoding
A1d. Vocal encoding

---

[9] I can only hope that I won't suffer the fate of Ernst Haeckel, who was accused of having tried to prove the identity of human and animal development by labeling a photograph of a pig's fetus as that of a human embryo. Otherwise, I'm indebted to Roger Fouts and Gorden Hewes for letting me have access to then unpublished material.

[10] "Proximal" is understood here as mechanically or chemically tactile (immediate), somewhat as represented in the works of Hall (1966), Sebeok (1967), and Wilson (1968). In proximal communication, the effectors, characteristically, supply their own mediating agents.

The postulates underlying the whole of A1 include Hockett's DF2 (broadcast transmission and directional reception) and DF3 (rapid fading), whereas A1b and A1d in particular correspond to DF1 (vocal-auditory channel). Since chimps, in addition to their ASL competence, are capable of understanding complex English sentences, it must be assumed that A1d is actually the only channel capacity lacking in chimps but present in men. Kortlandt (1968, 1973), Lenneberg (1962, 1967), and Lieberman, Crelin, and Klatt (1972) offer attractive explanations regarding this fact. Lenneberg (1967) furnishes interesting parallels in humans (and a conclusive corroboration of implications underlying Kortlandt's observations) when he says that: "[due to a congenital deformity,] children may acquire a complete understanding of language without ever having been able to produce intelligible words" (p. 66); "the development of language is quite independent of articulatory skills . . . the perfection of articulation cannot be predicted simply on the basis of general motor development" (pp. 127–128); "since knowledge of a language may be established in the absence of speaking skills, the former must be prior, and, in a sense, simpler than the latter. Speaking appears to require additional capacities, but these are accessory rather than critical for language development" (pp. 308–309, with an earlier reference to Premack and Schwartz, 1966, p. 305).

Total Feedback Control (DF5)

In all communication, total information is an additive vectorial combination of the information provided by all of the system's relevant components. Wiener has shown that a complete additive system like this cannot be stabilized by a single feedback. Distal communication, as a matter of fact, may employ three stages of feedback:

A2a.   Proprioceptive (or kinesthetic) broadcast control
A2b.   Exteroceptive broadcast control
A2c.   Feedback derived from decoding a response in successful communication

In stickleback courtship, as far as the distal components are concerned, A2b is lacking and the basic A2a is baked up by A2c alone.[11] In man and chimp, the basic A2a is necessarily backed up by A2b, whereas A2c in these animals may be required in some situations but totally cut out in others. This particular pattern of feedbacks allows them not only to record the performance or nonperformance of their own tasks, but also to be *en rapport* with the outer world *on a selective basis* in order to *know* what the existing circumstances

---

[11]The male stickleback, according to classical reasoning (cf. Hockett), does not see the colors of his own eye and belly (the static sustained signals) that are crucial in stimulating the female.

are. The latter constitutes, according to Wiener (1954), feedback of a higher order necessary to learning, since "past experience is used not only to regulate specific movements, but also whole policies of behavior . . ." (p. 33); "It differs from more elementary feedbacks in what Bertrand Russell would call its 'logical type' " (p. 59; cf. Wiener, 1961, p. 126). In fact, the notion of total feedback in man and chimp is so powerful that it must include Hockett's DF4 (interchangeability),[12] DF6 (specialization),[13] DF12 (code acquisition through learning),[14] and DF15 (reflexiveness). In other words, the network under discussion can involve reciprocal exchanges intraspecifically with individuals and organized groups of the same or related species; the network, however, can be short-circuited, reducing dialogue to monologue and metalogue. This line of reasoning is entirely consistent with Kortlandt's (1973, p. 14) observation that chimps do a lot of "thinking aloud" without needing any short-term "reward" for their performance in such a situation.

Code Capacity

The idea of "code capacity" is meaningful only to the extent that we can oppose it to "code acquisition." If this general requirement is not met, code ontogenesis *and* phylogenesis are dependent on physiological maturation alone without the "addition," along the way, of any learned "software" components. The optimal code is part of the system's hardware. In distal communication, however, extragenetically determined and congenital code aspects remain quite distinct. Moreover, the kind of code capacity we wish to investigate must be homeomorphic to human language capacity. This is to say that the code capacity we're looking for can operate only when conditions on A2 are optimal and conditions on A1 optimal or minimal.[15]

Three gradations of code flexibility are criterial in mapping natural code capacity in man and chimp:

B1. Capacity for predication
B2. Capacity for isolation
B3. Multiple codability

Predication implies that every "Sentence" in rule-governed coding behavior will have the pattern "Subject + Predicate." The notion of "Sen-

---

[12]Either adult participant can act out the signals appropriate to the other. This feature and the whole of A2 are prerequisites to B3.

[13]To the extent that this concept is not totally meaningless.

[14]This feature predetermines the meaningfulness of the parameters underlying feature framework B, whose capacitive margin will tell what sort of code or codes the system is able to handle.

[15]Minimal conditions on A1 are needed in order to stimulate human code acquisition (and maturation based on experience) in the presence of congenital channel deficiencies.

tence," however, can be meaningful only in relation to other "sentences" generated by the same code. The minimal requirement would be that "Subject" and "Predicate" be sets consisting of at least two "Concepts," and that "Concepts" be correlated to single surface labels. In this way, it would be possible to generate four different sentences and 12 narrative patterns that are not repetitions. Two sentences with no overlapping, such as

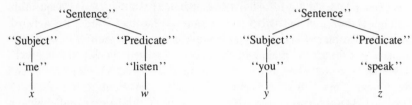

would be a representative sample from which to construct the optimal grammar. The model involves syntactic blending of the simplest kind (Bolinger, 1961), as well as narrative competence (Wittmann, 1975). The requirements for Hockett's DF9 (discreteness) and DF7 (semanticity) are equally met, which implies also a minimum of arbitrariness (DF8) and double articulation in the wider sense (DF13). B1 seems thus to be a very fundamental aspect of code capacity and should have appeared early in its development (cf. Bidwell, 1968).

The minimal units functioning in syntactic blending are formatives (as defined by Bolinger, 1948). The formatives in the sample sentences xw and yz are, as total gestalts, logocenematic, i.e., cenemes of word size. Isolation (B2) renders formatives cenematically and plerematically complex.[16] Isolation allows recursive definitions of formats in response to communicative needs conflicting with the tendency to reduce to a minimum mental and physical activity. The implied DF11 (productivity) leads to distinctions such as lexical/grammatical, generic–specific, and ultimately to DF10 (displacement).[17]

Multiple codability (B3 corresponding to Hockett's DF16), although to some extent inherent in optimal A2, constitutes capacity of a higher order than B1 and B2 together, whether cross-modal transfer of learning or code-

---

[16]Formatives are built out of recurrent partials that Hall (1959, pp. 106–110) calls "isolates" (phonemes in speech, kinemes in gesture, and so on). B2 now includes Martinet's double articulation in the narrow sense (DF13) and supposes arbitrariness of a higher order (DF8).

[17]Healy, 1973, doubts whether chimps could ever learn a phonemic language (i.e., truly talk). She is apparently unaware that ASL does have "structure" below the level of the formative, and she doesn't account for the chimp's ability to understand spoken English. Without that sort of underlying economy, the mind of the chimp would never have been able to generate such things as "dirty monkey."

switching on the same mode is involved. Bicodalism in chimps has definitely been observed by Kortlandt (1967) and Fouts, Chown, and Goodin (1973) (and by Carpenter, 1969, p. 51, for lower primates).[18] Bicodalism is equally involved when code surrogates (converting evanescent messages to frozen messages) develop under laboratory conditions (the cases of chimps Sarah and Lana). The general principle underlying bicodalism might be called "economy of alternate policies of behavior." Eventually, bicodalism in the individual and variable rules in the group (as defined by Labov, 1972),[19] will affect the extragenetic transmission of code structure and lead to code change and code diversity.[20] Thus, even the covariability of linguistic with social structure turns out to be a phenomenon common to the life of man and chimp.[21]

INTONATION IN GLOTTOGENESIS

As can be seen, the communicative capacities of man and chimp do meet Lenneberg's requirement of homeomorphism. Comparative evidence may therefore be helpful in glottogonic debating.

Lenneberg himself, on the basis of congenital anarthria observed in human subjects, comes to the conclusion (1967, p. 305) that speaking skills evidently are accessory rather than criterial for language development. Why, then, shouldn't the absence of speaking skills in chimps be interpreted by Hewes as meaning that human speaking skills must constitute, in a model of glottogenesis, a relatively recent addition to the overall code capacity as compared to the preexisting gestural skills?

As a last step, we may now attempt to determine how "suprasegmentals," intonation in the wider sense, insert into a model of "optimal" distal communication. Do primates, for instance, make use of suprasegmental modalities?

On examination, there can be no doubt that what we call "primate vocalizations" (as, for example, in Altmann, 1968) are the suprasegmentals

---

[18]Carpenter (1969, p. 51): "It's a reasonable hypothesis, therefore, that vocal responses are less plastic for learning and more fixed than their sensory perception and associated neurological processes. The latter can be learned for use in across species communicative behavior, and in interactions between individuals of different species as exemplified by these infant howler and spider monkeys."

[19]Indeed, the operation of variable rules can be extrapolated from the protocols of the Gardners and Fouts.

[20]As noted by Kortlandt (1967) for chimps and by Stokoe (1969) for human deaf-mutes.

[21]Although this discussion can only be an information presentation of a formal model for communicative capacity, it should be clear that B3 attempts to define inherent code variability whether intra- or interlingual in scope. Synonymizing, syntactic transforming, translating, and so on are all aspects of a general capacity for recoding messages relating to one social reality into structurally equivalent messages relating to another social reality.

we're looking for in primates (a fact not fully appreciated by Hewes). The apparent dissociation of segmental and suprasegmental modes observed for chimps in the wild is part of an intricate system of predator control (cf. Kortlandt, 1973). When such constraints are removed, as is the case in ASL-using chimps, normal communicative behavior exhibits a conjoint use of segmental and suprasegmental signs (even when the inhibition on the use of vocal segmentals persists). In optimally developed distal communication, suprasegmentals are thus suprasegmental to both gestural-visual and vocal-auditory coding.

Bolinger has shown that: 1) there is no valid reason to compartmentalize suprasegmentals, as signata, into cognitive and emotive; and 2) suprasegmentals, as signantia, are *voice-gestures*. Intonation thus constitutes an area of apparent transition, the compactness of which is more stable than we have expected so far. We might do well to amend our model of A1 so as to integrate voice-gesture as the essential pivot to cross-modal transfer of dominance from body-gesture to mouth-gesture, with congenital consequences on the encoding rather than the decoding side. Reformulated, the model looks like this:

A1a.   Visual-auditory decoding
A1b.   Body-gestural encoding
A1c.   Voice-gestural encoding
A1d.   Mouth-gestural encoding

The integration of visual and auditory modes of decoding into a single multimodal all-purpose decoding capacity (as operant in simultaneous listening and lipreading) underlies the acquisition of complex "gestural" encoding skills. "Gestural" encoding integrates, on various levels (A1b, A1c, A1d), skills of correlating "manners" and "places" of articulation, although control of these factors is more elusive on the level of voice-gesture. In other words, voice-gestural encoding is more complex than either body-gestural or mouth-gestural encoding.

The latter conclusion is crucial to our understanding of the evolution of optimally operant distal communication systems. If we want to explain the lack of A1d ability in chimps, we must assume either that the evolutionary design of the chimp's communicative capacity allows for the existence of congenital predispositions to congenital predispositions or that optimal designs may be altered through the addition of congenital inhibitions (in Kortlandt's sense).[22] Although the latter alternative seems to be more attrac-

---

[22]It might be worthwhile to mention that the chimp Viki actually overcame congenital inhibition in simulating human speech sounds in four isolated words. This would suggest that the lack of a supralaryngeal vocal tract in chimps (as posited by Lieberman) does not necessarily impede the removal of congenital inhibition to mouth gesturing.

tive from an angle of structural simplicity, both perspectives would have to admit that the communicative capacities of man and chimp are superficially different representations of one abstract structure of evolutionary design.[23]

REFERENCES

Altmann, S. A. 1968. Primates. In: T. A. Sebeok (ed.), Animal Communication: Techniques of Study and Results of Research, pp. 466–522. Indiana University Press, Bloomington.

Bidwell, C. E. 1968. Some typological considerations bearing upon language prehistory. Linguistics 44:5–10.

Bolinger, D. L. 1948. On defining the morpheme. Word 4:18–23.

Bolinger, D. L. 1961. Syntactic blends and other matters. Language 37:366–381.

Bolinger, D. L. 1964. Intonation as a universal. In: H. G. Lunt (ed.), Proceedings of the Ninth International Congress of Linguists, 1962, pp. 833–848. Mouton & Co., the Hague.

Bühler, K. 1934. Sprachtheorie: Die Darstellungsfunktion der Sprache. Fischer-Verlag, Jena.

Bryan, A. L. 1970. Reply. Curr. Anthropol. 11:166–167.

Carini, L. 1970. On the origins of language. Curr. Anthropol. 11:165–166.

Carpenter, C. R. 1969. Approaches to studies of the naturalistic communicative behavior in nonhuman primates. In: T. A. Sebeok and A. Ramsay (eds.), Approaches to Animal Communication, pp. 40–70. Mouton & Co., the Hague.

Chomsky, N. 1968. Language and Mind. Harcourt, Brace & World, New York.

Descartes, R. 1637. Discours de la Méthode. Leyden.

Fouts, R. S. 1973. Capacities for language in Great Apes. In: Proceedings of the IXth International Congress of Anthropological and Ethnological Sciences, Chicago, Ill. Mouton & Co., the Hague. In press.

Fouts, R. S., Chown, W., and Goodin, L. 1973. The use of vocal English to teach American Sign Language (ASL) to a chimpanzee: Translation from English to ASL. Paper presented at the Southwestern Psychological Association Meeting in Dallas, Texas, April, 1973.

Gardner, R. A., and Gardner, B. T. 1969. Teaching sign language to a chimpanzee. Science 165:664–672.

Gelb, I. J. 1952. A Study of Writing. University of Chicago Press, Chicago.

Hall, E. T. 1959. The Silent Language. Doubleday & Company, Inc., Garden City, N.Y.

Hall, E. T. 1966. The Hidden Dimension. Doubleday & Company, Inc., Garden City, New York.

Hall, R. A., Hockett, C. F., and Messing, G. M. 1973. Letter to the Editor. Language 49:984.

Healy, A. F. 1973. Can chimpanzees learn a phonemic language? J. Psycholing. Res. 2:167–170.

Hermann, E. 1942. Probleme der Frage. Akad. d. Wiss., Phil.-Hist. Kl., Göttingen. (Cf. the 1943 résumé in Cahiers Ferdinand de Saussure 3:40–41.)

---

[23]This work was supported in part by the Quebec Department of Education.

Hewes, G. W. 1971. Language Origins: A Bibliography. University of Colorado, Boulder.

Hewes, G. W. 1973. Primate communication and the gestural origin of language. Curr. Anthropol. 14:5-24.

Hockett, C. F. 1958. A Course in Modern Linguistics. Macmillan Publishing Company, Inc., New York.

Hockett, C. F. 1960. The origin of speech. Sci. Am. 203:88-96.

Hockett, C. F. 1963. The problem of universals in language. In: J. H. Greenberg (ed.), Universals of Language, pp. 1-29. MIT Press, Cambridge, Mass.

Hockett, C. F., and Stuart, S. A. 1968. A note on design features. In: T. A. Sebeok (ed.), Animal Communication. Techniques of Study and Results of Research, pp. 61-72. Indiana University Press, Bloomington.

Kortlandt, A. 1967. Experimentation with chimpanzees in the wild. In: D. Starck et al. (eds.), Progress in Primatology, pp. 208-224. Fischer, Stuttgart.

Kortlandt, A. 1968. Handgebrauch bei freilebenden Schimpansen. In: B. Rensch (ed.), Handgebrauch und Verständigung bei Affen und Frühmenschen. Huber, Stuttgart.

Kortlandt, A. 1973. Comments. Curr. Anthropol. 14:13-14.

Labov, W. 1972. Sociolinguistic Patterns. University of Pennsylvania Press, Philadelphia.

Lakoff, R. 1972. Language in Context. Language 48:907-927.

Lenneberg, E. H. 1962. Understanding language without ability to speak: A case report. J. Abnorm. Social Psychol. 65:419-425.

Lenneberg, E. H. 1967. Biological Foundations of Language. John Wiley & Sons, Inc., New York.

Lenneberg, E. H. 1971. Of language knowledge, apes, and brains. J. Psycholing. Res. 1:1-29.

Lieberman, P., Crelin, E., and Klatt, D. 1972. Phonetic ability and related anatomy of the newborn and adult human, Neanderthal Man, and the chimpanzee. Am. Anthropol. 74:287-307.

Nehring, A. 1964. Das Problem der Tiersprache in sprachtheoretischer Sicht. Die Sprache 10:202-240.

Premack, D. 1970. A functional analysis of language. J. Exp. Anal. Behav. 14:107-125.

Premack, D., and Schwartz, A. 1966. Preparations for discussing behaviorism with chimpanzee. In: F. Smith and G. A. Miller (eds.), The Genesis of Language: A Psycholinguistic Approach, pp. 295-335. MIT Press, Cambridge, Mass.

Révész, G. 1956. The Origins and Prehistory of Language. Philosophical Library, New York. (Translated from the German original, published 1946.)

Sebeok, T. A. 1967. On chemical signs. In: To Honor Roman Jakobson, Vol. 3, pp. 1775-1782. Mouton & Co., The Hague.

Sebeok, T. A. 1968. Goals and limitations of the study of animal communications. In: T. A. Sebeok (ed.), Animal Communication: Techniques of Study and Results of Research, pp. 3-14. Indiana University Press, Bloomington.

Stockwell, R. P. 1971. The role of intonation: Reconsiderations and other considerations. UCLA Working Papers in Phonetics 21:25-49.

Stokoe, W. C. 1969. Sign language diglossia. Stud. Linguist. 21:27-41.

Trager, G. L. 1958. Paralanguage: A first approximation. Stud. Linguist. 13:1-12.

Wiener, N. 1954. The Human Use of Human Beings: Cybernetics and Society. Houghton Mifflin Company, Boston.

Wiener, N. 1961. Cybernetics or Control and Communication in the Animal and the Machine. MIT Press, Cambridge, Mass.

Wilson, E. O. 1968. Chemical systems. In: T. A. Sebeok (ed.), Animal Communication: Techniques of Study and Results of Research, pp. 75-102. Indiana University Press, Bloomington.

Wittmann, H. 1970. The prosodic formatives of Modern German. Phonetica 22:1-10.

Wittmann, H. 1975. Théories des narrèmes et algorithmes narratifs. Poetics 4:19-28.

Wittmann, H. Introduction à la linguistique historique. Presses de l'Université du Québec, Montréal. In print.

22/ Grammatical Intonation in Child Language

Henning Wode

PURPOSE

The acquisition and development of grammatical intonation is probably one of the most neglected areas in present-day research on language acquisition. As far as I can see, reliable data are practically nonexistent. The main reason for this deplorable state of affairs seems to be that researchers on child language have so far failed to apply or develop models rich enough to cope fully with all of the complexities of suprasegmental analysis. Consequently, it is quite likely that we have in the past not been posing the proper questions.

In this paper, I explore and demonstrate some of the more basic potentialities inherent in an approach to the analysis and understanding of intonation that attempts to relate pitch, stress, and pause to linguistic structures such as morphosyntax, question-answer, and the like. My cover term for this is *grammatical intonation*. My claim is that a child has to master these various relationships if he is to master the intonation system of a language like English or German.

The approach is not described in full here (for details cf. Wode, 1966, 1968, 1972a, 1972b). Below, I merely illustrate some of its major features and principles in order to be able to illuminate the nature of the child's task if viewed within the framework of grammatical intonation. Since the principles seem to be equally applicable to a variety of languages, such as English, German, French, and possibly others, I had hoped to be able to include a review of additional cross-cultural evidence and some general conclusions based on it. However, appropriate data, even from a language as widely studied as English, are so scarce that no serious attempt to generalize can at present be undertaken. Consequently, the major part of this paper presents the highlights of the first stages in the acquisition of intonation by Lars, a monolingual German boy.

THE NATURE OF THE TASK: GRAMMATICAL INTONATION

Although numerous studies, recent and less recent, deal with intonation in child language in one way or another, the term tends to be applied to such a variety of different phenomena—utterance boundaries, interrogation, and paralinguistic features (annoyance, emphasis), to name just a few (cf. Crystal, 1973, for a survey)—that the term intonation has become too vague to be linguistically helpful. Moreover, many studies, it seems to me, have overlooked a very important point in any intonational analysis with respect to both fully fledged adult languages and language acquisition. The point concerns the type of relationship that may exist between the phonetic features proper and the various linguistic categories that are associated with them. Does one intonation or one intonational feature always imply the same distinction—for example, interrogation? Furthermore, does one intonation combine freely with any item in the linguistic system? My answer to both questions is no. In fact the complex interplay between intonation and morphosyntax also involves, it seems to me, such deep-rooted principles as structure dependence, so often discussed with reference to syntax (for instance, Chomsky, 1965).

Intonation and Meaning

It seems to me that intonation research in the past—and not only with respect to English and German—has been primarily concerned with classifying, identifying, and labeling the intonation of particular utterances. With few exceptions (cf., for instance, Halliday, 1967, but for some criticism cf. Wode, 1969), no attempts have been made to generalize on these findings in order to predict which "meaning" will result if such and such an intonation is combined with such and such a segmental carrier phrase. For instance, compare examples (1a) and (1b):

(1)   a.   'Meet my as'sistant ˳Mr. Peabody.[1]
       b.   'Meet my assistant Mr. 'Peabody.

If the phrase <u>Mr. Peabody</u> is regarded as a vocative, the intonation of (1a) carries no striking implications. In contrast, the intonation of (1b) high-

---

[1]The transcriptions in this article use the following marks:
ˋ Falling pitch.
ˊ Rising pitch.
ˈ ˳ High or low, more or less level pitch preceding ˋ or ˊ.
˳ Postcontour (i.e., tail intonation) following ˋ or ˊ and starting at approximately the height of the endpoint of the preceding ˋ or ˊ. (The transcription is refined and discussed more fully in "The Data," below.)
* Ungrammaticality.

lights the vocative, perhaps as an admonition or the like. If, however, the phrase Mr. Peabody is interpeted as being an apposition to the preceding NP my assistant, then the highlighting effect is reversed: (1a) now highlights my assistant, and (1b) represents the straightforward intonation with no particular implications.

Thus, in English as well as in other languages, the particular meaningful implications attributed to intonation cannot be regarded as invariably inherent in the particular intonation per se. Rather, they arise from a complex interplay between the segmental carrier phrase and the intonation proper. It is therefore important to indicate briefly the range of restrictions that may hold between certain types of segmental carrier phrases and various intonational features.

Intonation and Morphosyntax

Restrictions between stress and morphosyntax of various sorts are familiar from many handbooks, in particular as they relate to word stress. However, the stressing of words in longer utterances, say, sentences, has been studied less extensively (Wode, 1966). Comparable pitch restrictions have, to my knowledge, not been studied at length at all. I have no doubt that such restrictions do, in fact, exist. Compare, for instance, curses and vocatives in English and in German [examples (2) and (3)]:

(2) a. 'George 'clear `out
     b. ´George 'clear `out
     c. 'Hell 'clear `out
     d. * ´Hell 'clear `out
(3) a. `Larsi 'hau `ab (Larsi, clear out)
     b. ´Larsi 'hau `ab (Larsi, clear out)
     c. `Verdammt 'hau `ab (damn it, clear out)
     d. *´Verdammt 'hau `ab (damn it, clear out)

Although utterance-initial vocatives in English and in German may be spoken with a falling intonation [examples (2a) and (3a)] or a rising one [examples (2b) and (3b)], curses in the same position cannot have the rising pitch, irrespective of whether they are to be interrogated or not. Examples (2d) and (3d) are ungrammatical. Furthermore, the rising pitch in examples (2b) and (3b) does not imply interrogation, as it might do if produced in the utterance-final position of certain constructions.[2]

It is clear, then, that there are structure-dependent limitations in the occurrence of the various intonational features—including pitch—with re-

---

[2]Of course, one could redefine the term interrogation to include (2b) and (3b), perhaps as "incompleteness." This, however, makes the term vague, hence less useful.

spect to the morphosyntactic properties of a given string. Every construction can be regarded as having a particular set of intonations that can be associated with it. Furthermore, to illustrate that examples (2) and (3) are by no means marginal cases, I add example (4), which contains a carrier phrase with quite a different morphosyntactic structure:

(4) He has raised various economic religious and constitutional issues

Whereas example (4) can be intoned with a slight rise in pitch on economic and religious, no such a rise is possible on various. This holds true irrespective of the attitudinal or emotional intention that one may wish to convey.

Examples (1) through (4) illustrate distributional restrictions between morphosyntax and such smaller constituents as vocatives, curses, appositions, or adjectival modifiers. Other restrictions extend well beyond individual sentences to include, for instance, questions and answers to such sentences as those in examples (5) and (6):

(5) a. Who settled in Princeton in 16-something?
     b. The PILGRIMS settled in Princeton in 16-something.
(6) a. When did the pilgrims settle in Princeton?
     b. The pilgrims settled in Princeton in 16-SOMETHING.

The string (5b/6b) requires the intonation center (capital letters) on pilgrims in answer to example (5a), as in example (5b), but on something in answer to example (6a), as in example (6b). Example (6b) as a reply to example (5a) would be ungrammatical, just as would example (5b) as a reply to example (6a).

In summary, then, it seems obvious to me that even the analysis of the emotional aspects of intonation cannot be carried out successfully unless grammatical aspects of intonation are taken into consideration. The next section summarizes some of the devices that have been found useful to cope with these problems.

Descriptive Devices

The particular intonation "meanings" illustrated by examples (1a,b) can be regarded as due to a shift of the respective intonational features from unmarked or neutral to marked or emphatic position. Elsewhere I have tried to show for English (Wode, 1966, 1972a, 1972b) and German (Wode, 1968) that the neutral intonation can be generated for any string or text by reference to its morphosyntactic structure. More specifically, I have suggested that the neutral intonation can be appropriately specified, if intonation is treated in terms of hierarchically organized constructions—much as in syntax (Wode, 1972a). To simplify matters somewhat, an intonation minimally requires an intonation *center,* optionally a *pendant* (i.e., any segmental stretch preceding

Table 1.   The basic intonation construction of English, illustrating the constituents pendant, center, and postcontour (adapted from Wode, 1972a)

Example	Pendant	Center	Postcontour
(1a)	'Meet my as-	'sistant	Mr. Peabody
(1b)	'Meet my assistant Mr.	'Peabody	

the center), and, also optionally, a *postcontour* either embodied within the pendant or following the center (Table 1).[3]

Emphatic intonations can be treated as shifts of various intonational constituents from neutral to non-neutral position. English vocatives may serve as a (simple) illustration. Under neutral conditions, they have postcontour (tail) intonation if placed noninitially in an utterance; they do not if placed utterance-initially. Compare example (1a) above with example (1c) below:

(1c)   'Mr. 'Peabody 'meet my as'sistant.

If the center is shifted to noninitial vocatives, the particular highlighting effects pointed out with respect to example (1b) in "Intonation and Meaning," above, may result.

The Child's Task

Within the framework suggested above, the child's task will be to master the intionational construction(s), to acquire their co-occurrence with morphosyntax, including the area beyond the individual sentence, and to acquire the regularities governing neutral and emphatic shades of meaning.

In the remainder of this paper my main focus is on the acquisition of the intonational construction(s) and the relationship of some intonational constituents with morphosyntax, rather than with the number of pitch levels, tones, tunes, stresses, pauses, and so on. That is, I primarily report on how the intonational constituents center, pendant, and postcontour evolved in the speech of Lars. My starting point is the point when the child begins to produce recognizable morphosyntactic carrier phrases, however rudimentary, i.e., when one-word utterances first appear. I have nothing to say on "intonation at the prelinguistic stage" of development.

---

[3]The terms center and pendant are taken from Hockett (1958); the term postcontour is from Pike (1945). The above is a simplified description. It neglects hierarchical structuring in sequences of intonation (cf. Wode, 1972a).

THE DATA

The data come from a detailed longitudinal study of my son Lars, born in May, 1969, as the third of four children. He has been observed daily since he began to speak, and I have tape recordings as well as notes taken spontaneously at the scene of action. These notes include the child's productions, phonetic transcriptions, and his (most likely) intention. I am interested in all aspects of his linguistic development, intonation being only one of them. Ultimately, my aim is to develop an integrated theory that characterizes man's capacity for language acquisition. It is assumed that only man can acquire (human) languages, and that this capacity is not limited to L1 acquisition. Man can learn, forget, and relearn languages under a large variety of circumstances. Consequently, his capacity for language acquisition can only be characterized if the various types of language acquisition are brought within the scope of one integrated theory that describes both the commonalities and the differences, if any, between the various acquisitional types, including classroom teaching. (For details on these issues, see Wode, 1974.)[4]

THE DEVELOPMENT OF GRAMMATICAL INTONATION

The key notion is the familiar concept of developmental sequence. It is assumed that learners pass through an ordered set of developmental stages on their way toward mastering a language or a given target structure. Each stage is marked by not necessarily target-like developmental structures peculiar to that stage. The sequence of these stages is the developmental sequence. Children may vary as to the amount of time it takes them to pass from one stage to the next, but the order of these stages is fixed relative to each other. Also,

---

[4]This report is a revised version of Arbeitspapiere zum Spracherwerb No. 2, Universität Kiel, 1974. Since then the project has developed further. We now have data on L1 English, naturalistic (i.e., untutored) L2 English acquired by children with German as L1, naturalistic L2 German/L1 English, relearning of L2 English/L1 German, L2 English taught to German students, and pidgins of various sorts. The acquisitional types are compared for differences and parallels. The main results so far are: there are certain regularities that recur in all types of language acquisition; and other peculiarities are restricted to specific types. Learning a language requires a learning theory of its own. No type of language acquisition can be described in terms of behavioristic conditioning, nor in terms of a Piagetian type of approach based on conceptual or logical development. That is, just as the regularities in children's development of, say, gait cannot be explained by the development of visual perception, so the acquisition of the formal properties used in natural languages, such as word order or inflectional marking, cannot be explained by, say, the development of cognitive concepts or logical thinking. The ability to acquire such formal properties is species specific, and very likely biologically inborn, with *Homo sapiens*. Just as it takes a goose to be imprinted, it takes a human brain to handle the formal properties of linguistic devices. The actual neuropsychological mechanisms seem to function on a categorical basis. (For summaries and further references see Wode 1976, 1977a,b, 1978a-c.)

there may be some individual variations between learners, but such individual variation is not infinite, i.e., it occurs within predictable ranges (for details see Wode, 1978b).

Stage I:—The Holophrastic Stage: The Acquisition of the Intonation Center

During the holophrastic stage, the child produced texts where each different lexical item formed a separate intonation (tone group) with a pause of varying duration after each intonation. There seemed to be no organization across intonation boundaries that indicated any kind of structuring usually described in terms of linguistic structures. As for the intonation, there was some structuring, although it was confined to the domain of the individual intonation. I here discuss briefly the intonation center, the discrete two-term system ±inter(rogative), and the semigradient system of ±neutral.

The Intonation Center   Throughout the purely holophrastic stage the intonation center was formed by the individual lexical items. This was true for monosyllabic as well as for multisyllabic items. Under neutral conditions, the latter were stressed initially. For special emphasis (or playful amusement) other stresses could be added on noninitial syllables, or, alternatively, the stress could be shifted to noninitial syllables.

The development of stress contrasts is not pursued any further. Here I focus on pitch because numerous other intonational properties are acquired before the stress system is expanded. I distinguish the discrete opposition ±inter(rogative) and the gradient contrast of ±neutral.

Discreteness: ±inter   Investigators have frequently noted that children may have a binary system of rising (+inter) versus falling (−inter) pitch at or even before the holophrastic stage, however difficult it may be to describe precisely just what distinctions the child may be signaling when he uses a rising intonation.

With the child under observation here it is not quite clear whether the two-term system arose with both terms simultaneously or whether the falling pitch developmentally preceded the rising one. However, his older brother clearly had the binary system before he had acquired any contrasting segmental lexical items at all,[5] whereas his younger sister had a marked time lag

---

[5]He had a stereotyped dummy element [hagŋ] that, apparently, served no other purpose than to provide a segmental carrier for the rise versus fall of pitch. It seemed that he employed the up-glide as an attention-getting device, when, for instance, he wanted to join in the (adult) activities around him. The down-glide was heard only when no such desire was apparent, i.e., when, for instance, he was fully involved in his own activity and wanted no interference from outside. Cf. similarly Raffler-Engel, 1964.

during the holophrastic stage before she was ever heard to produce a rising pitch in any utterance.

For this paper it is assumed that the two terms arose simultaneously with this child. Although the system is termed ±inter, the label is not meant to imply that the child was asking questions in the adult sense of the term. I am quite sure that what he was signaling was probably a real difference for him, although equivalents to adult queries cover only part of the information he may have been trying to convey or elicit.

The system ±inter operates at the intonation center. The actual auditory feature associated with ±inter is the direction of the pitch movement, with +inter requiring an up-glide and −inter a down-glide.

However, the child also produced emphatic level intonations implying insistance (or obstinacy) where it was difficult to choose between up and down. This is an instance of the gradient system ±neutral.

Gradiency: ±neutral   This is the area where most ink has been spilt by previous researchers (see Crystal, 1973, for a survey), but where, unfortunately, little precision has been achieved. I am afraid I cannot do any better. I am sure that, to signal his intentions, Lars has used a variety of suprasegmental parameters like pitch height, abruptness of pitch change, loudness, drawling, and others. However, I find it impossible to establish any clear-cut, let alone one-to-one, relationships between the observable phonetic features and the child's most likely intentions. It seems that adequate categories for the classification of this wealth of vocalization have yet to be developed. Therefore, instead of adding more data that remain at present unanalyzable, I merely note that this child was certainly capable of implying shades of meaning that were not part of the lexical meaning of a word by altering, among other things, his intonation. The distinction of ±neutral is introduced to account for this ability. In the following I am not concerned with −neutral, i.e., emphatic intonations.

Stage II—Holophrastic Repetitions: The Acquisition of the Pendant

Before passing on to two-word utterances proper, another type of utterance must be considered, for which the term *holophrastic repetition* is suggested. To date, holophrastic repetitions do not seem to have received any attention in the literature.

While still at the genuinely holophrastic stage, children are known to optionally repeat a lexical item within one intonation, as in example (7):

(7)   Mama Mama Mama (calling for Mom)
Decke Decke Decke (blanket)
Apfel Apfel Apfel (apple)

Utterances like these are intonationally and semantically important. With the child under investigation here, the repeated items had the same referent throughout the utterances, i.e., the same Mom, the same blanket, and the same apple. At this stage, such utterances never referred to, say, different blankets, even if these were spread out in full view of the child. Optionally, strings like those in example (7) could be uttered as one intonation. Their status as ±inter was determined by the final token of the string. Thus the intonation center was located on the final token, and all of the preceding tokens formed the pendant. From the data on this child it appears that repetition strings are acquired subsequent to one-token holophrastic utterances and their intonational peculiarities.

Pitch Restrictions and Morphosyntax   Recall from examples (3c) and (3d) that, in German, initial curses are ungrammatical if spoken with a rise. Apparently, the child attended to this distinction already from the holophrastic stages—roughly since the age of 1;6-7 (1 year; 6-7 months, 0 days). Admonitions like "Mann" [man] or "Mensch" [mɛnθ][6] (both semantically interjectional admonitions) were never heard with a rising pitch.

Stage III—The Two-Word Stage: Vocatives and Postcontours

In passing from the holophrastic stages to two- or more word utterances, this child did not follow the course one would expect on the basis of the findings by Braine (1963), Brown and Fraser (1963), and Miller and Ervin (1964) for English, as well as those summarized by Slobin (1970) for other languages. That is, this child did not directly go on to produce pivots like those of Braine. Rather, before doing so, he began, *inter alia,* to systematically use postcontour intonations. These seem to be acquired by age 1;10. They appeared roughly at the same time with vocatives as well as under certain contextual conditions that are rather difficult to specify, but that, on the whole, seem to be quite parallel to those of adult German. The latter type are not treated here; I briefly discuss the vocatives.

The child differentiated the vocatives in much the same way as in adult German: in utterance-initial position, vocatives either form independent intonations or they are part of the pendant; in other positions they form postcontours, optionally cut off by a pause. Some examples are shown in Table 2, with postcontours marked by a lowered dash (_).

As is obvious from Table 2, vocatives can be pre- or postposed. Word order is random in this instance. Yet, pre- or postposition is marked by

---

[6]This utterance is modeled on German <u>Mensch</u> [mɛnʃ], literally meaning "human being." Colloquially it is very frequently used as an interjection roughly equivalent to <u>heck</u> or the like. Lars had a lisp at that time so that he substitutes [θ] for the target [ʃ].

Table 2. Examples of differentiation of vocatives by Lars

Example	Age	Child's utterance	Adult utterance	English translation
(a)	1;9,27	'Henning 'kletter	Henning, ich klettere	Henning, I am climbing
(b)	1;9,29	'Heiko 'arbeiten	Heiko, Henning arbeitet	Heiko, Henning is working
(c)	1;9,30	'rein_Mama 'Milch	Die Milch soll hier rein, Mama	The milk is to go in here, Mom
(d)	1;10,8	'groβ_Henning	Das ist groβ Henning	This is big, Henning
(e)	1;10,8	'schwimmt_Henning 'schwimmt	Das Schiff schwimmt, Henning, es schwimmt	The ship is moving, Henning, it moves
(f)	1;10,8	'beiβt 'beiβt_Henning 'beiβt	Der Luftballon beiβt, Henning, er beiβt	The balloon will bite, Henning, it will bite
(g)	1;10,22	'ne_Mama 'runter_Mama	Nein, Mama, ich will runter, Mama	No, Mom, I want to get down, Mom

340

intonation. The actual pitch features used by the child in uttering vocatives are, with preposed vocatives, ¦ (level), ‵ (falling), ′ (rising), or ˇ (falling-rising); with postposed vocatives the postcontours are level or they continue in the same direction as the pitch on the center. I have marked all these variants as _ .

As for the developmental sequence, with preposed vocatives the falling-rising pitch is rare at 1;10. It is used freely only later; with postposed vocatives, rising ones are rare and probably unproductive at 1;10. The latter must be distinguished from the low rise following a fall and indicating +inter. This usage is acquired still later. Thus the developmental sequence is: with preposed vocatives, level, rising, and falling pitch precede falling-rising; with postposed vocatives, level pitch or pitch continuing a preceding fall precede pitch continuing a rise; this pitch, in turn, precedes the fall followed by a rise to indicate +inter.

Summary: Developmental Sequence

The developmental sequence of the three major intonational constituents corresponds to the generality of the categories in the adult model as defined by their hierarchical status: center before pendant and postcontour last.

In addition, the child has grasped several basic insights relating to the intonation system of adult German. First, he has grasped the principle of correlating morphosyntax with intonation. If this view is not accepted with respect to stage 1, it should surely be accepted at the age represented by example (7) or Table 2. Second, the child's productions evidence the principle that there are syntagmatic relationships between intonational constituents. Consider, for instance, the status of the various pitch features associated with postcontours as conditioned by the pitch of the center. Third, there is the structure-dependent principle that not all intonations are equally permissible with all morphosyntactic carrier phrases. Recall the status of curses, as mentioned briefly in "Intonation and Meaning," above.

Thus it seems that the basic properties of the intonation system are already acquired during the holophrastic and the early two-word stages. In the development to come, the child will expand his production capacity by increasing the complexity of the structuring in accordance with the basic insights stated above. This development is not described here. Suffice it to give a few illustrative examples, as summarized in Table 3. After the acquisition of postcontours, the child develops other constructions of various sorts. All of them have their own intonational peculiarities. In particular, they differ in the position of the intonational constituents (see Table 3). Without going into details here, utterances like those in Table 3 demonstrate that, in his sub-

Table 3. Some utterance types and their intonation

Example	Age	Intonational constituents[a]		Child's utterance	English translation
		P	X		
(a1)	1;10,22	'mein	'Stuhl	mein Stuhl	my chair
(a2)	1;10,17	'mein	'Sin	meine Medizin	my drugs
		X	P		
(b1)	1;10,28	'mag	_nicht	das mag ich nicht	I don't like it
(b2)	2;0,1	'schmeckt	_nicht	das schmeckt nicht	it doesn't taste well
(b3)	2;0,1	'Larsi 'hat _nicht Aa Henning		Larsi(=ich) hat nicht Aa gemacht, Henning	Larsi(=I) haven't dirtied my pants, Henning
		X	X		
(c1)		'Heiko	'Blume	Heikos Blume	Heiko's flower
(c2)		'Heiko	'teilen	Ich teile mit Heiko	I'll let Heiko have his share
(c3)		'Heiko	'müde	Heiko ist müde	Heiko is tired

[a]P = pivot like that of Braine; X = open class like that of Braine (see Braine, 1963).

sequent development, the child extends his use of pendant, center, and post-contour productively to other constructions.

CROSS-CULTURAL EVIDENCE

Previous summaries (Weir, 1966; Crystal, 1973) have deplored the state of affairs of present-day research on suprasegmentals. They have noted the anecdotal character of many observations, and the preoccupation with the very early, in many cases even the prelinguistic, stage of development. I would like to add that most studies are concerned with the emotional aspects of suprasegmental features. Works that present systematic data on the acquisition of grammatical intonation (including pitch, stress, pause, and juncture), are very few in number, and the ones that I have been able to find all deal with English.

Age groups from 4;0 upwards have been covered by Hornby and Hass (1970), Hornby (1971), and Atkinson-King (1973). Hornby and Hass and Hornby are interested in the topic-comment distinction, with intonation as one of several linguistic means available in English to signal this distinction. Their work presents some evidence that children at 4;0 handle postcontours and centers in accordance with the adult model to signal topic and comment.

Atkinson-King (1973, with a valuable review of the literature) has investigated stress contrasts in compounds versus noncompounds, chiefly of the bláckbird versus bláck bírd type. Younger age groups apparently have attracted only incidental comments in such reports as Weir (1962), Braine (1963), Miller and Ervin (1964), and others. Most of these observations relate to postcontours.

Braine (1963) has noted suprasegmentally differentiated terminal vocatives in the speech of one of the three children he studied. Similarly, Carlson and Anisfield (1969) have observed an instance where a 2-year-old child added a vocative intoned as a postcontour to an utterance begun by another interlocutor.

Weir (1962, p. 113), reports that her son, at about age 2;6, used examples (8a) and (8b) in close sequence:

(8)   a.   'big two 'trucks
       b.   'three _trucks

Atkinson-King (1973, p. 13) cites similar evidence from Brown (1969). Little Eve, at approximately 1;10, "went around a circle of people, pointing to each person's nose and saying":

(9)   'That 'Papa _nose
       'That 'Mama _nose
       'That 'Eve _nose

Miller and Ervin (1964) thought that they could analyze an "accentual system" in the speech of one of their subjects and claimed that they could differentiate intonationally a locative construction from adjectival and possessive constructions. However, the conclusions are not borne out by the data Miller and Ervin present.

CONCLUSION

Three major points emerge: any conclusions of a more general nature, let alone along universalist lines, are premature. At present, we need detailed empirical but linguistically sober longitudinal studies on the acquisition of the intonation of various languages. In attempting such studies, researchers will have to develop models for the analysis of intonation that are much more powerful than those presently available. The acquisition of intonation cannot adequately be described simply as the mastery of features like pitch levels, pauses, and so on. Instead, it involves more abstract categories (or facts described by linguists in terms of such categories) like center, pendant, post-contour, structure dependencies between intonation, and various other levels of structure. The status of such categories, both in the adult model and in the children's unfolding linguistic system, is much more complex than one might suspect in light of the preoccupation with the emotional aspects of intonation so often encountered in previous studies.

REFERENCES

Atkinson-King, K. 1973. Children's Acquisition of Phonological Stress Contrasts. Working Papers in Phonetics 25, University of California, Los Angeles.

Braine, M. D. S. 1963. The ontogeny of English phrase structure: The first phase. Language 39:1–13.

Brown, R. 1969. A First Language, Stage 1. Unpublished paper, Harvard University. (Revised version in press)

Brown, R., and Fraser, C. 1963. The acquisition of syntax. In: C. N. Cofer and B. S. Musgrave (eds.), Verbal Behaviour and Learning: Problems and Processes, pp. 158–197. McGraw-Hill Book Company, New York.

Carlson, P., and Anisfield, M. 1969. Some observations on the linguistic competence of a two-year-old child. Child Dev. 40:569–575.

Chomsky, N. 1965. Aspects of the Theory of Syntax. MIT Press, Cambridge, Mass.

Crystal, D. 1973. Non-segmental phonology in language acquisition. A review of the issues. Lingua 31:1–45.

Halliday, M. A. K. 1967. intonation and Grammar in British English. Mouton & Co., The Hague.

Hockett, C. F. 1958. A Course in Modern Linguistics. Macmillan Publishing Company, Inc., New York.

Hornby, P. A. 1971. Surface structure and the topic-comment distinction. Child Dev. 42:1975–1988.

Hornby, P. A., and Hass, W. A. 1970. Use of contrastive stress by preschool children. J. Speech Hear. Res. 19:395-399.

Miller, W. R., and Ervin, S. M. 1964. The development of grammar in child language. Monogr. Soc. Res. Child Dev. 29:9-35.

Slobin, D. I. 1970. Universals of grammatical development in children. In: G. B. Flores d'Arcais and W. J. M. Levelt (eds.), Advances in Psycholinguistics, pp. 174-186. North-Holland Publishing Co., Amsterdam.

von Raffler-Engel, W. 1964. Die Entwicklung vom Laut zum Phonem in der Kindersprache. In: H. Zwirner and W. Bethge (eds.), Proceedings of the Fifth International Congress of Phonetic Sciences, Munster, 1964, pp. 482-486. Karger AG., S., Basel.

Weir, R. 1962. Language in the Crib. Mouton & Co., The Hague.

Weir, R. 1966. Some questions of the child's learning of phonology. In: F. Smith and G. A. Miller (eds.), The Genesis of Language, pp. 153-168. MIT Press, Cambridge, Mass.

Wode, H. 1966. Englische Satzintonation. Phonetica 15:129-218.

Wode, H. 1968. Pause und Pausenstellen im Deutschen. Acta Ling. Hafn. 11:147-169.

Wode, H. 1969. Critique of "Intonation and Grammar in British English," by M. A. K. Halliday. Phonetica 20:229-231.

Wode, H. 1972a. Zur Erzeugung der Tonhöhe englischer Syntagmata. Acta Univ. Carol. [Philol.] 1; Phonetica Pragensia III:271-280.

Wode, H. 1972b. The intonation of replies to wh-questions in English. In: A. Rigault and P. Charbonneau (eds.), Proceedings of the Seventh International Congress of Phonetic Sciences, pp. 1056-1061. Mouton & Co., The Hague.

Wode, H. 1974. Natürliche Zweitsprachigeit: Probleme, Aufgaben, Perspektiven. Ling. Berichte 32:15-36.

Wode, H. 1976. Developmental Sequences in Naturalistic L2 Acquisition. Working Papers on Bilingualism 11, 1-31. Reprinted in E. M. Hatch (ed.), 1978, Second Language Acquisition. A Book of Readings, pp. 101-117. Newburg House Pubs., Rowley, Mass.

Wode, H. 1977a. The L2 Acquisition of /r/. Phonetica 34:200-217.

Wode, H. 1977b. Lernerorientiertheit im Fremdsprachenunterricht: FU als Spracherwerb. In: H. Hunfeld (ed.), Neue Perspektiven der Fremdsprachendidaktik, Eichstätter Kolloquium zum Fremdsprachenunterricht 1977, pp. 17-23. Kronsberg.

Wode, H. 1978a. Free vs. Bound Forms in Three Types of Language Acquisition. ISB-Utrecht 3:6-22.

Wode, H. 1978b. The L1 vs. L2 Acquisition of English Interrogation. Working Papers on Bilingualism 15, pp. 37-57.

Wode, H. 1978c. Kognition, Sprachenlernen und Fremdsprachenunterricht. In: H. Detering and W. Högel (eds.), Festschrift für K. Lorenzen, pp. 188-197. Schrödel-Verlag, Hannover.

Index

methods used to determine prosodic
traits helpful in determination of, 112
prosodic traits helpful in determination of, of disjunctive expressions, 82, 85–90, 92–94,
97–104
role of melodic structure of syllables in determination of,
of disjunctive expressions,
113
Modality and attitude, 104–111
Modals, 162, 245
Models, relational, of tone-intonation
interplay, 9
Monolingual, 201, 331
Monosyllable(s), 169, 170
in Chinese transliteration of foreign
names, 43–44
in people's names, transliteration
of, in Chinese, 43–44
"More-or-less," intonation, 5
Morpheme, question, 253 *note*
Morphology, and vocal pitch, 7–8
Morphosyntax
and pitch restrictions, at stage of
holophrastic repetitions in
development of grammatical
intonation, 339
restrictions between stress and,
333–334
Mouth-gestural encoding, 326
Multiple codability, aspect of code
capacity, 324–325
Muscular mechanisms, role of, in the
control and production of
intonation, 187, 188–189
Music, speech melody in, 14–15
Muskogean, 17

Nasals, 4, 8
Natural selection, 188, 196
Neanderthal man, 197, 198
Negative, associated with the "tag,"
301–302
Neg-transportation, occurrence of,
302–303

Neural mechanisms
evolution of, "tuned" to acoustic
signals, 196
language-specific, innately determined, 187
"tuned" to acoustic patterns of
breath group, 196
Neurophonetics, and syllabization, 26
Neutral intonation, specification of,
334–335
Neutral questions, *see* Questions, disjunctive inclusive
see also Modality and attitude;
Questions, neutral
Noise, 3, 11
Nonstop intonation
pitch accents of, 258
use of, 259
Nonverifiable events
intonation patterns of reports of,
224
reports of, compared to reports of
verifiable events, 224
time link between, and reports of,
222
types of reports of, 221
Norwegian, 10
Noun Phrase(s), 45, 47, 48, 50, 51, 52
definite, 255
generic, 255
position of, in Spanish sentences
under Subject Formation (movement) rule, 47
under theory of informational
word order, 50
as "subject" in Spanish sentences,
47
as "subject," under Subject Formation (feature-assignment)
rule, 48
Nuclear glide
English, 279
fall (F), in English, 279, 280, 295
note
fall-rise (FR), in English, 279
rise (R), in English, 280
rise-fall (RF), in English, 279–280,
295 *and note*

of English, presuming phonetic syllabization, 27, 29–35
un-English syllabization, presuming an, 27, 28–29
Phonetology, English, segmental rules of, 25
Phonics, voice quality, 3
Phonological categories, 55
in relation to context, 56
Phonological interpretation, 117, 120 *note*
Phonological stress, 37
Phonology
and syllabization, 26
and vocal pitch, 7–8
Phrase(s), 5, 7
assertive, acoustic analysis of, 81–97
in Hungarian, 81, 104
boundaries, 9
declarative, discussion of frequency curves of, 89–90
declarative, results of *tronquage* method in analysis of, 84, 88, 89, 95, 97
disjunctive exclusive
defined, 104
tonal polarization in, 83, 84, 88, 105, 106
disjunctive inclusive
defined, 104
tonal polarization in, 83, 87, 105, 106, 107
in French, frequency curve of
disjunctive exclusive assertions, 105
disjunctive inclusive assertions, 84, 87, 88, 106, 107
disjunctive exclusive questions, 84, 106
disjunctive inclusive questions, 84, 85, 87, 88, 89, 106
in Hungarian, frequency curves of, 83
Ici ou là-bas, synthesis of, in the study of disjunctive expressions, 97–104

interrogative
acoustic analysis of, 81–97
in Hungarian, 81, 104
discussion of frequency curves of, 89–90
results of *tronquage* method in analysis of, 95, 96, 97
participial, preposing with inversion, 149, 152
rhythmic structure of, in comparison of rise/duration quotients, 91, 95
in Russian, 82, 104
spatial/temporal location, preposing, 160
Physiologic mechanisms
for changing fundamental frequency of phonation, 191
for structuring and constraining breath group form, 192–196
Physiology, basic vegetative constraints of human, structuring intonation, 188, 198
Pitch
association of change in, with stress, 71
association of stress with, by Chinese speakers of English, 41–42
curves, 5, 6
curves, contour of, 8
discrete, in holophrastic stage of development of grammatical intonation, 337–338
displacement
in English, 11–12
in Japanese, 11
in Spanish, 11
falling, semantic labels describing linguistic functions of, 239
fundamental (singing), 5, 6
at holophrastic repetitions stage of development of grammatical intonation, 339
level, relative, 6, 7
melodic, in English prosodic system, 177
notation, 10

ERRATA

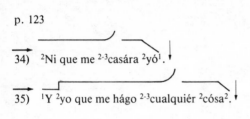

28) ^{1}No la $^{2\text{-}4}$co^{2}nózco^1.

31) ^{1}Que^{2}dáte a cenár con $^{2\text{-}2}$no^{2}sótros^1.

32) ^{2}Eran las diéz ménos cuárto de la $^{2\text{-}3}$nóche^2 . . .

p. 123

34) ^{2}Ni que me $^{2\text{-}3}$casára ^{2}yó^1.

35) ^{1}Y ^{2}yo que me hágo $^{2\text{-}3}$cualquiér ^{2}cósa^2.

p. 124

1. In general terms, the intonational system of Buenos Aires Spanish is less complex than the Tucuman and Cordoba ones, since, while the constituent elements of the first are limited to three terminal contours and three pitch levels that usually contrast in four positions (and exceptionally in five positions), in the Cordoba and Tucuman systems there are features of others kinds—the lengthening of the prestressed syllable, in the first case, and the secondary pitch level and the possibilities of a glide in the stressed syllable in the second one—that make their structure more complex.

p. 125

38) ^{2}En pri^{2+}mé^{3}ro!

p. 126, **REFERENCES**

Canellada, M. J. 1941. Notas de entonación extremeña. RFE 25:70–91.

Hockett, C. F. 1971. Curso de lingüística moderna, pp. 40–53. Traducido y adaptado al español por Emma Gregores y Jorge A. Suárez. Eudeba, Buenos Aires.

Lieberman, P., Sawashima, M., Harris, K. S., and Gay, T. 1970. The articulatory implementation of the breath-group and prominence. Language 46:312–328.

ERRATA

p. 120

14) ¹Seño²ríta As²⁺cá²ris.

15) ¹A ²dár ²⁺clá²ses?

16) ²Us²⁺téd.

17) ²Us²⁺téd!

18) ²Désde el áño que viéne son ²trés². . .

19) ²Háy que metér la ²máno?²

20) ²Són dós ²áños².

p. 121

21) ²Puéde írse ²sóla¹.

22) . . .²que se còntro²lá¹se.

23) ²Péro se vé que es muy càm²⁺bián²te.

24) . . .²que escri²bí¹an.

25) ²Díce que la encargáda lim²⁺piá²ba.

p. 122

27) ¹Ni ²qué ²⁻³ha²blár².

L. Waugh (ed.)/ *The Melody of Language*

ERRATA

The following corrections to chapter 8, "Three Intonational Systems of Argentinian Spanish," were submitted by the author after the book had gone to press.

p. 115, footnote 1

—Vos sos de pura nata cordobesa
—Y, escuchame LA TONAAADITA.
    (*Hortensia* Review, Cordoba, No. 30, March 1973.)

p. 115, footnote 2

 ²Cordoba, capital of the province that bears the same name, is located in the central region of Argentina, about 700 km northwest of Buenos Aires; it has a population of over 800,000. . .

p. 117 footnote 5

The David Crystal reference should be 1969. The Liberman et al. reference should be 1970.

p. 118

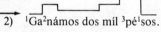

2) ¹Ga²námos dos míl ³pé¹sos.

3) ²Y a ³mí me llamó la aten³ción.

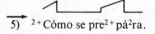

4) ¹Péro resúlta que con castelláno no ¹⁺pué¹de.

5) ²⁺Cómo se pre²⁺pá²ra.

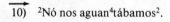

6) ²Y ²⁺ótra ³có²sa.

p. 119

10) ²Nó nos aguan⁴tábamos².

12) ²No es po³síble².

13) ²Hásta ²luégo².